About this book

This is the first adequate modern Burke 'reader', selecting from the total corpus of his political writings. Edited by Dr. Brian Hill, who worked on the standard multi-volume *Correspondence of Edmund Burke* (Cambridge and Chicago), it runs to some 145,000 words, includes a substantial introduction which incorporates a chronological account of Burke's politics, a summary of his ideas in a 'history of ideas' framework, and the book has informative prefaces to each extract and a full scholarly apparatus.

No political writer has been more quoted than Edmund Burke. Yet despite his enormous reputation, there has been no general agreement as to what he stood for. Regarded for most of his career as a dangerous opponent of the British government, a supporter of American rebels and a critic of British rule in India, he lived, after his outspoken attacks on French revolutionary ideas, to be regarded as the arch-defender of established authority. Since his death his ambiguous reputation has persisted as an enigma: in the nineteenth century, he was hailed as master by British liberals and radicals; in the twentieth he is regarded as the apostle by many of the New Conservative writers in the U.S.A.

This edition of his writings on government, politics and society seeks to present, impartially, a wide range of his views which were expressed in response to varying situations. His ideas are seen to have been drawn from more than one tradition of political philosophy. Burke is shown to be an eclectic thinker yet a consistent advocate of social morality, of moderation, and a friend of good responsi____ whatever quarter. He ____ an opponent of extren____ politics whether of the ____

D1219034

Dr B. W. Hill read history at Queen Mary College, University of London, graduating in 1957. From 1957 to 1961 he was a research student at King's College, Cambridge, preparing a thesis on 'The Career of Robert Harley, Earl of Oxford, 1702-1714'. In 1961 he was employed by the Institute of Historical Research to identify unpublished sources for Burke's speeches, and during the following year he served as a research and editorial assistant to the Cambridge/Chicago edition of *The Correspondence of Edmund Burke*. Since 1963 he has been lecturer in English History at the University of East Anglia. Dr Hill is the author of a number of important articles, and regularly reviews in *History* and *The Economist*.

EDMUND BURKE

On Government, Politics and Society

Selected and edited by
B. W. Hill

International Publications Service

Published in the U.S.A. 1976 by
International Publications Service
114 East 32nd Street
New York, N.Y. 10016
in association with Fontana

Edmund Burke on Government, Politics and Society
First published in 1975
by The Harvester Press Limited
in association with Fontana

Introduction, notes and this selection
copyright © B. W. Hill 1975

ISBN 0-8002-0161-2
Library of Congress Catalog Card Number: 75-23385

Library of Congress Cataloging in Publication Data

Burke, Edmund, 1729?-1797.
    Edmund Burke on government, politics, and society.

    Bibliography: p.
    Includes index.
    1. Political science--Collected works. 2. State,
The--Collected works. I. Hill, Brian W. II. Title.
JC176.B82522   320'.092'4   75-23385
ISBN 0-8002-0161-2

Typesetting by Wm. Collins & Co. Ltd.
London and Glasgow
Printed in Great Britain by Redwood Burn Limited
Trowbridge, Wiltshire
Bound by Cedric Chivers Limited, Portway, Bath

Contents

Textual Note

Editions of Burke's *Works* published during, or soon after his lifetime contained a number of footnotes by Burke himself or by his early editors. Such notes usually appeared in later editions and are retained in full in the present selection indicated by the symbols originally used, namely asterisks (*) and daggers (†). The present editor's additions to old notes are placed in square brackets. New notes are indicated by numbers. References to the *Works* given in this volume are in all cases for both the Boston (Little, Brown) 1865-67 and London (Bohn's British Classics) 1854-89 editions, as being the editions most commonly available to American and British readers respectively. The text used in the selections is that of the American edition.

ACKNOWLEDGEMENTS

I wish to thank Professor Thomas W. Copeland for reading the Introduction to this volume in an earlier and shorter draft, and for making many useful suggestions for its improvement. For translation of Burke's Latin quotations, use has been made of the excellent *Loeb Classical Library* editions. Also useful were the Everyman editions of *Burke's Speeches and Letters on American Affairs* and *Reflections on the French Revolution*, and Conor Cruise O'Brien's Penguin edition of *Reflections on the Revolution in France*.

Introduction: 'The Philosopher in Action'

B. W. HILL

I

Most men fall into easily identifiable categories in regard to their social, religious and political positions. Edmund Burke was not such a man. He came from an Irish family whose standing was at most that of small gentry, but he spent much of his life in the company of some of the wealthiest of the English aristocracy. Born of a mixed marriage, Catholic-Protestant, he chose his wife from a similar mixed background. Although a man of the highest talents he never rose above lower ministerial rank, and he was in office for a total of only twelve months in a parliamentary career which extended over twenty-eight years. His unusual background and uncertain status resulted in wide sympathies and an eclectic intellectual position. He has been placed in both the British empiricist and the natural law traditions of thought. And though he was, and still is considered one of the greatest writers on politics and government, there is no general agreement as to what he stood for. Nineteenth-century Liberals, for example, claimed him for their own,[1] while more recently he has been seen, particularly in the United States, as the philosopher of conservatism.[2]

The wide range of Burke's thought, and hence of his appeal, is immediately apparent in the extensive writings which he published over a long working lifetime. Such a range is not without its disadvantages, and Burke's reputation has often suffered from the imputation of inconsistency. For thinkers of the Left he is the champion of the weak who abandoned his life's work in 1790 when he wrote the *Reflections on the Revolution in France;* for those of the Right he is the philosopher who found his true bent at that time, after early indiscretions which are best overlooked. The assumption which is common to both these interpretations, that Burke's thought falls into a single political pattern despite some unfortunate inconsistencies, stems not only from a natural tendency to emphasize those writings and passages which, it is argued, support the particular case but also from the conviction that Burke's principal object was to advance an intellectual theory. Such an account overlooks the fact that Burke was, unlike most political philosophers, actively occupied in politics throughout the period of his major writings and acted as the spokesman of a political party. Burke was, it is true, a theorist, but of a rather special kind, for his aim was to advance many practicable theories rather than a single doctrinaire one. For while, as we will see, he upheld consistently certain fundamental moral values, as a practical politician he believed that abstract considerations must be tempered by the immediate realities of politics.

His own frequent and explicit statements make it very clear that he did not favour holding rigid theories of political behaviour. As a politician he was aware that the very diversity of situations in which men find themselves seldom permits of government on lines laid down by predetermined codes. 'I am no lover of names', he told the House of Commons; 'I contend for the substance of good and protecting government, let it come from what quarter it will'. From an early stage Burke drew a distinction between the functions of an abstract theorist and of one who was called upon to fit theory to practice. In his *Thoughts on the Cause of the Present Discontents* he contended:

> It is the business of the speculative philosopher to mark the proper ends of government. It is the business of the politician, who is the philosopher in action, to find out the proper means towards those ends, and to employ them with effect.

There was no doubt in his mind that he was himself not a 'speculative philosopher' but a politician, a 'philosopher in action'. Theoretical positions had no attraction for him. 'I have in general no very exalted opinion of the virtue of paper government, nor of any politics in which the plan is to be wholly separated from the execution'.[3] It is thus necessary always to consider Burke in the light of his own practical approach to politics. Only in this way can we avoid the extremes of abuse to which he has been subjected, at various times, by both the Left and the Right in politics.

But when all due allowance has been made for Burke's aggressively practical approach to political thought, it must be conceded that he contributed considerably to later misunderstandings of his philosophy by reason of the talent which he possessed, and frequently used, for coining neat aphorisms in support of his immediate contentions. His works have long been the happy hunting-ground of anthologists. Early in the field was the editor who published in 1804 two volumes of Burke's *Maxims and Opinions, Moral, Political and Economical*. In this handy, pocket-sized work, Burke's 'wisdom' was culled from his collected writings and neatly displayed – by subjects and in alphabetical order.

The antidote to the selective approach is for the reader to study Burke in the context of his times and in passages of reasonable length and diversity. For if ever there was a writer whose major intellectual effects were created in lengthy exposition, in a three-hour speech or a hundred-page pamphlet rather than in a neat generalization, Burke was that writer. The unit of his thought was the book rather than the chapter, the chapter rather than the paragraph, and the paragraph rather than the sentence.[4] His favourite literary method was, in his own words, to 'wind himself into' the details of a subject; to come at it from every angle, illustrate it with every pertinent example, and then to polish his exposition until it appeared as page upon page of flawless prose.

Ostensibly Burke's writings fall into two types, the speeches and the books or pamphlets. In practice this distinction is blurred, for he often composed his speeches with an eye to subsequent publication. Only by an occasional conventional aside, such as those addressed to the Speaker of the House of Commons, or by some compliment to the reader are we reminded of the origin of the texts. The distinction between the two types is further confused by Burke's frequent habit, in works written solely for publication, of nominally addressing himself to a particular reader. The best-known example is his selection of a little-known French legislator as the supposed recipient of the *Reflections on the Revolution in France*, a work which is accordingly written in the form of a letter. It was a method better suited to the polemic of the politician than to the terser, more abstract propositions of the political philosopher. In Burke's own day both the pamphlets and the published speeches were eagerly read, and they enjoyed a circulation which was remarkable for the time. His first major political pamphlet, the *Thoughts on the Cause of the Present Discontents*, sold over 3,000 copies in the two months after its first appearance.[5] But Burke's readership was not confined simply to those who purchased the individual publications, for newspapers, both national and local, and many periodicals often printed long unauthorized extracts from his publications. His views and arguments were thus much more widely known and discussed than sales alone would suggest.

For Burke's main speeches we are not dependent, as is the case with many other eighteenth-century debaters, on newspaper reports. He preferred to speak towards the end of a debate, so that during a late sitting of the House the reporters would often have slipped away to get their accounts to press before he rose; if he were generally known to intend to speak his reputation would hold many of them back, but this was not always the case, and many of his speeches are reported, if at all, in a short and uninformed paraphrase of information obtained at third hand. Fortunately Burke did not trust his reputation to the chances of unofficial and often inaccurate reportage; in the case of some of his greatest speeches he preserved the texts carefully and published them himself, often with explanatory prefaces and footnotes. Even in cases where full newspaper reports of his speeches survive, it is hardly surprising that these rarely match up to his own text since reporters were not permitted to write down speeches verbatim, and accounts derived from covertly-taken notes or reconstructed from memory tended to fall into a set pattern. From this journalistic idiom the freshness of Burke's ideas, the accuracy of his detailed information and the pungency of his delivery were saved, on many occasions, by his own fore-sight.

While it is clearly impossible for most readers to assimilate Burke's collected works in their entirety in the many-volumed editions published in the nineteenth century it is desirable, for reasons already outlined, that a broad cross-section of his writings should be examined to gain a fuller understanding of his thought. The aim of the present selection is not to illustrate a particular thesis or political viewpoint but to present some of Burke's profoundest statements, with a view to showing how he tried on diverse occasions to solve the age-old prob-lems of reconciling the claims of government with the needs of the governed. The following section of this Introduction attempts, by giving an outline of his life and career, to show how his speeches and pamphlets were written as a direct response to particular circumstances. A final section attempts to draw together the main strands of his ideas and to relate them to the history of political thought.

II

Edmund Burke was born in Dublin in 1729 and spent his childhood and young manhood in Ireland. He was brought up in the Anglican faith of his father, an attorney, but was almost equally familiar with the Roman Catholic faith of his mother and with the Quaker principles of a beloved schoolmaster, Abraham Shackleton, with whose son Richard he long re-mained on terms of close friendship. Burke's formal education was completed at Trinity College Dublin, from which he graduated in 1748, and for the next few years his ambitions were divided between law and journalism. In 1750 he went to London to study at the Middle Temple with the intention of returning eventually to Ireland to follow in his father's foot-steps, but by 1757 he had decided to remain in England as a man of letters. In that year he married Jane Nugent, the daughter of an Irish physician settled in London. Burke's

younger brother Richard and his distant cousin and friend
William Burke joined him soon after. In 1757 he established a
modest literary reputation for himself by publishing a treatise
on aesthetics, a subject in which he had long been interested,
*A Philosophical Inquiry into the Origin of our Ideas on the
Sublime and Beautiful*. But the work which occupied most of
his energies from 1758 until he gave it up to go into politics
was the *Annual Register*, a chronicle of current affairs with
extensive book reviews, which he founded for the publishers
Robert and James Dodsley.

The only publication of these early years in London which
is important for following his subsequent development as a
politician and political thinker was his *Vindication of Natural
Society*, published in 1756. The work was attributed on its
title page to 'a late noble author' and was a clever parody of
the distinctively pungent style of Henry St John, Viscount
Bolingbroke, who had been a major political and minor literary
and philosophical figure in the first half of the eighteenth
century. Bolingbroke, in common with other deists, had
rejected the traditional theology; the young Burke was concerned to discredit the attacks of such men by showing that
Church and State rested upon the same foundations, so that
assaults upon religion might well bring about the downfall of
the state and lead to anarchy. Burke's central premise, namely
that it was inexpedient to tamper with existing institutions
without good cause, was one which he was often to put forward
in his later works. But parody is a two-edged weapon, and it
proved to be an unfortunate medium for carrying this particular message. The pamphlet's criticism of all religious and
political institutions was so effective that when the true
authorship became known the odium which that criticism
engendered was to some extent transferred to Burke instead
of Bolingbroke. A year after first publication Burke felt
compelled to clarify the book's intention, in a preface to the
second edition, declaring that 'the design was to show that,
without the exertion of any considerable forces, the same
engines which were employed for the destruction of religion,
might be employed with equal success for the subversion of

government.' Despite this disclaimer of personal subversive intent a reputation for political unsoundness, and for over-cleverness and ambiguity, was to cling to him for the rest of his life.

Burke's failure in the *Vindication* to leave the clear impression that he was the true defender of existing political and social institutions becomes more understandable when we read the concluding section of the work. His matchless ability at pen portrayal betrayed deep-seated feelings; when he came to write, in the guise of Bolingbroke, of the evils of society he was carried away from his intention of defending that society. He thought only of the hundred thousand British miners: 'these unhappy wretches scarce ever see the light of the sun; they are buried in the bowels of the earth'; others were 'tortured without remission by the suffocating smoke, intense fires, and constant drudgery'. And beyond this 'slavery, with all its baseness and horror' at home lay the rest of the world, where 'millions daily bathed in the poisonous damps and destructive effluvia of lead, silver, copper and arsenic'. By contrast to such poverty the rich were 'by their artificial method of life bringing worse evils on themselves than their tyranny could possibly inflict on those below them'. The *Vindication* adumbrated the concern that became more sharply defined in his later writings for those who had to live in evil conditions under the control of the institutions of church and state which he was defending. Contemporaries were not slow to see this element in his thought, even though he had not intended to emphasize it. True, Burke finally attempted to pull his *Vindication* together by returning to his avowed object with a satirical attack on the enemies of religion. But the impression remained of a critical attitude towards an eighteenth-century convention whereby the evils of society were little questioned and remained, for preference, unmentioned. When we recall that Burke's later career was closely bound up with that of the second Marquess of Rockingham, the four hundred fires of whose Yorkshire home at Wentworth Woodhouse burned coal from his estates' private workings, we wonder not so much that Rockingham's aristo-

cratic circle distrusted Burke but that the Marquess himself
evidently did not share this distrust.

It was Burke's appointment as Rockingham's private
secretary in 1765 which ensured that his permanent career was
to be in politics. For several years before this date he had
sought a political patron. Rockingham was the leader of a
large group of politicians who had originally formed part of
the 'Old Corps' of the Whig party under the Duke of Newcastle, before the break-up of that party in 1762 when Newcastle had been dismissed from office to make way for Lord
Bute, the favourite of George III. But Bute did not last long,
and his immediate successor, George Grenville, held office
only a little longer. The King, being unable to persuade his
first choice, Wiliam Pitt, to take office at this juncture, was
forced to turn to Newcastle's political heir Rockingham. In
July 1765 the Rockingham Whigs re-entered the ministry,
with their leader at the Treasury. In need of a secretary or
man of business Rockingham received a strong recommendation to appoint Burke, who was thus brought into the centre
of national affairs in one movement. A seat in the House of
Commons was found for him, in Lord Verney's borough of
Wendover, and on 23 December 1765 he was elected at the
age of thirty-six.

Burke arrived in the Commons in time to take part in all
the leading events of Rockingham's short first administration,
including the repeal of Grenville's Stamp Act, the tax which
had been so bitterly opposed by the American colonists, and
the passing of the Declaratory Act, a vain attempt to appease
the King by restating Parliament's theoretical right to tax
the colonies. Before the ministry fell in July 1766, after prolonged failure to agree with George on methods and policies,
Burke was established as one of its leading speakers in the
lower house. This first session also ensured Burke's adherence
to Rockingham for the remainder of the latter's life. Offered a
position by the incoming administration of Pitt, now Earl of
Chatham, Burke replied in terms which amounted to refusal.
Twelve months earlier he had joined the Rockingham Whigs
almost by chance. Now he identified himself with all that they

stood for, and was preparing himself for the task of shaping their none-too-coherent ideas into a unified political creed.

The party with which Burke thus became definitely associated may be seen as an important link between the original Whig party, which had been founded mainly to restrict the power of the monarchy, and the revived party of the late eighteenth and early nineteenth centuries. When Burke first joined Rockingham the Whigs had recently been shattered by the determination of George III to govern without recourse to party, and fragmented by internecine quarrels. The followers of Rockingham constituted only one section of the party, and among their number were some prominent politicians who had formerly been classified under the now equally-broken old Tory party. That the Rockingham Whigs, with these initial disadvantages, were to make good their claim to be the true inheritors of Whig tradition and emerge as the nucleus of a revived Whig party was to be in no small measure due to Burke, who enthusiastically threw his literary and debating talents into their cause. At the time of their fall from office in 1766 they displayed little defiance of the crown and no political programme. Rather than accede to the King's wishes they had refused to work with the court party, thereby retaining their independence at the expense of losing their offices, and in a fumbling way they had adumbrated their future policy on the American problem; but they were by no means united either on the need for further opposition to the crown or on support for the colonists' position. Two years of inept administration by Chatham, in which that minister's personal sympathy for the colonists was frustrated by illness and by his adherence to the royal view that party government was unacceptable, brought the Rockinghams closer to clearing their vision. It was left to Burke, in 1769–1770, to produce their manifesto.

The events which provided the stimulus for his work were a fresh attempt to tax America, in the duties imposed by Chatham's unruly Chancellor of the Exchequer, Charles Townshend, and the Middlesex election case, in which the succeeding ministry of the Duke of Grafton provoked great

popular excitement by preventing the demagogue, John
Wilkes, from taking his seat in the Commons. Burke's first
attempt to deal with the political situation and to try to define
the Rockinghams' uncertain position was a pamphlet entitled
*Observations on a late Publication intitled the Present State of
the Nation* (1769), written in reply to a tract by Grenville
which had castigated the Rockinghams, among others, for the
political disruptions of the day. The tract had to be answered,
but a straightforward *apologia* was bound to be relatively weak
and negative in its impact. What was required was a positive
statement of what the party stood for. Such was the origin of
the *Thoughts on the Cause of the Present Discontents*, on which
Burke worked during the summer recess of 1769. His aim had
been to publish in time for the autumn session, but when the
House assembled his pamphlet was still undergoing final
revision. He intended that this statement, when it emerged,
should be as definitive as he could make it. Indeed, some
members of the party, among whom drafts were circulated
for approval, objected to the clarity of definition that Burke
proposed. Rockingham, however, was for a clear statement of
principles. The leader's view prevailed, and it was with the
virtual unanimity of the party that the pamphlet was published
finally in April 1770.

The *Present Discontents* has thus, from Burke's day to the
present, been regarded rightly as a party policy statement. In
it are outlined many of the policies which the Rockingham
Whigs were to put into practice during their second ministry
in 1782. The only aspect of their thinking which was to receive
significant additions during the intervening period was, in
fact, that which concerned the American problem. In the
heyday of Victorian constitutionalism it was common to
regard the pamphlet not only as a party manifesto but as a
blueprint for the two-party system itself. Although this view
has sometimes been questioned by modern scholars, who
point out that Burke nowhere explicitly envisages a permanent
alternation between parties and the virtual exclusion of the
crown from politics such as existed in the days of Gladstone
and Disraeli, there is nevertheless some justification for the

Victorian interpretation of Burke's intention. He set out to justify the combination or 'connection' of men in the form of a party as a remedy to the prevalence in the Commons of a court party. 'When bad men combine, the good must associate.' He was well aware that the two parties had dominated politics in the earlier part of the eighteenth century and had ceased only recently to have an effective existence. This situation had been brought about, he maintained, by the deliberate intention of George III to destroy the old parties in Parliament and rule through a compliant body of parliamentarians who were willing to accept court patronage. 'As, hitherto, business had gone through the hands of leaders of Whigs or Tories, men of talents to conciliate the people, and to engage their confidence; now the method was to be altered: and the lead was to be given to men of no sort of consideration or credit in the country.' The King, in his policy of ignoring the conventions of party government, had been aided by the somewhat shadowy constitutional status hitherto enjoyed by the parties themselves. Burke set out to state the rationale for the behaviour of his own party in opposition to the crown, and in so doing set out the way towards a new and more permanent two-party system in which the existence of a parliamentary opposition party would be recognized not only *de facto*, as it had been since the end of the seventeenth century, but *de jure* as a constitutionally desirable part of the system.

In contravention of long-established custom, Burke argued, the object of George III had been to ignore the recognized leaders of the party who formed the ministry and to 'draw *a line which should separate the court from the ministry*'. Much of the pamphlet was devoted to elaborating the theme that behind the ostensible ministry lay a core of real policy-makers answerable not to Parliament but to the King himself. This clique, variously described as an 'interior ministry', the 'interior managers' and 'the cabal', had for the last ten years been making ministries and unmaking them when the ministers refused to co-operate with court policy. Burke undoubtedly had chiefly in mind the experiences of Rockingham's own ministry, though he could also call upon the events of the Grenville, Chatham and Grafton administrations. For most opposition Whigs the chief culprit in these events had been the Earl of Bute, the favourite who had been placed in office at the beginning of the reign without either experience of government or any compensating abilities. But Bute, as Burke was aware, could not reasonably be blamed for all the royal excursions of the 1760s; he had left office for ever in 1763 and Burke may well have suspected, as is now known for certain, that Bute had little influence over George III after 1765. Hence Burke proclaimed his intention of avoiding 'personal reflections' on the Earl.

> Where there is a regular system of operations carried on, it is the system, and not any individual person who acts in it, that is truly dangerous . . . We should have been tried with it, if the Earl of Bute had never existed; and it will want neither a contriving head nor active members, when the Earl of Bute exists no longer.

It was not, indeed, Burke's intention to pillory individual members of the 'interior ministry', for the whole tenor of his charge was, despite his conventional disclaimers, that the King himself was responsible for the discontents of the day. George III might be portrayed as a misguided monarch betrayed by false servants into actions which were not acceptable to the nation at large, but few readers could fail to draw the conclusion that if any substantial reform were to take place the initiative must be the King's. Phrases like 'this unnatural infusion of a *system of favouritism*' and 'the dead repose of despotism', with Burke's scornful rejection of the idea that ministers should be supported for the sole reason '*that the King has thought proper to appoint them*', spoke for themselves.

In the middle section of the pamphlet, omitted in this selection, Burke expatiated on the way in which the system of 'double cabinet' had in his opinion brought about the mismanagement of public affairs and the discontent of the people, in the conduct of both foreign and domestic affairs. In many ways the weakest of his assertions, the existence of 'double cabinet' in a literal sense is not in evidence and has often been indignantly denied by historians. Burke, indeed, imputed to the crown a purposiveness of action which was, all too frequently, quite lacking. Nevertheless, the existence of a court party in Parliament and the prevalence of constitutional quarrels, especially in connection with the chequered career of Wilkes, could hardly be denied. Much of the detail of Burke's indictment of 'the system' came from events connected with this gentleman, especially the General Warrants case and the Middlesex election dispute, not without an eye to allying the Rockinghams with a popular cause. But Burke had to tread carefully. His own friends were far from wishing to see the triumph of all the reforms which Wilkes's radical supporters were beginning to demand. Hence he was quick to disavow any sympathy for such projects as more frequent general elections or the unlimited ejection of 'placemen' from the Commons; the Rockinghams had in mind only a limited abolition of offices held at the pleasure of the crown. Still less did he contemplate the abolition of rotten or close boroughs – many of which were controlled by his own party – or such extreme measures as manhood suffrage. Only by a long disquisition on the King's misuse of the civil list and by the hint that certain types of office were redundant did Burke make concession to the clamour for reform, thereby adumbrating the measures which he was to carry into effect during Rockingham's second ministry by means of the Civil Establishment Act.

The solution to state ills which Burke held constantly before his readers throughout *Present Discontents*, and to which he returned in his peroration, was the checking of royal influence by a party of well-disposed men, the natural guardians of the nation's liberties as understood since the Revolution of 1688. The court cabal had built its power on the break-up of the old Whig party; let a new party be built to take over the functions of the old. Burke was chary about claiming that it was still possible to revive the old Whig party: too many Whigs existed independently of the Rockingham 'connection'. But this connection was, he maintained, the only one which still carried the banner; the only 'honourable connection' as distinct from those self-seeking patronage groups which brought the name of party into bad repute. Only genuine party, or honourable connection, could resist the pressures of the court, for only they were united by principle rather than self-interest. Burke instanced the Whigs of Queen Anne's reign, as the supreme example of patriotic party endeavour, devoted to the safeguarding of the Protestant succession and the bringing of the House of Hanover to the throne in 1714. The Rockinghams were, he implied, directly in the tradition of the early Whigs. They were united by the same overriding principle, the maintenance of the settlement made at the Revolution of 1688–89. 'Party is a body of men united for promoting by their joint endeavours the national interest upon some particular principle in which they are all agreed.' Further, the purpose of honourable connection was 'to pursue every just method to put the men who hold their opinions into such a condition as may enable them to carry their common plans into execution, with all the power and authority of the state' – in short to get into office in order to resist the King.

The tocsin of party which Burke sounded was directed not only against undue interference in politics by the King but against the anti-party theory of the great Chatham, especially dangerous now that the latter was in opposition. The *Present Discontents* made clear that 'the cant of *Not men, but measures*', Chatham's doctrine that a ministry should be supported for the policies it espoused rather than for the men it contained, was not acceptable to the advocates of party government. The independent Whig such as Chatham himself, however well-meaning and popular, was no substitute, when it came to resisting despotism, for the united endeavours of a party of men who were willing to merge their individuality into a common endeavour.

Burke's position as one of the devisers of policy, if not one of the recognized leaders of his party, was confirmed by the publication of the *Present Discontents:* his place among the foremost parliamentarians of his generation was secured by his speeches and publications upon American affairs. Since Rockingham's repeal of the Stamp Act the British government had enjoyed relatively good relations with the colonists for only eighteen months. The situation changed in Chatham's administration. During his illness his colleagues fell apart, each pursuing separate policies. It was left to Townshend to introduce, in May 1767, a series of new duties on such essential imports into the colonies as glass, paper, lead and tea. This renewed attempt to recoup the mother country's shaky finances at their expense caused fresh uproar among the Americans, and resistance was only assuaged two years later when Grafton's ministry raised the duties, with the exception of that on tea which was retained to save face. Lord North, who as Chancellor had ushered through the removal of these duties, was able to avoid further entanglements for several years after he formed his own ministry in 1770, but in December 1773 a dangerous situation was again precipitated by the Boston Tea Party. Urged on by the King, the ministry immediately passed through Parliament a series of punitive acts to close the port of Boston, quarter troops within the city and amend the constitution of Massachusetts. The representatives of the colonies, meeting in a Congress at Philadelphia in 1774, rallied to the support of the afflicted New Englanders and breathed defiance at the home government. An explosion which had long been coming now only needed a spark to set it off.

Burke's main contribution to attempts to settle the American problem without unnecessary bloodshed consisted of his famous speeches in 1774 and 1775 on American Taxation and Conciliation with America, and his pamphlet of 1777 addressed to the Sheriffs of Bristol. Yet he moved only slowly towards the conclusion that the colonists must be permitted their independence. The Rockinghams were reluctant to abandon the principle of the Declaratory Act, though the Americans considered them, after Chatham, as the most sympathetic section of British opinion. Burke himself had been selected in 1770 by the Assembly of New York as their official Agent in London, and the duties which he undertook on their behalf did much to broaden his knowledge and understanding of their point of view. This understanding was progressively drawn upon in his speeches.

In many ways his first speech, that on American Taxation on 19 April 1774, was concerned with the fate of the Americans mainly as a stick with which to beat the government and other power groups at Westminster, and thus hardly marked his emergence as an imperial statesman. He reviewed the events of the last ten years in order to attack the attempts of successive ministries to settle the taxation problem. While maintaining the right of Parliament to impose taxes upon the colonists Burke vigorously denied the expediency of such measures. Grenville he castigated for initiating ill feeling, especially by the Stamp Act; upon Chatham's ministry he poured scorn for implementing the Townshend duties in defiance of its own stated intentions; North's repeal of the duties he condemned for its inconsistency in not including the duty on tea. In the course of the speech Burke began to develop the idea, which he was to carry further in the speech on Conciliation, that Britain had recently departed from a principle which had previously long been observed in her dealings with the colonies, that of legislating for purely mercantile reasons which would mutually benefit both home country and colonists. He blamed Grenville and Townshend in particular for departing from this overriding principle in favour of a policy of obtaining revenue, although implicit in his remarks was a greater censure of the King.

Why was Burke's attack on the government less sharp than his comments on Grenville, Townshend and Chatham? The Rockinghams could hope for little change of heart from the solid phalanx of voters who normally followed North in divisions; 'the low, pimping politics of a court' could be taken for granted. But there was still some hope of attracting independent MPs into the party, providing that a debating ascendancy could be secured in the Commons over the small but eloquent body of Chathamites. Burke was fighting for control of the opposition, but on the American question his position was difficult. While conceding the inexpediency of taxation he was obliged to demonstrate his party's continued adherence to the principle of Parliament's right to impose taxes, as laid down in their Declaratory Act. At this stage Chatham, who had long since endorsed the colonial claim that there should be no taxation without representation, undoubtedly had a better claim to be a friend of the Americans. Hence Burke's insistence, against the claims of Chatham's followers, that the repeal of the Stamp Act in 1766 had been the decision of Rockingham's own friends, irrespective of the wishes of Chatham himself. Hence too Burke's celebrated description of what he held to be the basic error made in the formation of Chatham's ministry in the same year, namely that it was not constructed upon a proper party basis:

> He made an administration so checkered and speckled, he put together a piece of joinery so crossly indented and whimsically dovetailed, a cabinet so variously inlaid, such a piece of diversified mosaic, such a tessellated pavement without cement, – here a bit of black stone and there a bit of white, patriots and courtiers, king's friends and republicans, Whigs and Tories, treacherous friends and open enemies, – that it was, indeed, a very curious show, but utterly unsafe to touch and unsure to stand on.

This attack on Chatham, reminiscent of similar passages in the *Present Discontents*, shows Burke in 1774 to be more concerned with parliamentary manoeuvre than with obtaining a united opposition front in support of the colonists.

Between his first and second major speeches on America Burke's ties with the colonists were further strengthened by an unexpected opportunity, in the general election of 1774, to represent the important mercantile community of Bristol, which had many connections with American cities. Although, as he made clear in his *Speech to the Electors of Bristol*, he reserved his right to take such action in Parliament as he thought fit, without reference to the close and binding restrictions which Bristol and many other radical constituencies were seeking to impose upon their representatives, Burke was for the moment at one with his new constituents in seeking an early solution to the American problems which had so often disrupted trade in the last decade.

In 1775, with his Speech on Conciliation delivered on 22 March, Burke was still not ready to renounce his party's stand on the matter of the Declaratory Act, but in other ways he had moved much closer to directly supporting the colonists. The speech ranks among his finest. Specifically disclaiming any intention to produce a detailed plan for the regulation of relations, Burke made instead a powerful bid to produce among his parliamentary colleagues a more generous concept of the home country's responsibilities, with a view to obtaining the repeal of the tea duty and the recent coercive acts.

Few British people of Burke's day had any concept that the colonies, which only one hundred years before had been straggling and stockaded outposts, had now become a large and prosperous nation; that in Philadelphia, indeed, they possessed the second largest city of the empire. Burke himself had only in recent years come to appreciate the significance of such facts, which he now strove to impart to his fellows by dint of illustration and information. His opening calculation that the population of the colonies had risen to two million of European descent, together with another half million Africans and others, was in itself sufficiently enlightening for those who had been taught to believe the Americans too insignificant for detailed consideration at Westminster. His account of the great value of American commerce to the empire as a whole must have come as a revelation to listeners who considered the colonies to be parasites on the home country. But lest some Members should be tempted by this information to think that America was worth retaining even by recourse to military force, Burke was at pains to emphasize that force never had been and never would be a viable solution to imperial problems within the general framework of British political ideas. The colonists, as descendants of Englishmen, held English ideas of liberty, and were as little likely to be constrained by forcible taxation as the home country itself had been in the past. The Americans, he reminded the House, were 'not only devoted to liberty, but to liberty according to English ideas and on English principles'.

In accordance with his usual dislike of 'paper government', Burke's proposals were of a general and declaratory, rather than a detailed and innovatory nature. They took a form which he often favoured as good parliamentary tactics, a series of motions any one of which taken alone would appear innocuous but which, if taken as a whole, added up to a sweeping indictment of current practices. The resolutions he proposed stressed, above all, that the colonies possessed their own elected assemblies with powers to raise revenue, and that these colonial assemblies had granted subsidies to the government at various times and represented a medium of taxation acceptable to the colonists. In fact Burke had moved some way towards recognition of the Americans' claim of no taxation without representation. But North's followers in the Commons were not deceived by the oblique nature of the suggested resolutions and rejected them *in toto*, together with Burke's other motions calling for the repeal of the Tea Act and coercive legislation and for the reform of colonial judicature.

Within a month of the delivery of this speech in Parliament the first shots were exchanged in the civil war which Burke had feared. After Independence was declared in 1776 he was again at the forefront of his party in his recognition of the realities of the situation, just as even before Independence he had foreseen that all hope of compromise was lost. 'We are a people who have just lost an Empire', he wrote to his chief supporter in Bristol five weeks before the Declaration. As a compassionate statesman he saw no point in prolonging a struggle which could only result either in loss of liberty to the Americans or in loss of any remaining dignity to the British. The Rockingham party as a whole, however, needed time to adjust to the idea of accepting Independence. The opening of the session in January 1777 saw their decision to secede from Parliament rather than face up to formulating a new policy to meet changed circumstances. Burke, loyal as usual, undertook to defend the secession to the public.

The medium he chose was an open letter to his own constituents. *A Letter to John Farr and John Harris Esqrs., Sheriffs of the City of Bristol, on the Affairs of America* was published in May 1777 in London and Bristol. In it Burke not only defended the Rockinghams' recent conduct but made his own final literary contribution to Anglo-American relations. His Bristol constituents were particularly uneasy because he had remained absent from the House during a proposed partial suspension of the Habeas Corpus Act to deal with the rebellious colonists. Burke's defence of himself and his party left his readers in no doubt that he disapproved of the suspension of this Act, and he attempted to defend the secession as a useful tactic. He placed the blame for the war squarely on the shoulders of the 'court faction' who dominated the government, and called openly for a 'formed American party in England' to whom the Americans could always look for support.

The pamphlet did much to convert the Rockinghams into the 'American party' Burke envisaged, though their conversion to support of Independence was not completed until the defeat of a British force at Saratoga the following October convinced them that there was no other solution to the American problem. Against the doubters, or constitutional purists, who believed that in the last count the colonists should conform to the wishes of the home government, Burke insisted that there existed no single definition of the relationship between the state and the individual, to which the individual must conform at all times and in all circumstances: 'social and civil freedom, like all other things in common life, are variously mixed and modified, enjoyed in very different degrees, and shaped into an infinite diversity of forms, according to the temper and circumstances of every community.' The Americans, living in communities very different from those in Britain, had found intolerable the form of social and civil freedom which suited Britain. This being the case, Burke could not fail to approve of independence as the best way of obtaining a better relationship between the countries involved. He had, he confessed:

so much trust in the inclinations and prejudices of mankind, and so little in anything else, that I should expect ten times more benefit to this kingdom from the affection of America, though under a separate establishment, than from her perfect submission to the crown and Parliament, accompanied with her terror, disgust and abhorrence.

Such was Burke's contribution to the problem of an imperial relationship which could no longer be sustained; and if his final view was reached by a hard path and came too late to save the first British Empire, it was not without value in teaching the British a better method when they came to build another.

The surrender of a British army at Yorktown in October 1781 convinced independent opinion in the Commons that the war was lost, and North's ministry fell in March of the following year. The King, forced to turn to the opposition, appointed a ministry led by Rockingham but including the Earl of Shelburne, who had become leader of the Chathamites since Chatham's death in 1778. The Rockinghams came to office pledged to limiting the patronage of the crown and ending the American war on the basis of independence. An extensive programme of legislation was carried for the former purpose, much of it drawn up by Burke, who occupied the post of Paymaster General. Over American affairs Charles James Fox, who had joined the party during the war, clashed with Shelburne over the latter's seeming preference for an imperial solution. On the Marquess of Rockingham's untimely death after only three months at the Treasury the ministry fell apart and the King took advantage of the situation to appoint Shelburne, rather than the party's nominee, the Duke of Portland, as Rockingham's successor. The Rockinghamite ministers thereupon resigned, with few exceptions, but Shelburne struggled on without them until early in 1783 when his negotiations with the Americans alienated not only the Rockinghams but also many who still looked for leadership to Lord North. The upshot was an agreement between Fox and North to set up, in April, a coalition ministry under Portland.

The events of the Fox-North Coalition, or Portland

Ministry, in which Portland became First Lord and Burke again Paymaster, proved to be a turning point for the old Rockingham Whigs and for Burke personally. The rapid rise of Fox as leader in the Commons, surpassing Burke in personal popularity, gave a new flamboyant appearance to the party's counsels; while the presence in the ministry of North and his friends introduced an alien element. Since Fox leaned towards radicalism and North was more conservative than the Rockinghams on many issues, the new ministry's views were far from unanimous. Indeed, in the view of many moderate observers the union of Fox and North, so lately parliamentary antagonists, was an inexplicable development. In the country at large the legend of the 'infamous Coalition' was born, while in Parliament the homogeneity of the party which Burke had helped to build largely disappeared.[7] Burke himself, without his patron, played a less important part in the party for the next few years except in one respect, the reform of the government of India.

On this important subject all members of the ministry felt, for the moment, that they could agree. After the recognition of an independent government in America, which Fox was now able to carry through Parliament, and the reform of government in Britain, which the Rockinghams believed they had successfully carried out by reducing the King's power of patronage in 1782, the government of India under the ineffective rule of the East India Company stood out as an anomaly and a scandal. As in the former issues it was Burke who took the lead, eager to right the wrongs suffered by India during George III's reign. As the leading member of a Select Committee of the Commons set up in 1781 to examine the Company's management of its heavy responsibilities he was deeply angered by the evidence of corruption and tyranny which was uncovered. Early in 1783 he pledged himself in the Commons 'to God, to his country, to that House, and to the unfortunate and plundered inhabitants of India, that he would bring to justice, as far as in him lay, the greatest delinquent that India ever saw' – Warren Hastings, Governor-General of Bengal.[8] The ministry's weakness prevented for the moment

the pursuit of Hastings, who had many friends in Parliament
and at court; but the reform of Indian government for the
future, by taking it out of the hands of East India Company
employees and making it the responsibility of the British
government or its nominees, seemed within the power of the
ministry. In the summer of 1783 Burke became the principal
draftsman of the bills for this purpose which were introduced
in the Commons by Fox in November.

The Foxites' proposals were the signal for a constitutional
crisis. George III was still smarting at the way in which
Rockingham and Portland had, in accordance with their
party's doctrines, constructed their ministries without
consultation on appointments and without regard to his views
on policy. While there were individual precedents for such
behaviour the comprehensive nature of the party's demands
had gone considerably ahead of general constitutional practice.
Though adverse circumstances had forced the King to bow
his head temporarily he had no intention of remaining quies-
cent. With the introduction of the India bills the leaders of
the court party, Charles Jenkinson and John Robinson,
advised him that the time had come to assert himself. The
Coalition was unpopular, and the bills could plausibly be
represented to the public as a fresh attack on the authority of
the crown by an opportunist and unprincipled set of politicians
who no longer constituted even the party that they had claimed
to be under Rockingham. The proposed legislation which
aroused most alarm was that which would have made the
seven commissioners appointed to rule India from London
irremovable during their first four years of office, except by
an address from either House of Parliament. The powers of
patronage in India which the Foxite commissioners might
build up during those initial four years would, the King's
supporters alleged, rival those of the crown itself in Britain
which the Rockinghams as a party had been at pains to
diminish as being against the national interest. As well as
appealing to public opinion on these grounds the court could
rely upon the powerful support of the East India Company
itself, especially through its adherents in Parliament, and of

the younger William Pitt, a rising luminary whose friend
Henry Dundas had been prevented by the ministry from
offering his own scheme for the reform of India. Once more
the fatal rivalry between the Rockinghamite and Chathamite
sections of the old Whig party threatened to bring about the
downfall of the king's opponents.

The task which confronted Burke in his first major speech
on the India issue, on 1 December 1783, was therefore not a
simple one of proving the East India Company's incapacity
to govern its vast territories; he had also to assume a defensive
position in the face of the campaign of propaganda and vilifica-
tion being mounted against his party on the score of constitutional impropriety. One of the principal accusations which
he had to refute was that the ministry, in proposing to remove
the long standing charter rights granted to the Company by
the crown, was in fact undermining one of the great bulwarks
of British liberties, the chartered rights of corporations and
individuals. If the Company's charter were revoked, claimed
the king's writers, the great medieval charters from Magna
Carta onwards might be the next to be challenged. The
assault by Charles II and James II on the charters of the
borough corporations, which had hastened the downfall of the
latter in 1688, was cited and neatly turned against the Foxites.
That such arguments were spurious did not make them less
effective in the prevailing climate of opinion, and Burke took
them seriously in the opening part of his speech. He drew a
necessary distinction between charters which were respected
as forming the basis of political liberty and those monopoly
charters, like that of the Company, which he claimed were
the very antithesis of the principles of the Great Charter of
King John and its like. Some charters reinforced men's
natural rights: others were drawn up to controvert and set
aside these rights. The Company's chartered existence had
done the latter for the inhabitants of India, the most extensive
colonial territory for which Britain now remained responsible
since the loss of America.

Throughout this and all his subsequent speeches on India
runs one of the most fundamental strands of Burke's thought,

his conviction of the dignity and importance of oppressed peoples and individuals; just as underdogs who came to him with tales of misfortune and oppression were always assured of a warm welcome and assistance, so the fate of populations of subordinate territories invariably awakened his sympathy. Nevertheless, he did not contemplate lightly the constitutional gravity of revoking what amounted to an entire system of government, however ineffective it might be. His concept of the sanctity of existing institutions, hallowed by prescriptive rights, which was to come to the fore a few years later in his defence of the French monarchy and church establishment, was already present. 'I feel an insuperable reluctance', he told the Commons, 'in giving my hand to destroy any established institution of government, upon a theory, however plausible it may be.' The case for reform had to be watertight:

> To justify us in taking the administration of their affairs out of the hands of the East India Company, on my principles, I must see several conditions. 1st, The object affected by the abuse should be great and important. 2nd, The abuse affecting this great object ought to be a great abuse. 3rd, it ought to be habitual, and not accidental. 4th, It ought to be utterly incurable in the body as it now stands constituted.

In his view all these conditions were present in the case of India. His approach, as in the speech on Conciliation with America, was to stimulate the imagination of his hearers as to the fate of a distant and populous province 'larger than the kingdom of France'. Interspersed with this stimulus was much detailed matter, though only a fraction of what he actually knew, on the way in which India had been governed. His contention was that the Company was not only greatly at fault but incorrigible. It was a conclusion which most of his listeners could endorse, and within a few months Pitt himself was to make a successful attempt to put the government of India into the hands of a Board of Control.

For Burke's scheme was not to be carried through by himself, or in quite the form which he had planned. The objection that it was devised for the benefit of a party proved too powerful. Burke, indeed, had hardly denied that the bill was a party measure, convinced as he was of the rectitude of his party's motives, and his argument on this score does not seem an exceptionable one to modern readers:

> As to the gain by party from the right honourable gentleman's bill, let it be shown that this supposed party advantage is pernicious to its object, and the objection is of weight; but until this is done (and this has not been attempted), I shall consider the sole objection from its tendency to promote the interest of a party as altogether contemptible. The kingdom is divided into parties, and it ever has been so divided, and it ever will be so divided; and if no system for relieving the subjects of this kingdom from oppression, and snatching its affairs from ruin, can be adopted, until it is demonstrated that no party can derive an advantage from it, no good can ever be done in this country.

But the country was unready to endorse this view. The bill passed the Commons but was rejected by the Lords after the King had made known in that House 'that whoever voted for the India Bill was not only not his friend, but would be considered by him as an enemy'.[9] On the rejection of the bill the king dismissed the Coalition and asked Pitt to form a new ministry. The view of the constitution implicit in George's actions was not one which later monarchs would be able to implement, but the considerable remaining patronage of the crown together with the support of public opinion enabled him on this occasion to dissolve Parliament and obtain a large majority for Pitt in the ensuing election of April 1784.

This election put an end to the Foxites' hopes of office for many years to come; and over the tactics they should pursue in opposition Fox and Burke soon began to diverge. Fox's ideas were the more realistic; he wished to play down the old issues which had proved to be the party's undoing and concentrate upon holding it together by his personal popularity, by an increasing formalization of party organization, and by opportunistic parliamentary tactics to take advantage of any slip which Pitt might make. This approach accorded ill with the rigid Rockinghamite concept of fixed principles which Burke continued to favour.

The two main principles which Burke wished to promote, in the new House as in the old, were restraint of the King's constitutional claims and reform of Indian government. In both matters Fox's desire to soft-pedal aroused his concern. The first difference between the two men arose over the tactics to be used in the debate on the opening speech from the throne. This speech took the offensive by speaking of the Coalition's recent actions as innovations in the constitution. But in the new House there was no hope of obtaining a vote condemning the Speech or the King's own recent actions. Burke therefore determined upon the unusual expedient of casting a condemnation in the form of a motion which would be recorded in the Journals of the Commons even though negatived. His motion took the Speaker over an hour to read from the Chair. Since the Coalition Ministry had possessed, at the time of its dismissal, a large majority in the Commons Burke treated the Speech as an attack not only on his own party but upon the lower house itself and insisted that, as the majority was the only body truly representative of the nation, the treatment of the India Bill by the King and by the House of Lords had flouted the nation. The Commons which was dissolved in March 1784 for continuing to support the Foxites after their dismissal was 'uncorrupt, independent and reforming' in its nature. For an election to be called three years before the end of the permitted term was distinctly unusual and of doubtful constitutional propriety; and Burke did not intend to allow these facts to pass unremarked or unrecorded.

The difficulty which Fox and the majority of the Whig party faced in deciding whether to support Burke's motion lay in the reflection that the King's actions, however constitutionally dubious, had been retrospectively sanctioned by the electorate. Burke had his answer: the King's and Pitt's success, he implied, was a further demonstration of the illicit influence exerted by the crown in elections. In private, however, he had to admit that the use of royal patronage or bribery had had only limited significance in an election which had aroused public opinion against Fox and North.[10] The motion was seconded by his friend William Windham but was not supported by other colleagues and was rejected without a debate. It was the first of many misunderstandings between Burke and his party. Nevertheless, his protest went down upon the official record, as he intended, and remained a silent but unforgotten condemnation of the last occasion on which a monarch successfully defied a majority of the Commons in open conflict.

Before the end of the first session Burke had the mortification of seeing Pitt obtain an East India Act which was in many respects very similar to his own unsuccessful bill. He took particular exception to the absence from the new measure of any clear statement concerning the nature of the misrule in India which the reform was intended to rectify, since the omission indicated that his own desire to punish some of the chief offenders was to be ignored by the new ministry. On 28 July 1784 he moved for an early consideration of the reports of the Select Committee, and of a Secret Committee in which Dundas had taken the lead, with a view to instituting proceedings against Warren Hastings. Again, however, the majority of the opposition were not willing to follow him in reviving an unpopular cause, and Fox with several others failed to stay in the House for the motion. Hastings, however culpable, had done much to secure and extend British rule in India. It was amid scenes of disorderly shouting and hooting that Burke wound up bitterly with a declaration of his own continued commitment to obtaining justice for India:

> He hoped a time would come when he should be heard, and heard with a decency which he well knew the subject deserved. But the House of Commons was gone, was annihilated. Did they imagine that because everything went at present as they wished, that therefore the world was blind, that posterity would be blind, to the evils they were entailing on the country? He protested the crimes, the political enormities, lately perpetuated and still to be perpetuated, by the British government in India, filled him with horror. To destroy this deplorable system he had toiled many a night when he might have

amused himself as others did. But the facts which he saw in the papers which, under the direction of Parliament, he was obliged to read, had left in his mind such an impression of horror as deprived him often of his sleep.[11]

Hastings continued to take up most of Burke's time for the next four years, and in February 1788 the former Governor-General was at last arraigned before the House of Lords on a series of articles drawn up by the opposition. The process by which this end was reached, however, was far from satisfactory to Burke. Fox had come to the conclusion that some major issue was, after all, needed to rally the party, and in the absence of any more suitable subject he fell back upon India. But for Burke the question of bringing Hastings to justice was a matter of political morality rather than party expedient, and he foresaw that little political advantage was to be gained from an impeachment. 'In a party-light, and as a question to draw numbers', he wrote, '. . . a worse cannot be chosen out of the whole bundle of political measures. It is therefore my opinion that the wisest course for Mr Fox to pursue is, not to consider it as such.'[12] Burke's judgement proved correct, for the charges against Hastings were not opposed by Pitt, who thus easily avoided identifying the ministry with misgovernment in India.

It was thus with already diminishing fervour that many of the leading members of the Whig party viewed the opening of the impeachment. But Burke's ardour was unremitting, and to him was given the honour of opening the case on 15 February 1788. Taking four days to deliver, his speech ranged over many aspects of Hastings' rule in India. He did not fail to point out that the defendant was only the chief among many who had made their fortune at the expense of those whom they controlled: 'you strike at the whole corps, if you strike at the head'. But the proceedings made only slow progress. Meeting on occasional days between other business the House of Lords had considered but two of the twenty articles by the end of the session in 1788. By this time too the Whigs were, with the exception of Burke and his small circle of followers such as Windham and Sir Gilbert Elliot, already tired of the trial and inclined to stop the case for the prosecution immediately. After discussion Burke's insistence on letting it run its full course prevailed, but at least one of his colleagues among the managers of the impeachment, the politician-playwright Richard Brinsley Sheridan, openly expressed a wish that 'Hastings would run away and Burke after him'.[13]

By 1789 the division within the Whigs, implicit since the death of Rockingham, was beginning to widen. In the winter of 1788–89 the King suffered from the first of the prolonged bouts of supposed madness, now known to be a symptom of porphyria, which were to incapacitate him increasingly in the remainder of his reign. In the expectation that a Regency would take place in the person of the Prince of Wales, who was a Foxite, the opposition prepared themselves for office. The ministerial arrangements which were mooted were of a nature which offended Burke deeply. He was to be given no higher office than that of Paymaster which he had held in 1782 and 1783; while his claim to be leading member of the Board of Control for India was to be blocked because of Fox's insistence on the difficulties which this would cause in relations between the Board and the East India Company.[14] The King's early recovery made the proposed arrangements abortive, but these had exacerbated the fraught tempers among the opposition. Before the next session Fox attempted to stop the impeachment, but was again outmanoeuvred by Burke. The trial was to drag on for a further six years. Before its end the general aspect of politics had been changed by the impact of the French Revolution, the Whig party had been split asunder, and Portland and Burke had led off more than half its members from Fox's leadership in 1794.

Burke's anger at the way in which he was ignored by the party during the Regency crisis was voiced in a letter which he wrote to Windham in its concluding stages; but even more in evidence were constitutional differences which divided him from Fox on this issue.[15] Hitherto Burke had found himself almost continuously in opposition to George III concerning the latter's view of the role of monarchy in British politics

Consequently, another aspect of Burke's position, his deep respect for the institution of monarchy itself, provided that its incumbents did not exceed the proper limits of its functions, had had little chance to come to the fore. It was the claim of the Prince of Wales to take his father's place during the latter's incapacity which permitted Burke's latent political ideas to be displayed more clearly. For when the ministry had attempted to impose restrictions on the Prince's power as Regent Burke had castigated them for claiming 'that the representative of the Kingly honours shall have no other power than the House of Commons shall think fit to allow him'.[16] In short, Burke went some way, during the crisis, towards that position in defence of royal prerogatives which he was to assume a few months later when the events of the French Revolution shocked and exhilarated Europe.

Burke's *Reflections on the Revolution in France* would, nevertheless, have been less decisive in condemnation of the French Revolution but for the general and, in the case of Fox, unqualified approval with which this was greeted in Britain. Fox's opinion of the fall of the Bastille was 'how much the greatest event it is that ever happened in the world! and how much the best!'[17] But the immediate cause of Burke's sitting down to compose a counterblast to the French Revolution was not Fox's reaction. For in January 1790 Burke had chanced upon the published form of a sermon which had been delivered to the Revolution Society of London, a body devoted to the memory of the Revolution of 1688, by the unitarian preacher and political pamphleteer Richard Price. Under the title *A Discourse on the Love of our Country* Price had welcomed the French Revolution in unmeasured terms as being akin to the 'Glorious Revolution' itself. The support of a radical dissenter, a breed for whom Burke had shown little love, for events in Europe which he already viewed with extreme suspicion proved to be the trigger mechanism which set off his greatest polemical endeavour. Through most of 1790 Burke remained at his desk, devouring public and private reports of affairs in France and casting his own fears into the rhetoric of the forthcoming *Reflections*.

Burke's attitude to the French Revolution, at a time when even Pitt was giving a moderate welcome to the setting up of a Constituent Assembly, was given a certain fillip by his position of isolation in British politics, but it was basically the expression of far deeper feelings. He had long campaigned against the abuse of governmental powers in Britain, in the American colonies and in India; but in so doing he had not lost sight of the need for good government in human society. Also he believed that all institutions were of slow, coral-like growth which could not easily be replaced if hastily done away with. In the *Vindication of Natural Society* he had satirized those who might wish to overset existing government in favour of 'natural society'. Even in the *Present Discontents*, his most extreme attack upon the King, he had never hinted at changing the form of British government but had only demanded a reform in the manner of its execution. Similarly, in supporting the Americans, Burke had hesitated long before advocating the extreme solution of independence, consenting to this only when there was no alternative; and in pleading the cause of oppressed India he had made very clear his aversion from overturning established governments unless they were utterly corrupt. The French monarchy of the *Ancien Régime*, as Burke saw it, was far from being this. Indeed, he wilfully closed his eyes to much that was totally incorrigible in the French body politic. What, of course, obscured his usual clarity of vision was that he could not see the new arrangements in France as any improvement on the old; and, further, he greatly feared the spread of French revolutionary ideas to Britain, where he believed that existing government was basically sound and exemplary. His early understanding of the spread of terror in the French provinces, the *grand peur*, convinced him that what was happening was not simply a mild constitutional change, such as the Revolution of 1688 or his own proposed reform of Indian government, but the spectre of social revolution.

The opening section of the *Reflections* was therefore devoted to demonstrating that recent events in France, including the transformation of the States-General summoned in May

1789 into a National Assembly in the following month, constituted not so much the establishment of a representative government on the English pattern as the first moves in a slide towards anarchy. Burke was soon led, however, into a discussion of the nature of the Glorious Revolution of 1688–89 with a view to showing that it was, by contrast, basically preservative in its aims and had deviated from the traditional pattern of English government no more than had been absolutely necessary. His love of delving into documents came into its own as he quoted extensively from the Declaration and Bill of Rights to show that monarchy had not been as lightly treated in the England of 1689 as in the France of 1789. He dismissed radicals like Price and 'the gentlemen of the Revolution Society' as belonging to the breed of extremists bred by the English Civil War, on whom the constitution had turned its back in 1689. Save for during the shortlived aberration of the Interregnum, Englishmen had been in the habit, Burke asserted, of considering their constitution as an entailed inheritance, not to be dissipated at will by any one generation. This precise analogy from the law of inheritance had a special significance for English readers, who were well acquainted with the legal processes by which great estates were held together.[18] Burke maintained that the shattering of the constitution, like the splintering of a long-established unit of property, was not the English way. In the eyes of many the doctrine was sufficient to exclude almost any possibility of change in political institutions.

Burke himself did not go so far as this, but there is no doubt that in the situation of 1790 he saw nothing but danger in the proposals of English reformers. Hence his insistence that the National Assembly was not to be compared with Parliament or, worse, used as a model for change in Britain. The Third Estate, the moving force of the new unicameral Assembly, were, he believed, very different from their supposed counterparts in the House of Commons. They were men of little experience and little substance, 'men formed to be instruments, not controls'. As usual Burke had investigated the French details closely and was therefore better able than most of his contemporaries to see the constituent elements, as well as the outward form of the new French legislature. After reading his analysis few could doubt that the National Assembly had a membership of a different type from the landed interest which dominated the Commons. Few could doubt either that the intentions of the Assembly towards the French King and royal family were very different from those entertained by most members of the Commons towards George III.

Integral with the sanctity of existing political institutions, in Burke's mind, was the inviolability of religious establishments. Much space was taken up in the *Reflections* by his description of the interdependence of Church and State, of the way in which this had continued to be recognized in Britain after 1688, and of the way it had been largely ignored by the constitution-makers of France. In Britain, he maintained, the school of deists had passed into obscurity, while in France similar doctrine in the hands of the *philosophes* had found widespread acceptance, undermining the church and upsetting the whole existing basis of society. That there had been irremediable corruptions in the French church he could no more accept than the suggestion that the French monarchy was an unsatisfactory vehicle of government. In both cases his assertions were questionable, to say the least, but fortunately the value of the *Reflections* is not, despite its title, derived from its analysis of French affairs but from its understanding of British political institutions and its exposition of the assumptions and half-understood theory which lay behind these.

After the *Reflections* Burke was to make one further major contribution to British political thought. He was satisfied that the *Reflections* had made his case against the English radicals who supported the French Revolution, but what of those of like mind within Parliament, within the Whig party itself? George III might read the book and recommend others to read it, but as the months went by there was still every sign that Burke was not considered a prophet by many of his colleagues. The climax came in May 1791 when Fox and Burke clashed in the Commons, each stating his own interpretation of the situation in France. Burke thereupon publicly renounced their friendship – though this was hardly the personal catastrophe which it has sometimes been represented since the two men had not, for some time, been on good terms. More importantly, Burke felt that he had become estranged from the party as a whole. This was not, in fact, the case, for the great aristocrats, led by Portland, who had formed the backbone of the old Rockingham party, were moving closer to his standpoint though they were reluctant to make an open break with Fox which would involve a split within the party. It was, nevertheless, with a strong feeling of isolation that Burke began to compose the pamphlet which was to refute the charges brought against him by the Foxites, and which have been made at intervals ever since, in particular that his behaviour was at variance with his own past career of opposition to the king.

The *Appeal from the New to the Old Whigs*, published in August 1791, was thus a personal apologia. But it was more than this, for in justifying his own position Burke not only rejected charges of personal inconsistency but turned back in self-justification to what he saw as the fundamentals of the Whig creed, the views promulgated by the party in the first generation after the Revolution of 1688. He selected as his texts the speeches by Whig lawyers at the trial of Dr Henry Sacheverell, a clergyman who had been impeached in 1710 for preaching the doctrine of non-resistance to kings. Burke had no difficulty in showing that the Whigs of Anne's reign had been extremely cautious in their statements, avowing only support for such a limited degree of resistance as had been needed to overset the direct line of the monarchy on the particular occasion of the Revolution. He thus made good his point that after 1689 the Whigs had, in the main, arrived early at the position that resistance to monarchy was to be treated as a unique event, and one not likely to be repeated. Many of Burke's party who had not been convinced by the polemic of the *Reflections* found the historical argument of the *Appeal* more satisfying. Almost three more years were to pass before the majority of the party finally broke with Fox, but Burke had opened the rift and events in France could be left to complete the severance. The September Massacres of 1792, the execution of the French royal family and the outbreak of war between Britain and revolutionary France early in 1793 came as hammer blows in support of Burke's contentions.

One of Burke's remaining preoccupations was his concern for his native Ireland. His past services had not been inconsiderable, and in particular much credit was due to him for the Rockingham ministry's measures in 1782 whereby Ireland's Parliament was given greater independence from the tutelage of Westminster. But the Irish legislature remained the instrument of the Protestant Ascendancy, and as such unrepresentative of the great majority of the Irish population who were Catholic. When the French Revolution with its atheistic tendencies had made English public opinion more sympathetic to downtrodden Catholicism, Burke saw an opportunity for obtaining a share in government for the Irish Catholics. Immersed as he was in Hastings' trial and in his denunciations of the Revolution, he delegated to his son Richard the practical work of negotiating an agreement between the Catholics and Pitt's government. In 1792 and 1793 relief bills were passed in the Dublin Parliament allowing Catholics to practise in the legal profession and granting to many the right to vote, to serve on magisterial benches and grand juries, and to hold most civil and military offices. But the right of Irish Catholics to sit in their own national Parliament was still withheld and became a ground of contention. The most likely opportunity for emancipation appeared to come when Burke's friend, Earl Fitzwilliam, was appointed to Ireland as Lord Lieutenant in 1794, soon after joining Pitt's government along with other Whigs under Portland. Richard Burke was expected to accompany Fitzwilliam to Ireland as his Chief Secretary, but died before he could take up the appointment. And when Fitzwilliam showed signs of promoting emancipation he was soon recalled by Pitt, though other reasons were emphasized. Thus ended one of Burke's dearest hopes, and the failure was perhaps accompanied by the reflection that his son's strenuous exertions in this cause had probably hastened his early death.

The remaining years of Burke's own life do not make happy reading. The final split in the Whig party in July 1794, with more than half its members in the Commons withdrawing themselves from Fox's leadership, was a triumph for Burke which can have brought him only qualified satisfaction after a political lifetime spent in promoting the party. The death of his younger brother in the same year as his son added to the dissolution of Edmund Burke's happy personal circle. In 1795 came the final acquittal of Hastings. By this time Burke had ceased to hope for an outstanding conviction, but the defendant's acquittal on all articles of impeachment was a bitter blow. The long-term value of the proceedings, in terms of the development of more responsible attitudes by British administrators in India, was as yet not visible. In one matter, however, Burke received some recognition, for after he retired from Parliament in 1794 he received a grant of £1,200 per annum from the civil list, a belated recognition by the government of his great and various services. He died at his home at Beaconsfield on 9 July 1797, survived by his wife but leaving no descendants.

III

In his own day most men who knew Burke agreed that he was a remarkable man. The opinion of Dr Johnson, delivered to Boswell, was that 'Burke, sir, is such a man that if you met him for the first time in a street where you were stopped by a drove of oxen, and you and he stepped aside to take shelter but for five minutes, he'd talk to you in such a manner that, when you parted, you would say, this is an extraordinary man.'[19] Most who had personal dealings with him were also agreed on the warmness of his character, his honesty and loyalty to his friends. The Duke of Grafton, for example, claimed that he was 'one on whom the thoroughest dependence may be given, where an obligation is owed'.[20] The man who had the highest claim upon his loyalty was the Marquess of Rockingham, and to the end of his life Burke continued to refer to his patron with feeling and respect. More than anyone else Rockingham seems to have been able to work with his prickly genius on terms of undiminished amity.

With the other aristocrats and rich men who formed the hard core of his party Burke was far less at ease. They stood for the stability in society which his intellect told him was ultimately for the good of the whole; but at the same time they often revealed a degree of social injustice and careless indifference to others whose fortunes they controlled which could not fail to disturb him. His celebrated outburst against the young fifth Duke of Bedford, a Foxite who had attacked him publicly, brought out vividly the conflicting strands in Burke's attitude to the English upper class. The aristocracy might be the 'great oaks' which beneficially shaded lesser social vegetation, but Burke could not supress his resentment at the chance of fortune which brought men like Bedford to positions of power by virtue of their rank, 'swaddled and dandled and rocked into a legislator'. Bedford's path could hardly have been more different from his own. At every turnpike met, Burke recalled, 'I was obliged to show my passport'.[21]

In his writings and speeches two commitments stand out, never reconciled and never entirely subduing each other, though one or other often dominate according to the need of the moment. One is to suffering humanity, clamouring for justice, compassion and life itself. The other is to society, formed of human beings in an intricate pattern which subordinates some men, elevates others and articulates the whole. Society is necessary for the survival of the species, yet it can and does inflict injury on many of its members. How are the claims to be reconciled? Should we save individuals even if this means damaging the organism of society, or preserve society intact and let the individuals suffer? Burke could countenance neither as the permanent solution. Where society as a whole had to be preserved he hoped that public and private charity, in which he was not personally lacking, would help to redress the injuries which could not be avoided. But this was rarely a satisfactory resolution, for there were some injuries inflicted by society which could only be salved by public action. Hence Burke's assumption of the role of paladin on behalf of the inhabitants of India. As he told the assembled Lords on the first day of Warren Hastings' impeachment:

> The business of this day is not the business of this man, it is not solely whether the prisoner at the bar be found innocent or guilty, but whether millions of mankind shall be made miserable or happy.

In the case of the American colonies he led his party, and eventually the nation, to recognition of Independence when this became inevitable, with the intention of reducing bloodshed and bitter feeling to a minimum. In Ireland his heartfelt sympathy for the subordinate majority, though they were not of his religion, had less direct effect in his own lifetime but was not forgotten at a later date. Only in the case of the French Revolution did he seem, to many of his contemporaries, to ignore humanity; and here his pity for the persecuted clergy and aristocracy blinded him to the less obvious but nonetheless real grievances of a large part of the population of France under the *Ancien Régime*.

In every cause which he took up, except that of France, Burke was dealing with nations under British rule whose destinies could be directly affected by the government, Parliament and political nation whose operation he understood so well. This political world of late eighteenth-century Britain did bear many resemblances to those of modern Britain, the United States and other English-speaking countries; but it also differed in a number of significant ways. Thus, Burke's frequent insistence on the importance of public opinion, which he urged upon his friends on every possible occasion, can give a misleading view of his attitude unless it is remembered that his concept of the political public was a narrow one by modern standards. In 1796 he estimated the size of the political nation as being around 400,000.[22] It is within such a context that his references to 'the people' must usually be understood

He believed that the House of Commons must listen to public opinion, as expressed by the electorate, the press and other pressures such as county meetings. At the time of the Middlesex election dispute of 1768–1769, when he considered that the Commons had succumbed to the control of the crown, he held that the voice of the people might override the votes and resolutions of the House. On the whole, however, he was satisfied that Parliament expressed the will of the political nation. For he held that the Revolution of 1688 had defined the complex relationship between the crown, the Commons and the House of Lords, and that the interposition of the people was little needed except when something or someone threatened to alter that relationship.

Though much of Burke's career was taken up with trying to eliminate the excessive degree of royal influence which, he believed, had grown up since the Glorious Revolution, his general attitude to change, particularly the reform of Parliament, was what might be expected from his veneration of the existing constitution. In the *Appeal from the New to the Old Whigs* he wrote of his own record in this respect:

> The reforms in representation, and the bills for shortening the duration of parliaments, he uniformly and steadily opposed for many years together, in contradiction to many of his best friends.[23]

And the contention was substantially true. Least of all did he wish to turn Parliament into an executive body that would replace the crown. Towards the end of his speech on Conciliation he remarked, after listing the string of resolutions which he proposed to move, that he could have thought of two or three more 'but they come rather too near detail, and to the province of executive government, which I wish Parliament always to superintend, never to assume'. Like most men of his day, in fact, Burke was a fervent believer in the excellence of the existing constitution so long as its precepts were properly understood and observed.

But if his political outlook was not that of the late nineteenth-century liberal it was once assumed to be, it offers no more comfort to modern conservatism, for Burke was far from being consistently a man of the Right within the framework of the system he upheld. When the French Revolution threatened Europe with anarchy his position was certainly far to the right in the spectrum of British opinion, but those writers who make him the prophet of unyielding conservatism on the strength of the *Reflections* and other works of that era ignore much that is characteristic and important in his thought. For the first twenty-four of his twenty-nine years in Parliament he opposed continually the royal executive and almost as constantly favoured those measures which were inimical to true conservative minds. Nor do Burke's writings substantiate the belief that he was uniformly on the side of authority. Regarding the Americans' stand he advised his constituents in 1777 that '*General* rebellions and revolts of an whole people ... are always *provoked*'. And even in the *Reflections*, the work on which his reputation as the philosopher of the Right is largely based, he was capable of such statements as:

> A state without the means of some change is without the means of its conservation. Without such means it might even risk the loss of that part of the Constitution which it wished the most religiously to preserve.

Burke was, in fact, always conscious of the conflicting claims of stability and reform.

How, on any particular occasion, did he decide which of these claims should predominate? In any assessment of Burke's ideas on government, politics and society, it is necessary to take into account not only the immediate circumstances and the political context that provoked the particular speeches and pamphlets, but the intellectual influences which moulded his fundamental assumptions and values. For although, as will be clear by now, his thought was, particularly during Rockingham's lifetime, often a rationalization, or at least an intelligent anticipation, of the policies of his party, it is obvious that Burke was far more deeply versed in the speculative traditions of western political thought than any of that party's leaders. He was widely read in the literary works of the Enlightenment, and was particularly influenced by Montesquieu. His acquaintance with the teaching of Locke, and of lesser Whig thinkers of the period of the 1688 Revolution, permeated his whole outlook. It is also clear that Burke had some acquaintance with medieval Christian political thought, and considerable knowledge of the classics of ancient Rome and Greece and the theories of the state advanced by their authors.

Until a generation or so ago Burke was commonly described by scholars as belonging to the British empiricist tradition of thought deriving from John Locke, whose contributions to philosophy, and to political thought in particular, had been made at the end of the seventeenth century.[24] In the eighteenth century nearly all British and American writers on these subjects owned and even gloried in their debt to Locke. His *Essay concerning Human Understanding* had familiarized men with a new theory of the nature of knowledge. Locke had invited his readers to consider that the mind of man did not come, as had been supposed, fully equipped with the power to perceive certain facts, and well stocked with 'innate' ideas. On the contrary, he claimed, the mind at birth was a blank, a *tabula rasa*, upon which the individual's personal experiences alone made an impression. Locke's doctrine thus accounted for human psychology in terms of external experience which structured and formed the mind, and hence swept away as unverifiable many of the ideas which had been built up for centuries around theological assertion. Though Locke himself believed that God could be perceived by the use of man's reasoning powers, many of his followers took his basic argument a stage further to reject traditional belief in God. But it was in his *Second Treatise of Civil Government* that Locke turned to the political aspect of man's experience. To explain the relationship between the rights of man and those of the state or government he adopted the postulate of an original historical condition of nature in which men had surrendered their rights to the state in order to obtain a measure of impartial protection against the untrammelled exercise of the

rights of others against themselves. This t
social contract, was government's fundamei
but, Locke maintained, the contract could onl
binding obligation as long as government perfc
which had been entrusted to it. If the state c
reason, to serve the best interests of its citizens
contract was void and individuals might conspire to set up a
new government. Such was the philosophy which had seen
James II off his throne in 1688. Locke's psychology of the
sensations, with its emphasis on the study of the observable,
together with his insistence upon social consent in government,
at the expense of the theological concept of kingly rule by
divine right, were integral parts of the intellectual heritage of
Burke and his contemporaries.

Nevertheless the general acceptance of Locke's teaching
sprang from the fact that this laid itself open to varying
interpretations. For example, with his rejection of innate
ideas influencing the mental processes, a rejection generally
taken by exponents of the cult of Reason to preclude the
existence of original sin, Locke had combined a stout defence
of the reasonableness of Christianity. And with his assertion
of the existence of a contract between government and the
governed he had combined a healthy respect for the existing
institutions of property and privilege. It is thus not surprising
that his views, or those of thinkers who drew directly upon his
work, were freely quoted at the time of the American War of
Independence by both the British government and its British
and American opponents, or that both the French revolutionaries and their British critics derived inspiration from the
same source. Burke, as a sympathizer with the Americans and
an enemy of the French Revolution, drew at different times
upon the varied opportunities of emphasis permissible to
Locke's disciples. In the former case his championship,
notably in the *Speech on Conciliation*, of the American colonial
assemblies against the intrusion of royal government and alien
taxation was analogous to the position of those English
politicians who had defied James and elevated the status of
Parliament in 1688; indeed the opposition of the Rockinghams

to George III was well justified by Locke's teaching. At the time of the French Revolution, with its attacks on property and its overthrow of the States General called by the French king (an assembly which Burke chose to consider as being, even after its long period in abeyance since the early seventeenth century, the equivalent of Britain's Parliament), his reaction could still be presented as legitimately reflecting important aspects of Locke's position as defender of the rights of property and of the integrity of representative assemblies.

Yet despite Burke's adherence to certain basic tenets of Locke, it is clear that he was by no means a mouthpiece for Lockeian doctrine. For where Locke placed emphasis upon the natural rights of man, including the right to abrogate the supposed social contract, Burke emphatically opposed those who upheld the rights of man during the American and French revolutionery periods.[25] While not entirely rejecting natural rights, Burke reserved them as a court of ultimate appeal against tyranny. As early as 1772 he was already clear that it was only 'when tyranny is extreme' that 'men resort to the rights of nature to shake it off'.[26] And when, nineteen years later, he wrote the *Appeal from the New to the Old Whigs* he was to come close to saying that the Revolution of 1688, which had placed men's natural rights above the claims of existing government, was un unrepeatable event.

Burke's divergencies from the thought which derived from Locke were not, however, confined to political theory. As early as the *Vindication of Natural Society* he attempted to demonstrate his aversion from *a priori* philosophy and from the cult of 'natural society', most completely embodied in Rousseau, which he believed were inimical to all religious and political institutions. On the evidence of these arguments, repeated more passionately at the time of the Revolution in France which he was convinced was largely inspired by subversive philosophical doctrines such as those of Rousseau, some modern scholars have drawn the conclusion that Burke was not, in any important sense, a child of the Enlightenment. Instead they see him as indebted to a different and older intellectual tradition which saw God, rather than utility, as the

ultimate source of all political obligation. Indeed, he has sometimes been seen as a direct successor to the natural law school
associated with St Thomas Aquinas. While there has been
disagreement among such scholars as to precisely what are the
criteria of a natural law philosopher, all are agreed in rejecting
the notion of Burke as a purely empirical thinker and in seeing
him instead as concerned with the problems of politics as an
aspect of the problems of a higher morality.[27]

Certainly Burke's references to natural law are at least as
numerous as his appeals to natural rights, and there is thus at
least the basis of a case for the new school of interpretation,
particularly when it is remembered that Burke was an admirer
of the sixteenth-century English theologian Richard Hooker,
who wrote within the natural law tradition. Nevertheless
recent writers, faced with the often cloudy nature of the
supposed links between a man of the late eighteenth century
and a medieval school of thought, have tended to discount the
natural law interpretation.[28] However these scholarly disagree-
ments are finally resolved – and it must be borne in mind that
both Locke and Montesquieu, whose writings contributed
substantially to Burke's thought, were not without some
affinities with the older tradition[29] – Burke's frequent appeals
to a law beyond positive laws and the 'laws' of Reason clearly
indicate that his avowedly practical approach to the problems
of government is tempered always by his perception of a
higher morality.

When we turn from attempting to trace the antecedents of
Burke's political thought to assessing its influence on later
generations the picture is equally confused. The late Professor
A. B. Cobban demonstrated that early nineteenth-century
Romantics, and the Lake poets in particular, owed some of
their social and political ideas to him.[30] But the Lake poets'
unusual amalgam of conservatism and social reform found
little response among their contemporaries. In the nineteenth-
century era of free trade and liberalism it was the utilitarian
and liberal aspects of his thought which were most emphasized.
Leslie Stephen, in his classic *History of English Thought in the
Eighteenth Century*, pronounced that Burke's 'views of

political economy were as far in advance of his time as his view of wider questions of policy', and regarded the *Reflections* as the only blot on an otherwise clean record – one which was best overlooked and forgiven as the work of old age. Burke had the right to remember at the end of his life, explained Stephen,

> that, throughout life he had, with one doubtful exception, taken the generous side. The exception – namely, his assault on the French Revolution – placed him for once on the side of the oppressors, and therefore brought him the reward denied to his earlier labours.[31]

The downfall of British Liberalism between the First and Second World Wars brought about the conditions needed for a new assessment of its supposed prophets, including Burke. Cobban, surveying the debris of eighteenth- and nineteenth-century civilization from the standpoint of the terrible year of 1929, was even forced to consider whether Burke had contributed to catastrophe by encouraging theories of nationality as the criterion of statehood; and although Cobban acquitted Burke of any theory justifying the aggressive nationalism of the late nineteenth and early twentieth centuries, he still emphasized the links between Burke's thought and that of the German idealist philosophers whose ideas were more culpable in this respect.[32] In 1930 the late Sir Lewis Namier carried reassessment a stage further, claiming that as the Rockinghams were basically hierarchical and authoritarian in their outlook, so Burke as their principal apologist was at bottom Tory in his assumptions.[33] It was this line of thought which was adopted and expanded after the Second World War and the onset of the Cold War by the American Right, who saw Burke as their major prophet in the struggle against communism.

What emerges from a consideration of the very varied schools of political thought which have been traced back to the influence of Burke, is that his own position was so much wider and more generous. For him the best political course depended upon circumstances, not on doctrine. As one perceptive scholar neatly put the truth of the matter, 'there is only one school of politics for which Burke can legitimately be claimed, and that is the school of Burke.'[34] Recognition of this fact will not only facilitate an approach to his ideas but may also lead to an appreciation of him as a political thinker of an independent status which has, despite his reputation, never been fully conceded.

Reasons for the general failure to place Burke in the same company as, for example, Hobbes, Locke and Mill, as a political thinker, must be sought principally in the two aspects of his work which set it radically apart from theirs: his writing was not produced in a compact form, much less in a single volume, and he was not a systematic thinker whose prime intention was to produce the appearance of consistency. His many statements on the theory of politics, embedded as they are in a wide variety of speeches and pamphlets, do not make as convenient reading as Locke's *Second Treatise* or Mill's *On Liberty*. His references to abstract concepts display many inconsistencies which cannot be glossed over in any serious assessment of his overall position; for his every appeal to natural law can be found another to practical needs, for every reference he made to man's natural rights can be provided another to man's duty to the state. Yet in reading Burke's speeches and pamphlets one does see certain guide-lines emerge, features of a core of political beliefs and assumptions which lie behind and give substance to his specific answers to particular problems.

The first and most obvious of his presuppositions about the purposes of the state was that these were ethical. For him every government was to be judged by its successes in securing the well-being of the governed. His standard by which political activity was to be measured was essentially the same as that applicable to individuals; 'the principles of true politicks', he wrote, 'are those of morality enlarged, and I neither now do or ever will admit of any other.'[35] His long and even malignant pursuit of Hastings, on behalf of the inhabitants of India, was based on no other belief than that the Governor-General had acted as a public man in such a way as would not be tolerated in a private citizen. To a scarcely lesser extent Burke's concern for the American colonists rested on his

n that the government was inclined to treat these
tizens not by the ordinary canons of political morality,
ld its nearer citizens in the British Isles, but by the
dictates of state expediency such as were usually reserved
(regrettably, in Burke's view) for subjects of another race.
For Burke it was only where politics and government were
morality writ large that they could begin to be defensible.

A second basic assumption in his thinking concerned men's
right to liberty, a right which could hardly be ignored in the
century of Locke, but which appeared to Burke a much more
complex matter, allowing greater flexibility but involving
greater dangers, than Locke had ever supposed. For Locke,
liberty had been to a large extent bound up with the preservation of property; and the Revolution of his own day, protecting
the propertied classes from the interference of Stuart monarchy, had not exceeded this concept. But Locke's doctrines
could also be construed, in other circumstances and in other
times, in a more truly revolutionary sense; so they became the
watchwords in turn of radicals in Britain, of rebels in the
American colonies, and of the revolutionaries in France.
Clearly in certain situations liberty could become a licence for
almost any socially disruptive activity. To avert the dangers
inherent in the lax use of the doctrine of liberty Burke was
constrained to point out that 'abstract liberty, like other mere
abstractions, is not be found', since in the last count 'liberty
inheres in some sensible* object'. In the city states of the
ancient world it had often turned primarily upon the right of
the election of magistrates; in English and American experience it turned upon the right to impose or withhold
taxation. By the time the Bastille had fallen and some of the
chateaux of the French provinces had been burned in 1789
Burke had further limited his definition of liberty, the 'splendid
flame' as he ironically called it. In a letter written in the
autumn of that year, and in a published work which appeared
eighteen months later, he argued that if liberty did not go
hand in hand with self-restraint it might well be forfeited.
Liberty was indeed 'the birthright of our species', but if men

* By 'sensible' Burke meant something like 'tangible'.

lowered themselves to the level of wild beasts they must give up that birthright:

> The liberty I mean is *social* freedom. It is that state of things in which Liberty is secured by the equality of Restraint; a constitution of things in which the liberty of no one man, and no body of men and no number of men can find means to trespass on the liberty of any person or any description of persons in the society. This kind of liberty is indeed but another name for Justice, ascertained by wise laws, and secured by well constructed institutions.

Where liberty and justice were separated, he further observed, neither were safe.[36]

The near-equation of liberty and justice brings us to another of Burke's basic considerations. His early training in law, and his subsequent political career in a nation which placed great emphasis upon the importance of constitutional precedent, accustomed him to consider political problems, especially those concerned with Britain, from the point of view of a constitutional lawyer. It has been suggested that his most famous doctrine, that of prescription or the wisdom of traditional institutions, derived from 'his continued employment and highly developed understanding of certain concepts which came from the common law (as he recognized) and were generally in use as part of the political language he spoke with his contemporaries.'[37] By invoking customary rights the British had long been used to defending themselves against the claims of sovereigns or of churches which would have deprived them of their liberties (or of their privileges) in the name of some higher good. In the *Present Discontents* Burke was able to draw upon his contemporaries' responsiveness to the dictates of constitutional custom in order to build a case against what he considered to be innovations introduced by George III; later, in the *Reflections*, he was to draw upon the same responsiveness in his crusade against the reformers. The argument from prescription, defending the *status quo* on the grounds that its very survival has proved its worth, has perhaps never been better stated than in the following passage from the *Reflections:*

> In states there are often some obscure and almost latent causes, things which appear at first view of little moment, on which a very great part of its prosperity or adversity may most essentially depend. The science of government being, therefore, so practical in itself, and intended for such practical purposes, a matter which requires experience, and even more experience than any person can gain in his whole life, however sagacious and observing he may be, it is with infinite caution that any man ought to venture upon pulling down an edifice which has answered in any tolerable degree for ages the common purposes of society, or on building it up again without having models and patterns of approved utility before his eyes.

Such sanctification of immemorial custom in government, even to the point of insisting that the worth of the institutions sanctified need not be immediately obvious, was in many ways analogous to the manner in which Burke's contemporaries regarded justice, as embodied in English law.

Closely related to the concept of custom as the chief determinant of society's workings was Burke's awareness of parallels between the development of social and natural bodies. His frequent references to human customs and institutions in the language of biological organisms have often been noted as examples of vivid metaphor. But phrases like 'a decomposition of the whole civil and political mass' and 'we have taken care not to inoculate any scion alien to the nature of the existing plant' are far more than rhetorical effects; they represented a deep-felt conviction that the institutions built by human endeavour were not mere artefacts but, in some manner, bodies with a life of their own. At the Restoration of 1660 and the Revolution of 1688, the English nation showed that they regarded their body politic in this light:

> in both cases they regenerated the deficient part of the old Constitution through the parts which were not impaired. They kept these old parts exactly as they were, that the part recovered might be suited to them.

Nor was it simply the constitution of the old country which he saw as an organism; in the *Speech on Conciliation* he told his hearers of his conviction that British and American interests could not be considered as separate since they formed part of a single body:

> But, it will be said, is not this American trade an unnatural protuberance, that has drawn the juices from the rest of the body? The reverse. It is the very food that has nourished every other part into its present magnitude.

To Burke it was the family which provided the link between human institutions and biological organisms. Here he drew heavily upon his personal experience, for the Burkes were at one and the same time a closely-knit and a widely-ranging cousinhood; in his conception of their family he made little distinction between his son or his brother, on the one hand, and his distant 'cousin' William or other Irish relations on the other. For Burke, in short, the clan was his family. It was, therefore, but a short step in his thinking from the extended family to the political 'connection' of friends (and, often enough, relations too), to the party, and even to the nation. In the *Reflections* he wrote:

> In this choice of inheritance we have given to our frame of polity the image of a relation in blood: binding up the Constitution of our country with our dearest domestic ties; adopting our fundamental laws into the bosom of our family affections; keeping inseparable, and cherishing with the warmth of all their combined and mutually reflecting charities, our state, our hearths, our sepulchres, and our altars.

By thus considering nations in the light of families Burke introduced into his political thought features not invariably found in the writings of political thinkers.[38] The emotions which usually went towards producing family unity could be aroused in hard-headed British parliamentarians on behalf of equally hard-headed American politicians. The sufferings of unknown and little understood Indian races could be presented to a British audience through the appeal of consanguinity. Above all, the codes of morality generally accepted as operating in the case of the individual could directly be applied, through the analogy of the family, to national and international relations.

Some of Burke's most basic conceptions arose from the fact that he approached politics equipped with a measure of historical vision unusual in his day. His largest formal contribution to the writing of history, the *Abridgement of English History*, a fragment written in 1757, was abandoned for reasons that are not entirely clear, and was not published in his lifetime. But he brought to almost everything he wrote an awareness of the historical process which provided, for his readers or hearers, a new insight into how the customs and institutions of their day had taken shape. The lessons which he could inculcate in this respect were the more necessary in that certain aspects of the thought of the day militated strongly against such an insight. The Age of Reason had rejected existing institutions of Church and State where they did not appear to meet the new requirement of utility. In so doing it ignored, often enough, the whole process of historical development which had produced such institutions. Although David Hume's *History of England* had brought to the study of history the idea of change and growth which was still largely absent from other British historians, and had perhaps thereby made a contribution to Burke's ideas on prescription, few politicians had thought out the implications of historical change as far as the practice of politics was concerned.

To discover the source of Burke's historical understanding it is necessary to recall his continual study of England's past, particularly of the evolution of the national government. The Revolution of 1688 had repulsed a direct attack by the Stuart monarchy on the independence of Parliament, resorting to such devices as the assertion of royal power to dispense with legislation and the issuing of charters to determine the nature of the electorate. But, with these abuses blocked, it was difficult for Britons in the 1760s to understand how royal power could again become dangerous; lacking a strong sense of change, they were not easily to be persuaded that Parliament's ultimate authority, assumed to have been established for all time in 1688, could be lost again. It took Burke to point out that 'every age has its own manners, and its politics dependent upon them; and the same attempts will not be made against a constitution fully formed and matured, that were used to destroy it in the cradle, or to resist its growth during its infancy'. Such was the intellectual groundwork behind his famous contention, in the *Present Discontents*, that the power of the crown, destroyed in the form of prerogative, was being restored in the form of influence and patronage. Burke's historical understanding could not only be used to protest at what Burke considered to be George III's constitutional innovations, it could equally well be displayed in argument against similar attempts by radical parliamentary reformers, though here indeed it merged into the argument from prescription:

> a nation is . . . an idea of continuity, which extends in time as well as in numbers and in space. And this is a choice not of one day . . . it is a constitution made by what is ten thousand times better than choice, it is made by the peculiar circumstances, occasions, tempers, dispositions, and moral, civil, and social habitudes of the people, which disclose themselves only in a long space of time.[39]

Burke's appreciation of the influence which history exerted upon contemporary societies and institutions was not limited to his pronouncements on the situation of Britain. Though his knowledge of the American colonies, India and France was more restricted than that he had of British history, and thereby he was sometimes led to erroneous conclusions, his instinct was still to study the present in terms of the past, and the established situation in terms of the way it had emerged over a long period of time. It was very much his conviction that the rebelling Americans shared with the British a long history of struggle for liberty against the encroachments of monarchical government, as well as his consciousness of the colonists' geographically-induced sense of separate identity, which lent strength to his pleas for conciliation. It was his knowledge

es of India had codes of law and bodies of custom
indigenous historical development which con-
that British government in India had failed
by ignoring them. And it was his probably
mistaken belief that French history over the past two centuries
would have permitted the setting up of constitutional monarchy in that country which lent especial force to his denunciations of the French Revolution.

Burke's importance as a political thinker is secure. Within
the history of political thought he is most convincingly seen
as a school in himself; he had no precursors or successors who
shared the full range of his ideas. He did not display a ready
consistency in providing abstract answers to political problems,
for he saw that politics and government rarely present their
problems in a manner capable of systematic answer. But, as we
have seen, the arguments and views that he held do stand upon
a set of related assumptions. Consistently he fought in-
humanity wherever he found it, whether it was the inhuman
despotism of the single ruler or the inhuman tyranny of the
mob. Thus among those censured by him were both kings
and governors, radicals and revolutionaries. All the objects of
his censure shared the characteristic of going beyond the
bounds of political morality. Burke's position is thus revealed
as that of an apostle of moderation: he is, in fact, an advocate
of the oldest maxim of politics or personal conduct, that of
adherence to the mean, the middle path. Those who would
follow his example, and arrive at a Burkeian solution to
modern problems, should not ask what he advocated in any
particular situation, on the assumption that that situation has
its exact parallel in the present one; rather they should
examine the current situation, consider all courses of possible
action, and reject the extremes by holding to the course of
morality and humanity.

Notes

1 The Gladstonian Liberal, John Morley, concluded his popular biography of Burke (1879) with the prescient hope that 'it seems probable that he will be more frequently and more seriously referred to within the next twenty years . . .' Since Morley's book was reprinted eight times during that period, his account doubtless bears a considerable responsibility for the Liberals' frequent use of Burke.

2 See, for instance, Russell Kirk, *The Conservative Mind from Burke to Santayana* (New York, 1953), and Leo Strauss, *Natural Right and History* (Chicago, 1953).

3 Introduction to *Speech on Conciliation with the Colonies* in *Works*, ii. 104–105 (Little, Brown), or i. 453 (Bohn).

4 William Hazlitt went further: 'There is no single speech of Mr Burke which can convey a satisfactory idea of his powers of mind: to do him justice, it would be necessary to quote all his works; the only specimen of Burke is, *all that he wrote,*' *Eloquence of the British Senate* (1807).

5 William B. Todd, *A Bibliography of Edmund Burke* (1964), pp. 73ff.

6 To Richard Champion, 30 May, 1776, *The Correspondence of Edmund Burke*, vol. iii, ed. George H. Guttridge (Cambridge and Chicago, 1961), p. 269.

7 For an early, if gentle critique of the sort of ideas which Fox was to bring into the party, see Burke's letter to him of 8 October 1777, below, pp. 207-9.

8 *The Parliamentary Register*, ix, 670–71.

9 Richard Plantagenet Temple-Nugent-Brydges-Chandos-Grenville, Duke of Buckingham and Chandos, *Memoirs of the Court and Cabinets of George III* (1853), i, 285.

10 'The people did not like our work; and they joined the Court to pull it down,' he wrote on 22 June 1784, *The Correspondence of Edmund Burke*, vol. v, eds. Holden Furber and P. J. Marshall (Cambridge and Chicago, 1968), p. 154.

11 *General Evening Post*, 31 July, 1784.

12 10 Dec., 1785, *Burke Corr.* v. 243.

13 Diary of Georgina, Duchess of Devonshire, 20 Nov. 1788, in Walter Sichel, *Sheridan* (1909), ii. 404.

14 Fox to Portland [20 Jan. 1789], British Museum Additional MS. 47561, f. 93.

15 [Circa 24 Jan., 1789], *Burke Corr.* v. 436–45.

16 *The Parliamentary Register*, xxv. 125–30, 22 Dec., 1788.

17 30 July, 1789, in Lord John Russell (ed.), *Memorials and Correspondence of Charles James Fox* (1853), ii. 361.

18 To speak of Burke's use of the entail, and of other legal devices in common use for the preservation of estates, as an 'analogy' does less than justice to his literary method, which was a complex of argument and imagery. As Professor James T. Boulton writes: 'Burke was not only a great thinker, he was also an imaginative writer who requires a response from the reader as a whole man and not simply as a creature of intellect. Consequently his exposition – the play of imaginative insights as well as the statement of logical argument – itself becomes "proof" in this special sense that it communicates, and affirms while communicating, the rich complexity of a philosophy of life; it does not merely demonstrate the truth of a set of propositions,' *The Language of Politics in the Age of Wilkes and Burke* (1963), p. 98.

19 James Boswell, *Journal of a Tour to the Hebrides*, 15 Aug., 1773.

20 Grafton to Chatham, 17 Oct., 1766, *Chatham Correspondence* (1839), III, iii.

21 *Letter to a Noble Lord* (1796) in *Works*, v. 193 (Little, Brown) or v. 124–5 (Bohn).

22 *Three Letters on a Regicide Peace, Letter I* (1796) in *Works*, v. 284 (Little, Brown) or v. 189–90 (Bohn).

23 *Works*, iv. 96 (Little, Brown) or iii. 27 (Bohn).

24 For a useful account of this interpretation, see Francis P. Canavan, *The Political Reason of Edmund Burke* (Durham, N.C., 1960), pp. 3–5.

25 Two radicals who were to be Burke's opponents at the time of the French Revolution, Richard Price and Thomas Paine, had already put forward interpretations of the doctrine of rights at the time of the Anglo-American conflict. Price's *Observations on the Nature of Civil Liberty*, published in February 1776, had provoked Burke's wrath by its attack on his party's middle position – see Burke to Champion [19 March 1776], *Burke Corr.*, iii. 254. Paine's *Common Sense*, published in America a month earlier than Price's pamphlet, went even further in proposing Independence,

and was influential in bringing about the Declaration of Independence.

26 *Speech on . . . the Acts of Uniformity* in *Works*, vii. 16 (Little, Brown) or vi. 99 (Bohn).

27 One of the latest and most moderate statements of the 'natural law' school of Burke interpretations is B. T. Wilkins, *The Problems of Burke's Political Philosophy* (Oxford, 1967). For an earlier and more extreme version of the thesis, see Peter J. Stanlis, *Edmund Burke and the Natural Law* (Ann Arbor, 1958).

28 See Frank O'Gorman, *Edmund Burke, His Political Philosophy* (1973). That Burke's doctrine of prescription derives from natural law tradition is doubted by J. G. A. Pocock, 'Burke and the Ancient Constitution – a problem in the history of ideas,' *The Historical Journal*, iii (1960), 125–43.

29 For Locke, see Wilkins, *op. cit.*, pp. 19ff. For Montesquieu, see C. P. Courtney, *Montesquieu and Burke* (Oxford, 1963), especially the suggestive passages on pp. 15–16.

30 Alfred Cobban, *Edmund Burke and the Revolt against the Eighteenth Century* (1929). Cobban was also responsible for first questioning Burke's debt to the Enlightenment, though he did not try to establish affinities between Burke's thought and 'natural law'. By the second edition (1960), however, Cobban believed that he had been over-critical of the eighteenth century and that he had underemphasized that 'the basic affiliations of Burke are with Locke and Montesquieu'.

31 Stephen, *History* (Harbinger ed., 1962), ii. 189.

32 Cobban, *op. cit.* In his Preface to the second edition, he somewhat modified this position.

33 '. . . had Burke been in office during the American Revolution, we might merely have had to antedate his counter-revolutionary Toryism by some twenty years,' *England in the Age of the American Revolution* (2nd ed. 1961), pp. 39–40.

34 Cobban, *op. cit.* (2nd ed. 1960), p. 39.

35 To Dr William Markham, *post* 9 Nov., 1771, *The Correspondence of Edmund Burke*, vol. ii, ed. L. S. Sutherland (Cambridge and Chicago, 1962), p. 282.

36 To Depont (Nov. 1789), *The Correspondence of Edmund Burke*, vol. vi, eds. A. B. Cobban and R. A. Smith (Cambridge and Chicago, 1969), pp. 40–42; *A Letter to a Member of the National Assembly* (1791) in *Works*, iv. 51 (Little, Brown), or ii. 555 (Bohn).

37 Pocock, *op. cit.*, p. 143.

38 Readers will, however, note a certain similarity between this aspect of Burke's thought and that of Sir Robert Filmer, whose *Patriarcha, or the Natural Power of Kings asserted* (1680) was attacked in Locke's *First Treatise of Government*.

39 *Speech on . . . the state of the Representation of the Commons in Parliament* in *Works*, vii. 95 (Little, Brown) or vi. 146–47 (Bohn).

A Vindication of Natural Society

Before Burke's entry into politics his public comments on political and social matters were neither numerous nor explicit. His first major published work gives perhaps the best example of his early thought, though it is not without its problems for the reader. *A Vindication of Natural Society* was not, like so many of his later writings, intended as political polemic; rather, it was Burke's first contribution to those speculative discussions which occupied so many thinkers in the eighteenth century concerning man's use of his reasoning powers, the nature of the society in which he lived, and the nature of the universe. In such discussions the authority of the churches and of the Bible itself had often been displaced by 'the religion of Nature'. The main object of Burke's essay was to defend traditional religious authorities from further assault by showing that the arguments of the rationalists could easily be turned against the State if they conquered the more vulnerable Church. The *Vindication* was a parody of the style of Bolingbroke, the deist writer and sometime Tory politician. Burke in this work pours scorn upon Bolingbroke's alleged championship of 'natural society' over 'artificial society' or civil institutions of government. But the catalogue of the weaknesses of society which Burke attributes to Bolingbroke is very characteristically Burke's own. Though he does not blame government for the evils which afflict mankind, the impression he leaves is rather of a society to be reformed than of a society to be protected. The uneasy balance exhibited in this pamphlet between Burke's concern for humanity and his desire to preserve existing institutions was to continue throughout his life and writings.

By setting out for the first time his aversion from the *a priori* philosophy of natural society and the rights of man, the *Vindication* defined the position which Burke was to occupy not only in relation to the English deists and their successors, the Unitarians, but also in relation to the leading thinkers of the continental Enlightenment. At this time began his lifelong admiration for Montesquieu whose *Lettres Persanes* had, like Burke's own satire, rejected the extreme interpretations of natural society. At the same time began his ambivalent relationship with Rousseau, with whose *Discours sur l'inégalité* published in 1755 he is likely to have been acquainted when he wrote the *Vindication*. Rousseau's subsequent attack on civil society and vindication of natural society, in *É nile*, was criticised in the *Annual Register* by Burke, who was later still to regard the great *philosophe* as a principal instigator of the French Revolution. Yet the two men had more than a little in common; neither was bound by rigid views on consistency, both were capable of wider sympathies than most of their contemporaries, and both were later to be placed in the pantheon of forerunners of nineteenth-century Romanticism.

From A Vindication of Natural Society: or, a View of the Miseries and Evils arising to Mankind from every Species of Artificial Society. In a Letter to Lord ***. By a late Noble Writer (1756).

Before we finish our examination of artificial society, I shall lead your lordship into a closer consideration of the relations which it gives birth to, and the benefits, if such they are, which result from these relations. The most obvious division of society is into rich and poor; and it is no less obvious, that the number of the former bear a great disproportion to those of the latter. The whole business of the poor is to administer to the idleness, folly, and luxury of the rich; and that of the rich, in return, is to find the best methods of confirming the slavery and increasing the burdens of the poor. In a state of nature, it is an invariable law, that a man's acquisitions are in proportion to his labors. In a state of artificial society, it is a law as constant and as invariable, that those who labor most enjoy the fewest things; and that those who labor not at all have the greatest number of enjoyments. A constitution of things this, strange and ridiculous beyond expression! We scarce believe a thing when we are told it, which we actually see before our eyes every day without being in the least surprised. I suppose that there are in Great Britain upwards of a hundred thousand people employed in lead, tin, iron, copper, and coal mines; these unhappy wretches scarce ever see the light of the sun; they are buried in the bowels of the earth; there they work at a severe and dismal task, without the least prospect of being delivered from it; they subsist upon the coarsest and worst sort of fare; they have their health miserably impaired, and their lives cut short, by being perpetually confined in the close vapor of these malignant minerals. A hundred thousand more at least are tortured without remission by the suffocating smoke, intense fires, and constant drudgery necessary in refining and managing the products of those mines. If any man informed us that two hundred thousand innocent persons were condemned to so intolerable slavery, how should we pity the unhappy sufferers, and how great would be our just indignation against those who inflicted so cruel and ignominious a punishment! This is an instance – I could not wish a stronger – of the numberless things which we pass by in their common dress, yet which shock us when they are nakedly represented. But this number, considerable as it is, and the slavery, with all its baseness and horror, which we have at home, is nothing to what the rest of the world affords of the same nature. Millions daily bathed in the poisonous damps and destructive effluvia of lead, silver, copper, and arsenic. To say nothing of those other employments, those stations of wretchedness and contempt, in which civil society has placed the numerous *enfans perdus* of her army. Would any rational man submit to one of the most tolerable of these drudgeries, for all the artificial enjoyments which policy has made to result from them? By no means. And yet need I suggest to your lordship, that those who find the means, and those who arrive at the end, are not at all the same persons? On considering the strange and unaccountable fancies and contrivances of artificial reason, I have somewhere called this earth the Bedlam of our system. Looking now upon the effects of some of those fancies, may we not with equal reason call it likewise the Newgate and the Bridewell of the universe? Indeed the blindness of one part of mankind co-operating with the frenzy and villany of the other, has been the real builder of this respectable fabric of political society: and as the blindness of mankind has caused their slavery, in return their state of slavery is made a pretence for continuing them in a state of blindness; for the politician will tell you gravely, that their life of servitude disqualifies the greater part of the race of man for a search of truth, and supplies them with no other than mean and insufficient ideas. This is but too true; and this is one of the reasons for which I blame such institutions.

In a misery of this sort, admitting some few lenitives, and those too but a few, nine parts in ten of the whole race of mankind drudge through life. It may be urged perhaps, in palliation of this, that at least the rich few find a considerable and real benefit from the wretchedness of the many. But is this so in fact? Let us examine the point with a little more attention. For this purpose the rich in all societies may be thrown into two classes. The first is of those who are powerful as well as rich, and conduct the operations of the vast political machine. The other is of those who employ their riches wholly in the acquisition of pleasure. As to the first sort, their continual care and anxiety, their toilsome days, and sleepless nights, are next to proverbial. These circumstances are sufficient almost to level their condition to that of the unhappy majority; but there are other circumstances which place them in a far lower condition. Not only their understandings labor continually, which is the severest labor, but their hearts are torn by the worst, most troublesome, and insatiable of all passions, by avarice, by ambition, by fear and jealousy. No part of the mind has rest. Power gradually extirpates from the mind every humane and gentle virtue. Pity, benevolence, friendship, are things almost unknown in high stations. *Veræ amicitiæ rarissime inveniuntur in iis qui in honoribus reque publica versantur*, says Cicero.[1] And indeed courts are the schools where cruelty, pride, dissimulation, and treachery are studied and taught in the most vicious perfection. This is a point so clear and acknowledged, that if it did not make a necessary part of my subject, I should pass it by entirely. And this has hindered me from drawing at full length, and in the most striking colors, this shocking picture of the degeneracy and wretchedness of human nature, in that part which is vulgarly thought its happiest and most amiable state. You know from what originals I could copy such pictures. Happy are they who know enough of them to know the little value of the possessors of such things, and of all that they possess; and happy they who have been snatched from that post of danger which they occupy, with the remains of their virtue; loss of honors, wealth, titles, and even the loss of one's country, is nothing in balance with so great an advantage.

Let us now view the other species of the rich, those who devote their time and fortunes to idleness and pleasure. How much happier are they? The pleasures which are agreeable to nature are within the reach of all, and therefore can form no distinction in favor of the rich. The pleasures which art forces up are seldom sincere, and never satisfying. What is worse, this constant application to pleasure takes away from the enjoyment, or rather turns it into the nature of a very burdensome and laborious business. It has consequences much more fatal. It produces a weak valetudinary state of body, attended by all those horrid disorders, and yet more horrid methods of cure, which are the result of luxury on the one hand, and the weak and ridiculous efforts of human art on the other. The pleasures of such men are scarcely felt as pleasures; at the same time that they bring on pains and diseases, which are felt but too severely. The mind has its share of the misfortune; it grows lazy and enervate, unwilling and unable to search for truth, and utterly uncapable of knowing, much less of relishing, real happiness. The poor by their excessive labor, and the rich by their enormous luxury,

[1] True friendships are rarely found among those who are occupied in the pursuit of honours and in public affairs. *De Amicitia*, 17.64.

are set upon a level, and rendered equally ignorant of any knowledge which might conduce to their happiness. A dismal view of the interior of all civil society! The lower part broken and ground down by the most cruel oppression; and the rich by their artificial method of life bringing worse evils on themselves than their tyranny could possibly inflict on those below them. Very different is the prospect of the natural state. Here there are no wants which nature gives, and in this state men can be sensible of no other wants, which are not to be supplied by a very moderate degree of labor; therefore there is no slavery. Neither is there any luxury, because no single man can supply the materials of it. Life is simple, and therefore it is happy.

I am conscious, my lord, that your politician will urge in his defence, that this unequal state is highly useful. That without dooming some part of mankind to extraordinary toil, the arts which cultivate life could not be exercised. But I demand of this politician, how such arts came to be necessary? He answers, that civil society could not well exist without them. So that these arts are necessary to civil society, and civil society necessary again to these arts. Thus are we running in a circle, without modesty, and without end, and making one error and extravagance an excuse for the other. My sentiments about these arts and their cause, I have often discoursed with my friends at large. Pope has expressed them in good verse, where he talks with so much force of reason and elegance of language, in praise of the state of nature:

'Then was not pride, nor arts that pride to aid,
Man walked with beast, joint tenant of the shade.'[1]

On the whole, my lord, if political society, in whatever form, has still made the many the property of the few; if it has introduced labors unnecessary, vices and diseases unknown, and pleasures incompatible with nature; if in all countries it abridges the lives of millions, and renders those of

[1] *An Essay on Man* (1732), Epistle III, lines 151-52. The first line should begin 'Pride then was not;'. The poem was dedicated to Bolingbroke.

millions more utterly abject and miserable, shall we still worship so destructive an idol, and daily sacrifice to it our health, our liberty, and our peace? Or shall we pass by this monstrous heap of absurd notions, and abominable practices, thinking we have sufficiently discharged our duty in exposing the trifling cheats, and ridiculous juggles of a few mad, designing, or ambitious priests? Alas! my lord, we labor under a mortal consumption, whilst we are so anxious about the cure of a sore finger. For has not this leviathan of civil power overflowed the earth with a deluge of blood, as if he were made to disport and play therein? We have shown that political society, on a moderate calculation, has been the means of murdering several times the number of inhabitants now upon the earth, during its short existence, not upwards of four thousand years in any accounts to be depended on. But we have said nothing of the other, and perhaps as bad, consequence of these wars, which have spilled such seas of blood, and reduced so many millions to a merciless slavery. But these are only the ceremonies performed in the porch of the political temple. Much more horrid ones are seen as you enter it. The several species of government vie with each other in the absurdity of their constitutions, and the oppression which they make their subjects endure. Take them under what form you please, they are in effect but a despotism, and they fall, both in effect and appearance too, after a very short period, into that cruel and detestable species of tyranny: which I rather call it, because we have been educated under another form, than that this is of worse consequences to mankind. For the free governments, for the point of their space, and the moment of their duration, have felt more confusion, and committed more flagrant acts of tyranny, than the most perfect despotic governments which we have ever known. Turn your eye next to the labyrinth of the law, and the iniquity conceived in its intricate recesses. Consider the ravages committed in the bowels of all commonwealths by ambition, by avarice, envy, fraud, open injustice, and pretended friendship; vices which could draw little support from a state of nature, but which blossom and flourish in the rankness of political society. Resolve our whole discourse; add to it all those reflections which your own good understanding shall suggest, and make a strenuous effort beyond the reach of vulgar philosophy, to confess that the cause of artificial society is more defenceless even than that of artificial religion; that it is as derogatory from the honor of the Creator, as subversive of human reason, and productive of infinitely more mischief to the human race.

If pretended revelations have caused wars where they were opposed, and slavery where they were received, the pretended wise inventions of politicians have done the same. But the slavery has been much heavier, the wars far more bloody, and both more universal by many degrees. Show me any mischief produced by the madness or wickedness of theologians, and I will show you a hundred resulting from the ambition and villany of conquerors and statesmen. Show me an absurdity in religion, and I will undertake to show you a hundred for one in political laws and institutions. If you say that natural religion is a sufficient guide without the foreign aid of revelation, on what principle should political laws become necessary? Is not the same reason available in theology and in politics? If the laws of nature are the laws of God, is it consistent with the Divine wisdom to prescribe rules to us, and leave the enforcement of them to the folly of human institutions? Will you follow truth but to a certain point?

We are indebted for all our miseries to our distrust of that guide which Providence thought sufficient for our condition, our own natural reason, which rejecting both in human and divine things, we have given our necks to the yoke of political and theological slavery. We have renounced the prerogative of man, and it is no wonder that we should be treated like beasts. But our misery is much greater than theirs, as the crime we commit in rejecting the lawful dominion of our reason is greater than any which they can commit. If, after all, you should confess all these things, yet plead the necessity of political institutions, weak and wicked as they are, I can argue with equal, perhaps superior, force, concerning the necessity of artificial religion; and every step you advance in your argument, you add a strength to mine. So that if we are resolved to submit our reason and our liberty to civil usurpation, we have nothing to do but to conform as quietly as we can to the vulgar notions which are connected with this, and take up the theology of the vulgar as well as their politics. But if we think this necessity rather imaginary than real, we should renounce their dreams of society, together with their visions of religion, and vindicate ourselves into perfect liberty.

You are, my lord, but just entering into the world; I am going out of it. I have played long enough to be heartily tired of the drama. Whether I have acted my part in it well or ill, posterity will judge with more candor than I, or than the present age, with our present passions, can possibly pretend to. For my part, I quit it without a sigh, and submit to the sovereign order without murmuring. The nearer we approach to the goal of life, the better we begin to understand the true value of our existence, and the real weight of our opinions. We set out much in love with both; but we leave much behind us as we advance. We first throw away the tales along with the rattles of our nurses: those of the priest keep their hold a little longer; those of our governors the longest of all. But the passions which prop these opinions are withdrawn one after another; and the light of cool reason, at the setting of our life, shows us what a false splendor played upon these objects during our more sanguine seasons. Happy, my lord, if instructed by my experience, and even by my errors, you come early to make such an estimate of things, as may give freedom and ease to your life. I am happy that such an estimate promises me comfort at my death.

On the Present Discontents

The ostensible purpose of the finest of Burke's early political pamphlets was to explain the disruptions which had occurred since George III had come to the throne a decade earlier, a period during which there had been no less than seven changes of ministry. Discontents there certainly were: a growing parliamentary opposition, much extra-parliamentary discontent manifested in popular support for the demagogue John Wilkes, bitter criticism of the king and of other public figures culminating in the letters of 'Junius' in the *Public Advertiser*, and a growing disregard of the Commons' prohibition of printed reports on its debates. But Burke's principal purpose was to justify the position of his own party, the Rockingham Whigs, in their opposition to the king and his ministers. Though systematic party activity had been common enough in practice it still lacked a theoretical justification with which to counter the undoubted right of the monarch to act as head of government within the fairly tolerant limits laid down by the Revolution Settlement of William III's reign. For Burke the political party or connection was the manifestation of man's potential for achievement through social action, and as such a higher form of activity than that of the individual politician. In the latter category Burke placed not only George III but also the leading political figure of the day William Pitt, Earl of Chatham, who was in opposition in 1770 but despised the party mentality of the Rockinghams. Like other Rockinghamite pamphlets the *Present Discontents* was approved and amended by the party leaders, but it was in every sense the product of Burke's own mind, which moulded the loose clay of his friends' ideas into a brilliant exposition of the party's policy. Traditionally the work has been considered as providing a defence of the party system. Although Burke did in fact provide a complete rationale for the existence of a party in opposition, he stopped short of postulating a permanent rotation of parties in office. This development, however, was implicit in his understanding of party politics of the past, and in his advocacy of the right of an opposition to force itself into office in order to carry out its policies.

From Thoughts on the Cause of the Present Discontents (1770).

It is an undertaking of some degree of delicacy to examine into the cause of public disorders. If a man happens not to succeed in such an inquiry, he will be thought weak and visionary; if he touches the true grievance, there is a danger that he may come near to persons of weight and consequence, who will rather be exasperated at the discovery of their errors, than thankful for the occasion of correcting them. If he should be obliged to blame the favorites of the people, he will be considered as the tool of power; if he censures those in power, he will be looked on as an instrument of faction. But in all exertions of duty something is to be hazarded. In cases of tumult and disorder, our law has invested every man, in some sort, with the authority of a magistrate. When the affairs of the nation are distracted, private people are, by the spirit of that law, justified in stepping a little out of their ordinary sphere. They enjoy a privilege, of somewhat more dignity and effect, than that of idle lamentation over the calamities of their country. They may look into them narrowly; they may reason upon them liberally; and if they should be so fortunate as to discover the true source of the mischief, and to suggest any probable method of removing it, though they may displease the rulers for the day, they are certainly of service to the cause of government. Government is deeply interested in everything which, even through the medium of some temporary uneasiness, may tend finally to compose the minds of the subject, and to conciliate their affections. I have nothing to do here with the abstract value of the voice of the people. But as long as reputation, the most precious possession of every individual, and as long as opinion, the great support of the state, depend entirely upon that voice, it can never be considered as a thing of little consequence either to individuals or to governments. Nations are not primarily ruled by laws: less by violence. Whatever original energy may be supposed either in force or regulation, the operation of both is, in truth, merely instrumental. Nations are governed by the same methods, and on the same principles, by which an individual without authority is often able to govern those who are his equals or his superiors; by a knowledge of their temper, and by a judicious management of it; I mean, – when public affairs are steadily and quietly conducted; not when government is nothing but a continued scuffle between the magistrate and the multitude; in which sometimes the one and sometimes the other is uppermost; in which they alternately yield and prevail, in a series of contemptible victories, and scandalous submissions. The temper of the people amongst whom he presides ought therefore to be the first study of a statesman. And the knowledge of this temper it is by no means impossible for him to attain, if he has not an interest in being ignorant of what it is his duty to learn.

To complain of the age we live in, to murmur at the present possessors of power, to lament the past, to conceive extravagant hopes of the future, are the common dispositions of the greatest part of mankind; indeed the necessary effects of the ignorance and levity of the vulgar. Such complaints and humors have existed in all times; yet as all times have *not* been alike, true political sagacity manifests itself in distinguishing that complaint which only characterizes the general infirmity of human nature, from those which are symptoms of the particular distemperature of our own air and season.

Nobody, I believe, will consider it merely as the language of spleen or disappointment, if I say, that there is something particularly alarming in the present conjuncture. There is hardly a man, in or out of power, who holds any other language. That government is at once dreaded and contemned; that the laws are despoiled of all their respected and salutary terrors; that their inaction is a subject of ridicule, and their exertion of abhorrence; that rank, and office and title, and all the solemn plausibilities of the world, have lost their reverence and effect; that our foreign politics are as much deranged as our domestic economy; that our dependencies are slackened in their affection, and loosened from their obedience; that we know neither how to yield nor how to enforce; that hardly anything above or below, abroad or at home, is sound and entire; but that disconnection and confusion, in offices, in parties, in families, in Parliament, in the nation, prevail beyond the disorders of any former time: these are facts universally admitted and lamented.

This state of things is the more extraordinary, because the great parties which formerly divided and agitated the kingdom are known to be in a manner entirely dissolved. No great external calamity has visited the nation; no pestilence or famine. We do not labor at present under any scheme of taxation new or oppressive in the quantity or in the mode. Nor are we engaged in unsuccessful war; in which, our misfortunes might easily pervert our judgment; and our minds, sore from the loss of national glory, might feel every blow of fortune as a crime in government.

It is impossible that the cause of this strange distemper should not sometimes become a subject of discourse. It is a compliment due, and which I willingly pay, to those who administer our affairs, to take notice in the first place of their speculation. Our ministers are of opinion, that the increase of our trade and manufactures, that our growth by colonization, and by conquest, have concurred to accumulate immense wealth in the hands of some individuals; and this again being dispersed among the people, has rendered them universally proud, ferocious, and ungovernable; that the insolence of some from their enormous wealth, and the boldness of others from a guilty poverty, have rendered them capable of the most atrocious attempts; so that they have trampled upon all subordination, and violently borne down the unarmed laws of a free government; barriers too feeble against the fury of a populace so fierce and licentious as ours. They contend, that no adequate provocation has been given for so spreading a discontent; our affairs having been conducted throughout with remarkable temper and consummate wisdom. The wicked industry of some libellers, joined to the intrigues of a few disappointed politicians, have, in their opinion, been able to produce this unnatural ferment in the nation.

Nothing indeed can be more unnatural than the present convulsions of this country, if the above account be a true one. I confess I shall assent to it with great reluctance, and only on the compulsion of the clearest and firmest proofs; because their account resolves itself into this short, but discouraging proposition, 'That we have a very good ministry, but that we are a very bad people'; that we set outselves to bite the hand that feeds us; that with a malignant insanity, we oppose the measures, and ungratefully vilify the persons, of those whose sole object is our own peace and prosperity. If a few puny libellers, acting under a knot of factious politicians, without virtue, parts, or character (such they are constantly represented by these gentlemen), are sufficient to excite this disturbance, very perverse must be the disposition of that people, amongst whom such a disturbance can be excited by such means. It is besides no small aggravation of the public misfortune, that the disease, on this hypothesis, appears to be without remedy. If the wealth of the nation be the cause of its turbulence, I imagine it is not proposed to introduce poverty, as a constable to keep the peace. If our dominions abroad are the roots which feed all this rank luxuriance of sedition, it is not intended to cut them off in order to famish the fruit. If our liberty has enfeebled the executive power, there is no design, I hope, to call in the aid of despotism, to fill up the deficiencies of law. Whatever may be intended, these things are not yet professed. We seem therefore to be driven to absolute despair; for we have no other materials to work upon, but those out of which God has been pleased to form the inhabitants of this island. If these be radically and essentially vicious, all that can be said is, that those men are very unhappy, to whose fortune or duty it falls to administer the affairs of this untoward people. I hear it indeed sometimes asserted, that a steady perseverance in the present measures, and a rigorous punishment of those who oppose them, will in course of time infallibly put an end to these disorders. But this, in my opinion, is said without much observation of our present disposition, and without any knowledge at all of the general nature of mankind. If the matter of which this nation is composed be so very fermentable as these gentlemen describe it, leaven never will be wanting to work it up, as long as discontent, revenge, and ambition, have existence in the world. Particular punishments are the cure for accidental distempers in the state; they inflame rather than allay those heats which arise from the settled mismanagement of the government, or from a natural indisposition in the people. It is of the utmost moment not to make mistakes in the use of strong measures; and firmness is then only a virtue when it accompanies the most perfect wisdom. In truth, inconstancy is a sort of natural corrective of folly and ignorance.

I am not one of those who think that the people are never in the wrong. They have been so, frequently and outrageously, both in other countries and in this. But I do say, that in all disputes between them and their rulers, the presumption is at least upon a par in favor of the people. Experience may perhaps justify me in going further. When popular discontents have been very prevalent, it may well be affirmed and supported, that there has been generally something found amiss in the constitution, or in the conduct of government. The people have no interest in disorder. When they do wrong, it is their error, and not their crime. But with the governing part of the state, it is far otherwise. They certainly may act ill by design, as well as by mistake. '*Les révolutions qui arrivent dans les grands états ne sont point un effect du hazard, ni du caprice des peuples. Rien ne révolte* les grands *d'un royaume comme* un gouvernement foible et dérangé. *Pour la* populace, *ce n'est jamais par envie d'attaquer qu'elle se soulève, mais par impatience de souffrir.*'* These are the words of a great man; of a minister of state; and a zealous assertor of monarchy. They are applied

---

* Mém. de Sully, tom. i. p. 133. [Cf. Burke's remark in his *Letter to the Sheriffs of Bristol:* '*General* rebellions and revolts of an whole people never were *encouraged*, now or at any time. They are always *provoked*.' (below, p. 190)].

to the *system of favoritism* which was adopted by Henry the
Third of France, and to the dreadful consequences it produced. What he says of revolutions, is equally true of all great
disturbances. If this presumption in favor of the subjects
against the trustees of power be not the more probable, I am
sure it is the more comfortable speculation; because it is more
easy to change an administration, than to reform a people.

Upon a supposition, therefore, that, in the opening of the
cause, the presumptions stand equally balanced between the
parties, there seems sufficient ground to entitle any person to
a fair hearing, who attempts some other scheme beside that
easy one which is fashionable in some fashionable companies,
to account for the present discontents. It is not to be argued
that we endure no grievance, because our grievances are not
of the same sort with those under which we labored formerly;
not precisely those which we bore from the Tudors, or
vindicated on the Stuarts. A great change has taken place in
the affairs of this country. For in the silent lapse of events as
material alterations have been insensibly brought about in the
policy and character of governments and nations, as those
which have been marked by the tumult of public revolutions.

It is very rare indeed for men to be wrong in their feelings
concerning public misconduct; as rare to be right in their
speculation upon the cause of it. I have constantly observed,
that the generality of people are fifty years, at least, behind-
hand in their politics. There are but very few who are capable
of comparing and digesting what passes before their eyes at
different times and occasions, so as to form the whole into a
distinct system. But in books everything is settled for them,
without the exertion of any considerable diligence or sagacity.
For which reason men are wise with but little reflection, and
good with little self-denial, in the business of all times except
their own. We are very uncorrupt and tolerably enlightened
judges of the transactions of past ages; where no passions
deceive, and where the whole train of circumstances, from the
trifling cause to the tragical event, is set in an orderly series
before us. Few are the partisans of departed tyranny; and to be
a Whig on the business of an hundred years ago, is very con-

sistent with every advantage of present servility. This retrospective wisdom, and historical patriotism, are things of wonderful convenience, and serve admirably to reconcile the old quarrel between speculation and practice. Many a stern republican, after gorging himself with a full feast of admiration of the Grecian commonwealths and of our true Saxon constitution, and discharging all the splendid bile of his virtuous indignation on King John and King James, sits down perfectly satisfied to the coarsest work and homeliest job of the day he lives in. I believe there was no professed admirer of Henry the Eighth among the instruments of the last King James; nor in the court of Henry the Eighth was there, I dare say, to be found a single advocate for the favorites of Richard the Second.

No complaisance to our court, or to our age, can make me believe nature to be so changed, but that public liberty will be among us as among our ancestors, obnoxious to some person or other; and that opportunities will be furnished for attempting, at least, some alteration to the prejudice of our constitution. These attempts will naturally vary in their mode according to times and circumstances. For ambition, though it has ever the same general views, has not at all times the same means, nor the same particular objects. A great deal of the furniture of ancient tyranny is worn to rags; the rest is entirely out of fashion. Besides, there are few statesmen so very clumsy and awkward in their business, as to fall into the identical snare which has proved fatal to their predecessors. When an arbitrary imposition is attempted upon the subject, undoubtedly it will not bear on its forehead the name of *Ship-money*. There is no danger that an extension of the *Forest laws* should be the chosen mode of oppression in this age. And when we hear any instance of ministerial rapacity, to the prejudice of the rights of private life, it will certainly not be the exaction of two hundred pullets, from a woman of fashion, for leave to lie with her own husband.*

* 'Uxor Hugonis de Nevill dat Domino Regi ducentas Gallinas eo quod possit jacere una nocte cum Domino suo Hugone de Nevill.' – Maddox, Hist. Exch. c. xiii. p. 326.

Every age has its own manners, and its politics dependent upon them; and the same attempts will not be made against a constitution fully formed and matured, that were used to destroy it in the cradle, or to resist its growth during its infancy.

Against the being of Parliament, I am satisfied, no designs have ever been entertained since the revolution. Every one must perceive, that it is strongly the interest of the court, to have some second cause interposed between the ministers and the people. The gentlemen of the House of Commons have an interest equally strong in sustaining the part of that inter-mediate cause. However they may hire out the *usufruct* of their voices, they never will part with the *fee and inheritance*. Accordingly those who have been of the most known devotion to the will and pleasure of a court have, at the same time, been most forward in asserting a high authority in the House of Commons. When they knew who were to use that authority, and how it was to be employed, they thought it never could be carried too far. It must be always the wish of an unconstitutional statesman, that a House of Commons, who are entirely dependent upon him, should have every right of the people entirely dependent upon their pleasure. It was soon dis-covered, that the forms of a free, and the ends of an arbitrary government, were things not altogether incompatible.

The power of the crown, almost dead and rotten as Prerogative, has grown up anew, with much more strength, and far less odium, under the name of Influence. An influence, which operated without noise and without violence; an influence, which converted the very antagonist into the instrument of power; which contained in itself a perpetual principle of growth and renovation; and which the distresses and the prosperity of the country equally tended to augment, was an admirable substitute for a prerogative, that, being only the offspring of antiquated prejudices, had moulded in its original stamina irresistible principles of decay and dissolution. The ignorance of the people is a bottom but for a temporary system; the interest of active men in the state is a foundation perpetual and infallible. However, some circumstances, arising, it must be confessed, in a great degree from accident, prevented the effects of this influence for a long time from breaking out in a manner capable of exciting any serious apprehensions. Although government was strong and flourished exceedingly, the *court* had drawn far less advantage than one would imagine from this great source of power.

At the revolution,[1] the crown, deprived, for the ends of the revolution itself, of many prerogatives, was found too weak to struggle against all the difficulties which pressed so new and unsettled a government. The court was obliged therefore to delegate a part of its powers to men of such interest as could support, and of such fidelity as would adhere to, its establishment. Such men were able to draw in a greater number to a concurrence in the common defence. This connection, necessary at first, continued long after convenient; and properly conducted might indeed, in all situations, be an useful instrument of government. At the same time, through the intervention of men of popular weight and character, the people possessed a security for their just proportion of importance in the state. But as the title to the crown grew stronger by long possession, and by the constant increase of its influence, these helps have of late seemed to certain persons no better than incumbrances. The powerful managers for government were not sufficiently submissive to the pleasure of the possessors of immediate and personal favor, sometimes from a confidence in their own strength, natural and acquired; sometimes from a fear of offending their friends, and weakening that lead in the country which gave them a consideration independent of the court. Men acted as if the court could receive, as well as confer, an obligation. The influence of government, thus divided in appearance between the court and the leaders of parties, became in many cases an accession rather to the popular than to the royal scale; and some part of that influence, which would otherwise have been possessed as in a sort of mortmain and unalienable domain, returned again to the great ocean from whence it arose, and circulated among the people. This method, therefore, of governing by men of

[1] i.e. the Revolution of 1688.

great natural interest or great acquired consideration was viewed in a very invidious light by the true lovers of absolute monarchy. It is the nature of despotism to abhor power held by any means but its own momentary pleasure; and to annihilate all intermediate situations between boundless strength on its own part, and total debility on the part of the people.

To get rid of all this intermediate and independent importance, and *to secure to the court the unlimited and uncontrolled use of its own vast influence, under the sole direction of its own private favor,* has for some years past been the great object of policy. If this were compassed, the influence of the crown must of course produce all the effects which the most sanguine partisans of the court could possibly desire. Government might then be carried on without any concurrence on the part of the people; without any attention to the dignity of the greater, or to the affections of the lower sorts. A new project was therefore devised by a certain set of intriguing men, totally different from the system of administration which had prevailed since the accession of the House of Brunswick. This project, I have heard, was first conceived by some persons in the court of Frederick Prince of Wales.

The earliest attempt in the execution of this design was to set up for minister, a person, in rank indeed respectable, and very ample in fortune; but who, to the moment of this vast and sudden elevation, was little known or considered in the kingdom.[1] To him the whole nation was to yield an immediate and implicit submission. But whether it was from want of firmness to bear up against the first opposition; or that things were not yet fully ripened, or that this method was not found the most eligible; that idea was soon abandoned. The instrumental part of the project was a little altered, to accommodate it to the time and to bring things more gradually and more surely to the one great end proposed.

The first part of the reformed plan was to draw *a line which*

---

[1] John Stuart, third Earl of Bute (1713–1792). Bute had become a Secretary of State in 1761 and First Lord of the Treasury in 1762. He resigned in 1763.

should separate the court from the ministry. Hitherto these names had been looked upon as synonymous; but for the future, court and administration were to be considered as things totally distinct. By this operation, two systems of administration were to be formed; one which should be in the real secret and confidence; the other merely ostensible to perform the official and executory duties of government. The latter were alone to be responsible; whilst the real advisers, who enjoyed all the power, were effectually removed from all the danger.

Secondly, *A party under these leaders was to be formed in favor of the court against the ministry:* this party was to have a large share in the emoluments of government, and to hold it totally separate from, and independent of, ostensible administration.

The third point, and that on which the success of the whole scheme ultimately depended, was *to bring Parliament to an acquiescence in this project.* Parliament was therefore to be taught by degrees a total indifference to the persons, rank, influence, abilities, connections, and character of the ministers of the crown. By means of a discipline, on which I shall say more hereafter, that body was to be habituated to the most opposite interests, and the most discordant politics. All connections and dependencies among subjects were to be entirely dissolved. As, hitherto, business had gone through the hands of leaders of Whigs or Tories, men of talents to conciliate the people, and to engage their confidence; now the method was to be altered: and the lead was to be given to men of no sort of consideration or credit in the country. This want of natural importance was to be their very title to delegated power. Members of Parliament were to be hardened into an insensibility to pride as well as to duty. Those high and haughty sentiments, which are the great support of independence, were to be let down gradually. Points of honor and precedence were no more to be regarded in Parliamentary decorum than in a Turkish army. It was to be avowed, as a constitutional maxim, that the king might appoint one of his footmen, or one of your footmen for minister; and that he ought to be, and that he would be, as well followed as the first name for rank or wisdom in the nation. Thus Parliament was to look on as if perfectly unconcerned, while a cabal of the closet and back-stairs was substituted in the place of a national administration.

With such a degree of acquiescence, any measure of any court might well be deemed thoroughly secure. The capital objects, and by much the most flattering characteristics of arbitrary power, would be obtained. Everything would be drawn from its holdings in the country to the personal favor and inclination of the prince. This favor would be the sole introduction to power, and the only tenure by which it was to be held; so that no person looking towards another, and all looking towards the court, it was impossible but that the motive which solely influenced every man's hopes must come in time to govern every man's conduct; till at last the servility became universal, in spite of the dead letter of any laws or institutions whatsoever.

How it should happen that any man could be tempted to venture upon such a project of government, may at first view appear surprising. But the fact is that opportunities very inviting to such an attempt have offered; and the scheme itself was not destitute of some arguments, not wholly unplausible, to recommend it. These opportunities and these arguments, the use that has been made of both, the plan for carrying this new scheme of government into execution, and the effects which it has produced, are, in my opinion, worthy of our serious consideration.

His Majesty came to the throne of these kingdoms with more advantages than any of his predecessors since the revolution. Fourth in descent, and third in succession of his royal family, even the zealots of hereditary right, in him, saw something to flatter their favorite prejudices; and to justify a transfer of their attachments, without a change in their principles. The person and cause of the Pretender were become contemptible; his title disowned throughout Europe; his party disbanded in England. His Majesty came, indeed, to the inheritance of a mighty war; but, victorious in every part of the globe, peace was always in his power, not to negotiate, but to dictate. No foreign habitudes or attachments withdrew him from the cultivation of his power at home. His revenue for the civil establishment, fixed (as it was then thought) at a large, but definite sum, was ample without being invidious. His influence, by additions from conquest, by an augmentation of debt, by an increase of military and naval establishment, much strengthened and extended. And coming to the throne in the prime and full vigor of youth, as from affection there was a strong dislike, so from dread there seemed to be a general averseness, from giving anything like offence to a monarch, against whose resentment opposition could not look for a refuge in any sort of reversionary hope.

These singular advantages inspired his Majesty only with a more ardent desire to preserve unimpaired the spirit of that national freedom, to which he owed a situation so full of glory. But to others it suggested sentiments of a very different nature. They thought they now beheld an opportunity (by a certain sort of statesmen never long undiscovered or unemployed) of drawing to themselves by the aggrandizement of a court faction, a degree of power which they could never hope to derive from natural influence or from honorable service; and which it was impossible they could hold with the least security, whilst the system of administration rested upon its former bottom. In order to facilitate the execution of their design, it was necessary to make many alterations in political arrangement, and a signal change in the opinions, habits, and connections of the greatest part of those who at that time acted in public.

In the first place, they proceeded gradually, but not slowly, to destroy everything of strength which did not derive its principal nourishment from the immediate pleasure of the court. The greatest weight of popular opinion and party connection were then with the Duke of Newcastle and Mr Pitt. Neither of these held their importance by the *new tenure* of the court; they were not therefore thought to be so proper as others for the services which were required by that tenure. It happened very favorably for the new system, that under a forced coalition there rankled an incurable alienation and disgust between the parties which composed the administration. Mr Pitt was first attacked. Not satisfied with removing him from power, they endeavored by various artifices to ruin his character. The other party seemed rather pleased to get rid of so oppressive a support; not perceiving, that their own fall was prepared by his, and involved in it. Many other reasons prevented them from daring to look their true situation in the face. To the great Whig families it was extremely disagreeable, and seemed almost unnatural, to oppose the administration of a prince of the House of Brunswick. Day after day they hesitated, and doubted, and lingered, expecting that other counsels would take place; and were slow to be persuaded, that all which had been done by the cabal was the effect not of humor, but of system. It was more strongly and evidently the interest of the new court faction, to get rid of the great Whig connections, than to destroy Mr Pitt. The power of that gentleman was vast indeed and merited; but it was in a great degree personal, and therefore transient. Theirs was rooted in the country. For, with a good deal less of popularity, they possessed a far more natural and fixed influence. Long possession of government; vast property; obligations of favors given and received; connection of office; ties of blood, of alliance, of friendship (things at that time supposed of some force); the name of Whig, dear to the majority of the people; the zeal early begun and steadily continued to the royal family: all these together formed a body of power in the nation, which was criminal and devoted. The great ruling principle of the cabal, and that which animated and harmonized all their proceedings, how various soever they may have been, was to signify to the world that the court would proceed upon its own proper forces only; and that the pretence of bringing any other into its service was an affront to it, and not a support. Therefore when the chiefs were removed, in order to go to the root, the whole party was put under a proscription, so general and severe, as to take their hard-earned bread from the lowest officers, in a manner which had never been known before, even in general revolutions. But it was thought necessary effectually to destroy all dependencies but one; and to show an example of the firmness and rigor with which the new system was to be supported.

Thus for the time were pulled down, in the persons of the Whig leaders and of Mr Pitt (in spite of the services of the one at the accession of the royal family, and the recent services of the other in the war), the *two only securities for the importance of the people; power arising from popularity; and power arising from connection.* Here and there indeed a few individuals were left standing, who gave security for their total estrangement from the odious principles of party connection and personal attachment; and it must be confessed that most of them have religiously kept their faith. Such a change could not however be made without a mighty shock to government.

To reconcile the minds of the people to all these movements, principles correspondent to them had been preached up with great zeal. Every one must remember that the cabal set out with the most astonishing prudery, both moral and political. Those, who in a few months after soused over head and ears into the deepest and dirtiest pits of corruption, cried out violently against the indirect practices in the electing and managing of Parliaments, which had formerly prevailed. This marvellous abhorrence which the court had suddenly taken to all influence, was not only circulated in conversation through the kingdom, but pompously announced to the public, with many other extraordinary things, in a pamphlet* which had all the appearance of a manifesto preparatory to some considerable enterprise. Throughout it was a satire, though in terms managed and decent enough, on the politics of the former reign. It was indeed written with no small art and address.

In this piece appeared the first dawning of the new system: there first appeared the idea (then only in speculation) of *separating the court from the administration;* of carrying everything from national connection to personal regards; and of forming a regular party for that purpose, under the name of *king's men.*

To recommend this system to the people, a perspective

* Sentiments of an Honest Man.

view of the court, gorgeously painted, and finely illuminated from within, was exhibited to the gaping multitude. Party was to be totally done away, with all its evil works. Corruption was to be cast down from court, as *Atè* was from heaven. Power was thenceforward to be the chosen residence of public spirit; and no one was to be supposed under any sinister influence, except those who had the misfortune to be in disgrace at court, which was to stand in lieu of all vices and all corruptions. A scheme of perfection to be realized in a monarchy far beyond the visionary republic of Plato. The whole scenery was exactly disposed to captivate those good souls, whose credulous morality is so invaluable a treasure to crafty politicians. Indeed there was wherewithal to charm everybody, except those few who are not much pleased with professions of super-natural virtue, who know of what stuff such professions are made, for what purposes they are designed, and in what they are sure constantly to end. Many innocent gentlemen, who had been talking prose all their lives without knowing anything of the matter, began at last to open their eyes upon their own merits, and to attribute their not having been lords of the treasury and lords of trade many years before, merely to the prevalence of party, and to the ministerial power, which had frustrated the good intentions of the court in favor of their abilities. Now was the time to unlock the sealed fountain of royal bounty, which had been infamously monopolized and huckstered, and to let it flow at large upon the whole people. The time was come, to restore royalty to its original splendor. *Mettre le Roy hors de page*, became a sort of watchword. And it was constantly in the mouths of all the runners of the court, that nothing could preserve the balance of the constitution from being overturned by the rabble, or by a faction of the nobility, but to free the sovereign effectually from that ministerial tyranny under which the royal dignity had been oppressed in the person of his Majesty's grandfather.

These were some of the many artifices used to reconcile the people to the great change which was made in the persons who composed the ministry, and the still greater which was made and avowed in its constitution. As to individuals, other methods were employed with them; in order so thoroughly to disunite every party, and even every family, that *no concert, order, or effect, might appear in any future opposition.* And in this manner an administration without connection with the people, or with one another, was first put in possession of government. What good consequences followed from it, we have all seen; whether with regard to virtue, public or private; to the ease and happiness of the sovereign; or to the real strength of government. But as so much stress was then laid on the necessity of this new project, it will not be amiss to take a view of the effects of this royal servitude and vile durance, which was so deplored in the reign of the late monarch, and was so carefully to be avoided in the reign of his successor. The effects were these.

In times full of doubt and danger to his person and family, George II maintained the dignity of his crown connected with the liberty of his people, not only unimpaired, but improved, for the space of thirty-three years. He overcame a dangerous rebellion, abetted by foreign force, and raging in the heart of his kingdoms; and thereby destroyed the seeds of all future rebellion that could arise upon the same principle. He carried the glory, the power, the commerce of England, to a height unknown even to this renowned nation in the times of its greatest prosperity: and he left his succession resting on the true and only true foundations of all national and all regal greatness; affection at home, reputation abroad, trust in allies, terror in rival nations. The most ardent lover of his country cannot wish for Great Britain a happier fate than to continue as she was then left. A people, emulous as we are in affection to our present sovereign, know not how to form a prayer to heaven for a greater blessing upon his virtues, or a higher state of felicity and glory, than that he should live, and should reign, and when Providence ordains it, should die, exactly like his illustrious predecessor.

A great prince may be obliged (though such a thing cannot happen very often) to sacrifice his private inclination to his public interest, A wise prince will not think that such a restraint implies a condition of servility; and truly, if such was the condition of the last reign, and the effects were also such as we have described, we ought, no less for the sake of the sovereign whom we love, than for our own, to hear arguments convincing indeed, before we depart from the maxims of that reign, or fly in the face of this great body of strong and recent experience.

One of the principal topics which was then, and has been since, much employed by that political* school, is an affected terror of the growth of an aristocratic power, prejudicial to the rights of the crown, and the balance of the constitution. Any new powers exercised in the House of Lords, or in the House of Commons, or by the crown, ought certainly to excite the vigilant and anxious jealousy of a free people. Even a new and unprecedented course of action in the whole legislature, without great and evident reason, may be a subject of just uneasiness. I will not affirm, that there may not have lately appeared in the House of Lords, a disposition to some attempts derogatory to the legal rights of the subject. If any such have really appeared, they have arisen, not from a power properly aristocratic, but from the same influence which is charged with having excited attempts of a similar nature in the House of Commons; which House, if it should have been betrayed into an unfortunate quarrel with its constituents, and involved in a charge of the very same nature, could have neither power nor inclination to repel such attempts in others. Those attempts in the House of Lords can no more be called aristocratic proceedings, than the proceedings with regard to the county of Middlesex in the House of Commons can with any sense be called democratical.[1]

It is true, that the peers have a great influence in the kingdom, and in every part of the public concerns. While they are

* See the political writings of the late Dr. Brown, and many others. [John Brown (1715–1766), in *An Estimate of the Manners and Principles of the Times* (1757), had argued that there was a general political degeneracy in Britain under the ministries of the 'Whig oligarchy'.]

[1] Viz. the Middlesex election case, 1768–1769, concerning the election of John Wilkes (1727–1797), whom the government had prevented from taking his seat.

men of property, it is impossible to prevent it, except by such means as must prevent all property from its natural operation: an event not easily to be compassed, while property is power; nor by any means to be wished, while the least notion exists of the method by which the spirit of liberty acts, and of the means by which it is preserved. If any particular peers, by their uniform, upright, constitutional conduct, by their public and their private virtues, have acquired an influence in the country; the people, on whose favor that influence depends, and from whom it arose, will never be duped into an opinion, that such greatness in a peer is the despotism of an aristocracy, when they know and feel it to be the effect and pledge of their own importance.

I am no friend to aristocracy, in the sense at least in which that word is usually understood. If it were not a bad habit to moot cases on the supposed ruin of the constitution, I should be free to declare, that if it must perish, I would rather by far see it resolved into any other form, than lost in that austere and insolent domination. But, whatever my dislikes may be, my fears are not upon that quarter. The question, on the influence of a court, and of a peerage, is not, which of the two dangers is the more eligible, but which is the more imminent. He is but a poor observer, who has not seen, that the generality of peers, far from supporting themselves in a state of independent greatness, are but too apt to fall into an oblivion of their proper dignity, and to run headlong into an abject servitude. Would to God it were true, that the fault of our peers were too much spirit. It is worthy of some observation that these gentlemen, so jealous of aristocracy, make no complaints of the power of those peers (neither few nor inconsiderable) who are always in the train of a court, and whose whole weight must be considered as a portion of the settled influence of the crown. This is all safe and right; but if some peers (I am very sorry they are not as many as they ought to be) set themselves, in the great concern of peers and commons, against a back-stairs influence and clandestine government, then the alarm begins; then the constitution is in danger of being forced into an aristocracy.

I rest a little the longer on this court topic, because it was much insisted upon at the time of the great change,[1] and has been since frequently revived by many of the agents of that party; for, whilst they are terrifying the great and opulent with the horrors of mob-government, they are by other managers attempting (though hitherto with little success) to alarm the people with a phantom of tyranny in the nobles. All this is done upon their favorite principle of disunion, of sowing jealousies amongst the different orders of the state, and of disjointing the natural strength of the kingdom; that it may be rendered incapable of resisting the sinister designs of wicked men, who have engrossed the royal power.

Thus much of the topics chosen by the courtiers to recommend their system; it will be necessary to open a little more at large the nature of that party which was formed for its support. Without this, the whole would have been no better than a visionary amusement, like the scheme of Harrington's political club,[2] and not a business in which the nation had a real concern. As a powerful party, and a party constructed on a new principle, it is a very inviting object of curiosity.

It must be remembered, that since the revolution, until the period we are speaking of, the influence of the crown had been always employed in supporting the ministers of state, and in carrying on the public business according to their opinions. But the party now in question is formed upon a very different idea. It is to intercept the favor, protection, and confidence of the crown in the passage to its ministers; it is to come between them and their importance in Parliament; it is to separate them from all their natural and acquired dependencies; it is intended as the control, not the support, of administration. The machinery of this system is perplexed in its movements, and false in its principle. It is formed on a supposition that the king is something external to his government; and that he may be honored and aggrandized, even by its debility and disgrace. The plan proceeds expressly on the idea of enfeebling

[1] i.e. at or soon after George III's accession in 1760.

[2] James Harrington (1611–1677), the political theorist, formed the Rota Club, 1659–1660, for the discussion of politics.

the regular executory power. It proceeds on the idea of weakening the state in order to strengthen the court. The scheme depending entirely on distrust, on disconnection, on mutability by principle, on systematic weakness in every particular member; it is impossible that the total result should be substantial strength of any kind.

As a foundation of their scheme, the cabal have established a sort of *rota* in the court. All sorts of parties, by this means, have been brought into administration; from whence few have had the good fortune to escape without disgrace; none at all without considerable losses. In the beginning of each arrangement no professions of confidence and support are wanting, to induce the leading men to engage. But while the ministers of the day appear in all the pomp and pride of power, while they have all their canvas spread out to the wind, and every sail filled with the fair and prosperous gale of royal favor, in a short time they find, they know not how, a current, which sets directly against them: which prevents all progress, and even drives them backwards. They grow ashamed and mortified in a situation, which, by its vicinity to power, only serves to remind them the more strongly of their insignificance. They are obliged either to execute the orders of their inferiors, or to see themselves opposed by the natural instruments of their office. With the loss of their dignity they lose their temper. In their turn they grow troublesome to that cabal which, whether it supports or opposes, equally disgraces and equally betrays them. It is soon found necessary to get rid of the heads of administration; but it is of the heads only. As there always are many rotten members belonging to the best connections, it is not hard to persuade several to continue in office without their leaders. By this means the party goes out much thinner than it came in; and is only reduced in strength by its temporary possession of power. Besides, if by accident, or in course of changes, that power should be recovered, the junto have thrown up a retrenchment of these carcasses, which may serve to cover themselves in a day of danger. They conclude, not unwisely, that such rotten members will become the first objects of disgust and resentment to their ancient connections.

They contrive to form in the outward administration two parties at the least; which, whilst they are tearing one another to pieces, are both competitors for the favor and protection of the cabal; and, by their emulation, contribute to throw everything more and more into the hands of the interior managers.

A minister of state will sometimes keep himself totally estranged from all his colleagues; will differ from them in their councils, will privately traverse, and publicly oppose, their measures. He will, however, continue in his employment. Instead of suffering any mark of displeasure, he will be distinguished by an unbounded profusion of court rewards and caresses; because he does what is expected, and all that is expected, from men in office. He helps to keep some form of administration in being, and keeps it at the same time as weak and divided as possible.

However, we must take care not to be mistaken, or to imagine that such persons have any weight in their opposition. When, by them, administration is convinced of its insignificancy, they are soon to be convinced of their own. They never are suffered to succeed in their opposition. They and the world are to be satisfied, that neither office, nor authority, nor property, nor ability, eloquence, counsel, skill, or union, are of the least importance; but that the mere influence of the court, naked of all support, and destitute of all management, is abundantly sufficient for all its own purposes.

When any adverse connection is to be destroyed, the cabal seldom appear in the work themselves. They find out some person of whom the party entertains a high opinion. Such a person they endeavor to delude with various pretences. They teach him first to distrust, and then to quarrel with his friends; among whom, by the same arts, they excite a similar diffidence of him; so that in this mutual fear and distrust, he may suffer himself to be employed as the instrument in the change which is brought about. Afterwards they are sure to destroy him in his turn, by setting up in his place some person in whom he he had himself reposed the greatest confidence, and who serves to carry off a considerable part of his adherents.

When such a person has broke in this manner with his connections, he is soon compelled to commit some flagrant act of iniquitous, personal hostility against some of them (such as an attempt to strip a particular friend of his family estate), by which the cabal hope to render the parties utterly irreconcilable. In truth, they have so contrived matters, that people have a greater hatred to the subordinate instruments than to the principal movers.

As in destroying their enemies they make use of instruments not immediately belonging to their corps, so in advancing their own friends they pursue exactly the same method. To promote any of them to considerable rank or emolument, they commonly take care that the recommendation shall pass through the hands of the ostensible ministry: such a recommendation might however appear to the world, as some proof of the credit of ministers, and some means of increasing their strength. To prevent this, the persons so advanced are directed, in all companies, industriously to declare, that they are under no obligations whatsoever to administration; that they have received their office from another quarter; that they are totally free and independent.

When the faction has any job of lucre to obtain, or of vengeance to perpetrate, their way is, to select, for the execution, those very persons to whose habits, friendships, principles, and declarations, such proceedings are publicly known to be the most adverse; at once to render the instruments the more odious, and therefore the more dependent, and to prevent the people from ever reposing a confidence in any appearance of private friendship or public principle.

If the administration seem now and then, from remissness, or from fear of making themselves disagreeable, to suffer any popular excesses to go unpunished, the cabal immediately sets up some creature of theirs to raise a clamor against the ministers, as having shamefully betrayed the dignity of government. Then they compel the ministry to become active in conferring rewards and honors on the persons who have been the instruments of their disgrace; and, after having first vilified them with the higher orders for suffering the laws to sleep over the licentiousness of the populace, they drive them (in order to make amends for their former inactivity) to some act of atrocious violence, which renders them completely abhorred by the people. They, who remember the riots which attended the Middlesex election, the opening of the present Parliament, and the transactions relative to Saint George's Fields, will not be at a loss for an application of these remarks.[1]

That this body may be enabled to compass all the ends of its institution, its members are scarcely ever to aim at the high and responsible offices of the state. They are distributed with art and judgment through all the secondary, but efficient, departments of office, and through the households of all the branches of the royal family: so as on one hand to occupy all the avenues to the throne; and on the other to forward or frustrate the execution of any measure, according to their own interests. For with the credit and support which they are known to have, though for the greater part in places which are only a genteel excuse for salary, they possess all the influence of the highest posts; and they dictate publicly in almost everything, even with a parade of superiority. Whenever they dissent (as it often happens) from their nominal leaders, the trained part of the senate, instinctively in the secret, is sure to follow them: provided the leaders, sensible of their situation, do not of themselves recede in time from their most declared opinions. This latter is generally the case. It will not be conceivable to any one who has not seen it, what pleasure is taken by the cabal in rendering these heads of office thoroughly contemptible and ridiculous. And when they are become so, they have then the best chance for being well supported.

The members of the court faction are fully indemnified for not holding places on the slippery heights of the kingdom, not only by the lead in all affairs, but also by the perfect security in which they enjoy less conspicuous, but very advantageous

[1] The 'Massacre of St. George's Fields', when the Foot Guards killed some members of a crowd of Wilkes' supporters in Southwark, occurred on 10 May 1768.

situations. Their places are in express legal tenure, or, in effect, all of them for life. Whilst the first and most respectable persons in the kingdom are tossed about like tennis-balls, the sport of a blind and insolent caprice, no minister dares even to cast an oblique glance at the lowest of their body. If an attempt be made upon one of this corps, immediately he flies to sanctuary, and pretends to the most inviolable of all promises. No conveniency of public arrangement is available to remove any one of them from the specific situation he holds; and the slightest attempt upon one of them, by the most powerful minister, is a certain preliminary to his own destruction.

Conscious of their independence, they bear themselves with a lofty air to the exterior ministers. Like janissaries, they derive a kind of freedom from the very condition of their servitude. They may act just as they please; provided they are true to the great ruling principle of their institution. It is, therefore, not at all wonderful, that people should be so desirous of adding themselves to that body, in which they may possess and reconcile satisfactions the most alluring, and seemingly the most contradictory; enjoying at once all the spirited pleasure of independence, and all the gross lucre and fat emoluments of servitude.

Here is a sketch, though a slight one, of the constitution, laws, and policy of this new court corporation. The name by which they choose to distinguish themselves, is that of *king's men* or the *king's friends*, by an invidious exclusion of the rest of his Majesty's most loyal and affectionate subjects. The whole system, comprehending the exterior and interior administrations, is commonly called, in the technical language of the court, *double cabinet*; in French or English, as you choose to pronounce it.

Whether all this be a vision of a distracted brain, or the invention of a malicious heart, or a real faction in the country, must be judged by the appearances which things have worn for eight years past. Thus far I am certain, that there is not a single public man, in or out of office, who has not, at some time or other, borne testimony to the truth of what I have now related. In particular, no persons have been more strong in their assertions, and louder and more indecent in their complaints, than those who compose all the exterior part of the present administration; in whose time that faction has arrived at such an height of power, and of boldness in the use of it, as may, in the end, perhaps bring about its total destruction.

It is true, that about four years ago, during the administration of the Marquis of Rockingham, an attempt was made to carry on government without their concurrence. However, this was only a transient cloud; they were hid but for a moment; and their constellation blazed out with greater brightness, and a far more vigorous influence, some time after it was blown over. An attempt was at that time made (but without any idea of proscription) to break their corps, to discountenance their doctrines, to revive connections of a different kind, to restore the principles and policy of the Whigs, to reanimate the cause of liberty by ministerial countenance; and then for the first time were men seen attached in office to every principle they had maintained in opposition. No one will doubt, that such men were abhorred and violently opposed by the court faction, and that such a system could have but a short duration.

It may appear somewhat affected, that in so much discourse upon this extraordinary party, I should say so little of the Earl of Bute, who is the supposed head of it. But this was neither owing to affectation nor inadvertence. I have carefully avoided the introduction of personal reflections of any kind. Much the greater part of the topics which have been used to blacken this nobleman are either unjust or frivolous. At best, they have a tendency to give the resentment of this bitter calamity a wrong direction, and to turn a public grievance into a mean, personal, or a dangerous national quarrel. Where there is a regular scheme of operations carried on, it is the system, and not any individual person who acts in it, that is truly dangerous. This system has not arisen solely from the ambition of Lord Bute, but from the circumstances which favored it, and from an indifference to the constitution which had been for some time growing among our gentry. We should have been tried with it, if the Earl of Bute had never existed; and it will want neither a contriving head nor active members, when the Earl of Bute exists no longer. It is not, therefore, to rail at Lord Bute, but firmly to embody against this court party and its practices, which can afford us any prospect of relief in our present condition.

Another motive induces me to put the personal consideration of Lord Bute wholly out of the question. He communicates very little in a direct manner with the greater part of our men of business. This has never been his custom. It is enough for him that he surrounds them with his creatures. Several imagine, therefore, that they have a very good excuse for doing all the work of this faction, when they have no personal connection with Lord Bute. But whoever becomes a party to an administration, composed of insulated individuals, without faith plighted, tie, or common principle; an administration constitutionally impotent, because supported by no party in the nation; he who contributes to destroy the connections of men and their trust in one another, or in any sort to throw the dependence of public counsels upon private will and favor, possibly may have nothing to do with the Earl of Bute. It matters little whether he be the friend or the enemy of that particular person. But let him be who or what he will, he abets a faction that is driving hard to the ruin of his country. He is sapping the foundation of its liberty, disturbing the sources of its domestic tranquillity, weakening its government over its dependencies, degrading it from all its importance in the system of Europe.

It is this unnatural infusion of a *system of favoritism* into a government which in a great part of its constitution is popular, that has raised the present ferment in the nation. The people, without entering deeply into its principles, could plainly perceive its effects, in much violence, in a great spirit of innovation, and a general disorder in all the functions of government. I keep my eye solely on this system; if I speak of those measures which have arisen from it, it will be so far only as they illustrate the general scheme. This is the fountain of all those bitter waters of which, through an hundred diff.rent conduits, we have drunk until we are ready to burst. The discretionary power of the crown in the formation of ministry, abused by bad or weak men, has given rise to a system, which, without directly violating the letter of any law, operates against the spirit of the whole constitution.

A plan of favoritism for our executory government is essentially at variance with the plan of our legislature. One great end undoubtedly of a mixed government like ours, composed of monarchy, and of controls, on the part of the higher people and the lower, is that the prince shall not be able to violate the laws. This is useful indeed and fundamental. But this, even at first view, is no more than a negative advantage; an armor merely defensive. It is therefore next in order, and equal in importance, *that the discretionary powers which are necessarily vested in the monarch, whether for the execution of the laws, or for the nomination to magistracy and office, or for conducting the affairs of peace and war, or for ordering the revenue, should all be exercised upon public principles and national grounds, and not on the likings or prejudices, the intrigues or policies, of a court.* This, I said, is equal in importance to the securing a government according to law. The laws reach but a very little way. Constitute government how you please, infinitely the greater part of it must depend upon the exercise of the powers which are left at large to the prudence and uprightness of ministers of state. Even all the use and potency of the laws depends upon them. Without them, your commonwealth is no better than a scheme upon paper; and not a living, active, effective constitution. It is possible that through negligence, or ignorance, or design artfully conducted, ministers may suffer one part of government to languish, another to be perverted from its purposes, and every valuable interest of the country to fall into ruin and decay, without possibility of fixing any single act on which a criminal prosecution can be justly grounded. The due arrangement of men in the active part of the state, far from being foreign to the purposes of a wise government, ought to be among its very first and dearest objects. When, therefore, the abettors of the new system tell us, that between them and their opposers there is nothing but a struggle for power, and that therefore we are no ways concerned in it; we must tell those who have the impudence to insult us in this manner, that, of all things, we ought to be the most concerned who, and what sort of men they are that hold the trust of everything that is dear to us. Nothing can render this a point of indifference to the nation, but what must either render us totally desperate, or soothe us into the security of idiots. We must soften into a credulity below the milkiness of infancy to think all men virtuous. We must be tainted with a malignity truly diabolical to believe all the world to be equally wicked and corrupt. Men are in public life as in private, some good, some evil. The elevation of the one, and the depression of the other, are the first objects of all true policy. But that form of government, which, neither in its direct institutions, nor in their immediate tendency, has contrived to throw its affairs into the most trustworthy hands, but has left its whole executory system to be disposed of agreeably to the uncontrolled pleasure of any one man, however excellent or virtuous, is a plan of polity defective not only in that member, but consequentially erroneous in every part of it.

In arbitrary governments, the constitution of the ministry follows the constitution of the legislature. Both the law and the magistrate are the creatures of will. It must be so. Nothing, indeed, will appear more certain, on any tolerable consideration of this matter, than that *every sort of government ought to have its administration correspondent to its legislature.* If it should be otherwise, things must fall into an hideous disorder. The people of a free commonwealth, who have taken such care that their laws should be the result of general consent, cannot be so senseless as to suffer their executory system to be composed of persons on whom they have no dependence, and whom no proofs of the public love and confidence have recommended to those powers, upon the use of which the very being of the state depends.

The popular election of magistrates, and popular disposition of rewards and honors, is one of the first advantages of a free state. Without it, or something equivalent to it, perhaps the people cannot long enjoy the substance of freedom; certainly none of the vivifying energy of good government. The frame of our commonwealth did not admit of such an actual election: but it provided as well, and (while the spirit of the constitution is preserved) better for all the effects of it than by the method of suffrage in any democratic state whatsoever. It had always, until of late, been held the first duty of Parliament *to refuse to support government, until power was in the hands of persons who were acceptable to the people, or while factions predominated in the court in which the nation had no confidence.* Thus all the good effects of popular election were supposed to be secured to us, without the mischiefs attending on perpetual intrigue, and a distinct canvass for every particular office throughout the body of the people. This was the most noble and refined part of our constitution. The people, by their representatives and grandees, were intrusted with a deliberative power in making laws; the king with the control of his negative. The king was intrusted with the deliberative choice and the election to office; the people had the negative in a Parliamentary refusal to support. Formerly this power of control was what kept ministers in awe of Parliaments, and Parliaments in reverence with the people. If the use of this power of control on the system and persons of administration is gone, everything is lost, Parliament and all. We may assure ourselves, that if Parliament will tamely see evil men take possession of all the strongholds of their country, and allow them time and means to fortify themselves, under a pretence of giving them a fair trial, and upon a hope of discovering, whether they will not be reformed by power, and whether their measures will not be better than their morals; such a Parliament will give countenance to their measures also, whatever that Parliament may pretend, and whatever those measures may be.

Every good political institution must have a preventive operation as well as a remedial. It ought to have a natural tendency to exclude bad men from government, and not to trust for the safety of the state to subsequent punishment alone; punishment, which has ever been tardy and uncertain;

and which, when power is suffered in bad hands, may chance to fall rather on the injured than the criminal.

Before men are put forward into the great trusts of the state, they ought by their conduct to have obtained such a degree of estimation in their country, as may be some sort of pledge and security to the public, that they will not abuse those trusts. It is no mean security for a proper use of power, that a man has shown by the general tenor of his actions, that the affection, the good opinion, the confidence of his fellow-citizens have been among the principal objects of his life; and that he has owed none of the gradations of his power or fortune to a settled contempt, or occasional forfeiture of their esteem.

That man who before he comes into power has no friends, or who coming into power is obliged to desert his friends, or who losing it has no friends to sympathize with him; he who has no sway among any part of the landed or commercial interest, but whose whole importance has begun with his office, and is sure to end with it, is a person who ought never to be suffered by a controlling Parliament to continue in any of those situations which confer the lead and direction of all our public affairs; because such a man *has no connection with the interest of the people*.

Those knots or cabals of men who have got together, avowedly without any public principle, in order to sell their conjunct iniquity at the higher rate, and are therefore universally odious, ought never to be suffered to domineer in the state; because they have *no connection with the sentiments and opinions of the people*.

These are considerations which in my opinion enforce the necessity of having some better reason, in a free country, and a free Parliament, for supporting the ministers of the crown, than that short one, *That the king has thought proper to appoint them*. There is something very courtly in this. But it is a principle pregnant with all sorts of mischief, in a constitution like ours, to turn the views of active men from the country to the court. Whatever be the road to power, that is the road which will be trod. If the opinion of the country be of no use as a means of power or consideration, the qualities which usually procure that opinion will be no longer cultivated. And whether it will be right, in a state so popular in its constitution as ours, to leave ambition without popular motives, and to trust all to the operation of pure virtue in the minds of kings, and ministers, and public men, must be submitted to the judgment and good sense of the people of England.

Indeed, in the situation in which we stand, with an immense revenue, an enormous debt, mighty establishments, government itself a great banker and a great merchant, I see no other way for the preservation of a decent attention to public interest in the representatives, but *the interposition of the body of the people itself*, whenever it shall appear, by some flagrant and notorious act, by some capital innovation, that these representatives are going to overleap the fences of the law, and to introduce an arbitrary power. This interposition is a most unpleasant remedy. But, if it be a legal remedy, it is intended on some occasion to be used; to be used then only, when it is evident that nothing else can hold the constitution to its true principles.

The distempers of monarchy were the great subjects of apprehension and redress, in the last century; in this the distempers of Parliament. It is not in Parliament alone that the remedy for Parliamentary disorders can be completed; hardly indeed can it begin there. Until a confidence in government is re-established, the people ought to be excited to a more strict and detailed attention to the conduct of their representatives. Standards for judging more systematically upon their conduct ought to be settled in the meetings of counties and corporations. Frequent and correct lists of the voters in all important questions ought to be procured.

By such means something may be done. By such means it may appear who those are, that, by an indiscriminate support of all administrations, have totally banished all integrity and confidence out of public proceedings; have confounded the best men with the worst; and weakened and dissolved, instead of strengthening and compacting, the general frame of government. If any person is more concerned for government and order, than for the liberties of his country; even he is equally concerned to put an end to this course of indiscriminate support. It is this blind and undistinguishing support, that feeds the spring of those very disorders, by which he is frightened into the arms of the faction which contains in itself the source of all disorders, by enfeebling all the visible and regular authority of the state. The distemper is increased by his injudicious and preposterous endeavors, or pretences, for the cure of it.

An exterior administration, chosen for its impotency, or after it is chosen purposely rendered impotent, in order to be rendered subservient, will not be obeyed. The laws themselves will not be respected, when those who execute them are despised: and they will be despised, when their power is not immediate from the crown, or natural in the kingdom. Never were ministers better supported in Parliament. Parliamentary support comes and goes with office, totally regardless of the man, or the merit. Is government strengthened? It grows weaker and weaker. The popular torrent gains upon it every hour. Let us learn from our experience. It is not support that is wanting to government, but reformation. When ministry rests upon public opinion, it is not indeed built upon a rock of adamant; it has, however, some stability. But when it stands upon private humor, its structure is of stubble, and its foundation is on quicksand. I repeat it again, – He that supports every administration subverts all government. The reason is this: The whole business in which a court usually takes an interest goes on at present equally well, in whatever hands, whether high or low, wise or foolish, scandalous or reputable; there is nothing therefore to hold it firm to any one body of men, or to any one consistent scheme of politics. Nothing interposes, to prevent the full operation of all the caprices and all the passions of a court upon the servants of the public. The system of administration is open to continual shocks and changes, upon the principles of the meanest cabal, and the most contemptible intrigue. Nothing can be solid and permanent. All good men at length fly with horror from such a service. Men of rank and ability, with the spirit which ought to animate such men in a free state, while they decline the jurisdiction of dark cabal on their actions and their fortunes, will, for both, cheerfully put themselves upon their country. They will trust an inquisitive and distinguishing Parliament; because it does inquire, and does distinguish. If they act well, they know, that, in such a Parliament they will be supported against any intrigue; if they act ill, they know that no intrigue can protect them. This situation, however awful, is honorable. But in one hour, and in the self-same assembly, without any assigned or assignable cause, to be precipitated from the highest authority to the most marked neglect, possibly into the greatest peril of life and reputation, is a situation full of danger, and destitute of honor. It will be shunned equally by every man of prudence, and every man of spirit.

Such are the consequences of the division of court from the administration; and of the division of public men among themselves. By the former of these, lawful government is undone; by the latter, all opposition to lawless power is rendered impotent. Government may in a great measure be restored, if any considerable bodies of men have honesty and resolution enough never to accept administration, unless this garrison of *king's men*, which is stationed, as in a citadel, to control and enslave it, be entirely broken and disbanded, and every work they have thrown up be levelled with the ground. The disposition of public men to keep this corps together, and to act under it, or to co-operate with it, is a touchstone by which every administration ought in future to be tried. There has not been one which has not sufficiently experienced the utter incompatibility of that faction with the public peace, and with all the ends of good government: since, if they opposed it, they soon lost every power of serving the crown; if they submitted to it, they lost all the esteem of their country. Until ministers give to the public a full proof of their entire alienation from that system, however plausible their pretences, we may be sure they are more intent on the emoluments than the duties of office. If they refuse to give this proof, we know of what stuff they are made. In this particular, it ought to be the electors' business to look to their representatives. The electors ought to esteem it no less culpable in their member to give a single vote in Parliament to such an administration, than to take an office under it; to endure it, than to act in it. The notorious infidelity and versatility of members of Parliament, in their opinions of men and things, ought in a particular manner to be considered by the electors in the inquiry which is recommended to them. This is one of the principal holdings of that destructive system, which has endeavored to unhinge all the virtuous, honorable, and useful connections in the kingdom.

This cabal has, with great success, propagated a doctrine which serves for a color to those acts of treachery; and whilst it receives any degree of countenance it will be utterly senseless to look for a vigorous opposition to the court party. The doctrine is this: That all political connections are in their nature factious, and as such ought to be dissipated and destroyed; and that the rule for forming administrations is mere personal ability, rated by the judgment of this cabal upon it, and taken by draughts from every division and denomination of public men. This decree was solemnly promulgated by the head of the court corps, the Earl of Bute himself, in a speech which he made, in the year 1766, against the then administration, the only administration which he has ever been known directly and publicly to oppose.[1]

It is indeed in no way wonderful, that such persons should make such declarations. That connection and faction are equivalent terms, is an opinion which has been carefully inculcated at all times by unconstitutional statesmen. The reason is evident. Whilst men are linked together, they easily and speedily communicate the alarm of any evil design. They are enabled to fathom it with common counsel, and to oppose it with united strength. Whereas, when they lie dispersed, without concert, order, or discipline, communication is

---

[1] Burke refers to Bute's speech in the House of Lords on the Repeal of the Stamp Act, on 17 March 1766. Bute declared himself in opposition to the Rockingham Ministry's policy on America.

uncertain, counsel difficult, and resistance impracticable.
Where men are not acquainted with each other's principles,
nor experienced in each other's talents, nor at all practised in
their mutual habitudes and dispositions by joint efforts in
business; no personal confidence, no friendship, no common
interest, subsisting among them; it is evidently impossible
that they can act a public part with uniformity, perseverance,
or efficacy. In a connection, the most inconsiderable man, by
adding to the weight of the whole, has his value, and his use;
out of it, the greatest talents are wholly unserviceable to the
public. No man, who is not inflamed by vainglory into enthusiasm, can flatter himself that his single, unsupported,
desultory, unsystematic endeavors are of power to defeat the
subtle designs and united cabals of ambitious citizens. When
bad men combine, the good must associate; else they will fall,
one by one, an unpitied sacrifice in a contemptible struggle.

It is not enough in a situation of trust in the commonwealth, that a man means well to his country; it is not enough
that in his single person he never did an evil act, but always
voted according to his conscience, and even harangued against
every design which he apprehended to be prejudicial to the
interests of his country. This innoxious and ineffectual
character, that seems formed upon a plan of apology and
disculpation, falls miserably short of the mark of public duty.
That duty demands and requires, that what is right should
not only be made known, but made prevalent; that what is
evil should not only be detected, but defeated. When the
public man omits to put himself in a situation of doing his duty
with effect, it is an omission that frustrates the purposes of
his trust almost as much as if he had formally betrayed it. It
is surely no very rational account of a man's life, that he has
always acted right; but has taken special care, to act in such a
manner that his endeavors could not possibly be productive
of any consequence.

I do not wonder that the behavior of many parties should
have made persons of tender and scrupulous virtue somewhat
out of humor with all sorts of connection in politics. I admit
that people frequently acquire in such confederacies a narrow,

bigoted, and proscriptive spirit; that they are apt to sink the idea of the general good in this circumscribed and partial interest. But, where duty renders a critical situation a necessary one, it is our business to keep free from the evils attendant upon it; and not to fly from the situation itself. If a fortress is seated in an unwholesome air, an officer of the garrison is obliged to be attentive to his health, but he must not desert his station. Every profession, not excepting the glorious one of a soldier, or the sacred one of a priest, is liable to its own particular vices; which, however, form no argument against those ways of life; nor are the vices themselves inevitable to every individual in those professions. Of such a nature are connections in politics; essentially necessary for the full performance of our public duty, accidentally liable to degenerate into faction. Commonwealths are made of families, free commonwealths of parties also; and we may as well affirm, that our natural regards and ties of blood tend inevitably to make men bad citizens, as that the bonds of our party weaken those by which we are held to our country.

Some legislators went so far as to make neutrality in party a crime against the state. I do not know whether this might not have been rather to overstrain the principle. Certain it is, the best patriots in the greatest commonwealths have always commended and promoted such connections. *Idem sentire de republica*,[1] was with them a principal ground of friendship and attachment; nor do I know any other capable of forming firmer, dearer, more pleasing, more honorable, and more virtuous habitudes. The Romans carried this principle a great way. Even the holding of offices together, the disposition of which arose from chance, not selection, gave rise to a relation which continued for life. It was called *necessitudo sortis*;[2] and it was looked upon with a sacred reverence. Breaches of any of these kinds of civil relation were considered as acts of the most distinguished turpitude. The whole people was distributed into political societies, in which they acted in support

[1] To think alike about politics.
[2] The bond of clientage or patronage, especially between officeholders.

of such interests in the state as they severally affected. For it was then thought no crime to endeavor by every honest means to advance to superiority and power those of your own sentiments and opinions. This wise people was far from imagining that those connections had no tie, and obliged to no duty; but that men might quit them without shame, upon every call of interest. They believed private honor to be the great foundation of public trust; that friendship was no mean step towards patriotism; that he who, in the common intercourse of life, showed he regarded somebody besides himself, when he came to act in a public situation, might probably consult some other interest than his own. Never may we become *plus sages que les sages*, as the French comedian has happily expressed it, wiser than all the wise and good men who have lived before us.[1] It was their wish, to see public and private virtues, not dissonant and jarring, and mutually destructive, but harmoniously combined, growing out of one another in a noble and orderly gradation, reciprocally supporting and supported. In one of the most fortunate periods of our history this country was governed by a *connection*; I mean, the great connection of Whigs in the reign of Queen Anne. They were complimented upon the principle of this connection by a poet who was in high esteem with them. Addison, who knew their sentiments, could not praise them for what they considered as no proper subject of commendation. As a poet who knew his business, he could not applaud them for a thing which in general estimation was not highly reputable. Addressing himself to Britain, –

> 'Thy favourites grow not up by fortune's sport,
> Or from the crimes or follies of a court.
> On the firm basis of desert they rise,
> From long-tried faith, and friendship's holy ties.'[2]

The Whigs of those days believed that the only proper method of rising into power was through hard essays of

[1] Molière, *La Critique de l'École des Femmes*, Act 1, scene 3: 'plus sages que celles qui sont sages'.
[2] 'The Campaign.'

practised friendship and experimented fidelity. At that time it was not imagined, that patriotism was a bloody idol, which required the sacrifice of children and parents, or dearest connections in private life, and of all the virtues that rise from those relations. They were not of that ingenious paradoxical morality, to imagine that a spirit of moderation was properly shown in patiently bearing the sufferings of your friends; or that disinterestedness was clearly manifested at the expense of other people's fortune. They believed that no men could act with effect, who did not act in concert; that no men could act in concert, who did not act with confidence; that no men could act with confidence, who were not bound together by common opinions, common affections, and common interests.

These wise men, for such I must call Lord Sunderland, Lord Godolphin, Lord Somers, and Lord Marlborough, were too well principled in these maxims upon which the whole fabric of public strength is built, to be blown off their ground by the breath of every childish talker. They were not afraid that they should be called an ambitious junto; or that their resolution to stand for all together should, by placemen, be interpreted into a scuffle for places.[1]

Party is a body of men united for promoting by their joint endeavors the national interest upon some particular principle in which they are all agreed. For my part, I find it impossible to conceive, that any one believes in his own politics, or thinks them to be of any weight, who refuses to adopt the means of having them reduced into practice. It is the business of the speculative philosopher to mark the proper ends of government. It is the business of the politician, who is the philosopher in action, to find out proper means towards those ends, and to employ them with effect. Therefore every honorable connection will avow it is their first purpose, to pursue every just method to put the men who hold their opinions into such a condition as may enable them to carry

[1] Of those named by Burke, only Sunderland and Somers were members of the group often called the Junto, along with Lords Halifax, Wharton and Orford. Godolphin and Marlborough often worked with the Junto in Queen Anne's reign.

their common plans into execution, with all the power and authority of the state. As this power is attached to certain situations, it is their duty to contend for these situations. Without a proscription of others, they are bound to give to their own party the preference in all things; and by no means, for private considerations, to accept any offers of power in which the whole body is not included; nor to suffer themselves to be led, or to be controlled, or to be overbalanced, in office or in council, by those who contradict the very fundamental principles on which their party is formed, and even those upon which every fair connection must stand. Such a generous contention for power, on such manly and honorable maxims, will easily be distinguished from the mean and interested struggle for place and emolument. The very style of such persons will serve to discriminate them from those numberless impostors, who have deluded the ignorant with professions incompatible with human practice, and have afterwards incensed them by practices below the level of vulgar rectitude.

It is an advantage to all narrow wisdom and narrow morals, that their maxims have a plausible air: and, on a cursory view, appear equal to first principles. They are light and portable. They are as current as copper coin; and about as valuable. They serve equally the first capacities and the lowest; and they are, at least, as useful to the worst men as to the best. Of this stamp is the cant of *Not men, but measures*;[1] a sort of charm by which many people get loose from every honorable engagement. When I see a man acting this desultory and disconnected part, with as much detriment to his own fortune as prejudice to the cause of any party, I am not persuaded that he is right; but I am ready to believe he is in earnest. I respect virtue in all its situations; even when it is found in the unsuitable company of weakness. I lament to see qualities, rare and valuable, squandered away without any public utility. But when a gentleman with great visible emoluments abandons the party in which he has long acted, and tells you, it is because

[1] A phrase often used by Chatham and his associates, signifying that politicians should not formulate their policies as a party but support or oppose measures for their intrinsic worth.

he proceeds upon his own judgment; that he acts on the merits of the several measures as they arise; and that he is obliged to follow his own conscience, and not that of others; he gives reasons which it is impossible to controvert, and discovers a character which it is impossible to mistake. What shall we think of him who never differed from a certain set of men until the moment they lost their power, and who never agreed with them in a single instance afterwards? Would not such a coincidence of interest and opinion be rather fortunate? Would it not be an extraordinary cast upon the dice, that a man's connections should degenerate into faction, precisely at the critical moment when they lose their power, or he accepts a place? When people desert their connections, the desertion is a manifest *fact*, upon which a direct simple issue lies, triable by plain men. Whether a *measure* of government be right or wrong, is *no matter of fact*, but a mere affair of opinion, on which men may, as they do, dispute and wrangle without end. But whether the individual *thinks* the measure right or wrong, is a point at still a greater distance from the reach of all human decision. It is therefore very convenient to politicians, not to put the judgment of their conduct on overt acts, cognizable in any ordinary court, but upon such matter as can be triable only in that secret tribunal, where they are sure of being heard with favor, or where at worst the sentence will be only private whipping.

I believe the reader would wish to find no substance in a doctrine which has a tendency to destroy all test of character as deduced from conduct. He will therefore excuse my adding something more, towards the further clearing up a point, which the great convenience of obscurity to dishonesty has been able to cover with some degree of darkness and doubt.

In order to throw an odium on political connection, these politicians suppose it a necessary incident to it, that you are blindly to follow the opinions of your party, when in direct opposition to your own clear ideas; a degree of servitude that no worthy man could bear the thought of submitting to; and such as, I believe, no connections (except some court factions) ever could be so senselessly tyrannical as to impose. Men thinking freely, will, in particular instances, think differently. But still as the greater part of the measures which arise in the course of public business are related to, or dependent on, some great, *leading*, *general principles in government*, a man must be peculiarly unfortunate in the choice of his political company, if he does not agree with them at least nine times in ten. If he does not concur in these general principles upon which the party is founded, and which necessarily draw on a concurrence in their application, he ought from the beginning to have chosen some other, more conformable to his opinions. When the question is in its nature doubtful, or not very material, the modesty which becomes an individual, and (in spite of our court moralists), that partiality which becomes a well-chosen friendship, will frequently bring on an acquiescence in the general sentiment. Thus the disagreement will naturally be rare; it will be only enough to indulge freedom, without violating concord, or disturbing arrangement. And this is all that ever was required for a character of the greatest uniformity and steadiness in connection. How men can proceed without any connection at all, is to me utterly incomprehensible. Of what sort of materials must that man be made, how must he be tempered and put together, who can sit whole years in Parliament, with five hundred and fifty of his fellow-citizens, amidst the storm of such tempestuous passions, in the sharp conflict of so many wits, and tempers, and characters, in the agitation of such mighty questions, in the discussion of such vast and ponderous interests, without seeing any one sort of men, whose character, conduct, or disposition, would lead him to associate himself with them, to aid and be aided, in any one system of public utility?

I remember an old scholastic aphorism, which says, 'that the man who lives wholly detached from others, must be either an angel or a devil.' When I see in any of these detached gentlemen of our times the angelic purity, power, and beneficence, I shall admit them to be angels. In the mean time we are born only to be men. We shall do enough if we form ourselves to be good ones. It is therefore our business carefully to cultivate in our minds, to rear to the most perfect vigor and maturity, every sort of generous and honest feeling, that belongs to our nature. To bring the dispositions that are lovely in private life into the service and conduct of the commonwealth; so to be patriots, as not to forget we are gentlemen. To cultivate friendships, and to incur enmities. To have both strong, but both selected: in the one, to be placable; in the other immovable. To model our principles to our duties and our situation. To be fully persuaded, that all virtue which is impracticable is spurious; and rather to run the risk of falling into faults in a course which leads us to act with effect and energy, than to loiter out our days without blame, and without use. Public life is a situation of power and energy; he trespasses against his duty who sleeps upon his watch, as well as he that goes over to the enemy.

There is, however, a time for all things. It is not every conjuncture which calls with equal force upon the activity of honest men; but critical exigencies now and then arise; and I am mistaken, if this be not one of them. Men will see the necessity of honest combination; but they may see it when it is too late. They may embody, when it will be ruinous to themselves, and of no advantage to the country; when, for want of such a timely union as may enable them to oppose in favor of the laws, with the laws on their side, they may at length find themselves under the necessity of conspiring, instead of consulting. The law, for which they stand, may become a weapon in the hands of its bitterest enemies; and they will be cast, at length, into that miserable alternative between slavery and civil confusion, which no good man can look upon without horror; an alternative in which it is impossible he should take either part, with a conscience perfectly at repose. To keep that situation of guilt and remorse at the utmost distance is, therefore, our first obligation. Early activity may prevent late and fruitless violence. As yet we work in the light. The scheme of the enemies of public tranquillity has disarranged, it has not destroyed us.

If the reader believes that there really exists such a faction as I have described; a faction ruling by the private inclinations of a court, against the general sense of the people; and that this faction, whilst it pursues a scheme for undermining all the foundations of our freedom, weakens (for the present at least) all the powers of executory government, rendering us abroad contemptible, and at home distracted; he will believe also, that nothing but a firm combination of public men against this body, and that, too, supported by the hearty concurrence of the people at large, can possibly get the better of it. The people will see the necessity of restoring public men to an attention to the public opinion, and of restoring the constitution to its original principles. Above all, they will endeavor to keep the House of Commons from assuming a character which does not belong to it. They will endeavor to keep that House, for its existence, for its powers, and its privileges, as independent of every other, and as dependent upon themselves, as possible. This servitude is to a House of Commons (like obedience to the Divine law) 'perfect freedom.' For if they once quit this natural, rational, and liberal obedience, having deserted the only proper foundation of their power, they must seek a support in an abject and unnatural dependence somewhere else. When, through the medium of this just connection with their constituents, the genuine dignity of the House of Commons is restored, it will begin to think of casting from it, with scorn, as badges of servility, all the false ornaments of illegal power, with which it has been, for some time, disgraced. It will begin to think of its old office of CONTROL. It will not suffer that last of evils to predominate in the country: men without popular confidence, public opinion, natural connection, or mutual trust, invested with all the powers of government.

When they have learned this lesson themselves, they will be willing and able to teach the court, that it is the true interest of the prince to have but one administration; and that one composed of those who recommend themselves to their sovereign through the opinion of their country, and not by their obsequiousness to a favorite. Such men will serve their sovereign with affection and fidelity; because his choice of them, upon such principles, is a compliment to their virtue. They will be able to serve him effectually; because they will add the weight of the country to the force of the executory power. They will be able to serve their king with dignity; because they will never abuse his name to the gratification of their private spleen or avarice. This, with allowances for human frailty, may probably be the general character of a ministry, which thinks itself accountable to the House of Commons; when the House of Commons thinks itself accountable to its constituents. If other ideas should prevail, things must remain in their present confusion, until they are hurried into all the rage of civil violence, or until they sink into the dead repose of despotism.

On American Taxation

In the aftermath of the Boston Tea Party, when the government was carrying through Parliament coercive acts against the New Englanders, one member of the Commons, Rose Fuller, sought to remove the root grievance, the duty upon the import of tea into the colonies. Other duties imposed by Town.hend's Revenue Act of 1767 had been abolished as early as 1769. Fuller's motion on 19 April 1774 gave Burke the opportunity for his first major statement on American affairs. If the other duties had been admitted to be inexpedient, he argued, Lord North's ministry ought to be prepared to give up the tea duty. Its retention for so long had been an expensive and unnecessary gesture: expensive in that it had soured the colonists, unnecessary in that the right of parliamentary taxation which it had been intended to uphold had already been clearly stated in the Rockingham Ministry's Declaratory Act of 1766. When Burke spoke, events had already overtaken him in that the Americans were no longer prepared to accept even a theoretical claim of right to impose taxes. But if he did not go far enough to please them, his advocacy of repeal of the tea duty went too far for the majority of the Commons, who rejected the motion. Burke's speech was much acclaimed for its eloquence, and was widely read when published in January 1775.

Nevertheless, Burke did no more than lightly outline the position which he was later to adopt on the American problem. At this stage his thought was occupied with misgovernment rather than with the question of replacing it by some positive alternative. Much of the speech is taken up with a denunciation of the successive British ministries which had taken up the attempt to tax the colonists. His opposition to these attempts was based not upon any political theory or slogan – such as the colonists' claim of 'no taxation without representation', which was approved of by Chatham as in keeping with the 'Revolution principles' of 1688 – but upon the fact that the historical relationship of the colonies with the mother country down to 1764 had not included serious attempts at taxation for revenue. 'Again, and again, revert to your old principles, ... leave America, if she has taxable matter in her, to tax herself', he told the assembled parliamentarians, adding however a disclaimer of support for the Americans on abstract grounds of rights: 'I am not here going into the distinctions of rights, nor attempting to mark their boundaries. I do not enter into these metaphysical distinctions; I hate the very sound of them' (see below, p. 150). Although he did not here develop the argument from prescription, his view was clearly that a good relationship between the British and the Americans, sanctified by a long historical development (in the hands of the Whig party) was being endangered by doctrinaire governmental innovations and by equally doctrinaire opposition to it.

From a Speech on American Taxation (*19 April 1774*)

Here began to dawn the first glimmerings of this new colony system. It appeared more distinctly afterwards, when it was devolved upon a person to whom, on other accounts, this country owes very great obligations.[1] I do believe that he had a very serious desire to benefit the public. But with no small study of the detail, he did not seem to have his view, at least equally, carried to the total circuit of our affairs. He generally considered his objects in lights that were rather too detached. Whether the business of an American revenue was imposed upon him altogether, – whether it was entirely the result of his own speculation, or, what is more probable, that his own ideas rather coincided with the instructions he had received,[2] –

[1] George Grenville (1712–1770), who as First Lord of the Treasury and Chancellor of the Exchequer, 1763–1765, carried the Stamp Act and legislation for tightening revenue collection in the colonies.

[2] Burke believed, as did many of his contemporaries, that Grenville's policy had been very agreeable to the king and probably

certain it is, that, with the best intentions in the world, he first brought this fatal scheme into form, and established it by Act of Parliament.

No man can believe, that, at this time of day, I mean to lean on the venerable memory of a great man, whose loss we deplore in common. Our little party differences have been long ago composed; and I have acted more with him, and certainly with more pleasure with him, than ever I acted against him. Undoubtedly Mr Grenville was a first-rate figure in this country. With a masculine understanding, and a stout and resolute heart, he had an application undissipated and unwearied. He took public business, not as a duty which he was to fulfil, but as a pleasure he was to enjoy; and he seemed to have no delight out of this House, except in such things as some way related to the business that was to be done within it. If he was ambitious, I will say this for him, his ambition was of a noble and generous strain. It was to raise himself, not by the low, pimping politics of a court, but to win his way to power through the laborious gradations of public service, and to secure himself a well-earned rank in Parliament by a thorough knowledge of its constitution and a perfect practice in all its business.

Sir, if such a man fell into errors, it must be from defects not intrinsical; they must be rather sought in the particular habits of his life, which, though they do not alter the groundwork of character, yet tinge it with their own hue. He was bred in a profession. He was bred to the law, which is, in my opinion, one of the first and noblest of human sciences, – a science which does more to quicken and invigorate the understanding than all the other kinds of learning put together; but it is not apt, except in persons very happily born, to open and to liberalize the mind exactly in the same proportion. Passing from that study, he did not go very largely into the world, but plunged into business, – I mean into the business of office, and the limited and fixed methods and forms established there. Much knowledge is to be had,

dictated by the latter through Charles Jenkinson (1727–1808), Grenville's Secretary to the Treasury.

undoubtedly, in that line; and there is no knowledge which is not valuable. But it may be truly said, that men too much conversant in office are rarely minds of remarkable enlargement. Their habits of office are apt to give them a turn to think the substance of business not to be much more important than the forms in which it is conducted. These forms are adapted to ordinary occasions; and therefore persons who are nurtured in office do admirably well as long as things go on in their common order; but when the high-roads are broken up, and the waters out, when a new and troubled scene is opened, and the file affords no precedent, then it is that a greater knowledge of mankind, and a far more extensive comprehension of things is requisite, than ever office gave, or than office can ever give. Mr Grenville thought better of the wisdom and power of human legislation than in truth it deserves. He conceived, and many conceived along with him, that the flourishing trade of this country was greatly owing to law and institution, and not quite so much to liberty; for but too many are apt to believe regulation to be commerce, and taxes to be revenue. Among regulations, that which stood first in reputation was his idol: I mean the Act of Navigation.[1] He has often professed it to be so. The policy of that act is, I readily admit, in many respects well understood. But I do say, that, if the act be suffered to run the full length of its principle, and is not changed and modified according to the change of times and the fluctuation of circumstances, it must do great mischief, and frequently even defeat its own purpose.

After the war, and in the last years of it, the trade of America had increased far beyond the speculations of the most sanguine imaginations. It swelled out on every side. It filled all its proper channels to the brim. It overflowed with a rich redundance, and breaking its banks on the right and on the left, it spread out upon some places where it was indeed improper, upon others where it was only irregular. It is the nature of all greatness not to be exact; and great trade will always be

[1] The Act of 1660, confirming that of 1651 in strengthening England's bid for commercial and colonial dominance.

attended with considerable abuses. The contraband will always keep pace in some measure with the fair trade. It should stand as a fundamental maxim, that no vulgar precaution ought to be employed in the cure of evils which are closely connected with the cause of our prosperity. Perhaps this great person turned his eyes somewhat less than was just towards the incredible increase of the fair trade, and looked with something of too exquisite a jealousy towards the contraband. He certainly felt a singular degree of anxiety on the subject, and even began to act from that passion earlier than is commonly imagined. For whilst he was First Lord of the Admiralty, though not strictly called upon in his official line, he presented a very strong memorial to the Lords of the Treasury (my Lord Bute was then at the head of the board), heavily complaining of the growth of the illicit commerce in America. Some mischief happened even at that time from this over-earnest zeal. Much greater happened afterwards, when it operated with greater power in the highest department of the finances. The bonds of the Act of Navigation were straitened so much that America was on the point of having no trade, either contraband or legitimate. They found, under the construction and execution then used, the act no longer tying, but actually strangling them. All this coming with new enumerations of commodities, with regulations which in a manner put a stop to the mutual coasting intercourse of the colonies, with the appointment of courts of admiralty under various improper circumstances, with a sudden extinction of the paper currencies, with a compulsory provision for the quartering of soldiers, – the people of America thought themselves proceeded against as delinquents, or, at best, as people under suspicion of delinquency, and in such a manner as they imagined their recent services in the war did not at all merit. Any of these innumerable regulations, perhaps, would not have alarmed alone; some might be thought reasonable; the multitude struck them with terror.

But the grand manœuvre in that business of new regulating the colonies was the fifteenth act of the fourth of George the

Third, which, besides containing several of the matters to which I have just alluded, opened a new principle.[1] And here properly began the second period of the policy of this country with regard to the colonies, by which the scheme of a regular plantation Parliamentary revenue was adopted in theory and settled in practice: a revenue not substituted in the place of, but superadded to, a monopoly; which monopoly was enforced at the same time with additional strictness, and the execution put into military hands.

This act, Sir, had for the first time the title of 'granting duties in the colonies and plantations of America,' and for the first time it was asserted in the preamble 'that it was *just* and *necessary* that a revenue should be raised there'; then came the technical words of 'giving and granting.' And thus a complete American revenue act was made in all the forms, and with a full avowal of the right, equity, policy, and even necessity, of taxing the colonies, without any formal consent of theirs. There are contained also in the preamble to that act these very remarkable words, – the Commons, &c., 'being desirous to make *some* provision in the *present* session of Parliament *towards* raising the said revenue.' By these words it appeared to the colonies that this act was but a beginning of sorrows, – that every session was to produce something of the same kind, – that we were to go on, from day to day, in charging them with such taxes as we pleased, for such a military force as we should think proper. Had this plan been pursued, it was evident that the provincial assemblies, in which the Americans felt all their portion of importance, and beheld their sole image of freedom, were *ipso facto* annihilated. This ill prospect before them seemed to be boundless in extent and endless in duration. Sir, they were not mistaken. The ministry valued themselves when this act passed, and when they gave notice of the Stamp Act, that both of the duties came very short of their ideas of American taxation. Great was the applause of this measure here. In England we cried out for new taxes on America, whilst they cried out that they were nearly crushed

[1] Grenville's Revenue (Sugar) Act of 1764, which was partly intended to raise revenue for the defence of the colonies.

with those which the war and their own grants had brought upon them.

Sir, it has been said in the debate, that, when the first American revenue act (the act in 1764, imposing the port-duties) passed, the Americans did not object to the principle. It is true they touched it but very tenderly. It was not a direct attack. They were, it is true, as yet novices, – as yet unaccustomed to direct attacks upon any of the rights of Parliament. The duties were port-duties, like those they had been accustomed to bear, – with this difference, that the title was not the same, the preamble not the same, and the spirit altogether unlike. But of what service is this observation to the cause of those that make it? It is a full refutation of the pretence for their present cruelty to America; for it shows, out of their own mouths, that our colonies were backward to enter into the present vexatious and ruinous controversy.

There is also another circulation abroad (spread with a malignant intention, which I cannot attribute to those who say the same thing in this House), that Mr Grenville gave the colony agents an option for their assemblies to tax themselves, which they had refused. I find that much stress is laid on this, as a fact. However, it happens neither to be true nor possible. I will observe, first, that Mr Grenville never thought fit to make this apology for himself in the innumerable debates that were had upon the subject. He might have proposed to the colony agents, that they should agree in some mode of taxation as the ground of an act of Parliament. But he never could have proposed that they should tax themselves on requisition, which is the assertion of the day. Indeed, Mr Grenville well knew that the colony agents could have no general powers to consent to it; and they had no time to consult their assemblies for particular powers, before he passed his first revenue act. If you compare dates, you will find it impossible. Burdened as the agents knew the colonies were at that time, they could not give the least hope of such grants. His own favorite governor was of opinion that the Americans were not then taxable objects.

'Nor was the time less favorable to the *equity* of such a taxation. I don't mean to dispute the reasonableness of America contributing to the charges of Great Britain, *when she is able*; nor, I believe, would the Americans themselves have disputed it at a *proper time and season*. But it should be considered, that the American governments themselves have, in the prosecution of the late war, contracted very large debts, which it will take some years to pay off, and in the mean time occasion very *burdensome taxes for that purpose* only. For instance, this government, which is as much beforehand as any, raises every year 37,500*l.* sterling for sinking their debt, and must continue it for four years longer at least before it will be clear.'

These are the words of Governor Bernard's[1] letter to a member of the old ministry, and which he has since printed.

Mr Grenville could not have made this proposition to the agents for another reason. He was of opinion, which he has declared in this House an hundred times, that the colonies could not legally grant any revenue to the crown, and that infinite mischiefs would be the consequence of such a power. When Mr Grenville had passed the first revenue act, and in the same session had made this House come to a resolution for laying a stamp-duty on America, between that time and the passing the Stamp Act into a law he told a considerable and most respectable merchant, a member of this House, whom I am truly sorry I do not now see in his place, when he represented against this proceeding, that, if the stamp-duty was disliked, he was willing to exchange it for any other equally productive, – but that, if he objected to the Americans being taxed by Parliament, he might save himself the trouble of the discussion, as he was determined on the measure. This is the fact, and, if you please, I will mention a very unquestionable authority for it.

Thus, Sir, I have disposed of this falsehood. But falsehood has a perennial spring. It is said that no conjecture could be made of the dislike of the colonies to the principle. This is as

[1] Francis Bernard (1711?–1779), Governor of Massachusetts 1760–1769.

untrue as the other, After the resolution of the House, and before the passing of the Stamp Act, the colonies of Massachusetts Bay and New York did send remonstrances objecting to this mode of Parliamentary taxation. What was the consequence? They were suppressed, they were put under the table, notwithstanding an order of Council to the contrary, by the ministry which composed the very Council that had made the order; and thus the House proceeded to its business of taxing without the least regular knowledge of the objections which were made to it. But give that House its due, it was not over-desirous to receive information or to hear remonstrance. On the 15th of February, 1765, whilst the Stamp Act was under deliberation, they refused with scorn even so much as to receive four petitions presented from so respectable colonies as Connecticut, Rhode Island, Virginia, and Carolina, besides one from the traders of Jamaica. As to the colonies, they had no alternative left to them but to disobey, or to pay the taxes imposed by that Parliament, which was not suffered, or did not suffer itself, even to hear them remonstrate upon the subject.

This was the state of the colonies before his Majesty thought fit to change his ministers. It stands upon no authority of mine. It is proved by uncontrovertible records. The honorable gentleman[1] has desired some of us to lay our hands upon our hearts and answer to his queries upon the historical part of this consideration, and by his manner (as well as my eyes could discern it) he seemed to address himself to me.

Sir, I will answer him as clearly as I am able, and with great openness: I have nothing to conceal. In the year sixty-five, being in a very private station, far enough from any line of business, and not having the honor of a seat in this House, it was my fortune, unknowing and unknown to the then ministry, by the intervention of a common friend, to become connected with a very noble person, and at the head of the Treasury Department.[2] It was, indeed, in a situation of little

[1] Charles Wolfran Cornwall (1735-1789), who spoke before Burke, was not in sympathy with the colonists.

[2] Charles Watson-Wentworth (1730-1782), second Marquess of

rank and no consequence, suitable to the mediocrity of my talents and pretensions, – but a situation near enough to enable me to see, as well as others, what was going on; and I did see in that noble person such sound principles, such an enlargement of mind, such clear and sagacious sense, and such unshaken fortitude, as have bound me, as well as others much better than me, by an inviolable attachment to him from that time forward. Sir, Lord Rockingham very early in that summer received a strong representation from many weighty English merchants and manufacturers, from governors of provinces and commanders of men-of-war, against almost the whole of the American commercial regulations, – and particularly with regard to the total ruin which was threatened to the Spanish trade.[1] I believe, Sir, the noble lord soon saw his way in this business. But he did not rashly determine against acts which it might be supposed were the result of much deliberation. However, Sir, he scarcely began to open the ground, when the whole veteran body of office took the alarm. A violent outcry of all (except those who knew and felt the mischief) was raised against any alteration. On one hand, his attempt was a direct violation of treaties and public law; on the other, the Act of Navigation and all the corps of trade-laws were drawn up in array against it.

The first step the noble lord took was, to have the opinion of his excellent, learned, and ever-lamented friend, the late Mr Yorke, then Attorney-General, on the point of law.[2] When he knew that formally and officially which in substance he had known before, he immediately dispatched orders to redress the grievance. But I will say it for the then minister, he is of that constitution of mind, that I know he would have issued, on the same critical occasion, the very same orders, if the acts of trade had been, as they were not, directly against him, and

---

Rockingham, Burke's patron and leader, was First Lord in 1765–1766 and again in 1782.

[1] i.e. the trade of Jamaica with Spanish America, which had much concerned the 'West India interest' in Parliament.

[2] Charles Yorke (1722–1770).

would have cheerfully submitted to the equity of Parliament for his indemnity.

On the conclusion of this business of the Spanish trade, the news of the troubles on account of the Stamp Act arrived in England. It was not until the end of October that these accounts were received. No sooner had the sound of that mighty tempest reached us in England, than the whole of the then opposition, instead of feeling humbled by the unhappy issue of their measures, seemed to be infinitely elated, and cried out, that the ministry, from envy to the glory of their predecessors, were prepared to repeal the Stamp Act. Near nine years after, the honorable gentleman takes quite opposite ground, and now challenges me to put my hand to my heart and say whether the ministry had resolved on the repeal till a considerable time after the meeting of Parliament. Though I do not very well know what the honorable gentleman wishes to infer from the admission or from the denial of this fact on which he so earnestly adjures me, I do put my hand on my heart and assure him that they did *not* come to a resolution directly to repeal. They weighed this matter as its difficulty and importance required. They considered maturely among themselves. They consulted with all who could give advice or information. It was not determined until a little before the meeting of Parliament; but it was determined, and the main lines of their own plan marked out, before that meeting. Two questions arose. (I hope I am not going into a narrative troublesome to the House.)

[A cry of 'Go on, go on!']

The first of the two considerations was, whether the repeal should be total, or whether only partial, – taking out everything burdensome and productive, and reserving only an empty acknowledgment, such as a stamp on cards or dice. The other question was, on what principle the act should be repealed. On this head also two principles were started. One, that the legislative rights of this country with regard to America were not entire, but had certain restrictions and limitations. The other principle was, that taxes of this kind were contrary to the fundamental principles of commerce on which the colonies were founded, and contrary to every idea of political equity, – by which equity we are bound as much as possible to extend the spirit and benefit of the British Constitution to every part of the British dominions. The option, both of the measure and of the principle of repeal, was made before the session; and I wonder how any one can read the king's speech at the opening of that session, without seeing in that speech both the repeal and the Declaratory Act very sufficiently crayoned out. Those who cannot see this can see nothing.

Surely the honorable gentleman will not think that a great deal less time than was then employed ought to have been spent in deliberation, when he considers that the news of the troubles did not arrive till towards the end of October. The Parliament sat to fill the vacancies on the 14th day of December, and on business the 14th of the following January.

Sir, a partial repeal, or, as the *bon-ton* of the court then was, a *modification*, would have satisfied a timid, unsystematic, procrastinating ministry, as such a measure has since done such a ministry. A modification is the constant resource of weak, undeciding minds. To repeal by a denial of our right to tax in the preamble (and this, too, did not want advisers) would have cut, in the heroic style, the Gordian knot with a sword. Either measure would have cost no more than a day's debate. But when the total repeal was adopted, and adopted on principles of policy, of equity, and of commerce, this plan made it necessary to enter into many and difficult measures. It became necessary to open a very large field of evidence commensurate to these extensive views. But then this labor did knights' service. It opened the eyes of several to the true state of the American affairs; it enlarged their ideas; it removed prejudices; and it conciliated the opinions and affections of men. The noble lord who then took the lead in administration, my honorable friend* under me, and a right honorable gentleman† (if he will not reject his share, and it was a large one, of this business) exerted the most laudable industry in bringing before you the fullest, most impartial, and least garbled body of evidence that ever was produced to this

* Mr. Dowdeswell.   † General Conway.

House. I think the inquiry lasted in the committee for six weeks;[1] and at its conclusion, this House, by an independent, noble, spirited, and unexpected majority, by a majority that will redeem all the acts ever done by majorities in Parliament, in the teeth of all the old mercenary Swiss of state, in despite of all the speculators and augurs of political events, in defiance of the whole embattled legion of veteran pensioners and practised instruments of a court, gave a total repeal to the Stamp Act, and (if it had been so permitted) a lasting peace to this whole empire.

I state, Sir, these particulars, because this act of spirit and fortitude has lately been, in the circulation of the season, and in some hazarded declamations in this House, attributed to timidity. If, Sir, the conduct of ministry, in proposing the repeal, had arisen from timidity with regard to themselves, it would have been greatly to be condemned. Interested timidity disgraces as much in the cabinet as personal timidity does in the field. But timidity with regard to the well-being of our country is heroic virtue. The noble lord who then conducted affairs, and his worthy colleagues, whilst they trembled at the prospect of such distresses as you have since brought upon yourselves were not afraid steadily to look in the face that glaring and dazzling influence at which the eyes of eagles have blenched. He looked in the face one of the ablest, and, let me say, not the most scrupulous oppositions, that perhaps ever was in this House; and withstood it, unaided by even one of the usual supports of administration. He did this, when he repealed the Stamp Act. He looked in the face a person he had long respected and regarded, and whose aid was then particularly wanting: I mean Lord Chatham. He did this when he passed the Declaratory Act.

It is now given out, for the usual purposes, by the usual emissaries, that Lord Rockingham did not consent to the repeal of this act until he was bullied into it by Lord Chatham;

[1] The Committee of the Whole House dealing with American affairs in January–February 1766 was chaired by Rose Fuller (1708?–1777). The principal American witness heard by the committee was Benjamin Franklin, the Agent for Pennsylvania.

and the reporters have gone so far as publicly to assert, in an hundred companies, that the honorable gentleman under the gallery,* who proposed the repeal in the American committee, had another set of resolutions in his pocket, directly the reverse of those he moved. These artifices of a desperate cause are at this time spread abroad, with incredible care, in every part of the town, from the highest to the lowest companies; as if the industry of the circulation were to make amends for the absurdity of the report.

Sir, whether the noble lord is of a complexion to be bullied by Lord Chatham, or by any man, I must submit to those who know him. I confess, when I look back to that time, I consider him as placed in one of the most trying situations in which, perhaps, any man ever stood. In the House of Peers there were very few of the ministry, out of the noble lord's own particular connection (except Lord Egmont, who acted, as far as I could discern, an honorable and manly part), that did not look to some other future arrangement, which warped his politics. There were in both Houses new and menacing appearances, that might very naturally drive any other than a most resolute minister from his measure or from his station. The household troops openly revolted. The allies of ministry (those, I mean, who supported some of their measures, but refused responsibility for any) endeavored to undermine their credit, and to take ground that must be fatal to the success of the very cause which they would be thought to countenance. The question of the repeal was brought on by ministry in the committee of this House in the very instant when it was known that more than one court negotiation was carrying on with the heads of the opposition. Everything, upon every side, was full of traps and mines. Earth below shook; heaven above menaced; all the elements of ministerial safety were dissolved. It was in the midst of this chaos of plots and counterplots, it was in the midst of this complicated warfare against public opposition and private treachery, that the firmness of that noble person was put to the proof. He never stirred from his ground: no, not an inch. He remained fixed and determined, in principle,

* General Conway.

in measure, and in conduct. He practised no managements. He secured no retreat. He sought no apology.

I will likewise do justice – I ought to do it – to the honorable gentleman who led us in this House.* Far from the duplicity wickedly charged on him, he acted his part with alacrity and resolution. We all felt inspired by the example he gave us, down even to myself, the weakest in that phalanx. I declare for one, I knew well enough (it could not be concealed from anybody) the true state of things; but, in my life, I never came with so much spirits into this House. It was a time for a *man* to act in. We had powerful enemies; but we had faithful and determined friends, and a glorious cause. We had a great battle to fight; but we had the means of fighting: not as now, when our arms are tied behind us. We did fight that day, and conquer.

I remember, Sir, with a melancholy pleasure, the situation of the honorable gentleman* who made the motion for the repeal: in that crisis, when the whole trading interest of this empire, crammed into your lobbies, with a trembling and anxious expectation, waited, almost to a winter's return of light, their fate from your resolutions. When at length you had determined in their favor, and your doors thrown open showed them the figure of their deliverer in the well-earned triumph of his important victory, from the whole of that grave multitude there arose an involuntary burst of gratitude and transport. They jumped upon him like children on a long absent father. They clung about him as captives about their redeemer. All England, all America, joined in his applause. Nor did he seem insensible to the best of all earthly rewards, the love and admiration of his fellow-citizens. *Hope elevated and joy brightened his crest.*[1] I stood near him; and his face, to use the expression of the Scripture of the first martyr, 'his face was as if it had been the face of an angel.' I do not know how others feel; but if I had stood in that situation, I never would have exchanged it for all that kings in their profusion could

* General Conway.
[1] Milton, *Paradise Lost*, ix. 633–34: 'Hope elevates, and joy Brightens his crest.'

bestow. I did hope that that day's danger and honor would have been a bond to hold us all together forever. But, alas! that, with other pleasing visions, is long since vanished.

Sir, this act of supreme magnanimity has been represented as if it had been a measure of an administration that, having no scheme of their own, took a middle line, pilfered a bit from one side and a bit from the other. Sir, they took *no* middle lines. They differed fundamentally from the schemes of both parties; but they preserved the objects of both. They preserved the authority of Great Britain; they preserved the equity of Great Britain. They made the Declaratory Act; they repealed the Stamp Act. They did both *fully*: because the Declaratory Act was *without qualification*; and the repeal of the Stamp Act *total*. This they did in the situation I have described.

Now, Sir, what will the adversary say to both these acts? If the principle of the Declaratory Act was not good, the principle we are contending for this day is monstrous. If the principle of the repeal was not good, why are we not at war for a real, substantial, effective revenue? If both were bad, why has this ministry incurred all the inconveniences of both and of all schemes? why have they enacted, repealed, enforced, yielded, and now attempt to enforce again?

Sir, I think I may as well now as at any other time speak to a certain matter of fact not wholly unrelated to the question under your consideration. We, who would persuade you to revert to the ancient policy of this kingdom, labor under the effect of this short current phrase, which the court leaders have given out to all their corps, in order to take away the credit of those who would prevent you from that frantic war you are going to wage upon your colonies. Their cant is this: 'All the disturbances in America have been created by the repeal of the Stamp Act.' I suppress for a moment my indignation at the falsehood, baseness, and absurdity of this most audacious assertion. Instead of remarking on the motives and character of those who have issued it for circulation, I will clearly lay before you the state of America, antecedently to that repeal, after the repeal, and since the renewal of the schemes of American taxation.

It is said, that the disturbances, if there were any before the repeal, were slight, and without difficulty or inconvenience might have been suppressed. For an answer to this assertion I will send you to the great author and patron of the Stamp Act, who, certainly meaning well to the authority of this country, and fully apprised of the state of that, made, before a repeal was so much as agitated in this House, the motion which is on your journals, and which, to save the clerk the trouble of turning to it, I will now read to you. It was for an amendment to the address of the 17th of December, 1765.

'To express our just resentment and indignation at the *outrageous tumults and insurrections* which have been excited and carried on in North America, and at the resistance given, by *open* and *rebellious* force, to the execution of the laws in that part of his Majesty's dominions; to assure his Majesty, that his faithful Commons, animated with the warmest duty and attachment to his royal person and government, ... will firmly and effectually support his Majesty in all such measures as shall be necessary for preserving and securing the legal dependence of the colonies upon this their mother country,' etc., etc.

Here was certainly a disturbance preceding the repeal, – such a disturbance as Mr Grenville thought necessary to qualify by the name of an *insurrection*, and the epithet of a *rebellious* force: terms much stronger than any by which those who then supported his motion have ever since thought proper to distinguish the subsequent disturbances in America. They were disturbances which seemed to him and his friends to justify as strong a promise of support as hath been usual to give in the beginning of a war with the most powerful and declared enemies. When the accounts of the American governors came before the House, they appeared stronger even than the warmth of public imagination had painted them: so much stronger, that the papers on your table bear me out in saying that all the late disturbances, which have been at one time the minister's motives for the repeal of five out of six of the new court taxes, and are now his pretences for refusing to repeal that sixth, did not amount – why do I compare them?– no, not to a tenth part of the tumults and violence which prevailed long before the repeal of that act.

Ministry cannot refuse the authority of the commander-in-chief, General Gage, who, in his letter of the 4th of November, from New York, thus represents the state of things:–

'It is difficult to say, from the *highest to the lowest*, who has not been *accessory* to this *insurrection*, either by writing, or *mutual agreements* to oppose the act, by what they are pleased to term all legal opposition to it. Nothing effectual has been proposed, either to prevent or quell the tumult. *The rest of the provinces are in the same situation*, as to a positive refusal to take the stamps, and threatening those who shall take them *to plunder and murder them*; and this affair stands *in all the provinces*, that, unless the act from its own nature enforce itself, nothing but a *very* considerable military force can do it.'

It is remarkable, Sir, that the persons who formerly trumpeted forth the most loudly the violent resolutions of assemblies, the universal insurrections, the seizing and burning the stamped papers, the forcing stamp officers to resign their commissions under the gallows, the rifling and pulling down of the houses of magistrates, and the expulsion from their country of all who dared to write or speak a single word in defence of the powers of Parliament, – these very trumpeters are now the men that represent the whole as a mere trifle, and choose to date all the disturbances from the repeal of the Stamp Act, which put an end to them. Hear your officers abroad, and let them refute this shameless falsehood, who, in all their correspondence, state the disturbances as owing to their true causes, the discontent of the people from the taxes. You have this evidence in your own archives; and it will give you complete satisfaction, if you are not so far lost to all Parliamentary ideas of information as rather to credit the lie of the day than the records of your own House.

Sir, this vermin of court reporters, when they are forced into day upon one point, are sure to burrow in another: but they shall have no refuge; I will make them bolt out of all their holes. Conscious that they must be baffled, when they attribute a precedent disturbance to a subsequent measure, they take other ground, almost as absurd, but very common in modern practice, and very wicked; which is, to attribute the ill effect of ill-judged conduct to the arguments which had been used to dissuade us from it. They say, that the opposition made in Parliament to the Stamp Act, at the time of its passing, encouraged the Americans to their resistance. This has even formally appeared in print in a regular volume from an advocate of that faction, – a Dr Tucker.[1] This Dr Tucker is already a dean, and his earnest labors in this vineyard will, I suppose, raise him to a bishopric. But this assertion, too, just like the rest, is false. In all the papers which have loaded your table, in all the vast crowd of verbal witnesses that appeared at your bar, witnesses which were indiscriminately produced from both sides of the House, not the least hint of such a cause of disturbance has ever appeared. As to the fact of a strenuous opposition to the Stamp Act, I sat as a stranger in your gallery when the act was under consideration. Far from anything inflammatory, I never heard a more languid debate in this House. No more than two or three gentlemen, as I remember, spoke against the act, and that with great reserve and remarkable temper. There was but one division in the whole progress of the bill; and the minority did not reach to more than 39 or 40. In the House of Lords I do not recollect that there was any debate or division at all. I am sure there was no protest. In fact, the affair passed with so very, very little noise, that in town they scarcely knew the nature of what you were doing. The opposition to the bill in England never could have done this mischief, because there scarcely ever was less of opposition to a bill of consequence.

Sir, the agents and distributors of falsehoods have, with their usual industry, circulated another lie, of the same nature with the former. It is this: that the disturbances arose from the account which had been received in America of the change in the ministry. No longer awed, it seems, with the spirit of

[1] Josiah Tucker (1712–1799), Dean of Gloucester, *Four Tracts* . . . (Gloucester, 1774).

the former rulers, they thought themselves a match for what
our calumniators choose to qualify by the name of so feeble
a ministry as succeeded. Feeble in one sense these men
certainly may be called: for, with all their efforts, and they
have made many, they have not been able to resist the distempered vigor and insane alacrity with which you are rushing
to your ruin. But it does so happen, that the falsity of this
circulation is (like the rest) demonstrated by indisputable dates
and records.

So little was the change known in America, that the letters
of your governors, giving an account of these disturbances
long after they had arrived at their highest pitch, were all
directed to the *old ministry*, and particularly to the *Earl of
Halifax*, the Secretary of State corresponding with the
colonies,[1] without once in the smallest degree intimating the
slightest suspicion of any ministerial revolution whatsoever.
The ministry was not changed in England until the 10th day
of July, 1765. On the 14th of the preceding June, Governor
Fauquier, from Virginia,[2] writes thus, – and writes thus to the
Earl of Halifax: – 'Government is set at *defiance*, not having
strength enough in her hands to enforce obedience to the
laws of the community. – The private distress, which every
man feels, increases the *general dissatisfaction* at the duties laid
by the *Stamp Act*, which breaks out and shows itself upon
every trifling occasion.' The general dissatisfaction had
produced some time before, that is, on the 29th of May,
several strong public resolves against the Stamp Act; and those
resolves are assigned by Governor Bernard as the cause of the
insurrections in Massachusetts Bay, in his letter of the 15th of
August, still addressed to the Earl of Halifax; and he continued to address such accounts to that minister quite to the
7th of September of the same year. Similar accounts, and of as
late a date, were sent from other governors, and all directed to
Lord Halifax. Not one of these letters indicates the slightest
idea of a change, either known or even apprehended.

[1] George Montagu Dunk (1716–1771), second earl of Halifax,
served under both Bute and Grenville.
[2] Francis Fauquier (1704?–1768), Lieutenant-Governor of Virginia.

Thus are blown away the insect race of courtly falsehoods! Thus perish the miserable inventions of the wretched runners for a wretched cause, which they have fly-blown into every weak and rotten part of the country, in vain hopes, that, when their maggots had taken wing, their importunate buzzing might sound something like the public voice!

Sir, I have troubled you sufficiently with the state of America before the repeal. Now I turn to the honorable gentleman who so stoutly challenges us to tell whether, after the repeal, the provinces were quiet. This is coming home to the point. Here I meet him directly, and answer most readily, *They were quiet.* And I, in my turn, challenge him to prove when, and where, and by whom, and in what numbers, and with what violence, the other laws of trade, as gentlemen assert, were violated in consequence of your concession, or that even your other revenue laws were attacked. But I quit the vantage-ground on which I stand, and where I might leave the burden of the proof upon him: I walk down upon the open plain, and undertake to show that they were not only quiet, but showed many unequivocal marks of acknowledgment and gratitude. And to give him every advantage, I select the obnoxious colony of Massachusetts Bay, which at this time (but without hearing her) is so heavily a culprit before Parliament: I will select their proceedings even under circumstances of no small irritation. For, a little imprudently, I must say, Governor Bernard mixed in the administration of the lenitive of the repeal no small acrimony arising from matters of a separate nature. Yet see, Sir, the effect of that lenitive, though mixed with these bitter ingredients, – and how this rugged people can express themselves on a measure of concession.

'If it is not now in our power,' (say they, in their address to Governor Bernard), 'in so full a manner as will be expected, to show our respectful gratitude to the mother country, or to make a dutiful, affectionate return to the indulgence of the King and Parliament, it shall be no fault of ours; for this we intend, and hope shall be able fully to effect.'

Would to God that this temper had been cultivated, managed, and set in action! Other effects than those which we have since felt would have resulted from it. On the requisition for compensation to those who had suffered from the violence of the populace, in the same address they say, – 'The recommendation enjoined by Mr Secretary Conway's letter, and in consequence thereof made to us, we shall embrace the first convenient opportunity to consider and act upon.' They did consider; they did act upon it. They obeyed the requisition. I know the mode has been chicaned upon; but it was substantially obeyed, and much better obeyed than I fear the Parliamentary requisition of this session will be, though enforced by all your rigor and backed with all your power. In a word, the damages of popular fury were compensated by legislative gravity. Almost every other part of America in various ways demonstrated their gratitude. I am bold to say, that so sudden a calm recovered after so violent a storm is without parallel in history. To say that no other disturbance should happen from any other cause is folly. But as far as appearances went, by the judicious sacrifice of one law you procured an acquiescence in all that remained. After this experience, nobody shall persuade me, when an whole people are concerned, that acts of lenity are not means of conciliation.

I hope the honorable gentleman has received a fair and full answer to his question.

I have done with the third period of your policy, – that of your repeal, and the return of your ancient system, and your ancient tranquillity and concord. Sir, this period was not as long as it was happy. Another scene was opened, and other actors appeared on the stage. The state, in the condition I have described it, was delivered into the hands of Lord Chatham, a great and celebrated name, – a name that keeps the name of this country respectable in every other on the globe. It may be truly called

Clarum et venerabile nomen
Gentibus, et muluum nostræ quod proderat urbi.[1]

Sir, the venerable age of this great man, his merited rank,

[1] A distinguished and venerable name to the people, and one which has been of much service to our city. Lucan, *Pharsalia* ix. 203.

his superior eloquence, his splendid qualities, his eminent
services, the vast space he fills in the eye of mankind, and,
more than all the rest, his fall from power, which, like death,
canonizes and sanctifies a great character, will not suffer me to
censure any part of his conduct. I am afraid to flatter him; I
am sure I am not disposed to blame him. Let those who have
betrayed him by their adulation insult him with their male-
volence. But what I do not presume to censure I may have
leave to lament. For a wise man, he seemed to me at that time
to be governed too much by general maxims. I speak with the
freedom of history, and I hope without offence. One or two of
these maxims, flowing from an opinion not the most indulgent
to our unhappy species, and surely a little too general, led him
into measures that were greatly mischievous to himself, and
for that reason, among others, perhaps fatal to his country, –
measures, the effects of which, I am afraid, are forever incurable. He made an administration so checkered and speckled,
he put together a piece of joinery so crossly indented and
whimsically dovetailed, a cabinet so variously inlaid, such a
piece of diversified mosaic, such a tessellated pavement without
cement, – here a bit of black stone and there a bit of white,
patriots and courtiers, king's friends and republicans, Whigs
and Tories, treacherous friends and open enemies, – that it
was, indeed, a very curious show, but utterly unsafe to touch
and unsure to stand on. The colleagues whom he had assorted
at the same boards stared at each other, and were obliged to
ask, – 'Sir, your name?' – 'Sir, you have the advantage of me.'
– 'Mr Such-a-one.' – 'I beg a thousand pardons.' – I venture
to say, it did so happen that persons had a single office divided
between them, who had never spoke to each other in their
lives, until they found themselves, they knew not how,
pigging together, heads and points, in the same truckle-bed.*

* Supposed to allude to the Right Honourable Lord North, and
George Cooke, Esq., who were made joint paymasters in the summer
of 1766, on the removal of the Rockingham administration. [George
Cooke (c. 1705–1768) had been a Chathamite, while North had left
office with Grenville in 1765 and voted against the repeal of the Stamp
Act. The two men were therefore diametrically opposed to each other
on American policy.]

Sir, in consequence of this arrangement, having put so much the larger part of his enemies and opposers into power, the confusion was such that his own principles could not possibly have any effect or influence in the conduct of affairs. If ever he fell into a fit of the gout, or if any other cause withdrew him from public cares, principles directly the contrary were sure to predominate. When he had executed his plan, he had not an inch of ground to stand upon. When he had accomplished his scheme of administration, he was no longer a minister.

When his face was hid but for a moment, his whole system was on a wide sea without chart or compass. The gentlemen, his particular friends, who, with the names of various departments of ministry, were admitted to seem as if they acted a part under him, with a modesty that becomes all men, and with a confidence in him which was justified even in its extravagance by his superior abilities, had never in any instance presumed upon any opinion of their own. Deprived of his guiding influence, they were whirled about, the sport of every gust, and easily driven into any port; and as those who joined with them in manning the vessel were the most directly opposite to his opinions, measures, and character, and far the most artful and most powerful of the set, they easily prevailed, so as to seize upon the vacant, unoccupied, and derelict minds of his friends, and instantly they turned the vessel wholly out of the course of his policy. As if it were to insult as well as to betray him, even long before the close of the first session of his administration, when everything was publicly transacted, and with great parade, in his name, they made an act declaring it highly just and expedient to raise a revenue in America. For even then, Sir, even before this splendid orb was entirely set, and while the western horizon was in a blaze with his descending glory, on the opposite quarter of the heavens arose another luminary, and for his hour became lord of the ascendant.

This light, too, is passed and set forever. You understand, to be sure, that I speak of Charles Townshend, officially the reproducer of this fatal scheme, whom I cannot even now remember without some degree of sensibility. In truth, Sir, he was the delight and ornament of this House, and the charm of every private society which he honored with his presence. Perhaps there never arose in this country, nor in any country, a man of a more pointed and finished wit, and (where his passions were not concerned) of a more refined, exquisite, and penetrating judgment. If he had not so great a stock as some have had, who flourished formerly, of knowledge long treasured up, he knew, better by far than any man I ever was acquainted with, how to bring together within a short time all that was necessary to establish, to illustrate, and to decorate that side of the question he supported. He stated his matter skilfully and powerfully. He particularly excelled in a most luminous explanation and display of his subject. His style of argument was neither trite and vulgar, nor subtle and abstruse. He hit the House just between wind and water. And not being troubled with too anxious a zeal for any matter in question, he was never more tedious or more earnest than the preconceived opinions and present temper of his hearers required, to whom he was always in perfect unison. He conformed exactly to the temper of the House; and he seemed to guide, because he was always sure to follow it.

I beg pardon, Sir, if, when I speak of this and of other great men, I appear to digress in saying something of their characters. In this eventful history of the revolutions of America, the characters of such men are of much importance. Great men are the guideposts and landmarks in the state. The credit of such men at court or in the nation is the sole cause of all the public measures. It would be an invidious thing (most foreign, I trust, to what you think my disposition) to remark the errors into which the authority of great names has brought the nation, without doing justice at the same time to the great qualities whence that authority arose. The subject is instructive to those who wish to form themselves on whatever of excellence has gone before them. There are many young members in the House (such of late has been the rapid succession of public men) who never saw that prodigy, Charles Townshend, nor of course know what a ferment he was able to excite in everything by the violent ebullition of his mixed virtues and failings. For failings he had undoubtedly, – many of us remember them; we are this day considering the effect of them. But he had no failings which were not owing to a noble cause, – to an ardent, generous, perhaps an immoderate passion for fame: a passion which is the instinct of all great souls. He worshipped that goddess, wheresoever she appeared; but he paid his particular devotions to her in her favorite habitation, in her chosen temple, the House of Commons. Besides the characters of the individuals that compose our body, it is impossible, Mr Speaker, not to observe that this House has a collective character of its own. That character, too, however imperfect, is not unamiable. Like all great public collections of men, you possess a marked love of virtue and an abhorrence of vice. But among vices there is none which the House abhors in the same degree with *obstinacy*. Obstinacy, Sir, is certainly a great vice; and in the changeful state of political affairs it is frequently the cause of great mischief. It happens, however, very unfortunately, that almost the whole line of the great and masculine virtues, constancy, gravity, magnanimity, fortitude, fidelity, and firmness, are closely allied to this disagreeable quality, of which you have so just an abhorrence; and, in their excess, all these virtues very easily fall into it. He who paid such a punctilious attention to all your feelings certainly took care not to shock them by that vice which is the most disgustful to you.

That fear of displeasing those who ought most to be pleased betrayed him sometimes into the other extreme. He had voted, and, in the year 1765, had been an advocate for the Stamp Act. Things and the disposition of men's minds were changed. In short, the Stamp Act began to be no favorite in this House. He therefore attended at the private meeting in which the resolutions moved by a right honorable gentleman were settled: resolutions leading to the repeal. The next day he voted for that repeal; and he would have spoken for it, too, if an illness (not, as was then given out, a political, but, to my knowledge, a very real illness) had not prevented it.

The very next session, as the fashion of this world passeth away, the repeal began to be in as bad an odor in this House as the Stamp Act had been in the session before. To conform to the temper which began to prevail, and to prevail mostly amongst those most in power, he declared, very early in the winter, that a revenue must be had out of America. Instantly he was tied down to his engagements by some, who had no objection to such experiments, when made at the cost of persons for whom they had no particular regard. The whole body of courtiers drove him onward. They always talked as if the king stood in a sort of humiliated state, until something of the kind should be done.

Here this extraordinary man, then Chancellor of the Exchequer, found himself in great straits. To please universally was the object of his life; but to tax and to please, no more than to love and to be wise, is not given to men. However, he attempted it. To render the tax palatable to the partisans of American revenue, he made a preamble stating the necessity of such a revenue. To close with the American distinction, this revenue was *external* or port-duty; but again, to soften it to the other party, it was a duty of *supply*. To gratify the *colonists*, it was laid on British manufactures; to satisfy the *merchants of Britain*, the duty was trivial, and (except that on tea, which touched only the devoted East India Company) on none of the grand objects of commerce. To counterwork the American contraband, the duty on tea was reduced from a shilling to three-pence; but to secure the favor of those who would tax America, the scene of collection was changed, and, with the rest, it was levied in the colonies. What need I say more? This fine-spun scheme had the usual fate of all exquisite policy. But the original plan of the duties, and the mode of executing that plan, both arose singly and solely from a love of our applause. He was truly the child of the House. He never thought, did, or said anything, but with a view to you. He every day adapted himself to your disposition, and adjusted himself before it as at a looking-glass.

He had observed (indeed, it could not escape him) that several persons, infinitely his inferiors in all respects, had formerly rendered themselves considerable in this House by one method alone. They were a race of men (I hope in God the species is extinct) who, when they rose in their place, no man living could divine, from any known adherence to parties, to opinions, or to principles, from any order or system in their politics, or from any sequel or connection in their ideas, what part they were going to take in any debate. It is astonishing how much this uncertainty, especially at critical times, called the attention of all parties on such men. All eyes were fixed on them, all ears open to hear them; each party gaped, and looked alternately for their vote, almost to the end of their speeches. While the House hung in this uncertainty, now the *hear-hims* rose from this side, now they rebellowed from the other; and that party to whom they fell at length from their tremulous and dancing balance always received them in a tempest of applause. The fortune of such men was a temptation too great to be resisted by one to whom a single whiff of incense withheld gave much greater pain than he received delight in the clouds of it which daily rose about him from the prodigal superstition of innumerable admirers. He was a candidate for contradictory honors; and his great aim was, to make those agree in admiration of him who never agreed in anything else.

Hence arose this unfortunate act, the subject of this day's debate: from a disposition which, after making an American revenue to please one, repealed it to please others, and again revived it in hopes of pleasing a third, and of catching something in the ideas of all.

This revenue act of 1767 formed the fourth period of American policy. How we have fared since then: what woful variety of schemes have been adopted; what enforcing, and what repealing; what bullying, and what submitting; what doing, and undoing; what straining, and what relaxing; what assemblies dissolved for not obeying, and called again without obedience; what troops sent out to quell resistance, and, on meeting that resistance, recalled; what shiftings, and changes, and jumblings of all kinds of men at home, which left no possibility of order, consistency, vigor, or even so much as a decent unity of color, in any one public measure – It is a tedious, irksome task. My duty may call me to open it out

some other time; on a former occasion* I tried your temper
on a part of it; for the present I shall forbear.

After all these changes and agitations, your immediate
situation upon the question on your paper is at length brought
to this. You have an act of Parliament stating that 'it is
expedient to raise a revenue in America.' By a partial repeal
you annihilated the greatest part of that revenue which this
preamble declares to be so expedient. You have substituted
no other in the place of it. A Secretary of State has disclaimed,
in the king's name, all thoughts of such a substitution in
future.[1] The principle of this disclaimer goes to what has been
left, as well as what has been repealed. The tax which lingers
after its companions (under a preamble declaring an American
revenue expedient, and for the sole purpose of supporting the
theory of that preamble) militates with the assurance authentic-
ally conveyed to the colonies, and is an exhaustless source of
jealousy and animosity. On this state, which I take to be a fair
one, – not being able to discern any grounds of honor, advantage, peace, or power, for adhering, either to the act or to
the preamble, I shall vote for the question which leads to the
repeal of both.

If you do not fall in with this motion, then secure something
to fight for, consistent in theory and valuable in practice. If
you must employ your strength, employ it to uphold you in
some honorable right or some profitable wrong. If you are
apprehensive that the concession recommended to you,
though proper, should be a means of drawing on you further,
but unreasonable claims, – why, then employ your force in
supporting that reasonable concession against those unreasonable demands. You will employ it with more grace, with
better effect, and with great probable concurrence of all the
quiet and rational people in the provinces, who are now united

* Resolutions in May, 1770. [On 9 May 1770 Burke had introduced
eight proposed resolutions for censuring the ministry's treatment of
American affairs.]

[1] Wills Hill (1718–1793), Viscount Hillsborough, as Secretary of
State for the Colonies sent, in May 1769, a circular letter to the colonial
governors announcing the impending repeal of most of the Townshend
duties and also making, Burke believed, the assertion in question.

with and hurried away by the violent, – having, indeed, different dispositions, but a common interest. If you apprehend that on a concession you shall be pushed by metaphysical process to the extreme lines, and argued out of your whole authority, my advice is this: when you have recovered your old, your strong, your tenable position, then face about, – stop short, – do nothing more, – reason not at all, – oppose the ancient policy and practice of the empire as a rampart against the speculations of innovators on both sides of the question, – and you will stand on great, manly, and sure ground. On this solid basis fix your machines, and they will draw worlds towards you.

Your ministers, in their own and his Majesty's name, have already adopted the American distinction of internal and external duties. It is a distinction, whatever merit it may have, that was originally moved by the Americans themselves; and I think they will acquiesce in it, if they are not pushed with too much logic and too little sense, in all the consequences: that is, if external taxation be understood, as they and you understand it, when you please, to be not a distinction of geography, but of policy; that it is a power for regulating trade, and not for supporting establishments. The distinction, which is as nothing with regard to right, is of most weighty consideration in practice. Recover your old ground, and your old tranquillity; try it; I am persuaded the Americans will compromise with you. When confidence is once restored, the odious and suspicious *summum jus* will perish of course. The spirit of practicability, of moderation, and mutual convenience will never call in geometrical exactness as the arbitrator of an amicable settlement. Consult and follow your experience. Let not the long story with which I have exercised your patience prove fruitless to your interests.

For my part, I should choose (if I could have my wish) that the proposition of the honorable gentleman* for the repeal could go to America without the attendance of the penal bills. Alone I could almost answer for its success. I cannot be certain of its reception in the bad company it may keep. In

* Mr Fuller.

such heterogeneous assortments, the most innocent person will lose the effect of his innocency. Though you should send out this angel of peace, yet you are sending out a destroying angel too; and what would be the effect of the conflict of these two adverse spirits, or which would predominate in the end, is what I dare not say: whether the lenient measures would cause American passion to subside, or the severe would increase its fury, – all this is in the hand of Providence. Yet now, even now, I should confide in the prevailing virtue and efficacious operation of lenity, though working in darkness and in chaos, in the midst of all this unnatural and turbid combination: I should hope it might produce order and beauty in the end.

Let us, Sir, embrace some system or other before we end this session. Do you mean to tax America, and to draw a productive revenue from thence? If you do, speak out: name, fix, ascertain this revenue; settle its quantity; define its objects; provide for its collection; and then fight, when you have something to fight for. If you murder, rob; if you kill, take possession; and do not appear in the character of madmen as well as assassins, violent, vindictive, bloody, and tyrannical, without an object. But may better counsels guide you!

Again, and again, revert to your old principles, – seek peace and ensue it, – leave America, if she has taxable matter in her, to tax herself. I am not here going into the distinctions of rights, nor attempting to mark their boundaries. I do not enter into these metaphysical distinctions; I hate the very sound of them. Leave the Americans as they anciently stood, and these distinctions, born of our unhappy contest, will die along with it. They and we, and their and our ancestors, have been happy under that system. Let the memory of all actions in contradiction to that good old mode, on both sides, be extinguished forever. Be content to bind America by laws of trade: you have always done it. Let this be your reason for binding their trade. Do not burden them by taxes: you were not used to do so from the beginning. Let this be your reason for not taxing. These are the arguments of states and kingdoms. Leave the rest to the schools; for there only they may be discussed with safety. But if, intemperately, unwisely, fatally, you sophisticate and poison the very source of government, by urging subtle deductions, and consequences odious to those you govern, from the unlimited and illimitable nature of supreme sovereignty, you will teach them by these means to call that sovereignty itself in question. When you drive him hard, the boar will surely turn upon the hunters. If that sovereignty and their freedom cannot be reconciled, which will they take? They will cast your sovereignty in your face. Nobody will be argued into slavery. Sir, let the gentlemen on the other side call forth all their ability; let the best of them get up and tell me what one character of liberty the Americans have, and what one brand of slavery they are free from, if they are bound in their property and industry by all the restraints you can imagine on commerce, and at the same time are made pack-horses of every tax you choose to impose, without the least share in granting them. When they bear the burdens of unlimited monopoly, will you bring them to bear the burdens of unlimited revenue too? The Englishman in America will feel that this is slavery: that it is *legal* slavery will be no compensation either to his feelings or his understanding.

A noble lord,* who spoke some time ago, is full of the fire of ingenuous youth; and when he has modelled the ideas of a lively imagination by further experience, he will be an ornament to his country in either House. He has said that the Americans are our children, and how can they revolt against their parent? He says, that, if they are not free in their present state, England is not free; because Manchester, and other considerable places, are not represented. So, then, because some towns in England are not represented, America is to have no representative at all. They are 'our children'; but when children ask for bread, we are not to give a stone. Is it because the natural resistance of things, and the various mutations of time, hinders our government, or any scheme of government, from being any more than a sort of approximation to the right, is it therefore that the colonies are to recede from it infinitely? When this child of ours wishes to assimilate

* Lord Carmarthen.

to its parent, and to reflect with a true filial resemblance the beauteous countenance of British liberty, are we to turn to them the shameful parts of our constitution? are we to give them our weakness for their strength, our opprobrium for their glory, and the slough of slavery, which we are not able to work off, to serve them for their freedom?

If this be the case, ask yourselves this question: Will they be content in such a state of slavery? If not, look to the consequences. Reflect how you are to govern a people who think they ought to be free, and think they are not. Your scheme yields no revenue; it yields nothing but discontent, disorder, disobedience: and such is the state of America, that, after wading up to your eyes in blood, you could only end just where you begun, – that is, to tax where no revenue is to be found, to – My voice fails me: my inclination, indeed, carries me no further; all is confusion beyond it.

Well, Sir, I have recovered a little, and before I sit down I must say something to another point with which gentlemen urge us. What is to become of the Declaratory Act, asserting the entireness of British legislative authority, if we abandon the practice of taxation?

For my part, I look upon the rights stated in that act exactly in the manner in which I viewed them on its very first proposition, and which I have often taken the 'iberty, with great humility, to lay before you. I look, I s y, on the imperial rights of Great Britain, and the privileges which the colonists ought to enjoy under these rights, to be just the most reconcilable things in the world. The Parliament of Great Britain sits at the head of her extensive empire in two capacities. One as the local legislature of this island, providing for all things at home, immediately, and by no other instrument than the executive power. The other, and I think her nobler capacity, is what I call her *imperial character*; in which, as from the throne of heaven, she superintends all the several inferior legislatures, and guides and controls them all without annihilating any. As all these provincial legislatures are only coordinate to each other, they ought all to be subordinate to her; else they can neither preserve mutual peace, nor hope for mutual justice, nor effectually afford mutual assistance. It is necessary to coerce the negligent, to restrain the violent, and to aid the weak and deficient, by the overruling plenitude of her power. She is never to intrude into the place of the others, whilst they are equal to the common ends of their institution. But in order to enable Parliament to answer all these ends of provident and beneficent superintendence, her powers must be boundless. The gentlemen who think the powers of Parliament limited may please themselves to talk of requisitions. But suppose the requisitions are not obeyed? What! shall there be no reserved power in the empire, to supply a deficiency which may weaken, divide, and dissipate the whole? We are engaged in war, – the Secretary of State calls upon the colonies to contribute, – some would do it, I think most would cheerfully furnish whatever is demanded, – one or two, suppose, hang back, and, easing themselves, let the stress of the draft lie on the others, – surely it is proper that some authority might legally say, 'Tax yourselves for the common supply, or Parliament will do it for you.' This backwardness was, as I am told, actually the case of Pennsylvania for some short time towards the beginning of the last war, owing to some internal dissensions in the colony. But whether the fact were so or otherwise, the case is equally to be provided for by a competent sovereign power. But then this ought to be no ordinary power, nor ever used in the first instance. This is what I meant, when I have said, at various times, that I consider the power of taxing in Parliament as an instrument of empire, and not as a means of supply.

Such, Sir, is my idea of the Constitution of the British Empire, as distinguished from the Constitution of Britain; and on these grounds I think subordination and liberty may be sufficiently reconciled through the whole, – whether to serve a refining speculatist or a factious demagogue I know not, but enough surely for the ease and happiness of man.

Sir, whilst we held this happy course, we drew more from the colonies than all the impotent violence of despotism ever could extort from them. We did this abundantly in the last war; it has never been once denied; and what reason have we to imagine that the colonies would not have proceeded in supplying government as liberally, if you had not stepped in and hindered them from contributing, by interrupting the channel in which their liberality flowed with so strong a course, – by attempting to take, instead of being satisfied to receive? Sir William Temple says, that Holland has loaded itself with ten times the impositions which it revolted from Spain rather than submit to.[1] He says true. Tyranny is a poor provider. It knows neither how to accumulate nor how to extract.

I charge, therefore, to this new and unfortunate system the loss not only of peace, of union, and of commerce, but even of revenue, which its friends are contending for. It is morally certain that we have lost at least a million of free grants since the peace. I think we have lost a great deal more; and that those who look for a revenue from the provinces never could have pursued, even in that light, a course more directly repugnant to their purposes.

Now, Sir, I trust I have shown, first on that narrow ground which the honorable gentleman measured, that you are like to lose nothing by complying with the motion, except what you have lost already. I have shown afterwards, that in time of peace you flourished in commerce, and, when war required it, had sufficient aid from the colonies, while you pursued your ancient policy; that you threw everything into confusion, when you made the Stamp Act; and that you restored everything to peace and order, when you repealed it. I have shown that the revival of the system of taxation has produced the very worst effects; and that the partial repeal has produced, not partial good, but universal evil. Let these considerations, founded on facts, not one of which can be denied, bring us back to our reason by the road of our experience.

I cannot, as I have said, answer for mixed measures: but surely this mixture of lenity would give the whole a better chance of success. When you once regain confidence, the way will be clear before you. Then you may enforce the Act of

[1] Sir William Temple (1628–1699), *Observations upon . . . the Netherlands* (1672), chap. 2.

Navigation, when it ought to be enforced. You will yourselves open it, where it ought still further to be opened. Proceed in what you do, whatever you do, from policy, and not from rancor. Let us act like men, let us act like statesmen. Let us hold some sort of consistent conduct. It is agreed that a revenue is not to be had in America. If we lose the profit, let us get rid of the odium.

On this business of America, I confess I am serious, even to sadness. I have had but one opinion concerning it, since I sat, and before I sat in Parliament. The noble lord* will, as usual, probably, attribute the part taken by me and my friends in this business to a desire of getting his places. Let him enjoy this happy and original idea. If I deprived him of it, I should take away most of his wit, and all his argument. But I had rather bear the brunt of all his wit, and indeed blows much heavier, than stand answerable to God for embracing a system that tends to the destruction of some of the very best and fairest of His works. But I know the map of England as well as the noble lord, or as any other person; and I know that the way I take is not the road to preferment. My excellent and honorable friend under me on the floor† has trod that road with great toil for upwards of twenty years together. He is not yet arrived at the noble lord's destination. However, the tracks of my worthy friend are those I have ever wished to follow; because I know they lead to honor. Long may we tread the same road together, whoever may accompany us, or whoever may laugh at us on our journey! I honestly and solemnly declare, I have in all seasons adhered to the system of 1766 for no other reason than that I think it laid deep in your truest interests, – and that, by limiting the exercise, it fixes on the firmest foundations a real, consistent, well-grounded authority in Parliament. Until you come back to that system, there will be no peace for England.

* Lord North.
† Mr Dowdeswell [William Dowdeswel¹ (1721–1775), a leading member of the Rockingham party, sat on the front bench, on the floor of the Commons.]

Speech to the Electors of Bristol

Burke's election for the popular constituency of Bristol was something of an accident. Despite the presence of some strong supporters among the mercantile community there he would not have been elected but for the last-minute withdrawal of another candidate. Arriving after the commencement of the poll he was elected along with the radicals' candidate Henry Cruger, defeating two other contestants. At the conclusion of the proceedings Burke made the usual speech of thanks, following Cruger who had headed the poll. Burke differed from his new colleague in being unwilling to accept the right of a constituency to give instructions to its Members of Parliament, and made this clear at once. He particularly feared being bound to campaign for radical reform measures. At the next general election he was forced to withdraw his candidature and fall back upon Rockingham's borough of Malton. Burke's defence, in this speech, of parliamentarians' right to make their own initiatives, based upon their judgement of the matter in hand, has been quoted often in the course of two centuries, and is as valid today as it ever was. But it should be pointed out that Burke's own political career often illustrates a contrary argument: as the polemicist of a party he had to concede that a Member of Parliament might have to sink his individual judgement in the collective wisdom of the party.

From a Speech to the Electors of Bristol, on his being declared by the Sheriffs duly elected (3 November 1774)

I am sorry I cannot conclude without saying a word on a topic touched upon by my worthy colleague.[1] I wish that

---

[1] Henry Cruger (1739–1827), one of the few American-born Members of Parliament in this period.

topic had been passed by at a time when I have so little leisure to discuss it. But since he has thought proper to throw it out, I owe you a clear explanation of my poor sentiments on that subject.

He tells you that 'the topic of instructions has occasioned much altercation and uneasiness in this city'; and he expresses himself (if I understand him rightly) in favor of the coercive authority of such instructions.

Certainly, Gentlemen, it ought to be the happiness and glory of a representative to live in the strictest union, the closest correspondence, and the most unreserved communication with his constituents. Their wishes ought to have great weight with him; their opinions high respect; their business unremitted attention. It is his duty to sacrifice his repose, his pleasure, his satisfactions, to theirs, – and above all, ever, and in all cases, to prefer their interest to his own.

But his unbiased opinion, his mature judgment, his enlightened conscience, he ought not to sacrifice to you, to any man, or to any set of men living. These he does not derive from your pleasure, – no, nor from the law and the Constitution. They are a trust from Providence, for the abuse of which he is deeply answerable. Your representative owes you, not his industry only, but his judgment; and he betrays, instead of serving you, if he sacrifices it to your opinion.

My worthy colleague says, his will ought to be subservient to yours. If that be all, the thing is innocent. If government were a matter of will upon any side, yours, without question, ought to be superior. But government and legislation are matters of reason and judgment, and not of inclination; and what sort of reason is that in which the determination precedes the discussion, in which one set of men deliberate and another decide, and where those who form the conclusion are perhaps three hundred miles distant from those who hear the arguments?

To deliver an opinion is the right of all men; that of constituents is a weighty and respectable opinion, which a representative ought always to rejoice to hear, and which he ought always most seriously to consider. But *authoritative* instructions, *mandates* issued, which the member is bound blindly and implicitly to obey, to vote, and to argue for, though contrary to the clearest conviction of his judgment and conscience, – these are things utterly unknown to the laws of this land, and which arise from a fundamental mistake of the whole order and tenor of our Constitution.

Parliament is not a *congress* of ambassadors from different and hostile interests, which interests each must maintain, as an agent and advocate, against other agents and advocates; but Parliament is a *deliberative* assembly of *one* nation, with *one* interest, that of the whole – where not local purposes, not local prejudices, ought to guide, but the general good, resulting from the general reason of the whole. You choose a member, indeed; but when you have chosen him, he is not member of Bristol, but he is a member of *Parliament*. If the local constituent should have an interest or should form an hasty opinion evidently opposite to the real good of the rest of the community, the member for that place ought to be as far as any other from any endeavor to give it effect. I beg pardon for saying so much on this subject; I have been unwillingly drawn into it; but I shall ever use a respectful frankness of communication with you. Your faithful friend, your devoted servant, I shall be to the end of my life: a flatterer you do not wish for. On this point of instructions, however, I think it scarcely possible we ever can have any sort of difference. Perhaps I may give you too much, rather than too little trouble.

Speech on Conciliation with the Colonies

The assembling of a new House after the general election of 1774 brought no relaxation to the strain on Anglo-American relations. Lord North's ministry busied itself with new bills to restrain colonial trade, and when North himself announced on 20 February his private plan for conciliating the colonies this pleased neither his colleagues nor the colonists. A month later Burke produced his own plan of conciliation. By a fortunate chance a bill to restrain the trade of the New England colonies which had already been passed and sent up to the Lords was returned, as the result of an amendment there, on the day Burke was due to speak. The possibility of getting this bill rejected at the eleventh hour gave his speech an added note of urgency as he strove to convince his fellow Members of the expediency of a more understanding and lenient attitude towards the Americans. But the bill passed and his resolutions were rejected. Two months later, just as Burke published his speech for the benefit of a wider audience, news arrived in England of the outbreak of hostilities at Concord Bridge and Lexington.

The speech is notable for its further development of an idea already outlined in the *Speech on American Taxation*, namely that government should be dependent on the character of the people governed. In pointing out that this character could be formed by topography and climate as well as by history, Burke displayed the influence of Montesquieu's *Esprit des Lois*, a work which he much admired.

From the Speech on moving his Resolutions for Conciliation with the Colonies (*22 March 1775*)

The proposition is peace. Not peace through the medium of

war; not peace to be hunted through the labyrinth of intricate and endless negotiations; not peace to arise out of universal discord, fomented from principle, in all parts of the empire; not peace to depend on the juridical determination of perplexing questions, or the precise marking the shadowy boundaries of a complex government. It is simple peace, sought in its natural course and in its ordinary haunts. It is peace sought in the spirit of peace, and laid in principles purely pacific. I propose, by removing the ground of the difference, and by restoring the *former unsuspecting confidence of the colonies in the mother country*, to give permanent satisfaction to your people, – and (far from a scheme of ruling by discord) to reconcile them to each other in the same act and by the bond of the very same interest which reconciles them to British government.

My idea is nothing more. Refined policy ever has been the parent of confusion, – and ever will be so, as long as the world endures. Plain good intention, which is as easily discovered at the first view as fraud is surely detected at last, is, let me say, of no mean force in the government of mankind. Genuine simplicity of heart is an healing and cementing principle. My plan, therefore, being formed upon the most simple grounds imaginable, may disappoint some people, when they hear it. It has nothing to recommend it to the pruriency of curious ears. There is nothing at all new and captivating in it. It has nothing of the splendor of the project which has been lately laid upon your table by the noble lord in the blue riband.*

* 'That when the governor, council, and assembly, or general court, of any of his Majesty's provinces or colonies in America shall *propose* to make provision, *according to the condition, circumstances*, and *situation* of such province or colony, for contributing their *proportion* to the *common defence*, (such *proportion* to be raised under the authority of the general court or general assembly of such province or colony, and disposable by Parliament,) and shall *engage* to make provision also for the support of the civil government and the administration of justice in such province or colony, it will be proper, *if such proposal shall be approved by his Majesty and the two Houses of Parliament*, and for so long as such provision shall be made accordingly, to forbear, *in respect of such province or colony*, to levy any duty, tax, or assessment, or to impose any farther duty, tax, or assessment, except only such

It does not propose to fill your lobby with squabbling colony agents, who will require the interposition of your mace at every instant to keep the peace amongst them. It does not institute a magnificent auction of finance, where captivated provinces come to general ransom by bidding against each other, until you knock down the hammer, and determine a proportion of payments beyond all the powers of algebra to equalize and settle.

The plan which I shall presume to suggest derives, however, one great advantage from the proposition and registry of that noble lord's project. The idea of conciliation is admissible. First, the House, in accepting the resolution moved by the noble lord, has admitted, notwithstanding the menacing front of our address, notwithstanding our heavy bill of pains and penalties, that we do not think ourselves precluded from all ideas of free grace and bounty.

The House has gone farther: it has declared conciliation admissible *previous* to any submission on the part of America. It has even shot a good deal beyond that mark, and has admitted that the complaints of our former mode of exerting the right of taxation were not wholly unfounded. That right thus exerted is allowed to have had something reprehensible in it, – something unwise, or something grievous; since, in the midst of our heat and resentment, we, of ourselves, have proposed a capital alteration, and, in order to get rid of what seemed so very exceptionable, have instituted a mode that is altogether new, – one that is, indeed, wholly alien from all the ancient methods and forms of Parliament.

The *principle* of this proceeding is large enough for my purpose. The means proposed by the noble lord for carrying his ideas into execution, I think, indeed, are very indifferently suited to the end; and this I shall endeavor to show you before I sit down. But, for the present, I take my ground on the

---

duties as it may be expedient to continue to levy or to impose for the regulation of commerce: the net produce of the duties last mentioned to be carried to the account of such province or colony respectively.' – Resolution moved by Lord North in the Committee, and agreed to by the House, 27th February, 1775. [The italics are Burke's.]

admitted principle. I mean to give peace. Peace implies reconciliation; and where there has been a material dispute, reconciliation does in a manner always imply concession on the one part or on the other. In this state of things I make no difficulty in affirming that the proposal ought to originate from us. Great and acknowledged force is not impaired, either in effect or in opinion, by an unwillingness to exert itself. The superior power may offer peace with honor and with safety. Such an offer from such a power will be attributed to magnanimity. But the concessions of the weak are the concessions of fear. When such a one is disarmed, he is wholly at the mercy of his superior; and he loses forever that time and those chances which, as they happen to all men, are the strength and resources of all inferior power.

The capital leading questions on which you must this day decide are these two: First, whether you ought to concede; and secondly, what your concession ought to be. On the first of these questions we have gained (as I have just taken the liberty of observing to you) some ground. But I am sensible that a good deal more is still to be done. Indeed, Sir, to enable us to determine both on the one and the other of these great questions with a firm and precise judgment, I think it may be necessary to consider distinctly the true nature and the peculiar circumstances of the object which we have before us: because, after all our struggle, whether we will or not, we must govern America according to that nature and to those circumstances, and not according to our own imaginations, not according to abstract ideas of right, by no means according to mere general theories of government, the resort to which appears to me, in our present situation, no better than arrant trifling. I shall therefore endeavor, with your leave, to lay before you some of the most material of these circumstances in as full and as clear a manner as I am able to state them.

The first thing that we have to consider with regard to the nature of the object is the number of people in the colonies. I have taken for some years a good deal of pains on that point. I can by no calculation justify myself in placing the number below two millions of inhabitants of our own European blood and color, – besides at least 500,000 others, who form no inconsiderable part of the strength and opulence of the whole. This, Sir, is, I believe, about the true number. There is no occasion to exaggerate, where plain truth is of so much weight and importance. But whether I put the present numbers too high or too low is a matter of little moment. Such is the strength with which population shoots in that part of the world, that, state the numbers as high as we will, whilst the dispute continues, the exaggeration ends. Whilst we are discussing any given magnitude, they are grown to it. Whilst we spend our time in deliberating on the mode of governing two millions, we shall find we have millions more to manage. Your children do not grow faster from infancy to manhood than they spread from families to communities, and from villages to nations.

I put this consideration of the present and the growing numbers in the front of our deliberation, because, Sir, this consideration will make it evident to a blunter discernment than yours, that no partial, narrow, contracted, pinched, occasional system will be at all suitable to such an object. It will show you that it is not to be considered as one of those *minima* which are out of the eye and consideration of the law, – not a paltry excrescence of the state, – not a mean dependent, who may be neglected with little damage and provoked with little danger. It will prove that some degree of care and caution is required in the handling such an object; it will show that you ought not, in reason, to trifle with so large a mass of the interests and feelings of the human race. You could at no time do so without guilt; and be assured you will not be able to do it long with impunity.

But the population of this country, the great and growing population, though a very important consideration, will lose much of its weight, if not combined with other circumstances. The commerce of your colonies is out of all proportion beyond the numbers of the people. This ground of their commerce, indeed, has been trod some days ago, and with great ability, by a distinguished person,* at your bar. This gentleman,

* Mr Glover. [Richard Glover (1712–1785), who had recently

after thirty-five years, – it is so long since he first appeared at the same place to plead for the commerce of Great Britain, – has come again before you to plead the same cause, without any other effect of time than that to the fire of imagination and extent of erudition, which even then marked him as one of the first literary characters of his age, he has added a consummate knowledge in the commercial interest of his country, formed by a long course of enlightened and discriminating experience.

Sir, I should be inexcusable in coming after such a person with any detail, if a great part of the members who now fill the House had not the misfortune to be absent when he appeared at your bar. Besides, Sir, I propose to take the matter at periods of time somewhat different from his. There is, if I mistake not, a point of view from whence, if you will look at this subject, it is impossible that it should not make an impression upon you.

I have in my hand two accounts: one a comparative state of the export trade of England to its colonies, as it stood in the year 1704, and as it stood in the year 1772; the other a state of the export trade of this country to its colonies alone, as it stood in 1772, compared with the whole trade of England to all parts of the world (the colonies included) in the year 1704. They are from good vouchers: the latter period from the accounts on your table; the earlier from an original manuscript of Davenant,[1] who first established the Inspector-General's office, which has been ever since his time so abundant a source of Parliamentary information.

The export trade to the colonies consists of three great branches: the African, which, terminating almost wholly in the colonies, must be put to the account of their commerce; the West Indian; and the North American. All these are so interwoven, that the attempt to separate them would tear to pieces the contexture of the whole, and, if not entirely destroy, would very much depreciate, the value of all the parts. I

---

appeared at the bar of the House of Commons as agent for the West India merchants.]

[1] Charles Davenant (1656–1714), pamphleteer and economist, was Inspector-General of Imports and Exports 1705–1714.

therefore consider these three denominations to be, what in effect they are, one trade.

The trade to the colonies, taken on the export side, at the beginning of this century, that is, in the year 1704, stood thus:—

Exports to North America and the West Indies	£483,265
To Africa	86,665
	£569,930

In the year 1772, which I take as a middle year between the highest and lowest of those lately laid on your table, the account was as follows:—

To North America and the West Indies . .	£4,791,734
To Africa	866,398
To which if you add the export trade from Scotland, which had in 1704 no existence . .	364,000
	£6,024,171

From five hundred and odd thousand, it has grown to six millions. It has increased no less than twelvefold. This is the state of the colony trade, as compared with itself at these two periods, within this century; – and this is matter for meditation. But this is not all. Examine my second account. See how the export trade to the colonies alone in 1772 stood in the other point of view, that is, as compared to the whole trade of England in 1704.

The whole export trade of England, including that to the colonies, in 1704	£6,509,000
Export to the colonies alone, in 1772 . . .	6,024,000
Difference	£485,000

The trade with America alone is now within less than 500,000*l.* of being equal to what this great commercial nation, England, carried on at the beginning of this century with the whole world! If I had taken the largest year of those on your table, it would rather have exceeded. But, it will be said, is not this American trade an unnatural protuberance, that has drawn the juices from the rest of the body? The reverse. It is the very food that has nourished every other part into its present magnitude. Our general trade has been greatly augmented, and augmented more or less in almost every part to which it ever extended, but with this material difference: that of the six millions which in the beginning of the century constituted the whole mass of our export commerce the colony trade was but one twelfth part; it is now (as a part of sixteen millions) considerably more than a third of the whole. This is the relative proportion of the importance of the colonies at these two periods: and all reasoning concerning our mode of treating them must have this proportion as its basis, or it is a reasoning weak, rotten, and sophistical.

Mr Speaker, I cannot prevail on myself to hurry over this great consideration. It is good for us to be here. We stand where we have an immense view of what is, and what is past. Clouds indeed, and darkness, rest upon the future. Let us, however, before we descend from this noble eminence, reflect that this growth of our national prosperity has happened within the short period of the life of man. It has happened within sixty-eight years. There are those alive whose memory might touch the two extremities. For instance, my Lord Bathurst might remember all the stages of the progress.[1] He was in 1704 of an age at least to be made to comprehend such things. He was then old enough *acta parentum jam legere, et quæ sit poterit cognoscere virtus.*[2] Suppose, Sir, that the angel of this auspicious youth, foreseeing the many virtues which made him one of the most amiable, as he is one of the most fortunate men of his age, had opened to him in vision, that, when, in the fourth generation, the third prince of the House of Brunswick had sat twelve years on the throne of that nation

[1] Allen Bathurst (1684–1775), first Earl Bathurst, had first entered Parliament as a Tory Member in 1705.

[2] To study the actions of his forebears and know the meaning of virtue (Virgil, *Ecl.* iv. 26).

which (by the happy issue of moderate and healing councils) was to be made Great Britain, he should see his son,[1] Lord Chancellor of England, turn back the current of hereditary dignity to its fountain, and raise him to an higher rank of peerage, whilst he enriched the family with a new one, – if, amidst these bright and happy scenes of domestic honor and prosperity, that angel should have drawn up the curtain, and unfolded the rising glories of his country, and whilst he was gazing with admiration on the then commercial grandeur of England, the genius should point out to him a little speck, scarce visible in the mass of the national interest, a small seminal principle rather than a formed body, and should tell him, – 'Young man, there is America, – which at this day serves for little more than to amuse you with stories of savage men and uncouth manners, yet shall, before you taste of death, show itself equal to the whole of that commerce which now attracts the envy of the world. Whatever England has been growing to by a progressive increase of improvement, brought in by varieties of people, by succession of civilizing conquests and civilizing settlements in a series of seventeen hundred years, you shall see as much added to her by America in the course of a single life!' If this state of his country had been foretold to him, would it not require all the sanguine credulity of youth, and all the fervid glow of enthusiasm, to make him believe it? Fortunate man, he has lived to see it! Fortunate indeed, if he lives to see nothing that shall vary the prospect, and cloud the setting of his day!

Excuse me, Sir, if, turning from such thoughts, I resume this comparative view once more. You have seen it on a large scale; look at it on a small one. I will point out to your attention a particular instance of it in the single province of Pennsylvania. In the year 1704, that province called for 11,459*l.* in value of your commodities, native and foreign. This was the whole. What did it demand in 1772? Why, nearly fifty times as much; for in that year the export to Pennsylvania was

[1] Henry Bathurst (1714–1794) had become Baron Apsley and Lord Chancellor in 1771.

507,909*l.*, nearly equal to the export to all the colonies together in the first period.

I choose, Sir, to enter into these minute and particular details; because generalities, which in all other cases are apt to heighten and raise the subject, have here a tendency to sink it. When we speak of the commerce with our colonies, fiction lags after truth, invention is unfruitful, and imagination cold and barren.

So far, Sir, as to the importance of the object in the view of its commerce, as concerned in the exports from England. If I were to detail the imports, I could show how many enjoyments they procure which deceive the burden of life, how many materials which invigorate the springs of national industry and extend and animate every part of our foreign and domestic commerce. This would be a curious subject indeed, – but I must prescribe bounds to myself in a matter so vast and various.

I pass, therefore, to the colonies in another point of view, – their agriculture. This they have prosecuted with such a spirit, that, besides feeding plentifully their own growing multitude, their annual export of grain, comprehending rice, has some years ago exceeded a million in value. Of their last harvest, I am persuaded, they will export much more. At the beginning of the century some of these colonies imported corn from the mother country. For some time past the Old World has been fed from the New. The scarcity which you have felt would have been a desolating famine, if this child of your old age, with a true filial piety, with a Roman charity, had not put the full breast of its youthful exuberance to the mouth of its exhausted parent.

As to the wealth which the colonies have drawn from the sea by their fisheries, you had all that matter fully opened at your bar. You surely thought those acquisitions of value, for they seemed even to excite your envy; and yet the spirit by which that enterprising employment has been exercised ought rather, in my opinion, to have raised your esteem and admiration. And pray, Sir, what in the world is equal to it? Pass by the other parts, and look at the manner in which the people of

New England have of late carried on the whale-fishery. Whilst we follow them among the tumbling mountains of ice, and behold them penetrating into the deepest frozen recesses of Hudson's Bay and Davis's Straits, whilst we are looking for them beneath the arctic circle, we hear that they have pierced into the opposite region of polar cold, that they are at the antipodes, and engaged under the frozen serpent of the South. Falkland Island, which seemed too remote and romantic an object for the grasp of national ambition, is but a stage and resting-place in the progress of their victorious industry. Nor is the equinoctial heat more discouraging to them than the accumulated winter of both the poles. We know, that, whilst some of them draw the line and strike the harpoon on the coast of Africa, others run the longitude, and pursue their gigantic game along the coast of Brazil. No sea but what is vexed by their fisheries. No climate that is not witness to their toils. Neither the perseverance of Holland, nor the activity of France, nor the dexterous and firm sagacity of English enterprise, ever carried this most perilous mode of hardy industry to the extent to which it has been pushed by this recent people, – a people who are still, as it were, but in the gristle, and not yet hardened into the bone of manhood. When I contemplate these things, – when I know that the colonies in general owe little or nothing to any care of ours, and that they are not squeezed into this happy form by the constraints of watchful and suspicious government, but that, through a wise and salutary neglect, a generous nature has been suffered to take her own way to perfection, – when I reflect upon these effects, when I see how profitable they have been to us, I feel all the pride of power sink, and all presumption in the wisdom of human contrivances melt and die away within me, – my rigor relents, – I pardon something to the spirit of liberty.

I am sensible, Sir, that all which I have asserted in my detail is admitted in the gross, but that quite a different conclusion is drawn from it. America, gentlemen say, is a noble object, – it is an object well worth fighting for. Certainly it is, if fighting a people be the best way of gaining them.

Gentlemen in this respect will be led to their choice of means by their complexions and their habits. Those who understand the military art will of course have some predilection for it. Those who wield the thunder of the state may have more confidence in the efficacy of arms. But I confess, possibly for want of this knowledge, my opinion is much more in favor of prudent management than of force, – considering force not as an odious, but a feeble instrument, for preserving a people so numerous, so active, so growing, so spirited as this, in a profitable and subordinate connection with us.

First, Sir, permit me to observe, that the use of force alone is but *temporary*. It may subdue for a moment; but it does not remove the necessity of subduing again: and a nation is not governed which is perpetually to be conquered.

My next objection is its *uncertainty*. Terror is not always the effect of force, and an armament is not a victory. If you do not succeed, you are without resource: for, conciliation failing, force remains; but, force failing, no further hope of reconciliation is left. Power and authority are sometimes bought by kindness; but they can never be begged as alms by an impoverished and defeated violence.

A further objection to force is, that you *impair the object* by your very endeavors to preserve it. The thing you fought for is not the thing which you recover, but depreciated, sunk, wasted, and consumed in the contest. Nothing less will content me than *whole America*. I do not choose to consume its strength along with our own; because in all parts it is the British strength that I consume. I do not choose to be caught by a foreign enemy at the end of this exhausting conflict, and still less in the midst of it. I may escape, but I can make no insurance against such an event. Let me add, that I do not choose wholly to break the American spirit; because it is the spirit that has made the country.

Lastly, we have no sort of *experience* in favor of force as an instrument in the rule of our colonies. Their growth and their utility has been owing to methods altogether different. Our ancient indulgence has been said to be pursued to a fault. It may be so; but we know, if feeling is evidence, that our fault was more tolerable than our attempt to mend it, and our sin far more salutary than our penitence.

These, Sir, are my reasons for not entertaining that high opinion of untried force by which many gentlemen, for whose sentiments in other particulars I have great respect, seem to be so greatly captivated. But there is still behind a third consideration concerning this object, which serves to determine my opinion on the sort of policy which ought to be pursued in the mangement of America, even more than its population and its commerce: I mean its *temper and character*.

In this character of the Americans a love of freedom is the predominating feature which marks and distinguishes the whole: and as an ardent is always a jealous affection, your colonies become suspicious, restive, and untractable, whenever they see the least attempt to wrest from them by force, or shuffle from them by chicane, what they think the only advantage worth living for. This fierce spirit of liberty is stronger in the English colonies, probably, than in any other people of the earth, and this from a great variety of powerful causes; which, to understand the true temper of their minds, and the direction which this spirit takes, it will not be amiss to lay open somewhat more largely.

First, the people of the colonies are descendants of Englishmen. England, Sir, is a nation which still, I hope, respects, and formerly adored, her freedom. The colonists emigrated from you when this part of your character was most predominant; and they took this bias and direction the moment they parted from your hands. They are therefore not only devoted to liberty, but to liberty according to English ideas and on English principles. Abstract liberty, like other mere abstractions, is not to be found. Liberty inheres in some sensible object; and every nation has formed to itself some favorite point, which by way of eminence becomes the criterion of their happiness. It happened, you know, Sir, that the great contests for freedom in this country were from the earliest times chiefly upon the question of taxing. Most of the contests in the ancient commonwealths turned primarily on the right of election of magistrates, or on the balance among

the several orders of the state. The question of money was not
with them so immediate. But in England it was otherwise.
On this point of taxes the ablest pens and most eloquent
tongues have been exercised, the greatest spirits have acted
and suffered. In order to give the fullest satisfaction concerning the importance of this point, it was not only necessary
for those who in argument defended the excellence of the
English Constitution to insist on this privilege of granting
money as a dry point of fact, and to prove that the right had
been acknowledged in ancient parchments and blind usages to
reside in a certain body called an House of Commons: they
went much further: they attempted to prove, and they succeeded, that in theory it ought to be so, from the particular
nature of a House of Commons, as an immediate representative of the people, whether the old records had delivered this
oracle or not. They took infinite pains to inculcate, as a
fundamental principle, that in all monarchies the people must
in effect themselves, mediately or immediately, possess the
power of granting their own money, or no shadow of liberty
could subsist. The colonies draw from you, as with their
life-blood, these ideas and principles. Their love of liberty,
as with you, fixed and attached on this specific point of taxing.
Liberty might be safe or might be endangered in twenty other
particulars without their being much pleased or alarmed.
Here they felt its pulse; and as they found that beat, they
thought themselves sick or sound. I do not say whether they
were right or wrong in applying your general arguments to
their own case. It is not easy, indeed, to make a monopoly of
theorems and corollaries. The fact is, that they did thus apply
those general arguments; and your mode of governing them,
whether through lenity or indolence, through wisdom or
mistake, confirmed them in the imagination, that they, as
well as you, had an interest in these common principles.

They were further confirmed in this pleasing error by the
form of their provincial legislative assemblies. Their governments are popular in an high degree: some are merely popular;
in all, the popular representative is the most weighty; and this
share of the people in their ordinary government never fails to

insnire them with lofty sentiments, and with a strong aversion from whatever tends to deprive them of their chief importance.

You will now, Sir, perhaps imagine that I am on the point of proposing to you a scheme for a representation of the colonies in Parliament. Perhaps I might be inclined to entertain some such thought; but a great flood stops me in my course. *Opposuit Natura.* I cannot remove the eternal barriers of the creation. The thing, in that mode, I do not know to be possible. As I meddle with no theory, I do not absolutely assert the impracticability of such a representation; but I do not see my way to it; and those who have been more confident have not been more successful. However, the arm of public benevolence is not shortened; and there are often several means to the same end. What Nature has disjoined in one way wisdom may unite in another. When we cannot give the benefit as we would wish, let us not refuse it altogether. If we cannot give the principal, let us find a substitute. But how? where? what substitute?

Fortunately, I am not obliged, for the ways and means of this substitute, to tax my own unproductive invention. I am not even obliged to go to the rich treasury of the fertile framers of imaginary commonwealths: not to the Republic of Plato, not to the Utopia of More, not to the Oceana of Harrington. It is before me, – it is at my feet, –

> 'And the rude swain
> Treads daily on it with his clouted shoon.'[1]

I only wish you to recognize, for the theory, the ancient constitutional policy of this kingdom with regard to representation, as that policy has been declared in acts of Parliament, – and as to the practice, to return to that mode which an uniform experience has marked out to you as best, and in which you walked with security, advantage, and honor, until the year 1763.

[1] Milton, *Comus*, i. 634–35: 'and the dull swain Treads on it daily with his clouted shoon.'

My resolutions, therefore, mean to establish the equity and justice of a taxation of America by *grant*, and not by *imposition*; to mark the *legal competency* of the colony assemblies for the support of their government in peace, and for public aids in time of war; to acknowledge that this legal competency has had *a dutiful and beneficial exercise*, and that experience has shown *the benefit of their grants*, and *the futility of Parliamentary taxation, as a method of supply.*

These solid truths compose six fundamental propositions. There are three more resolutions corollary to these. If you admit the first set, you can hardly reject the others. But if you admit the first, I shall be far from solicitous whether you accept or refuse the last. I think these six massive pillars will be of strength sufficient to support the temple of British concord. I have no more doubt than I entertain of my existence, that, if you admitted these, you would command an immediate peace, and, with but tolerable future management, a lasting obedience in America. I am not arrogant in this confident assurance. The propositions are all mere matters of fact; and if they are such facts as draw irresistible conclusions even in the stating, this is the power of truth, and not any management of mine.

Sir, I shall open the whole plan to you together, with such observations on the motions as may tend to illustrate them, where they may want explanation.

The first is a resolution, – 'That the colonies and plantations of Great Britain in North America, consisting of fourteen separate governments, and containing two millions and upwards of free inhabitants, have not had the liberty and privilege of electing and sending any knights and burgesses, or others, to represent them in the high court of Parliament.'

This is a plain matter of fact, necessary to be laid down, and (excepting the description) it is laid down in the language of the Constitution; it is taken nearly *verbatim* from acts of Parliament.

The second is like unto the first, – 'That the said colonies and plantations have been made liable to, and bounden by, several subsidies, payments, rates, and taxes, given and

granted by Parliament, though the said colonies and plantations have not their knights and burgesses in the said high
court of Parliament, of their own election, to represent the
condition of their country; by lack whereof they have been
often-times touched and grieved by subsidies, given, granted,
and assented to, in the said court, in a manner prejudicial to
the common wealth, quietness, rest, and peace of the subjects
inhabiting within the same.'

Is this description too hot or too cold, too strong or too
weak? Does it arrogate too much to the supreme legislature?
Does it lean too much to the claims of the people? If it runs
into any of these errors, the fault is not mine. It is the language
of your own ancient acts of Parliament.

> Non meus hic sermo, sed quæ præcepit Ofellus
> Rusticus, abnormis sapiens.[1]

It is the genuine produce of the ancient, rustic, manly, home-
bred sense of this country. I did not dare to rub off a particle
of the venerable rust that rather adorns and preserves than
destroys the metal. It would be a profanation to touch with a
tool the stones which construct the sacred altar of peace. I
would not violate with modern polish the ingenuous and noble
roughness of these truly constitutional materials. Above all
things, I was resolved not to be guilty of tampering, – the
odious vice of restless and unstable minds. I put my foot in
the tracks of our forefathers, where I can neither wander nor
stumble. Determining to fix articles of peace, I was resolved
not to be wise beyond what was written; I was resolved to use
nothing else than the form of sound words, to let others
abound in their own sense, and carefully to abstain from all
expressions of my own. What the law has said, I say. In all
things else I am silent. I have no organ but for her words.
This, if it be not ingenious, I am sure is safe.

There are, indeed, words expressive of grievance in this
second resolution, which those who are resolved always to be
in the right will deny to contain matter of fact, as applied to

[1] 'Now this is no talk of mine, but is the teaching of Ofellus, a
peasant, a philosopher unschooled.' Horace, *Satires*, II. 2–3.

the present case; although Parliament thought them true with regard to the Counties of Chester and Durham.[1] They will deny that the Americans were ever 'touched and grieved' with the taxes. If they consider nothing in taxes but their weight as pecuniary impositions, there might be some pretence for this denial. But men may be sorely touched and deeply grieved in their privileges, as well as in their purses. Men may lose little in property by the act which takes away all their freedom. When a man is robbed of a trifle on the highway, it is not the twopence lost that constitutes the capital outrage. This is not confined to privileges. Even ancient indulgences withdrawn, without offence on the part of those who enjoyed such favors, operate as grievances. But were the Americans, then, not touched and grieved by the taxes, in some measure, merely as taxes? If so, why were they almost all either wholly repealed or exceedingly reduced? Were they not touched and grieved even by the regulating duties of the sixth of George the Second?[2] Else why were the duties first reduced to one third in 1764, and afterwards to a third of that third in the year 1766? Were they not touched and grieved by the Stamp Act? I shall say they were, until that tax is revived. Were they not touched and grieved by the duties of 1767, which were likewise repealed, and which Lord Hillsborough tells you (for the ministry) were laid contrary to the true principle of commerce? Is not the assurance given by that noble person to the colonies of a resolution to lay no more taxes on them an admission that taxes would touch and grieve them? Is not the resolution of the noble lord in the blue riband,[3] now standing on your journals, the strongest of all proofs that Parliamentary subsidies really touched and grieved them? Else why all these changes, modifications, repeals, assurances, and resolutions?

The next proposition is, – 'That, from the distance of the

[1] The parliamentary seats of Cheshire and Durham were created relatively late, in the reigns of Henry VIII and Charles II respectively, on their petition concerning the disadvantages of lack of representation.

[2] Sir Robert Walpole's 'Molasses Act' of 1733.

[3] The customary term for Lord North.

said colonies, and from other circumstances, no method hath hitherto been devised for procuring a representation in Parliament for the said colonies.'

This is an assertion of a fact. I go no further on the paper; though, in my private judgment, an useful representation is impossible; I am sure it is not desired by them, nor ought it, perhaps, by us: but I abstain from opinions.

The fourth resolution is, – 'That each of the said colonies hath within itself a body, chosen, in part or in the whole, by the freemen, freeholders, or other free inhabitants thereof, commonly called the General Assembly, or General Court, with powers legally to raise, levy, and assess, according to the several usages of such colonies, duties and taxes towards defraying all sorts of public services.'

This competence in the colony assemblies is certain. It is proved by the whole tenor of their acts of supply in all the assemblies, in which the constant style of granting is, 'An aid to his Majesty'; and acts granting to the crown have regularly, for near a century, passed the public offices without dispute. Those who have been pleased paradoxically to deny this right, holding that none but the British Parliament can grant to the crown, are wished to look to what is done, not only in the colonies, but in Ireland, in one uniform, unbroken tenor, every session. Sir, I am surprised that this doctrine should come from some of the law servants of the crown. I say, that, if the crown could be responsible, his Majesty, – but certainly the ministers, and even these law officers themselves, through whose hands the acts pass biennially in Ireland, or annually in the colonies, are in an habitual course of committing impeachable offences. What habitual offenders have been all Presidents of the Council all Secretaries of State, all First Lords of Trade, all Attorneys and all Solicitors General! However, they are safe, as no one impeaches them; and there is no ground of charge against them, except in their own unfounded theories.

The fifth resolution is also a resolution of fact, – 'That the said general assemblies, general courts, or other bodies legally qualified as aforesaid, have at sundry times freely granted several large subsidies and public aids for his Majesty's service, according to their abilities, when required thereto by letter from one of his Majesty's principal Secretaries of State; and that their right to grant the same, and their cheerfulness and sufficiency in the said grants, have been at sundry times acknowledged by Parliament.'

To say nothing of their great expenses in the Indian wars, and not to take their exertion in foreign ones, so high as the supplies in the year 1695, not to go back to their public contributions in the year 1710, I shall begin to travel only where the journals give me light, – resolving to deal in nothing but fact authenticated by Parliamentary record, and to build myself wholly on that solid basis.

On the 4th of April, 1748,* a committee of this House came to the following resolution:–

'*Resolved*, That it is the opinion of this committee, *that it is just and reasonable*, that the several provinces and colonies of Massachusetts Bay, New Hampshire, Connecticut, and Rhode Island be reimbursed the expenses they have been at in taking and securing to the crown of Great Britain the island of Cape Breton and its dependencies.'

These expenses were immense for such colonies. They were above 200,000*l.* sterling: money first raised and advanced on their public credit.

On the 28th of January, 1756,* a message from the king came to us, to this effect:– 'His Majesty, being sensible of the zeal and vigor with which his faithful subjects of certain colonies in North America have exerted themselves in defence of his Majesty's just rights and possessions, recommends it to this House to take the same into their consideration, and to enable his Majesty to give them such assistance as may be a *proper reward and encouragement.*'

On the 3rd of February, 1756,† the House came to a suitable resolution, expressed in words nearly the same as those of the message; but with the further addition, that the money then voted was as an *encouragement* to the colonies to exert themselves with vigor. It will not be necessary to go through

* Journals of the House, Vol. XXV.
* Journals of the House, Vol. XXVII.   † Ibid.

all the testimonies which your own records have given to the truth of my resolutions. I will only refer you to the places in the journals:–

Vol. XXVII. – 16th and 19th May, 1757.

Vol. XXVIII. – June 1st, 1758, – April 26th and 30th, 1759, – March 26th and 31st, and April 28th, 1760, – Jan. 9th and 20th, 1761.

Vol. XXIX. – Jan. 22nd and 26th, 1762, – March 14th and 17th, 1763.

Sir, here is the repeated acknowledgment of Parliament, that the colonies not only gave, but gave to satiety. This nation has formally acknowledged two things: first, that the colonies had gone beyond their abilities, Parliament having thought it necessary to reimburse them; secondly, that they had acted legally and laudably in their grants of money, and their maintenance of troops, since the compensation is expressly given as reward and encouragement. Reward is not bestowed for acts that are unlawful; and encouragement is not held out to things that deserve reprehension. My resolution, therefore, does nothing more than collect into one proposition what is scattered through your journals. I give you nothing but your own; and you cannot refuse in the gross what you have so often acknowledged in detail. The admission of this, which will be so honorable to them and to you, will, indeed, be mortal to all the miserable stories by which the passions of the misguided people have been engaged in an unhappy system. The people heard, indeed, from the beginning of these disputes, one thing continually dinned in their ears: that reason and justice demanded, that the Americans, who paid no taxes, should be compelled to contribute. How did that fact, of their paying nothing, stand, when the taxing system began? When Mr Grenville began to form his system of American revenue, he stated in this House that the colonies were then in debt two million six hundred thousand pounds sterling money, and was of opinion they would discharge that debt in four years. On this state, those untaxed people were actually subject to the payment of taxes to the amount of six hundred and fifty thousand a year. In fact, however, Mr

Grenville was mistaken. The funds given for sinking the debt did not prove quite so ample as both the colonies and he expected. The calculation was too sanguine: the reduction was not completed till some years after, and at different times in different colonies. However, the taxes after the war continued too great to bear any addition, with prudence or propriety; and when the burdens imposed in consequence of former requisitions were discharged, our tone became too high to resort again to requisition. No colony, since that time, ever has had any requisition whatsoever made to it.

We see the sense of the crown, and the sense of Parliament, on the productive nature of a *revenue by grant*. Now search the same journals for the produce of the *revenue by imposition*. Where is it? – let us know the volume and the page. What is the gross, what is the net produce? To what service is it applied? How have you appropriated its surplus? – What! can none of the many skilful index-makers that we are now employing find any trace of it? – Well, let them and that rest together. – But are the journals, which say nothing of the revenue, as silent on the discontent? – Oh, no! a child may find it. It is the melancholy burden and blot of every page.

I think, then, I am, from those journals, justified in the sixth and last resolution, which is, – 'That it hath been found by experience, that the manner of granting the said supplies and aids by the said general assemblies hath been more agreeable to the inhabitants of the said colonies, and more beneficial and conducive to the public service, than the mode of giving and granting aids and subsidies in Parliament, to be raised and paid in the said colonies.'

This makes the whole of the fundamental part of the plan. The conclusion is irresistible. You cannot say that you were driven by any necessity to an exercise of the utmost rights of legislature. You cannot assert that you took on yourselves the task of imposing colony taxes, from the want of another legal body that is competent to the purpose of supplying the exigencies of the state without wounding the prejudices of the people. Neither is it true that the body so qualified, and having that competence, had neglected the duty.

The question now, on all this accumulated matter, is, – Whether you will choose to abide by a profitable experience or a mischievous theory? whether you choose to build on imagination or fact? whether you prefer enjoyment or hope? satisfaction in your subjects, or discontent?

If these propositions are accepted, everything which has been made to enforce a contrary system must, I take it for granted, fall along with it. On that ground, I have drawn the following resolution, which, when it comes to be moved, will naturally be divided in a proper manner:– 'That it may be proper to repeal an act, made in the seventh year of the reign of his present Majesty, intituled, "An act for granting certain duties in the British colonies and plantations in America; for allowing a drawback of the duties of customs, upon the exportation from this kingdom, of coffee and cocoa-nuts, of the produce of the said colonies or plantations; for discontinuing the drawbacks payable on China earthen ware exported to America; and for more effectually preventing the clandestine running of goods in the said colonies and plantations." – And also, that it may be proper to repeal an act, made in the fourteenth year of the reign of his present Majesty. intituled, "An act to discontinue, in such manner and for such time as are therein mentioned, the landing and discharging, lading or shipping, of goods, wares, and merchandise, at the town and within the harbor of Boston, in the province of Massachusetts Bay, in North America." – And also, that it may be proper to repeal an act, made in the fourteenth year of the reign of his present Majesty, intituled, "An act for the impartial administration of justice, in the cases of persons questioned for any acts done by them, in the execution of the law, or for the suppression of riots and tumults, in the province of the Massachusetts Bay, in New England." – And also, that it may be proper to repeal an act, made in the fourteenth year of the reign of his present Majesty, intituled, "An act for the better regulating the government of the province of the Massachusetts Bay, in New England." – And also, that it may be proper to explain and amend an act, made in the thirty-fifth year of the reign of King Henry the Eighth, intituled,

"An act for the trial of treasons committed out of the king's dominions." [1]

I wish, Sir, to repeal the Boston Port Bill, because (independently of the dangerous precedent of suspending the rights of the subject during the king's pleasure) it was passed, as I apprehend, with less regularity, and on more partial principles, than it ought. The corporation of Boston was not heard before it was condemned. Other towns, full as guilty as she was, have not had their ports blocked up. Even the Restraining Bill of the present session does not go to the length of the Boston Port Act. The same ideas of prudence, which induced you not to extend equal punishment to equal guilt, even when you were punishing, induce me, who mean not to chastise, but to reconcile, to be satisfied with the punishment already partially inflicted.

Ideas of prudence and accommodation to circumstances prevent you from taking away the charters of Connecticut and Rhode Island, as you have taken away that of Massachusetts Colony, though the crown has far less power in the two former provinces than it enjoyed in the latter, and though the abuses have been full as great and as flagrant in the exempted as in the punished. The same reasons of prudence and accommodation have weight with me in restoring the charter of Massachusetts Bay. Besides, Sir, the act which changes the charter of Massachusetts is in many particulars so exceptionable, that, if I did not wish absolutely to repeal, I would by all means desire to alter it; as several of its provisions tend to the subversion of all public and private justice. Such, among others, is the power in the governor to change the sheriff at his pleasure, and to make a new returning officer for every special cause. It is shameful to behold such a regulation standing among English laws.

The act for bringing persons accused of committing murder

---

[1] i.e., in addition to calling for the repeal of the Tea Act and the coercive legislation of 1774, Burke wished for the amendment of a treason statute of Henry VIII's reign allowing trial in England for offences committed abroad, which had been invoked in 1769 as a threat against the colonists.

under the orders of government to England for trial is but temporary. That act has calculated the probable duration of our quarrel with the colonies, and is accommodated to that supposed duration. I would hasten the happy moment of reconciliation, and therefore must, on my principle, get rid of that most justly obnoxious act.

The act of Henry the Eighth for the trial of treasons I do not mean to take away, but to confine it to its proper bounds and original intention: to make it expressly for trial of treasons (and the greatest treasons may be committed) in places where the jurisdiction of the crown does not extend.

Having guarded the privileges of local legislature, I would next secure to the colonies a fair and unbiased judicature; for which purpose, Sir, I propose the following resolution:— 'That, from the time when the general assembly, or general court, of any colony or plantation in North America shall have appointed by act of assembly duly confirmed, a settled salary to the offices of the chief justice and other judges of the superior courts, it may be proper that the said chief justice and other judges of the superior courts of such colony shall hold his and their office and offices during their good behavior, and shall not be removed therefrom, but when the said removal shall be adjudged by his Majesty in council, upon a hearing on complaint from the general assembly, or on a complaint from the governor, or the council, or the house of representatives, severally, of the colony in which the said chief justice and other judges have exercised the said offices.'

The next resolution relates to the courts of admiralty. It is this:— 'That it may be proper to regulate the courts of admiralty or vice-admiralty, authorized by the 15th chapter of the 4th George the Third,[1] in such a manner as to make the same more commodious to those who sue or are sued in the said courts, and to provide for the more decent maintenance of the judges of the same.'

[1] The Revenue Act of 5 April 1764, which set up a new and superior Vice-Admiralty Court at Halifax, Nova Scotia, a naval base where customs cases could be tried beyond the influence of the American colonists.

These courts I do not wish to take away: they are in themselves proper establishments. This court is one of the capital securities of the Act of Navigation. The extent of its jurisdiction, indeed, has been increased; but this is altogether as proper, and is, indeed, on many accounts, more eligible, where new powers were wanted, than a court absolutely new. But courts incommodiously situated, in effect, deny justice; and a court partaking in the fruits of its own condemnation is a robber. The Congress complain, and complain justly, of this grievance.*

These are the three consequential propositions. I have thought of two or three more; but they come rather too near detail, and to the province of executive government, which I wish Parliament always to superintend, never to assume. If the first six are granted, congruity will carry the latter three. If not, the things that remain unrepealed will be, I hope, rather unseemly incumbrances on the building than very materially detrimental to its strength and stability.

Here, Sir, I should close, but that I plainly perceive some objections remain, which I ought, if possible, to remove. The first will be, that, in resorting to the doctrine of our ancestors, as contained in the preamble to the Chester act, I prove too much: that the grievance from a want of representation, stated in that preamble, goes to the whole of legislation as well as to taxation; and that the colonies, grounding themselves upon that doctrine, will apply it to all parts of legislative authority.

To this objection, with all possible deference and humility, and wishing as little as any man living to impair the smallest particle of our supreme authority, I answer, that *the words are the words of Parliament, and not mine*; and that all false and inconclusive inferences drawn from them are not mine; for I heartily disclaim any such inference. I have chosen the words of

---

* The Solicitor-General informed Mr B., when the resolutions were separately moved, that the grievance of the judges partaking of the profits of the seizure had been redressed by office; accordingly the resolution was amended. [The amendment omitted the words 'and to provide for the more decent maintenance of the judges of the same.']

an act of Parliament, which Mr Grenville, surely a tolerably zealous and very judicious advocate for the sovereignty of Parliament, formerly moved to have read at your table in confirmation of his tenets. It is true that Lord Chatham considered these preambles as declaring strongly in favor of his opinions. He was a no less powerful advocate for the privileges of the Americans. Ought I not from hence to presume that these preambles are as favorable as possible to both, when properly understood: favorable both to the rights of Parliament, and to the privilege of the dependencies of this crown? But, Sir, the object of grievance in my resolution I have not taken from the Chester, but from the Durham act, which confines the hardship of want of representation to the case of subsidies, and which therefore falls in exactly with the case of the colonies. But whether the unrepresented counties were *de jure* or *de facto* bound the preambles do not accurately distinguish, nor, indeed, was it necessary: for, whether *de jure* or *de facto*, the legislature thought the exercise of the power of taxing, as of right, or as of fact without right, equally a grievance, and equally oppressive.

I do not know that the colonies have, in any general way, or in any cool hour, gone much beyond the demand of immunity in relation to taxes. It is not fair to judge of the temper or dispositions of any man or any set of men, when they are composed and at rest, from their conduct or their expressions in a state of disturbance and irritation. It is, besides, a very great mistake to imagine that mankind follow up practically any speculative principle, either of government or of freedom, as far as it will go in argument and logical illation. We Englishmen stop very short of the principles upon which we support any given part of our Constitution, or even the whole of it together. I could easily, if I had not already tired you, give you very striking and convincing instances of it. This is nothing but what is natural and proper. All government, indeed every human benefit and enjoyment, every virtue and every prudent act, is founded on compromise and barter. We balance inconveniences; we give and take; we remit some rights, that we may enjoy others; and we choose rather to be happy citizens than subtle disputants. As we must give away some natural liberty, to enjoy civil advantages, so we must sacrifice some civil liberties, for the advantages to be derived from the communion and fellowship of a great empire. But, in all fair dealings, the thing bought must bear some proportion to the purchase paid. None will barter away the immediate jewel of his soul. Though a great house is apt to make slaves haughty, yet it is purchasing a part of the artificial importance of a great empire too dear, to pay for it all essential rights, and all the intrinsic dignity of human nature. None of us who would not risk his life rather than fall under a government purely arbitrary. But although there are some amongst us who think our Constitution wants many improvements to make it a complete system of liberty, perhaps none who are of that opinion would think it right to aim at such improvement by disturbing his country and risking everything that is dear to him. In every arduous enterprise, we consider what we are to lose, as well as what we are to gain; and the more and better stake of liberty every people possess, the less they will hazard in a vain attempt to make it more. These are *the cords of man.* Man acts from adequate motives relative to his interest, and not on metaphysical speculations. Aristotle, the great master of reasoning, cautions us and with great weight and propriety, against this species of delusive geometrical accuracy in moral arguments, as the most fallacious of all sophistry.

The Americans will have no interest contrary to the grandeur and glory of England, when they are not oppressed by the weight of it; and they will rather be inclined to respect the acts of a superintending legislature, when they see them the acts of that power which is itself the security, not the rival of their secondary importance. In this assurance my mind most perfectly acquiesces, and I confess I feel not the least alarm from the discontents which are to arise from putting people at their ease; nor do I apprehend the destruction of this empire from giving, by an act of free grace and indulgence, to two millions of my fellow-citizens some share of those rights upon which I have always been taught to value myself.

It is said, indeed, that this power of granting, vested in

American assemblies, would dissolve the unity of the empire, – which was preserved entire, although Wales, and Chester, and Durham were added to it. Truly, Mr Speaker, I do not know what this unity means; nor has it ever been heard of, that I know, in the constitutional policy of this country. The very idea of subordination of parts excludes this notion of simple and undivided unity. England is the head; but she is not the head and the members too. Ireland has ever had from the beginning a separate, but not an independent legislature, which, far from distracting, promoted the union of the whole. Everything was sweetly and harmoniously disposed through both islands for the conservation of English dominion and the communication of English liberties. I do not see that the same principles might not be carried into twenty islands, and with the same good effect. This is my model with regard to America, as far as the internal circumstances of the two countries are the same. I know no other unity of this empire than I can draw from its example during these periods, when it seemed to my poor understanding more united than it is now, or than it is likely to be by the present methods.

A Letter to the Sheriffs of Bristol

Burke's last major, and shortest contribution to discussion of the problem of Anglo-American relations contained a clearer statement of his political ideas than either of its predecessors. It came nearly a year after the American Declaration of Independence, and Burke was now prepared to concede almost everything that the Americans wanted, in the cause of future good understanding between the old and new nations. His reasons for moving towards independence as the only possible solution were mainly practical, and the pamphlet is notable for its attack on the 'speculative philosophers' who had, he considered, driven the two sides to the point of no return. Against the rigid constitutional theorists in Britain who had been unable to see the difference between the legal power of Parliament and its practical possibilities he argued that 'many things indubitably included in the abstract idea of that power, and which carry no absolute injustice in themselves, yet being contrary to the opinions and feelings of the people, can as little be exercised as if Parliament in that case had been possessed of no right at all.' Against the rationalist thinkers who had produced the extreme doctrines of the rights of man, and had guided the colonists to the Declaration, which though now irreversible had not been necessary, he was similarly stern: 'the *extreme* of liberty (which is not its abstract perfection, but its real fault) obtains nowhere, nor ought to obtain anywhere; because extremes, as we all know, in every point which relates either to our duties or satisfactions in life, are destructive both to virtue and enjoyment. Liberty, too, must be limited in order to be possessed.' But whatever his aversion from the rationalist arguments for revolt, Burke himself put forward in the *Letter* a criterion which justified his later overt support for Independence: 'in effect, to follow, not to force, the public inclination, – to give a direction, a form, a technical dress, and a specific sanction, to the general sense of the community, is the true end of legislature'. He believed that physical force would not solve the political problem, and that the 'general sense of the community' in the colonies had rejected British legislation.

From A Letter to John Farr and John Harris Esqrs., Sheriffs of the City of Bristol, on the Affairs of America (1777)

When any community is subordinately connected with another, the great danger of the connection is the extreme pride and self-complacency of the superior, which in all matters of controversy will probably decide in its own favor. It is a powerful corrective to such a very rational cause of fear, if the inferior body can be made to believe that the party inclination or political views of several in the principal state will induce them in some degree to counteract this blind and tyrannical partiality. There is no danger that any one acquiring consideration or power in the presiding state should carry this leaning to the inferior too far. The fault of human nature is not of that sort. Power, in whatever hands, is rarely guilty of too strict limitations on itself. But one great advantage to the support of authority attends such an amicable and protecting connection: that those who have conferred favors obtain influence, and from the foresight of future events can persuade men who have received obligations sometimes to return them. Thus, by the mediation of those healing principles (call them good or evil), troublesome discussions are brought to some sort of adjustment, and every hot controversy is not a civil war.

But, if the colonies (to bring the general matter home to us) could see that in Great Britain the mass of the people is melted into its government, and that every dispute with the ministry must of necessity be always a quarrel with the nation, they can stand no longer in the equal and friendly relation of fellow-citizens to the subjects of this kingdom. Humble as this relation may appear to some, when it is once broken, a strong tie is dissolved. Other sort of connections will be sought. For there are very few in the world who will not prefer an useful ally to an insolent master.

Such discord has been the effect of the unanimity into which so many have of late been seduced or bullied, or into the appearance of which they have sunk through mere despair. They have been told that their dissent from violent measures is an encouragement to rebellion. Men of great presumption and little knowledge will hold a language which is contradicted by the whole course of history. *General* rebellions and revolts of an whole people never were *encouraged*, now or at any time. They are always *provoked*. But if this unheard-of doctrine of the encouragement of rebellion were true, if it were true that an assurance of the friendship of numbers in this country towards the colonies could become an encouragement to them to break off all connection with it, what is the inference? Does anybody seriously maintain, that, charged with my share of the public councils, I am obliged not to resist projects which I think mischievous, lest men who suffer should be encouraged to resist? The very tendency of such projects to produce rebellion is one of the chief reasons against them. Shall that reason not be given? Is it, then, a rule, that no man in this nation shall open his mouth in favor of the colonies, shall defend their rights, or complain of their sufferings, – or when war finally breaks out, no man shall express his desires of peace? Has this been the law of our past, or is it to be the terms of our future connection? Even looking no further than ourselves, can it be true loyalty to any government, or true patriotism towards any country, to degrade their solemn councils into servile drawing-rooms, to flatter their pride and passions rather than to enlighten their reason, and to prevent them from being cautioned against violence lest others should be encouraged to resistance? By such acquiescence great kings and mighty nations have been undone; and if any are at this day in a perilous situation from rejecting truth and listening to flattery, it would rather become them to reform the errors under which they suffer than to reproach those who forewarned them of their danger.

But the rebels looked for assistance from this country. –

They did so, in the beginning of this controversy, most certainly; and they sought it by earnest supplications to government, which dignity rejected, and by a suspension of commerce, which the wealth of this nation enabled you to despise. When they found that neither prayers nor menaces had any sort of weight, but that a firm resolution was taken to reduce them to unconditional obedience by a military force, they came to the last extremity. Despairing of us, they trusted in themselves. Not strong enough themselves, they sought succor in France.[1] In proportion as all encouragement here lessened, their distance from this country increased. The encouragement is over; the alienation is complete.

In order to produce this favorite unanimity in delusion, and to prevent all possibility of a return to our ancient happy concord, arguments for our continuance in this course are drawn from the wretched situation itself into which we have been betrayed. It is said, that, being at war with the colonies, whatever our sentiments might have been before, all ties between us are now dissolved, and all the policy we have left is to strengthen the hands of government to reduce them. On the principle of this argument, the more mischiefs we suffer from any administration, the more our trust in it is to be confirmed. Let them but once get us into a war, and then their power is safe, and an act of oblivion passed for all their misconduct.

But is it really true that government is always to be strengthened with the instruments of war, but never furnished with the means of peace? In former times, ministers, I allow, have been sometimes driven by the popular voice to assert by arms the national honor against foreign powers. But the wisdom of the nation has been far more clear, when those ministers have been compelled to consult its interests by treaty. We all know that the sense of the nation obliged the court of Charles the Second to abandon the *Dutch war*[2]: a war, next to the present, the most impolitic which we ever carried on. The good

---

[1] France was already giving monetary assistance to the colonies. In 1778 she entered the war against Britain.

[2] In 1674.

people of England considered Holland as a sort of dependency on this kingdom; they dreaded to drive it to the protection or subject it to the power of France by their own i nconsiderate hostility. They paid but little respect to the court jargon of that day; nor were they inflamed by the pretended rivalship of the Dutch in trade, – by the massacre at Amboyna,[1] acted on the stage to provoke the public vengeance, – nor by declamations against the ingratitude of the United Provinces for the benefits England had conferred up on them in their infant state. They were not moved from their evident interest by all these arts; nor was it enough to tell them, they were at war, that they must go through with it, and that the cause of the dispute was lost in the consequences. The people of England were then, as they are now, called upon to make government strong. They thought it a great deal better to make it wise and honest.

When I was amongst my constituents at the last summer assizes, I remember that men of all descriptions did then express a very strong desire for peace, and no slight hopes of attaining it from the commission sent out by my Lord Howe.[2] And it is not a little remarkable, that, in proportion as every person showed a zeal for the court measures, he was then earnest in circulating an opinion of the extent of the supposed powers of that commission. When I told them that Lord Howe had no powers to treat, or to promise satisfaction on any point whatsoever of the controversy, I was hardly credited, – so strong and general was the desire of terminating this war by the method of accommodation. As far as I could discover, this was the temper then prevalent through the kingdom. The king's forces, it must be observed, had at that time been obliged to evacuate Boston. The superiority of the former campaign rested wholly with the colonists. If such powers of treaty were to be wished whilst success was very doubtful,

[1] A Dutch murder of English traders in 1623, at Amboyna in the Moluccas.

[2] Admiral Richard Howe (1726–1799), Viscount Howe, was sent in 1776 to offer peace terms on the basis of North's proposals of February 1775. The terms were rejected.

how came they to be less so, since his Majesty's arms have been crowned with many considerable advantages? Have these successes induced us to alter our mind, as thinking the season of victory not the time for treating with honor or advantage? Whatever changes have happened in the national character, it can scarcely be our wish that terms of accommodation never should be proposed to our enemy, except when they must be attributed solely to our fears. It has happened, let me say unfortunately, that we read of his Majesty's commission for making peace, and his troops evacuating his last town in the Thirteen Colonies, at the same hour and in the same gazette. It was still more unfortunate that no commission went to America to settle the troubles there, until several months after an act had been passed to put the colonies out of the protection of this government, and to divide their trading property, without a possibility of restitution, as spoil among the seamen of the navy. The most abject submission on the part of the colonies could not redeem them. There was no man on that whole continent, or within three thousand miles of it, qualified by law to follow allegiance with protection or submission with pardon. A proceeding of this kind has no example in history. Independency, and independency with an enmity (which, putting ourselves out of the question, would be called natural and much provoked), was the inevitable consequence. How this came to pass the nation may be one day in an humor to inquire.

All the attempts made this session to give fuller powers of peace to the commanders in America were stifled by the fatal confidence of victory and the wild hopes of unconditional submission. There was a moment favorable to the king's arms, when, if any powers of concession had existed on the other side of the Atlantic, even after all our errors, peace in all probability might have been restored. But calamity is unhappily the usual season of reflection; and the pride of men will not often suffer reason to have any scope, until it can be no longer of service.

I have always wished, that as the dispute had its apparent origin from things done in Parliament, and as the acts passed

E.B.   G there had provoked the war, that the foundations of peace should be laid in Parliament also. I have been astonished to find that those whose zeal for the dignity of our body was so hot as to light up the flames of civil war should even publicly declare that these delicate points ought to be wholly left to the crown. Poorly as I may be thought affected to the authority of Parliament, I shall never admit that our constitutional rights can ever become a matter of ministerial negotiation.

I am charged with being an American. If warm affection towards those over whom I claim any share of authority be a crime, I am guilty of this charge. But I do assure you (and they who know me publicly and privately will bear witness to me), that, if ever one man lived more zealous than another for the supremacy of Parliament and the rights of this imperial crown, it was myself. Many others, indeed, might be more knowing in the extent of the foundation of these rights. I do not pretend to be an antiquary, a lawyer, or qualified for the chair of professor in metaphysics. I never ventured to put your solid interests upon speculative grounds. My having constantly declined to do so has been attributed to my incapacity for such disquisitions; and I am inclined to believe it is partly the cause. I never shall be ashamed to confess, that, where I am ignorant, I am diffident. I am, indeed, not very solicitous to clear myself of this imputed incapacity; because men even less conversant than I am in this kind of subtleties, and placed in stations to which I ought not to aspire, have, by the mere force of civil discretion, often conducted the affairs of great nations with distinguished felicity and glory.

When I first came into a public trust, I found your Parliament in possession of an unlimited legislative power over the colonies. I could not open the statute-book without seeing the actual exercise of it, more or less, in all cases whatsoever. This possession passed with me for a title. It does so in all human affairs. No man examines into the defects of his title to his paternal estate or to his established government. Indeed, common sense taught me that a legislative authority not actually limited by the express terms of its foundation, or by its own subsequent acts, cannot have its powers parcelled out by argumentative distinctions, so as to enable us to say that here they can and there they cannot bind. Nobody was so obliging as to produce to me any record of such distinctions, by compact or otherwise, either at the successive formation of the several colonies or during the existence of any of them. If any gentlemen were able to see how one power could be given up (merely on abstract reasoning) without giving up the rest, I can only say that they saw further than I could. Nor did I ever presume to condemn any one for being clear-sighted when I was blind. I praise their penetration and learning, and hope that their practice has been correspondent to their theory.

I had, indeed, very earnest wishes to keep the whole body of this authority perfect and entire as I found it, – and to keep it so, not for our advantage solely, but principally for the sake of those on whose account all just authority exists: I mean the people to be governed. For I thought I saw that many cases might well happen in which the exercise of every power comprehended in the broadest idea of legislature might become, in its time and circumstances, not a little expedient for the peace and union of the colonies amongst themselves, as well as for their perfect harmony with Great Britain. Thinking so (perhaps erroneously, but being honestly of that opinion), I was at the same time very sure that the authority of which I was so jealous could not, under the actual circumstances of our plantations, be at all preserved in any of its members, but by the greatest reserve in its application, particularly in those delicate points in which the feelings of mankind are the most irritable. They who thought otherwise have found a few more difficulties in their work than (I hope) they were thoroughly aware of, when they undertook the present business. I must beg leave to observe, that it is not only the invidious branch of taxation that will be resisted, but that no other given part of legislative rights can be exercised, without regard to the general opinion of those who are to be governed. That general opinion is the vehicle and organ of legislative omnipotence. Without this, it may be a theory to entertain the mind, but it is nothing in the direction of affairs. The completeness of the legislative authority of Parliament *over this kingdom* is not questioned; and yet many things indubitably included in the abstract idea of that power, and which carry no absolute injustice in themselves, yet being contrary to the opinions and feelings of the people, can as little be exercised as if Parliament in that case had been possessed of no right at all. I see no abstract reason, which can be given, why the same power which made and repealed the High Commission Court and the Star-Chamber might not revive them again; and these courts, warned by their former fate, might possibly exercise their powers with some degree of justice. But the madness would be as unquestionable as the competence of that Parliament which should attempt such things. If anything can be supposed out of the power of human legislature, it is religion; I admit, however, that the established religion of this country has been three or four times altered by act of Parliament, and therefore that a statute binds even in that case. But we may very safely affirm, that, notwithstanding this apparent omnipotence, it would be now found as impossible for King and Parliament to alter the established religion of this country as it was to King James alone, when he attempted to make such an alteration without a Parliament. In effect, to follow, not to force, the public inclination, – to give a direction, a form, a technical dress, and a specific sanction, to the general sense of the community, is the true end of legislature.

It is so with regard to the exercise of all the powers which our Constitution knows in any of its parts, and indeed to the substantial existence of any of the parts themselves. The king's negative to bills is one of the most indisputed of the royal prerogatives; and it extends to all cases whatsoever. I am far from certain, that if several laws, which I know, had fallen under the stroke of that sceptre, that the public would have had a very heavy loss. But it is not the *propriety* of the exercise which is in question. The exercise itself is wisely forborne.[1] Its repose may be the preservation of its existence; and its

[1] The royal veto had not been used since the reign of Queen Anne, who used it only once.

existence may be the means of saving the Constitution itself, on an occasion worthy of bringing it forth.

As the disputants whose accurate and logical reasonings have brought us into our present condition think it absurd that powers or members of any constitution should exist, rarely, if ever, to be exercised, I hope I shall be excused in mentioning another instance that is material. We know that the Convocation of the Clergy had formerly been called, and sat with nearly as much regularity to business as Parliament itself.[1] It is now called for form only. It sits for the purpose of making some polite ecclesiastical compliments to the king, and, when that grace is said, retires and is heard of no more. It is, however, *a part of the Constitution*, and may be called out into act and energy, whenever there is occasion, and whenever those who conjure up that spirit will choose to abide the consequences. It is wise to permit its legal existence: it is much wiser to continue it a legal existence only. So truly has prudence (constituted as the god of this lower world) the entire dominion over every exercise of power committed into its hands! And yet I have lived to see prudence and conformity to circumstances wholly set at nought in our late controversies, and treated as if they were the most contemptible and irrational of all things. I have heard it an hundred times very gravely alleged, that, in order to keep power in wind, it was necessary, by preference, to exert it in those very points in which it was most likely to be resisted and the least likely to be productive of any advantage.

These were the considerations, Gentlemen, which led me early to think, that, in the comprehensive dominion which the Divine Providence had put into our hands, instead of troubling our understandings with speculations concerning the unity of empire and the identity or distinction of legislative powers, and inflaming our passions with the heat and pride of controversy, it was our duty, in all soberness, to conform our government to the character and circumstances of the several

[1] Down to 1717 the Convocation of Canterbury (here referred to) had met fairly frequently; the violently Tory policies of its lower house had caused its virtual suspension by Whig ministries.

people who composed this mighty and strangely diversified mass. I never was wild enough to conceive that one method would serve for the whole, that the natives of Hindostan and those of Virginia could be ordered in the same manner, or that the Cutchery court and the grand jury of Salem could be regulated on a similar plan. I was persuaded that government was a practical thing, made for the happiness of mankind, and not to furnish out a spectacle of uniformity to gratify the schemes of visionary politicians. Our business was to rule, not to wrangle; and it would have been a poor compensation that we had triumphed in a dispute, whilst we lost an empire.

If there be one fact in the world perfectly clear, it is this, – 'that the disposition of the people of America is wholly averse to any other than a free government'; and this is indication enough to any honest statesman how he ought to adapt whatever power he finds in his hands to their case. If any ask me what a free government is, I answer, that, for any practical purpose, it is what the people think so, – and that they, and not I, are the natural, lawful, and competent judges of this matter. If they practically allow me a greater degree of authority over them than is consistent with any correct ideas of perfect freedom, I ought to thank them for so great a trust, and not to endeavor to prove from thence that they have reasoned amiss, and that, having gone so far, by analogy they must hereafter have no enjoyment but by my pleasure.

If we had seen this done by any others, we should have concluded them far gone in madness. It is melancholy, as well as ridiculous, to observe the kind of reasoning with which the public has been amused, in order to divert our minds from the common sense of our American policy. There are people who have split and anatomized the doctrine of free government, as if it were an abstract question concerning metaphysical liberty and necessity, and not a matter of moral prudence and natural feeling. They have disputed whether liberty be a positive or a negative idea; whether it does not consist in being governed by laws, without considering what are the laws, or who are the makers; whether man has any rights by Nature; and whether all the property he enjoys be not the alms of his government, and his life itself their favor and indulgence. Others, corrupting religion as these have perverted philosophy, contend that Christians are redeemed into captivity, and the blood of the Saviour of mankind has been shed to make them the slaves of a few proud and insolent sinners. These shocking extremes provoking to extremes of another kind, speculations are let loose as destructive to all authority as the former are to all freedom; and every government is called tyranny and usurpation which is not formed on their fancies. In this manner the stirrers-up of this contention, not satisfied with distracting our dependencies and filling them with blood and slaughter, are corrupting our understandings: they are endeavoring to tear up, along with practical liberty, all the foundations of human society, all equity and justice, religion and order.

Civil freedom, Gentlemen, is not, as many have endeavored to persuade you, a thing that lies hid in the depth of abstruse science. It is a blessing and a benefit, not an abstract speculation; and all the just reasoning that can be upon it is of so coarse a texture as perfectly to suit the ordinary capacities of those who are to enjoy, and of those who are to defend it. Far from any resemblance to those propositions in geometry and metaphysics which admit no medium, but must be true or false in all their latitude, social and civil freedom, like all other things in common life, are variously mixed and modified, enjoyed in very different degrees, and shaped into an infinite diversity of forms, according to the temper and circumstances of every community. The *extreme* of liberty (which is its abstract perfection, but its real fault) obtains nowhere, nor ought to obtain anywhere; because extremes, as we all know, in every point which relates either to our duties or satisfactions in life, are destructive both to virtue and enjoyment. Liberty, too, must be limited in order to be possessed. The degree of restraint it is impossible in any case to settle precisely. But it ought to be the constant aim of every wise public counsel to find out by cautious experiments, and rational, cool endeavors, with how little, not how much, of this restraint the community can subsist: for liberty is a good to be improved, and not an evil to be lessened. It is not only a private blessing of the first order, but the vital spring and energy of the state itself, which has just so much life and vigor as there is liberty in it. But whether liberty be advantageous or not (for I know it is a fashion to decry the very principle), none will dispute that peace is a blessing; and peace must, in the course of human affairs, be frequently bought by some indulgence and toleration at least to liberty: for, as the Sabbath (though of divine institution) was made for man, not man for the Sabbath, government, which can claim no higher origin or authority, in its exercise at least, ought to conform to the exigencies of the time, and the temper and character of the people with whom it is concerned, and not always to attempt violently to bend the people to their theories of subjection. The bulk of mankind, on their part, are not excessively curious concerning any theories whilst they are really happy; and one sure symptom of an ill-conducted state is the propensity of the people to resort to them.

But when subjects, by a long course of such ill conduct, are once thoroughly inflamed, and the state itself violently distempered, the people must have some satisfaction to their feelings more solid than a sophistical speculation on law and government. Such was our situation: and such a satisfaction was necessary to prevent recourse to arms; it was necessary towards laying them down; it will be necessary to prevent the taking them up again and again. Of what nature this satisfaction ought to be I wish it had been the disposition of Parliament seriously to consider. It was certainly a deliberation that called for the exertion of all their wisdom.

I am, and ever have been, deeply sensible of the difficulty of reconciling the strong presiding power, that is so useful towards the conservation of a vast, disconnected, infinitely diversified empire, with that liberty and safety of the provinces which they must enjoy (in opinion and practice at least), or they will not be provinces at all. I know, and have long felt, the difficulty of reconciling the unwieldy haughtiness of a great ruling nation, habituated to command, pampered by enormous wealth, and confident from a long course of prosperity and victory, to the high spirit of free dependencies, animated with the first glow and activity of juvenile heat, and assuming to themselves, as their birthright, some part of that very pride which oppresses them. They who perceive no difficulty in reconciling these tempers (which, however, to make peace, must some way or other be reconciled) are much above my capacity, or much below the magnitude of the business. Of one thing I am perfectly clear: that it is not by deciding the suit, but by compromising the difference, that peace can be restored or kept. They who would put an end to such quarrels by declaring roundly in favor of the whole demands of either party have mistaken, in my humble opinion, the office of a mediator.

The war is now of full two years' standing: the controversy of many more. In different periods of the dispute, different methods of reconciliation were to be pursued. I mean to trouble you with a short state of things at the most important of these periods, in order to give you a more distinct idea of our policy with regard to this most delicate of all objects. The colonies were from the beginning subject to the legislature of Great Britain on principles which they never examined; and we permitted to them many local privileges, without asking how they agreed with that legislative authority. Modes of administration were formed in an insensible and very unsystematic manner. But they gradually adapted themselves to the varying condition of things. What was first a single kindgom stretched into an empire; and an imperial superintendency, of some kind or other, became necessary. Parliament, from a mere representative of the people, and a guardian of popular privileges for its own immediate constituents, grew into a mighty sovereign. Instead of being a control on the crown on its own behalf, it communicated a sort of strength to the royal authority, which was wanted for the conservation of a new object, but which could not be safely trusted to the crown alone. On the other hand, the colonies, advancing by equal steps, and governed by the same necessity, had formed within themselves, either by royal instruction or royal charter, assemblies so exceedingly resembling a parliament, in all their forms, functions, and powers that it was impossible they should not imbibe some opinion of a similar authority.

At the first designation of these assemblies, they were probably not intended for anything more (nor perhaps did they think themselves much higher) than the municipal corporations within this island, to which some at present love to compare them. But nothing in progression can rest on its original plan. We may as well think of rocking a grown man in the cradle of an infant. Therefore, as the colonies prospered and increased to a numerous and mighty people, spreading over a very great tract of the globe, it was natural that they should attribute to assemblies so respectable in their formal constitution some part of the dignity of the great nations which they represented. No longer tied to by-laws, these assemblies made acts of all sorts and in all cases whatsoever. They levied money, not for parochial purposes, but upon regular grants to the crown, following all the rules and principles of a parliament, to which they approached every day more and more nearly. Those who think themselves wiser than Providence and stronger than the course of Nature may complain of all this variation, on the one side or the other, as their several humors and prejudices may lead them. But things could not be otherwise; and English colonies must be had on these terms, or not had at all. In the mean time neither party felt any inconvenience from this double legislature, to which they had been formed by imperceptible habits, and old custom, the great support of all the governments in the world. Though these two legislatures were sometimes found perhaps performing the very same functions, they did not very grossly or systematically clash. In all likelihood this arose from mere neglect, possibly from the natural operation of things, which, left to themselves, generally fall into their proper order. But whatever was the cause, it is certain that a regular revenue, by the authority of Parliament, for the support of civil and military establishments, seems not to have been thought of until the colonies were too proud to submit, too strong to be forced, too enlightened not to see all the consequencies which must arise from such a system.

If ever this scheme of taxation was to be pushed against the inclinations of the people, it was evident that discussions must arise, which would let loose all the elements that composed this double constitution, would show how much each of their members had departed from its original principles, and would discover contradictions in each legislature, as well to its own first principles as to its relation to the other, very difficult, if not absolutely impossible, to be reconciled.

Therefore, at the first fatal opening of this contest, the wisest course seemed to be to put an end as soon as possible to the immediate causes of the dispute, and to quiet a discussion, not easily settled upon clear principles, and arising from claims which pride would permit neither party to abandon, by resorting as nearly as possible to the old, successful course. A mere repeal of the obnoxious tax, with a declaration of the legislative authority of this kingdom, was then fully sufficient to procure peace to *both sides*. Man is a creature of habit, and, the first breach being of very short continuance, the colonies fell back exactly into their ancient state. The Congress has used an expression with regard to this pacification which appears to me truly significant. After the repeal of the Stamp Act, 'the colonies fell,' says this assembly, 'into their ancient state of *unsuspecting confidence in the mother country*.' This unsuspecting confidence is the true centre of gravity amongst mankind, about which all the parts are at rest. It is this *unsuspecting confidence* that removes all difficulties, and reconciles all the contradictions which occur in the complexity of all ancient puzzled political establishments. Happy are the rulers which have the secret of preserving it!

The whole empire has reason to remember with eternal gratitude the wisdom and temper of that man[1] and his excellent associates, who, to recover this confidence, formed a plan of pacification in 1766. That plan, being built upon the nature of man, and the circumstances and habits of the two countries, and not on any visionary speculations, perfectly

[1] Rockingham.

answered its end, as long as it was thought proper to adhere to it. Without giving a rude shock to the dignity (well or ill understood) of this Parliament, they gave perfect content to our dependencies. Had it not been for the mediatorial spirit and talents of that great man between such clashing pretensions and passions, we should then have rushed headlong (I know what I say) into the calamities of that civil war in which, by departing from his system, we are at length involved; and we should have been precipitated into that war at a time when circumstances both at home and abroad were far, very far, more unfavorable unto us than they were at the breaking out of the present troubles.

I had the happiness of giving my first votes in Parliament for that pacification. I was one of those almost unanimous members who, in the necessary concessions of Parliament, would as much as possible have preserved its authority and respected its honor. I could not at once tear from my heart prejudices which were dear to me, and which bore a resemblance to virtue. I had then, and I have still, my partialities. What Parliament gave up I wished to be given as of grace and favor and affection, and not as a restitution of stolen goods. High dignity relented as it was soothed; and a benignity from old acknowledged greatness had its full effect on our dependencies. Our unlimited declaration of legislative authority produced not a single murmur. If this undefined power has become odious since that time, and full of horror to the colonies, it is because the *unsuspicious confidence* is lost, and the parental affection, in the bosom of whose boundless authority they reposed their privileges, is become estranged and hostile.

It will be asked, if such was then my opinion of the mode of pacification, how I came to be the very person who moved, not only for a repeal of all the late coercive statutes, but for mutilating, by a positive law, the entireness of the legislative power of Parliament, and cutting off from it the whole right of taxation. I answer, Because a different state of things requires a different conduct. When the dispute had gone to these last extremities (which no man labored more to prevent than I did), the concessions which had satisfied in the beginning could satisfy no longer; because the violation of tacit faith required explicit security. The same cause which has introduced all formal compacts and covenants among men made it necessary: I mean habits of soreness, jealousy, and distrust. I parted with it as with a limb, but as a limb to save the body: and I would have parted with more, if more had been necessary; anything rather than a fruitless, hopeless, unnatural civil war. This mode of yielding would, it is said, give way to independency without a war. I am persuaded, from the nature of things, and from every information, that it would have had a directly contrary effect. But if it had this effect, I confess that I should prefer independency without war to independency with it; and I have so much trust in the inclinations and prejudices of mankind, and so little in anything else, that I should expect ten times more benefit to this kingdom from the affection of America, though under a separate establishment, than from her perfect submission to the crown and Parliament, accompanied with her terror, disgust, and abhorrence. Bodies tied together by so unnatural a bond of union as mutual hatred are only connected to their ruin.

Letter to Fox

After being in office during the early part of North's ministry Fox fell out with the king and was finally dismissed in 1774. On American affairs he generally joined with the opposition, but he refused to take part in the Rockinghams' secession from Parliament. In the summer of 1777 he joined a house party at Chatsworth in Derbyshire, where the Cavendish brothers foregathered with other leading members of the party from the north of England. Nevertheless while still there Fox wrote somewhat critically to Burke 'I have been staying here some time with very pleasant and very amiable people but altogether as unfit to storm a citadel as they would be proper for the defence of it.' Despite his impatience with the aristocratic clique who were at the centre of the party Fox would be a useful addition to their strength through his ability and parliamentary eloquence. Burke set out in his reply to win Fox over, and though his arguments probably had little influence upon Fox they are revealing of Burke's own relationship with his leaders. 'I am quite convinced that they are the honestest public men that ever appeared in this country, and I am sure that they are the wisest, by far, of those who appear in it at present.' Burke's advice to Fox to 'lay your foundations deep in public opinion' proved to be good over the next five years, when public opinion moved gradually towards the Rockingham's views. Thereafter, however, Burke's views of his party's rectitude ceased to be generally shared by the public, so that Burke and Fox had to choose between public honesty, as seen by the party, and the pursuit of public favour.

From a Letter to Charles James Fox (8 October 1777)

In this temper of the people, I do not wholly wonder that our Northern friends look a little towards events.[1] In war, particularly, I am afraid it must be so. There is something so weighty and decisive in the events of war, something that so completely overpowers the imagination of the vulgar, that all counsels must in a great degree be subordinate to and attendant on them. I am sure it was so in the last war, very eminently. So that, on the whole, what with the temper of the people, the temper of our own friends, and the domineering necessities of war, we must quietly give up all ideas of any settled, pre-concerted plan. We shall be lucky enough, if, keeping ourselves attentive and alert, we can contrive to profit of the occasions as they arise: though I am sensible that those who are best provided with a general scheme are fittest to take advantage of all contigencies. However, to act with any people with the least degree of comfort, I believe we must contrive a little to assimilate to their character. We must gravitate towards them, if we would keep in the same system, or expect that they should approach towards us. They are, indeed, worthy of much concession and management. I am quite convinced that they are the honestest public men that ever appeared in this country, and I am sure that they are the wisest, by far, of those who appear in it at present. None of those who are continually complaining of them, but are themselves just as chargeable with all their faults, and have a decent stock of their own into the bargain. They (our friends) are, I admit, as you very truly represent them, but indifferently qualified for storming a citadel. After all, God knows whether this citadel is to be stormed by them, or by anybody else, by the means they use, or by any means. I know that as they are, abstractedly speaking, to blame, so there are those who cry

---

[1] Fox had written that opinion at Chatsworth had been for waiting upon events before forming a parliamentary strategy for the next session.

out against them for it, not with a friendly complaint, as we do, but with the bitterness of enemies. But I know, too, that those who blame them for want of enterprise have shown no activity at all against the common enemy: all their skill and all their spirit have been shown only in weakening, dividing, and indeed destroying their allies. What they are and what we are is now pretty evidently experienced; and it is certain, that, partly by our common faults, but much more by the difficulties of our situation, and some circumstances of unavoidable misfortune, we are in little better than a sort of *cul-de-sac*. For my part, I do all I can to give ease to my mind in this strange position. I remember, some years ago, when I was pressing some points with great eagerness and anxiety, and complaining with great vexation to the Duke of Richmond[1] of the little progress I make, he told me kindly, and I believe very truly, that, though he was far from thinking so himself, other people could not be persuaded I had not some latent private interest in pushing these matters, which I urged with an earnestness to extreme, and so much approaching to passion. He was certainly in the right. I am thoroughly resolved to give, both to myself and to my friends, less vexation on these subjects than hitherto I have done, – much less, indeed.

If *you* should grow too earnest, you will be still more inexcusable than I was. Your having entered into affairs so much younger ought to make them too familiar to you to be the cause of much agitation, and you have much more before you for your work. Do not be in haste. Lay your foundations deep in public opinion. Though (as you are sensible) I have never given you the least hint of advice about joining yourself in a declared connection with our party, nor do I now, yet, as I love that party very well, and am clear that you are better able to serve them than any man I know, I wish that things should be so kept as to leave you mutually very open to one another in all changes and contingencies; and I wish this the rather, because, in order to be very great, as I am anxious that you should be (always presuming that you are disposed to make a

[1] Charles Lennox (1735–1806), third Duke of Richmond, was at this time closely associated with the Rockinghams.

good use of power), you will certainly want some better support than merely that of the crown. For I much doubt, whether, with all your parts, you are the man formed for acquiring real interior favor in this court, or in any; I therefore wish you a firm ground in the country; and I do not know so firm and so sound a bottom to build on as our party. – Well, I have done with this matter; and you think I ought to have finished it long ago.

On Fox's East India Bill

On 18 November 1783 Charles James Fox, now in office and leader of the former Rockingham Whigs since the death of Rockingham in 1782, was given leave to introduce two bills for the reform of government in India. In the ensuing fortnight the bills' opponents, including the East India Company, made extraordinary efforts to stir public opinion against the proposals, and particularly against the bill 'for vesting the Affairs of the East India Company in the hands of certain Commissioners'. Only the transfer of political control from the Company to ministerially-appointed commissioners could, urged the Foxites, bring about the total reform of the Indian administration which most people now considered necessary. Burke, the actual author of the bill, set out in his speech to refute opposition allegations that the Foxites were undermining liberty and creating new corruption by seizing Indian patronage for themselves. He rested the case for his proposed reforms on the various reports of the Commons' Select Committee and Secret Committee on Indian affairs, both of which had been set up two years earlier, and his remarks assumed that his parliamentary listeners had read those reports. Many of his accusations of mismanagement and misconduct against the Company's employees were to be repeated in greater detail in the subsequent impeachment of its senior servant Warren Hastings, Governor-General of Bengal. Much of the interest of the present speech lies not in the detail of Burke's allegations, which were often prejudiced by his overwhelming indignation, but in the concept of a government's responsibility to the governed to which he was to return again and again. That the government of India had been delegated to the East India Company did not, he maintained, exonerate Parliament from guilt for the excesses committed by the Company, 'and for us passively to bear with oppressions committed under the sanction of our own authority is in truth and reason for this House to be an active accomplice in the abuse'. In urging that responsibility for governing India should be taken up by Parliament, Burke put forward an interesting variant of the Lockeian argument on contract: 'I ground myself, therefore, on this principle:– that, if the abuse is proved, the contract is broken, and we re-enter into all our rights, that is, into the exercise of all our duties.' In place of Locke's imagined contract between the governor and the governed, Burke puts the charter which (though issued by the crown) he regards as a compact between Parliament, seen as responsible to the people of India, and the Company, seen as an undesirable government.

From a Speech upon Mr Fox's East India Bill
(*1 December 1783*)

Mr Speaker, – I thank you for pointing to me. I really wished much to engage your attention in an early stage of the debate. I have been long very deeply, though perhaps ineffectually, engaged in the preliminary inquiries, which have continued without intermission for some years. Though I have felt, with some degree of sensibility, the natural and inevitable impressions of the several matters of fact, as they have been successively disclosed, I have not at any time attempted to trouble you on the merits of the subject, and very little on any of the points which incidentally arose in the course of our proceedings. But I should be sorry to be found totally silent upon this day. Our inquiries are now come to their final issue. It is now to be determined whether the three years of laborious Parliamentary research, whether the twenty years of patient Indian suffering, are to produce a substantial reform in our Eastern administration; or whether our knowledge of the grievances has abated our zeal for the correction of them, and our very inquiry into the evil was only a pretext to elude the remedy which is demanded from us by humanity, by justice, and by every principle of true policy. Depend upon it, this business cannot be indifferent to our fame. It will turn out a matter of great disgrace or great glory to the whole British nation. We are on a conspicuous stage, and the world marks our demeanor.

I am therefore a little concerned to perceive the spirit and temper in which the debate has been all along pursued upon one side of the House. The declamation of the gentlemen who oppose the bill has been abundant and vehement; but they have been reserved and even silent about the fitness or unfitness of the plan to attain the direct object it has in view. By some gentlemen it is taken up (by way of exercise, I presume) as a point of law, on a question of private property and corporate franchise; by others it is regarded as the petty intrigue of a faction at court, and argued merely as it tends to set this man a little higher or that a little lower in situation and power. All the void has been filled up with invectives against coalition,[1] with allusions to the loss of America, with the activity and inactivity of ministers. The total silence of these gentlemen concerning the interest and well-being of the people of India, and concerning the interest which this nation has in the commerce and revenues of that country, is a strong indication of the value which they set upon these objects.

It has been a little painful to me to observe the intrusion into this important debate of such company as *quo warranto*, and *mandamus*, and *certiorari*[2]: as if we were on a trial about mayors and aldermen and capital burgesses, or engaged in a suit concerning the borough of Penryn, or Saltash, or St Ives, or St Mawes. Gentlemen have argued with as much heat and passion as if the first things in the world were at stake; and their topics are such as belong only to matter of the lowest and meanest litigation. It is not right, it is not worthy of us, in

---

[1] The ministry consisted of a coalition of the followers of Fox and North; in the opinion of many an 'Infamous Coalition'.

[2] Mandatory writs issued by the high courts to inferior courts or to individuals. The *quo warranto* had achieved great notoriety under Charles II and James II as a means of withdrawing the charters of corporate bodies.

this manner to depreciate the value, to degrade the majesty, of this grave deliberation of policy and empire.

For my part, I have thought myself bound, when a matter of this extraordinary weight came before me, not to consider (as some gentlemen are so fond of doing) whether the bill originated from a Secretary of State for the Home Department or from a Secretary for the Foreign, from a minister of influence or a minister of the people, from Jacob or from Esau.* I asked myself, and I asked myself nothing else, what part it was fit for a member of Parliament, who has supplied a mediocrity of talents by the extreme of diligence, and who has thought himself obliged by the research of years to wind himself into the inmost recesses and labyrinths of the Indian detail, – what part, I say, it became such a member of Parliament to take, when a minister of state, in conformity to a recommendation from the throne, has brought before us a system for the better government of the territory and commerce of the East. In this light, and in this only, I will trouble you with my sentiments.

It is not only agreed, but demanded, by the right honorable gentleman,† and by those who act with him, that a *whole* system ought to be produced; that it ought not to be an *half-measure*; that it ought to be no *palliative*, but a legislative provision, vigorous, substantial, and effective. – I believe that no man who understands the subject can doubt for a moment that those must be the conditions of anything deserving the name of a reform in the Indian government; that anything short of them would not only be delusive, but, in this matter, which admits no medium, noxious in the extreme.

To all the conditions proposed by his adversaries the mover of the bill perfectly agrees; and on his performance of them he rests his cause. On the other hand, not the least objection has been taken with regard to the efficiency, the vigor, or the completeness of the scheme. I am therefore warranted to

* An allusion made by Mr Powis. [Thomas Powys (1743–1800) Member for Northamptonshire, had been foremost in opposing the bill as an invasion of the chartered rights of the East India Company.]
† Mr Pitt.

assume, as a thing admitted, that the bills accomplish what both sides of the House demanded as essential. The end is completely answered, so far as the direct and immediate object is concerned.

But though there are no direct, yet there are various collateral objections made: objections from the effects which this plan of reform for Indian administration may have on the privileges of great public bodies in England; from its probable influence on the constitutional rights, or on the freedom and integrity, of the several branches of the legislature.

Before I answer these objections, I must beg leave to observe, that, if we are not able to contrive some method of governing India *well*, which will not of necessity become the means of governing Great Britain *ill*, a ground is laid for their eternal separation, but none for sacrificing the people of that country to our Constitution. I am, however, far from being persuaded that any such incompatibility of interest does at all exist. On the contrary, I am certain that every means effectual to preserve India from oppression is a guard to preserve the British Constitution from its worst corruption. To show this, I will consider the objections, which, I think, are four.

1st, That the bill is an attack on the chartered rights of men.

2ndly, That it increases the influence of the crown.

3rdly, That it does *not* increase, but diminishes, the influence of the crown, in order to promote the interests of certain ministers and their party.

4thly, That it deeply affects the national credit.

As to the first of these objections, I must observe that the phrase of 'the chartered rights *of men*' is full of affectation, and very unusual in the discussion of privileges conferred by charters of the present description. But it is not difficult to discover what end that ambiguous mode of expression, so often reiterated, is meant to answer.

The rights of *men* – that is to say, the natural rights of mankind – are indeed sacred things; and if any public measure is proved mischievously to affect them, the objection ought to be fatal to that measure, even if no charter at all could be set up against it. If these natural rights are further affirmed and declared by express covenants, if they are clearly defined and secured against chicane, against power and authority, by written instruments and positive engagements, they are in a still better condition: they partake not only of the sanctity of the object so secured, but of that solemn public faith itself which secures an object of such importance. Indeed, this formal recognition, by the sovereign power, of an original right in the subject, can never be subverted, but by rooting up the holding radical principles of government, and even of society itself. The charters which we call by distinction *great* are public instruments of this nature: I mean the charters of King John and King Henry the Third. The things secured by these instruments may, without any deceitful ambiguity, be very fitly called the *chartered rights of men.*

These charters have made the very name of a charter dear to the heart of every Englishman. But, Sir, there may be, and there are, charters, not only different in nature, but formed on principles *the very reverse* of those of the Great Charter. Of this kind is the charter of the East India Company. *Magna Charta* is a charter to restrain power and to destroy monopoly. The East India charter is a charter to establish monopoly and to create power. Political power and commercial monopoly are *not* the rights of men; and the rights to them derived from charters it is fallacious and sophistical to call 'the chartered rights of men.' These chartered rights (to speak of such charters and of their effects in terms of the greatest possible moderation) do at least suspend the natural rights of mankind at large, and in their very frame and constitution are liable to fall into a direct violation of them.

It is a charter of this latter description (that is to say, a charter of power and monopoly) which is affected by the bill before you. The bill, Sir, does without question affect it: it does affect it essentially and substantially. But, having stated to you of what description the chartered rights are which this bill touches, I feel no difficulty at all in acknowledging the existence of those chartered rights in their fullest extent. They belong to the Company in the surest manner, and they are secured to that body by every sort of public sanction. They are stamped by the faith of the king; they are stamped by the faith of Parliament: they have been bought for money, for money honestly and fairly paid; they have been bought for valuable consideration, over and over again.

I therefore freely admit to the East India Company their claim to exclude their fellow-subjects from the commerce of half the globe. I admit their claim to administer an annual territorial revenue of seven millions sterling, to command an army of sixty thousand men, and to dispose (under the control of a sovereign, imperial discretion, and with the due observance of the natural and local law) of the lives and fortunes of thirty millions of their fellow-creatures. All this they possess by charter, and by Acts of Parliament (in my opinion), without a shadow of controversy.

Those who carry the rights and claims of the Company the furthest do not contend for more than this; and all this I freely grant. But, granting all this, they must grant to me, in my turn, that all political power which is set over men, and that all privilege claimed or exercised in exclusion of them, being wholly artificial, and for so much a derogation from the natural equality of mankind at large, ought to be some way or other exercised ultimately for their benefit.

If this is true with regard to every species of political dominion and every description of commercial privilege, none of which can be original, self-derived rights, or grants for the mere private benefit of the holders, then such rights, or privileges, or whatever else you choose to call them, are all in the strictest sense *a trust*: and it is of the very essence of every trust to be rendered *accountable*, – and even totally to *cease*, when it substantially varies from the purposes for which alone it could have a lawful existence.

This I conceive, Sir, to be true of trusts of power vested in the highest hands, and of such as seem to hold of no human creature. But about the application of this principle to subordinate *derivative* trusts I do not see how a controversy can be maintained. To whom, then, would I make the East India Company accountable? Why, to Parliament, to be sure, – to

Parliament, from whom their trust was derived, – to Parliament, which alone is capable of comprehending the magnitude of its object, and its abuse, and alone capable of an effectual legislative remedy. The very charter, which is held out to exclude Parliament from correcting malversation with regard to the high trust vested in the Company, is the very thing which at once gives a title and imposes a duty on us to interfere with effect, wherever power and authority originating from ourselves are perverted from their purposes, and become instruments of wrong and violence.

If Parliament, Sir, had nothing to do with this charter, we might have some sort of Epicurean excuse to stand aloof, indifferent spectators of what passes in the Company's name in India and in London. But if we are the very cause of the evil, we are in a special manner engaged to the redress; and for us passively to bear with oppressions committed under the sanction of our own authority is in truth and reason for this House to be an active accomplice in the abuse.

That the power, notoriously grossly abused, has been bought from us is very certain. But this circumstance, which is urged against the bill, becomes an additional motive for our interference, lest we should be thought to have sold the blood of millions of men for the base consideration of money. We sold, I admit, all that we had to sell, – that is, our authority, not our control. We had not a right to make a market of our duties.

I ground myself, therefore, on this principle:– that, if the abuse is proved, the contract is broken, and we re-enter into all our rights, that is, into the exercise of all our duties. Our own authority is, indeed, as much a trust originally as the Company's authority is a trust derivatively; and it is the use we make of the resumed power that must justify or condemn us in the resumption of it. When we have perfected the plan laid before us by the right honorable mover, the world will then see what it is we destroy, and what it is we create. By that test we stand or fall; and by that test I trust that it will be found, in the issue, that we are going to supersede a charter abused to the full extent of all the powers which it could abuse, and exercised in the plenitude of despotism, tyranny, and corruption, – and that in one and the same plan we provide a real chartered security for *the rights of men*, cruelly violated under that charter.

This bill, and those connected with it, are intended to form the *Magna Charta* of Hindostan. Whatever the Treaty of Westphalia is to the liberty of the princes and free cities of the Empire, and to the three religions there professed, – whatever the Great Charter, the Statute of Tallage, the Petition of Right, and the Declaration of Right are to Great Britain, these bills are to the people of India. Of this benefit I am certain their condition is capable: and when I know that they are capable of more, my vote shall most assuredly be for our giving to the full extent of their capacity of receiving; and no charter of dominion shall stand as a bar in my way to their charter of safety and protection.

The strong admission I have made of the Company's rights (I am conscious of it) binds me to do a great deal. I do not presume to condemn those who argue *a priori* against the propriety of leaving such extensive political powers in the hands of a company of merchants. I know much is, and much more may be, said against such a system.' But, with my particular ideas and sentiments, I cannot go that way to work. I feel an insuperable reluctance in giving my hand to destroy any established institution of government, upon a theory, however plausible it may be. My experience in life teaches me nothing clear upon the subject. I have known merchants with the sentiments and the abilities of great statesmen, and I have seen persons in the rank of statesmen with the conceptions and character of peddlers. Indeed, my observation has furnished me with nothing that is to be found in any habits of life or education, which tends wholly to disqualify men for the functions of government, but that by which the power of exercising those functions is very frequently obtained: I mean a spirit and habits of low cabal and intrigue; which I have never, in one instance, seen united with a capacity for sound and manly policy.

To justify us in taking the administration of their affairs

out of the hands of the East India Company, on my principles, I must see several conditions. 1st, The object affected by the abuse should be great and important. 2nd, The abuse affecting this great object ought to be a great abuse. 3rd, It ought to be habitual, and not accidental. 4th, It ought to be utterly incurable in the body as it now stands constituted. All this ought to be made as visible to me as the light of the sun, before I should strike off an atom of their charter.

As I have dwelt so long on these who are indirectly under the Company's administration, I will endeavor to be a little shorter upon the countries immediately under this charter-government. These are the Bengal provinces. The condition of these provinces is pretty fully detailed in the Sixth and Ninth Reports, and in their Appendixes.[1] I will select only such principles and instances as are broad and general. To your own thoughts I shall leave it to furnish the detail of oppressions involved in them. I shall state to you, as shortly as I am able, the conduct of the Company:– 1st, towards the landed interests;– next, the commercial interests;– 3rdly, the native government;– and lastly, to their own government.

Bengal, and the provinces that are united to it, are larger than the kingdom of France, and once contained, as France does contain, a great and independent landed interest, composed of princes, of great lords, of a numerous nobility and gentry, of freeholders, of lower tenants, of religious communities, and public foundations. So early as 1769, the Company's servants perceived the decay into which these provinces had fallen under English administration, and they made a strong representation upon this decay, and what they apprehended to be the causes of it. Soon after this representation, Mr Hastings became President of Bengal. Instead of administering a remedy to this melancholy disorder, upon the heels of a dreadful famine, in the year 1772, the succor

---

[1] The sixth report of the Select Committee dealt with Warren Hastings' administration in Bengal. The ninth report, largely the work of Burke himself, was a comprehensive indictment of the administration in India.

which the new President and the Council lent to this afflicted nation was – shall I be believed in relating it? – the landed interest of a whole kingdom, of a kingdom to be compared to France, was set up to public auction! They set up (Mr Hastings set up) the whole nobility, gentry, and freeholders to the highest bidder. No preference was given to the ancient proprietors. They must bid against every usurer, every temporary adventurer, every jobber and schemer, every servant of every European, – or they were obliged to content themselves, in lieu of their extensive domains, with their house, and such a pension as the state auctioneers thought fit to assign. In this general calamity, several of the first nobility thought (and in all appearance justly) that they had better submit to the necessity of this pension, than continue, under the name of zemindars, the objects and instruments of a system by which they ruined their tenants and were ruined themselves. Another reform has since come upon the back of the first; and a pension having been assigned to these unhappy persons, in lieu of their hereditary lands, a new scheme of economy has taken place, and deprived them of that pension.

The menial servants of Englishmen, persons (to use the emphatical phrase of a ruined and patient Eastern chief) '*whose fathers they would not have set with the dogs of their flock*' entered into their patrimonial lands. Mr Hastings's banian was, after this auction, found possessed of territories yielding a rent of one hundred and forty thousand pounds a year.

Such an universal proscription, upon any pretence, has few examples. Such a proscription, without even a pretence of delinquency, has none. It stands by itself. It stands as a monument to astonish the imagination, to confound the reason of mankind. I confess to you, when I first came to know this business in its true nature and extent, my surprise did a little suspend my indignation. I was in a manner stupefied by the desperate boldness of a few obscure young men, who, having obtained, by ways which they could not comprehend, a power of which they saw neither the purposes nor the limits, tossed about, subverted, and tore to pieces, as if it were in the gambols of a boyish unluckiness and malice, the most established rights, and the most ancient and most revered institutions, of ages and nations. Sir, I will not now trouble you with any detail with regard to what they have since done with these same lands and landholders, only to inform you that nothing has been suffered to settle for two seasons together upon any basis, and that the levity and inconstancy of these mock legislators were not the least afflicting parts of the oppressions suffered under their usurpation; nor will anything give stability to the property of the natives, but an administration in England at once protecting and stable. The country sustains, almost every year, the miseries of a revolution. At present, all is uncertainty, misery, and confusion. There is to be found through these vast regions no longer one landed man who is a resource for voluntary aid or an object for particular rapine. Some of them were not long since great princes; they possessed treasures, they levied armies. There was a zemindar[1] in Bengal (I forget his name), that, on the threat of an invasion, supplied the subah[2] of these provinces with the loan of a million sterling. The family at this day wants credit for a breakfast at the bazaar.

I shall now say a word or two on the Company's care of the commercial interest of those kingdoms. As it appears in the Reports that persons in the highest stations in Bengal have adopted, as a fixed plan of policy, the destruction of all intermediate dealers between the Company and the manufacturer, native merchants have disappeared of course. The spoil of the revenues is the sole capital which purchases the produce and manufactures, and through three or four foreign companies transmits the official gains of individuals to Europe. No other commerce has an existence in Bengal. The transport of its plunder is the only traffic of the country. I wish to refer you to the Appendix to the Ninth Report for a full acount of the manner in which the Company have protected the commercial interests of their dominions in the East.

As to the native government and the administration of justice, it subsisted in a poor, tottering manner for some years.

[1] Landed proprietor.   [2] Overlord.

In the year 1781 a total revolution took place in that establishment. In one of the usual freaks of legislation of the Council of Bengal, the whole criminal jurisdiction of these courts, called the Phoujdary Judicature, exercised till then by the principal Mussulmen, was in one day, without notice, without consultation with the magistrates or the people there, and without communication with the Directors or Ministers here, totally subverted. A new institution took place, by which this jurisdiction was divided between certain English servants of the Company and the Gentoo zemindars of the country, the latter of whom never petitioned for it, nor, for aught that appears, ever desired this boon. But its natural use was made of it: it was made a pretence for new extortions of money.

The natives had, however, one consolation in the ruin of their judicature: they soon saw that it fared no better with the English government itself. That, too, after destroying every other, came to its period. This revolution may well be rated for a most daring act, even among the extraordinary things that have been doing in Bengal since our unhappy acquisition of the means of so much mischief.

An establishment of English government for civil justice, and for the collection of revenue, was planned and executed by the President and Council of Bengal, subject to the pleasure of the Directors, in the year 1772. According to this plan, the country was divided into six districts, or provinces. In each of these was established a provincial council, which administered the revenue; and of that council, one member, by monthly rotation, presided in the courts of civil resort, with an appeal to the council of the province, and thence to Calcutta. In this system (whether in other respects good or evil) there were some capital advantages. There was, in the very number of persons in each provincial council, authority, communication, mutual check, and control. They were obliged, on their minutes of consultation, to enter their reasons and dissents; so that a man of diligence, of research, and tolerable sagacity, sitting in London, might from these materials, be enabled to form some judgment of the spirit of what was going on on the furthest banks of the Ganges and Burrampooter.

The Court of Directors so far ratified this establishment (which was consonant enough to their general plan of government), that they gave precise orders that no alteration should be made in it without their consent. So far from being apprised of any design against this constitution, they had reason to conceive that on trial it had been more and more approved by their Council-General, at least by the Governor-General, who had planned it. At the time of the revolution, the Council-General was nominally in two persons, virtually in one. At that time measures of an arduous and critical nature ought to have been forborne, even if, to the fullest council, this specific measure had not been prohibited by the superior authority. It was in this very situation that one man had the hardiness to conceive and the temerity to execute a total revolution in the form and the persons composing the government of a great kingdom. Without any previous step, at one stroke, the whole constitution of Bengal, civil and criminal, was swept away. The counsellors were recalled from their provinces; upwards of fifty of the principal officers of government were turned out of employ, and rendered dependent on Mr Hastings for their immediate subsistence, and for all hope of future provision. The chief of each council, and one European collector of revenue, was left in each province.

But here, Sir, you may imagine a new government, of some permanent description, was established in the place of that which had been thus suddenly overturned. No such thing. Lest these chiefs, without councils, should be conceived to form the ground-plan of some future government, it was publicly declared that their continuance was only temporary and permissive. The whole subordinate British administration of revenue was then vested in a committee in Calcutta, all creatures of the Governor-General; and the provincial management, under the permissive chief, was delivered over to native officers.

But that the revolution and the purposes of the revolution might be complete, to this committee were delegated, not only the functions of all the inferior, but, what will surprise the House, those of the supreme administration of revenue also. Hitherto the Governor-General and Council had, in their revenue department, administered the finances of those kingdoms. By the new scheme they are delegated to this committee, who are only to report their proceedings for approbation.

The key to the whole transaction is given in one of the instructions to the committee, – 'that it is not necessary that they should enter dissents.' By this means the ancient plan of the Company's administration was destroyed; but the plan of concealment was perfected. To that moment the accounts of the revenues were tolerably clear, – or at least means were furnished for inquiries, by which they might be rendered satisfactory. In the obscure and silent gulf of this committee everything is now buried. The thickest shades of night surround all their transactions. No effectual means of detecting fraud, mismanagement, or misrepresentation exist. The Directors, who have dared to talk with such confidence on their revenues, know nothing about them. What used to fill volumes is now comprised under a few dry heads on a sheet of paper. The natives, a people habitually made to concealment, are the chief managers of the revenue throughout the provinces. I mean by natives such wretches as your rulers select out of them as most fitted for their purposes. As a proper keystone to bind the arch, a native, one Gunga Govind Sing, a man turned out of his employment by Sir John Clavering[1] for malversation in office, is made the corresponding secretary, and, indeed, the great moving principle of their new board.

As the whole revenue and civil administration was thus subverted, and a clandestine government substituted in the place of it, the judicial institution underwent a like revolution. In 1772 there had been six courts, formed out of the six provincial councils. Eighteen new ones are appointed in their place, with each a judge, taken from the *junior* servants of the Company. To maintain these eighteen courts, a tax is levied

[1] General Sir John Clavering (1722–1777), a member of the Supreme Council set up under North's Regulating Act of 1773 to exercise restraint upon the Governor-General of Bengal, was an opponent of Hastings.

on the sums in litigation, of two and one half per cent on the great, and of five per cent on the less. This money is all drawn from the provinces to Calcutta. The chief justice (the same who stays in defiance of a vote of this House, and of his Majesty's recall) is appointed at once the treasurer and disposer of these taxes, levied without any sort of authority from the Company, from the Crown, or from Parliament.[1]

In effect, Sir, every legal, regular authority, in matters of revenue, of political administration, of criminal law, of civil law, in many of the most essential parts of military discipline, is laid level with the ground; and an oppressive, irregular, capricious, unsteady, rapacious, and peculating despotism, with a direct disavowal of obedience to any authority at home, and without any fixed maxim, principle, or rule of proceeding to guide them in India, is at present the state of your charter-government over great kingdoms.

As the Company has made this use of their trust, I should ill discharge mine, if I refused to give my most cheerful vote for the redress of these abuses, by putting the affairs of so large and valuable a part of the interests of this nation and of mankind into some steady hands, possessing the confidence and assured of the support of this House, until they can be restored to regularity, order, and consistency.

I have touched the heads of some of the grievances of the people and the abuses of government. But I hope and trust you will give me credit, when I faithfully assure you that I have not mentioned one fourth part of what has come to my knowledge in your committee; and further, I have full reason to believe that not one fourth part of the abuses are come to my knowledge, by that or by any other means. Pray consider what I have said only as an index to direct you in your inquiries.

If this, then, Sir, has been the use made of the trust of political powers, internal and external, given by you in the charter, the next thing to be seen is the conduct of the Com-

---

[1] Sir Elijah Impey (1732–1809), Chief Justice of Bengal, had been recalled to defend himself against charges of misconduct. He later returned to England, was impeached and acquitted.

pany with regard to the commercial trust. And here I will make a fair offer:– If it can be proved that they have acted wisely, prudently, and frugally, as merchants, I shall pass by the whole mass of their enormities as statesmen. That they have not done this their present condition is proof sufficient. Their distresses are said to be owing to their wars. This is not wholly true. But if it were, is not that readiness to engage in wars, which distinguishes them, and for which the Committee of Secrecy has so branded their politics, founded on the falsest principles of mercantile speculation?

The principle of buying cheap and selling dear is the first, the great foundation of mercantile dealing. Have they ever attended to this principle? Nay, for years have they not actually authorized in their servants a total indifference as to the prices they were to pay?

A great deal of strictness in driving bargains for whatever we contract is another of the principles of mercantile policy. Try the Company by that test. Look at the contracts that are made for them. Is the Company so much as a good commissary to their own armies? I engage to select for you, out of the innumerable mass of their dealings, all conducted very nearly alike, one contract only the excessive profits on which during a short term would pay the whole of their year's dividend. I shall undertake to show that upon two others the inordinate profits given, with the losses incurred in order to secure those profits, would pay a year's dividend more.

It is a third property of trading-men to see that their clerks do not divert the dealings of the master to their own benefit. It was the other day only, when their Governor and Council taxed the Company's investment with a sum of fifty thousand pounds, as an inducement to persuade only seven members of the Board of Trade to give their *honor* that they would abstain from such profits upon that investment, as they must have violated their *oaths*, if they had made at all.

It is a fourth quality of a merchant to be exact in his accounts. What will be thought, when you have fully before you the mode of accounting made use of in the Treasury of Bengal? I hope you will have it soon. With regard to one of their agencies, when it came to the material part, the prime cost of the goods on which a commission of fifteen per cent was allowed, to the astonishment of the factory to whom the commodities were sent, the Accountant-General reports that he did not think himself authorized to call for *vouchers* relative to this and other particulars, – because the agent was upon his *honor* with regard to them. A new principle of account upon honor seems to be regularly established in their dealings and their treasury, which in reality amounts to an entire annihilation of the principle of all accounts.

It is a fifth property of a merchant, who does not meditate a fraudulent bankruptcy, to calculate his probable profits upon the money he takes up to vest in business. Did the Company, when they bought goods on bonds bearing eight per cent interest, at ten and even twenty per cent discount, even ask themselves a question concerning the possibility of advantage from dealing on these terms?

The last quality of a merchant I shall advert to is the taking care to be properly prepared, in cash or goods in the ordinary course of sale, for the bills which are drawn on them. Now I ask, whether they have ever calculated the clear produce of any given sales, to make them tally with the four million of bills which are come and coming upon them, so as at the proper periods to enable the one to liquidate the other. No, they have not. They are now obliged to borrow money of their own servants to purchase their investment. The servants stipulate five per cent on the capital they advance, if their bills should not be paid at the time when they become due; and the value of the rupee on which they charge this interest is taken at two shillings and a penny. Has the Company ever troubled themselves to inquire whether their sales can bear the payment of that interest, and at that rate of exchange? Have they once considered the dilemma in which they are placed, – the ruin of their credit in the East Indies, if they refuse the bills, – the ruin of their credit and existence in England, if they accept them?

Indeed, no trace of equitable government is found in their politics, not one trace of commercial principle in their mercantile dealing: and hence is the deepest and maturest wisdom of Parliament demanded, and the best resources of this kingdom must be strained, to restore them, – that is, to restore the countries destroyed by the misconduct of the Company, and to restore the Company itself, ruined by the consequences of their plans for destroying what they were bound to preserve.

I required, if you remember, at my outset, a proof that these abuses were habitual. But surely this is not necessary for me to consider as a separate head; because I trust I have made it evident beyond a doubt, in considering the abuses themselves, that they are regular, permanent, and systematical.

I am now come to my last condition, without which, for one, I will never readily lend my hand to the destruction of any established government, which is, – that, in its present state, the government of the East India Company is absolutely incorrigible.

Of this great truth I think there can be little doubt, after all that has appeared in this House. It is so very clear, that I must consider the leaving any power in their hands, and the determined resolution to continue and countenance every mode and every degree of peculation, oppression, and tyranny, to be one and the same thing. I look upon that body incorrigible, from the fullest consideration both of their uniform conduct and their present real and virtual constitution.

If they had not constantly been apprised of all the enormities committed in India under their authority, if this state of things had been as much a discovery to them as it was to many of us, we might flatter ourselves that the detection of the abuses would lead to their reformation. I will go further. If the Court of Directors had not uniformly condemned every act which this House or any of its committees had condemned, if the language in which they expressed their disapprobation against enormities and their authors had not been much more vehement and indignant than any ever used in this House, I should entertain some hopes. If they had not, on the other hand, as uniformly commended all their servants who had done their duty and obeyed their orders as they had heavily censured those who rebelled, I might say, These people have been in an error, and when they are sensible of it they will mend. But when I reflect on the uniformity of their support to the objects of their uniform censure, and the state of insignificance and disgrace to which all of those have been reduced whom they approved, and that even utter ruin and premature death have been among the fruits of their favor, I must be convinced, that in this case, as in all others, hypocrisy is the only vice that never can be cured.

Attend, I pray you, to the situation and prosperity of Benfield,[1] Hastings, and others of that sort. The last of these has been treated by the Company with an asperity of reprehension that has no parallel. They lament 'that the power of disposing of their property for perpetuity should fall into such hands.' Yet for fourteen years, with little interruption, he has governed all their affairs, of every description, with an absolute sway. He has had himself the means of heaping up immense wealth; and during that whole period, the fortunes of hundreds have depended on his smiles and frowns. He himself tells you he is incumbered with two hundred and fifty young gentlemen, some of them of the best families in England, all of whom aim at returning with vast fortunes to Europe in the prime of life. He has, then, two hundred and fifty of your children as his hostages for your good behavior; and loaded for years, as he has been, with the execrations of the natives, with the censures of the Court of Directors, and struck and blasted with resolutions of this House, he still maintains the most despotic power ever known in India. He domineers with an overbearing sway in the assemblies of his pretended masters; and it is thought in a degree rash to venture to name his offences in this House, even as grounds of a legislative remedy.

On the other hand, consider the fate of those who have met with the applauses of the Directors. Colonel Monson,[2] one of the best of men, had his days shortened by the applauses,

---

[1] Paul Benfield (1741–1810), a 'nabob' returned 'from India with a considerable fortune, was M.P. for Cricklade.

[2] George Monson (1730–1776) was, like Clavering, a member of the Supreme Council and an opponent of Hastings.

destitute of the support, of the Company. General Clavering, whose panegyric was made in every dispatch from England, whose hearse was bedewed with the tears and hung round with the eulogies of the Court of Directors, burst an honest and indignant heart at the treachery of those who ruined him by their praises. Uncommon patience and temper supported Mr Francis[1] a while longer under the baneful influence of the commendation of the Court of Directors. His health, however, gave way at length; and in utter despair, he returned to Europe. At his return, the doors of the India House were shut to this man who had been the object of their constant admiration. He has, indeed, escaped with life; but he has forfeited all expectation of credit, consequence, party, and following. He may well say, '*Me nemo ministro fur erit, atque ideo nulli comes exeo.*' This man, whose deep reach of thought, whose large legislative conceptions, and whose grand plans of policy make the most shining part of our Reports, from whence we have all learned our lessons, if we have learned any good ones, – this man, from whose materials those gentlemen who have least acknowledged it have yet spoken as from a brief, – this man, driven from his employment, discountenanced by the Directors, has had no other reward, and no other distinction, but that inward 'sunshine of the soul' which a good conscience can always bestow upon itself. He has not yet had so much as a good word, but from a person too insignificant to make any other return for the means with which he has been furnished for performing his share of a duty which is equally urgent on us all.

Add to this, that, from the highest in place to the lowest, every British subject, who, in obedience to the Company's orders, has been active in the discovery of peculations, has been ruined. They have been driven from India. When they made their appeal at home, they were not heard; when they attempted to return, they were stopped. No artifice of fraud,

---

[1] Philip Francis (1740–1818), Hastings' greatest opponent on the Council, was wounded by him in a duel and became Burke's chief adviser in the subsequent impeachment of Hastings.

no violence of power, has been omitted to destroy them in character as well as in fortune.

Worse, far worse, has been the fate of the poor creatures, the natives of India, whom the hypocrisy of the Company has betrayed into complaint of oppression and discovery of peculation. The first women in Bengal, the Ranny of Rajeshahi, the Ranny of Burdwan, the Ranny of Ambooah, by their weak and thoughtless trust in the Company's honor and protection, are utterly ruined: the first of these women, a person of princely rank, and once of correspondent fortune, who paid above two hundred thousand a year quit-rent to the state, is, according to very credible information, so completely beggared as to stand in need of the relief of alms. Mahomed Reza Khân, the second Mussulman in Bengal, for having been distinguished by the ill-omened honor of the countenance and protection of the Court of Directors, was, without the pretence of any inquiry whatsoever into his conduct, stripped of all his employments, and reduced to the lowest condition. His ancient rival for power, the Rajah Nundcomar, was, by an insult on everything which India holds respectable and sacred, hanged in the face of all his nation by the judges you sent to protect that people: hanged for a pretended crime, upon an *ex post facto* British act of Parliament, in the midst of his evidence against Mr Hastings. The accuser they saw hanged.[1] The culprit, without acquittal or inquiry, triumphs on the ground of that murder: a murder, not of Nundcomar only, but of all living testimony, and even of evidence yet unborn. From that time not a complaint has been heard from the natives against their governors. All the grievances of India have found a complete remedy.

Men will not look to acts of Parliament, to regulations, to declarations, to votes, and resolutions. No, they are not such fools. They will ask, What is the road to power, credit, wealth, and honors? They will ask, What conduct ends in neglect, disgrace, poverty, exile, prison, and gibbet? These will teach

---

[1] The fate of Maharaja Nandakumar, hanged for forgery in 1775 after accusing Hastings of corruption, became a principal charge against both Hastings and Impey in their impeachments.

them the course which they are to follow. It is your distribution of these that will give the character and tone to your government. All the rest is miserable grimace.

When I accuse the Court of Directors of this habitual treachery in the use of reward and punishment, I do not mean to include all the individuals in that court. There have been, Sir, very frequently men of the greatest integrity and virtue amongst them; and the contrariety in the declarations and conduct of that court has arisen, I take it, from this, – that the honest Directors have, by the force of matter of fact on the records, carried the reprobation of the evil measures of the servants in India. This could not be prevented, whilst these records stared them in the face; nor were the delinquents, either here or there, very solicitous about their reputation, as long as they were able to secure their power. The agreement of their partisans to censure them blunted for a while the edge of a severe proceeding. It obtained for them a character of impartiality, which enabled them to recommend with some sort of grace, what will always carry a plausible appearance, those treacherous expedients called moderate measures. Whilst these were under discussion, new matter of complaint came over, which seemed to antiquate the first. The same circle was here trod round once more; and thus through years they proceeded in a compromise of censure for punishment, until, by shame and despair, one after another, almost every man who preferred his duty to the Company to the interest of their servants has been driven from that court.

This, Sir, has been their conduct: and it has been the result of the alteration which was insensibly made in their constitution. The change was made insensibly; but it is now strong and adult, and as public and declared as it is fixed beyond all power of reformation: so that there is none who hears me that is not as certain as I am, that the Company, in the sense in which it was formerly understood, has no existence.

The question is not, what injury you may do to the proprietors of India stock; for there are no such men to be injured. If the active, ruling part of the Company, who form the General Court, who fill the offices and direct the measures (the rest tell for nothing), were persons who held their stock as a means of their subsistence, who in the part they took were only concerned in the government of India for the rise or fall of their dividend, it would be indeed a defective plan of policy. The interest of the people who are governed by them would not be their primary object, – perhaps a very small part of their consideration at all. But then they might well be depended on, and perhaps more than persons in other respects preferable, for preventing the peculations of their servants to their own prejudice. Such a body would not easily have left their trade as a spoil to the avarice of those who received their wages. But now things are totally reversed. The stock is of no value, whether it be the qualification of a Director or Proprietor; and it is impossible that it should. A Director's qualification may be worth about two thousand five hundred pounds, – and the interest, at eight per cent, is about one hundred and sixty pounds a year. Of what value is that, whether it rise to ten, or fall to six, or to nothing, to him whose son, before he is in Bengal two months, and before he descends the steps of the Council-Chamber, sells the grant of a single contract for forty thousand pounds? Accordingly, the stock is bought up in qualifications. The vote is not to protect the stock, but the stock is bought to acquire the vote; and the end of the vote is to cover and support, against justice, some man of power who has made an obnoxious fortune in India, or to maintain in power those who are actually employing it in the acquisition of such a fortune, – and to avail themselves, in return, of his patronage, that he may shower the spoils of the East, 'barbaric pearl and gold,' on them, their families, and dependants. So that all the relations of the Company are not only changed, but inverted. The servants in India are not appointed by the Directors, but the Directors are chosen by them. The trade is carried on with their capitals. To them the revenues of the country are mortgaged. The seat of the supreme power is in Calcutta. The house in Leadenhall Street is nothing more than a 'change for their agents, factors, and deputies to meet in, to take care of their affairs and support their interests, – and this so avowedly, that we see the known agents of the delinquent servants marshalling and disciplining their forces, and the prime spokesmen in all their assemblies.

Everything has followed in this order, and according to the natural train of events. I will close what I have to say on the incorrigible condition of the Company, by stating to you a few facts that will leave no doubt of the obstinacy of that corporation, and of their strength too, in resisting the reformation of their servants. By these facts you will be enabled to discover the sole grounds upon which they are tenacious of their charter.

It is now more than two years, that upon account of the gross abuses and ruinous situation of the Company's affairs (which occasioned the cry of the whole world long before it was taken up here), that we instituted two committees to inquire into the mismanagements by which the Company's affairs had been brought to the brink of ruin. These inquiries had been pursued with unremitting diligence, and a great body of facts was collected and printed for general information. In the result of those inquiries, although the committees consisted of very different descriptions, they were unanimous. They joined in censuring the conduct of the Indian administration, and enforcing the responsibility upon two men, whom this House, in consequence of these reports, declared it to be the duty of the Directors to remove from their stations, and recall to Great Britain, – '*because they had acted in a manner repugnant to the honor and policy of this nation, and thereby brought great calamities on India and enormous expenses on the East India Company.*'

Here was no attempt on the charter. Here was no question of their privileges. To vindicate their own honor, to support their own interests, to enforce obedience to their own orders, – these were the sole object of the monitory resolution of this House. But as soon as the General Court could assemble, they assembled to demonstrate who they really were. Regardless of the proceedings of this House, they ordered the Directors not to carry into effect any resolution they might come to for the removal of Mr Hastings and Mr Hornby.[1] The Directors, still retaining some shadow of respect to this House, instituted an inquiry themselves, which continued from June to October, and, after an attentive perusal and full consideration of papers, resolved to take steps for removing the persons who had been the objects of our resolution, but not without a violent struggle against evidence. Seven Directors went so far as to enter a protest against the vote of their court. Upon this the General Court takes the alarm: it reassembles; it orders the Directors to rescind their resolution, that is, not to recall Mr Hastings and Mr Hornby, and to despise the resolution of the House of Commons. Without so much as the pretence of looking into a single paper, without the formality of instituting any committee of inquiry, they superseded all the labors of their own Directors and of this House.

It will naturally occur to ask, how it was possible that they should not attempt some sort of examination into facts, as a color for their resistance to a public authority proceeding so very deliberately, and exerted, apparently at least, in favor of their own. The answer, and the only answer which can be given, is, that they were afraid that their true relation should be mistaken. They were afraid that their patrons and masters in India should attribute their support of them to an opinion of their cause, and not to an attachment to their power. They were afraid it should be suspected that they did not mean blindly to support them in the use they made of that power. They determined to show that they at least were set against reformation: that they were firmly resolved to bring the territories, the trade, and the stock of the Company to ruin, rather than be wanting in fidelity to their nominal servants and real masters, in the ways they took to their private fortunes.

Even since the beginning of this session, the same act of audacity was repeated, with the same circumstances of contempt of all the decorum of inquiry on their part, and of all the proceedings of this House. They again made it a request

[1] The recall of William Hornby, President of Bombay, along with that of Hastings, had been called for by resolution of the Commons on 28 May 1782, on Dundas's motion.

to their favorite, and your culprit, to keep his post, – and
thanked and applauded him, without calling for a paper which
could afford light into the merit or demerit of the transaction,
and without giving themselves a moment's time to consider,
or even to understand, the articles of the Mahratta peace.
The fact is, that for a long time there was a struggle, a faint
one indeed, between the Company and their servants. But it
is a struggle no longer. For some time the superiority has been
decided. The interests abroad are become the settled preponderating weight both in the Court of Proprietors and the
Court of Directors. Even the attempt you have made to inquire
into their practices and to reform abuses has raised and
piqued them to a far more regular and steady support. The
Company has made a common cause and identified themselves
with the destroyers of India. They have taken on themselves
all that mass of enormity; they are supporting what you have
reprobated; those you condemn they applaud, those you
order home to answer for their conduct they request to stay,
and thereby encourage to proceed in their practices. Thus the
servants of the East India Company triumph, and the representatives of the people of Great Britain are defeated.[1]

I therefore conclude, what you all conclude, that this body,
being totally perverted from the purposes of its institution, is
utterly incorrigible; and because they are incorrigible, both
in conduct and constitution, power ought to be taken out of
their hands, – just on the same principles on which have been
made all the just changes and revolutions of government that
have taken place since the beginning of the world.

I will now say a few words to the general principle of the
plan[2] which is set up against that of my right honorable friend.
It is to recommit the government of India to the Court of
Directors. Those who would commit the reformation of India
to the destroyers of it are the enemies to that reformation.
They would make a distinction between Directors and

[1] The gestures of support for Hastings in the General Court had
taken place on 7 November, only three weeks before Burke's speech,
and were the Company's response to the impending Bill.

[2] i.e. Dundas's plan.

Proprietors, which, in the present state of things, does not, cannot exist. But a right honorable gentleman says, he would keep the present government of India in the Court of Directors, and would, to curb them, provide salutary regulations. Wonderful! That is, he would appoint the old offenders to correct the old offences; and he would render the vicious and the foolish wise and virtuous by salutary regulations. He would appoint the wolf as guardian of the sheep; but he has invented a curious muzzle, by which this protecting wolf shall not be able to open his jaws above an inch or two at the utmost. Thus his work is finished. But I tell the right honorable gentleman, that controlled depravity is not innocence, and that it is not the labor of delinquency in chains that will correct abuses. Will these gentlemen of the direction animadvert on the partners of their own guilt? Never did a serious plan of amending of any old tyrannical establishment propose the authors and abettors of the abuses as the reformers of them. If the undone people of India see their old oppressors in confirmed power, even by the reformation, they will expect nothing but what they will certainly feel, – a continuance, or rather an aggravation, of all their former sufferings. They look to the seat of power, and to the persons who fill it; and they despise those gentlemen's regulations as much as the gentlemen do who talk of them.

But there is a cure for everything. Take away, say they, the Court of Proprietors, and the Court of Directors will do their duty. Yes, – as they have done it hitherto. That the evils in India have solely arisen from the Court of Proprietors is grossly false. In many of them the Directors were heartily concurring; in most of them they were encouraging, and sometimes commanding; in all they were conniving.

But who are to choose this well-regulated and reforming Court of Directors? – Why, the very Proprietors who are excluded from all management, for the abuse of their power. They will choose, undoubtedly, out of themselves, men like themselves; and those who are most forward in resisting your authority, those who are most engaged in faction or interest with the delinquents abroad, will be the objects of their selection. But gentlemen say, that, when this choice is made, the Proprietors are not to interfere in the measures of the Directors, whilst those Directors are busy in the control of their common patrons and masters in India. No, indeed, I believe they will not desire to interfere. They will choose those whom they know may be trusted, safely trusted, to act in strict conformity to their common principles, manners, measures, interests, and connections. They will want neither monitor nor control. It is not easy to choose men to act in conformity to a public interest against their private; but a sure dependence may be had on those who are chosen to forward their private interest at the expense of the public. But if the Directors should slip, and deviate into rectitude, the punishment is in the hands of the General Court, and it will surely be remembered to them at their next election.

If the government of India wants no reformation, but gentlemen are amusing themselves with a theory, conceiving a more democratic or aristocratic mode of government for these dependencies, or if they are in a dispute only about patronage, the dispute is with me of so little concern that I should not take the pains to utter an affirmative or negative to any proposition in it. If it be only for a theoretical amusement that they are to propose a bill, the thing is at best frivolous and unnecessary. But if the Company's government is not only full of abuse, but is one of the most corrupt and destructive tyrannies that probably ever existed in the world (as I am sure it is), what a cruel mockery would it be in me, and in those who think like me, to propose this kind of remedy for this kind of evil!

I now come to the third objection,[1] – that this bill will increase the influence of the crown. An honorable gentleman has demanded of me, whether I was in earnest when I proposed to this House a plan for the reduction of that influence.[2] Indeed, Sir, I was much, very much, in earnest. My heart was deeply concerned in it; and I hope the public has not lost the

[1] Correctly the second objection – see above, p. 214.
[2] i.e. Burke's Civil Establishment Act, first proposed in 1780 and passed in the Rockingham administration of 1782.

effect of it. How far my judgment was right, for what concerned personal favor and consequence to myself, I shall not presume to determine; nor is its effect upon *me* of any moment. But as to this bill, whether it increases the influence of the crown, or not, is a question I should be ashamed to ask. If I am not able to correct a system of oppression and tyranny, that goes to the utter ruin of thirty millions of my fellow-creatures and fellow-subjects, but by some increase to the influence of the crown, I am ready here to declare that I, who have been active to reduce it, shall be at least as active and strenuous to restore it again. I am no lover of names; I contend for the substance of good and protecting government, let it come from what quarter it will.

But I am not obliged to have recourse to this expedient. Much, very much, the contrary, I am sure that the influence of the crown will by no means aid a reformation of this kind, which can neither be originated nor supported but by the uncorrupt public virtue of the representatives of the people of England. Let it once get into the ordinary course of administration, and to me all hopes of reformation are gone. I am far from knowing or believing that this bill will increase the influence of the crown. We all know that the crown has ever had some influence in the Court of Directors, and that it has been extremely increased by the acts of 1773 and 1780. The gentlemen[1] who, as part of their reformation, propose 'a more active control on the part of the crown,' which is to put the Directors under a Secretary of State specially named for that purpose, must know that their project will increase it further. But that old influence has had, and the new will have, incurable inconveniences, which cannot happen under the Parliamentary establishment proposed in this bill. An honorable gentleman,* not now in his place, but who is well acquainted with the India Company, and by no means a friend

---

[1] Principally Dundas, though Burke was probably thinking also of Jenkinson and Pitt as contributors to Dundas's proposals.

* Governor Johnstone [George Johnstone (c. 1730–1787), M.P. for Lostwithiel, was a proprietor and later a director of the East India Company. He had once been Governor of West Florida.]

to this bill, has told you that a ministerial influence has always been predominant in that body, – and that to make the Directors pliant to their purposes, ministers generally caused persons meanly qualified to be chosen Directors. According to his idea, to secure subserviency, they submitted the Company's affairs to the direction of incapacity. This was to ruin the Company in order to govern it. This was certainly influence in the very worst form in which it could appear. At best it was clandestine and irresponsible. Whether this was done so much upon system as that gentleman supposes, I greatly doubt. But such in effect the operation of government on that court unquestionably was; and such, under a similar constitution, it will be forever. Ministers must be wholly removed from the management of the affairs of India, or they will have an influence in its patronage. The thing is inevitable. Their scheme of a new Secretary of State, 'with a more vigorous control,' is not much better than a repetition of the measure which we know by experience will not do. Since the year 1773 and the year 1780, the Company has been under the control of the Secretary of State's office, and we had then three Secretaries of State. If more than this is done, then they annihilate the direction which they pretend to support; and they augment the influence of the crown, of whose growth they affect so great an horror. But in truth this scheme of reconciling a direction really and truly deliberative with an office really and substantially controlling is a sort of machinery that can be kept in order but a very short time. Either the Directors will dwindle into clerks, or the Secretary of State, as hitherto has been the course, will leave everything to them, often through design, often through neglect. If both should affect activity, collision, procrastination, delay, and, in the end, utter confusion, must ensue.

But, Sir, there is one kind of influence far greater than that of the nomination to office. This gentlemen in opposition have totally overlooked, although it now exists in its full vigor; and it will do so, upon their scheme, in at least as much force as it does now. That influence this bill cuts up by the roots. I mean the *influence of protection*. I shall explain myself. – The office given to a young man going to India is of trifling consequence. But he that goes out an insignificant boy in a few years returns a great nabob. Mr Hastings says he has two hundred and fifty of that kind of raw materials, who expect to be speedily manufactured into the merchantable quality I mention. One of these gentlemen, suppose, returns hither laden with odium and with riches. When he comes to England, he comes as to a prison, or as to a sanctuary; and either is ready for him, according to his demeanor. What is the influence in the grant of any place in India, to that which is acquired by the protection or compromise with such guilt, and with the command of such riches, under the dominion of the hopes and fears which power is able to hold out to every man in that condition? That man's whole fortune, half a million perhaps, becomes an instrument of influence, without a shilling of charge to the civil list: and the influx of fortunes which stand in need of this protection is continual. It works both ways: it influences the delinquent, and it may corrupt the minister. Compare the influence acquired by appointing, for instance, even a Governor-General, and that obtained by protecting him. I shall push this no further. But I wish gentlemen to roll it a little in their own minds.

The bill before you cuts off this source of influence. Its design and main scope is, to regulate the administration of India upon the principles of a court of judicature, – and to exclude, as far as human prudence can exclude, all possibliity of a corrupt partiality, in appointing to office, or supporting in office, or covering from inquiry and punishment, any person who has abused or shall abuse his authority. At the board, as appointed and regulated by this bill, reward and punishment cannot be shifted and reversed by a whisper. That commission becomes fatal to cabal, to intrigue, and to secret representation, those instruments of the ruin of India. He that cuts off the means of premature fortune, and the power of protecting it when acquired, strikes a deadly blow at the great fund, the bank, the capital stock of Indian influence, which cannot be vested anywhere, or in any hands, without most dangerous consequences to the public.

The third and contradictory objection is, that this bill does not increase the influence of the crown; on the contrary, that the just power of the crown will be lessened, and transferred to the use of a party, by giving the patronage of India to a commission nominated by Parliament and independent of the crown. The contradiction is glaring, and it has been too well exposed to make it necessary for me to insist upon it. But passing the contradiction, and taking it without any relation, of all objections that is the most extraordinary. Do not gentlemen know that the crown has not at present the grant of a single office under the Company, civil or military, at home or abroad? So far as the crown is concerned, it is certainly rather a gainer; for the vacant offices in the new commission are to be filled up by the king.

It is argued, as a part of the bill derogatory to the prerogatives of the crown, that the commissioners named in the bill are to continue for a short term of years, too short in my opinion, – and because, during that time, they are not at the mercy of every predominant faction of the court. Does not this objection lie against the present Directors, – none of whom are named by the crown, and a proportion of whom hold for this very term of four years? Did it not lie against the Governor-General and Council named in the act of 1773, – who were invested by name, as the present commissioners are to be appointed in the body of the act of Parliament, who were to hold their places for a term of years, and were not removable at the discretion of the crown? Did it not lie against the reappointment, in the year 1780, upon the very same terms? Yet at none of these times, whatever other objections the scheme might be liable to, was it supposed to be a derogation to the just prerogative of the crown, that a commission created by act of Parliament should have its members named by the authority which called it into existence. This is not the disposal by Parliament of any office derived from the authority of the crown, or now disposable by that authority. It is so far from being anything new, violent, or alarming, that I do not recollect, in any Parliamentary commission, down to the commissioners of the land-tax, that it has ever been otherwise.

The objection of the tenure for four years is an objection to all places that are not held during pleasure; but in that objection I pronounce the gentlemen, from my knowledge of their complexion and of their principles, to be perfectly in earnest. The party (say these gentlemen) of the minister who proposes this scheme will be rendered powerful by it; for he will name his party friends to the commission. This objection against party is a party objection; and in this, too, these gentlemen are perfectly serious. They see, that, if, by any intrigue, they should succeed to office, they will lose the *clandestine* patronage, the true instrument of clandestine influence, enjoyed in the name of subservient Directors, and of wealthy, trembling Indian delinquents. But as often as they are beaten off this ground, they return to it again. The minister will name his friends, and persons of his own party. Whom should he name? Should he name his adversaries? Should he name those whom he cannot trust? Should he name those to execute his plans who are the declared enemies to the principles of his reform? His character is here at stake. If he proposes for his own ends (but he never will propose) such names as, from their want of rank, fortune, character, ability, or knowledge, are likely to betray or to fall short of their trust, he is in an independent House of Commons, – in an House of Commons which has, by its own virtue, destroyed the instruments of Parliamentary subservience. This House of Commons would not endure the sound of such names. He would perish by the means which he is supposed to pursue for the security of his power. The first pledge he must give of his sincerity in this great reform will be in the confidence which ought to be reposed in those names.

For my part, Sir, in this business I put all indirect considerations wholly out of my mind. My sole question, on each clause of the bill, amounts to this:– Is the measure proposed required by the necessities of India? I cannot consent totally to lose sight of the real wants of the people who are the objects of it, and to hunt after every matter of party squabble that may be started on the several provisions. On the question of the duration of the commission I am clear and decided. Can I, can any one who has taken the smallest trouble to be informed concerning the affairs of India, amuse himself with so strange an imagination as that the habitual despotism and oppression, that the monopolies, the peculations, the universal destruction of all the legal authority of this kingdom, which have been for twenty years maturing to their present enormity, combined with the distance of the scene, the boldness and artifice of delinquents, their combination, their excessive wealth, and the faction they have made in England, can be fully corrected in a shorter term than four years? None has hazarded such an assertion; none who has a regard for his reputation will hazard it.

Sir, the gentlemen, whoever they are, who shall be appointed to this commission, have an undertaking of magnitude on their hands, and their stability must not only be, but it must be thought, real; and who is it will believe that anything short of an establishment made, supported, and fixed in its duration, with all the authority of Parliament, can be thought secure of a reasonable stability? The plan of my honorable friend is the reverse of that of reforming by the authors of the abuse. The best we could expect from them is, that they should not continue their ancient, pernicious activity. To those we could think of nothing but applying *control*; as we are sure that even a regard to their reputation (if any such thing exists in them) would oblige them to cover, to conceal, to suppress, and consequently to prevent all cure of the grievances of India. For what can be discovered which is not to their disgrace? Every attempt to correct an abuse would be a satire on their former administration. Every man they should pretend to call to an account would be found their instrument, or their accomplice. They can never see a beneficial regulation, but with a view to defeat it. The shorter the tenure of such persons, the better would be the chance of some amendment.

But the system of the bill is different. It calls in persons in no wise concerned with any act censured by Parliament, – persons generated with, and for, the reform, of which they are themselves the most essential part. To these the chief regulations in the bill are helps, not fetters: they are authorities to support, not regulations to restrain them. From these we look for much more than innocence. From these we expect zeal, firmness, and unremitted activity. Their duty, their character, binds them to proceedings of vigor; and they ought to have a tenure in their office which precludes all fear, whilst they are acting up to the purposes of their trust, – a tenure without which none will undertake plans that require a series and system of acts. When they know that they cannot be whispered out of their duty, that their public conduct cannot be censured without a public discussion, that the schemes which they have begun will not be committed to those who will have an interest and credit in defeating and disgracing them, then we may entertain hopes. The tenure is for four years, or during their good behavior. That good behavior is as long as they are true to the principles of the bill; and the judgment is in either House of Parliament. This is the tenure of your judges; and the valuable principle of the bill is to make a judicial adminis- tration for India. It is to give confidence in the execution of a duty which requires as much perseverance and fortitude as can fall to the lot of any that is born of woman.

As to the gain by party from the right honorable gentleman's bill, let it be shown that this supposed party advantage is pernicious to its object, and the objection is of weight; but until this is done (and this has not been attempted), I shall consider the sole objection from its tendency to promote the interest of a party as altogether contemptible. The kingdom is divided into parties, and it ever has been so divided, and it ever will be so divided; and if no system for relieving the subjects of this kindgom from oppression, and snatching its affairs from ruin, can be adopted, until it is demonstrated that no party can derive an advantage from it, no good can ever be done in this country. If party is to derive an advantage from the reform of India (which is more than I know or believe), it ought to be that party which alone in this kingdom has its reputation, nay, its very being, pledged to the protection and preservation of that part of the empire. Great fear is expressed that the commissioners named in this bill will show some regard to a minister out of place. To men made like the objectors this must appear criminal. Let it, however, be remembered by others, that, if the commissioners should be his friends, they cannot be his slaves. But dependants are not in a condition to adhere to friends, nor to principles, nor to any uniform line of conduct. They may begin censors, and be obliged to end accomplices. They may be even put under the direction of those whom they were appointed to punish.

The fourth and last objection is, that the bill will hurt public credit. I do not know whether this requires an answer. But if it does, look to your foundations. The sinking fund is the pillar of credit in this country; and let it not be forgot, that the distresses, owing to the mismanagement, of the East India Company, have already taken a million from that fund by the non-payment of duties. The bills drawn upon the Company, which are about four millions, cannot be accepted without the consent of the Treasury. The Treasury, acting under a Parliamentary trust and authority, pledges the public for these millions. If they pledge the public, the public must have a security in its hands for the management of this interest, or the national credit is gone. For otherwise it is not only the East India Company, which is a great interest, that is undone, but, clinging to the security of all your funds, it drags down the rest, and the whole fabric perishes in one ruin. If this bill does not provide a direction of integrity and of ability competent to that trust, the objection is fatal; if it does, public credit must depend on the support of the bill.

It has been said, If you violate this charter, what security has the charter of the Bank, in which public credit is so deeply concerned, and even the charter of London, in which the rights of so many subjects are involved? I answer, In the like case they have no security at all, – no, no security at all. If the Bank should, by every species of mismanagement, fall into a state similar to that of the East India Company, – if it should be oppressed with demands it could not answer, engagements which it could not perform, and with bills for which it could not procure payment, – no charter should protect the mismanagement from correction, and such public grievances from redress. If the city of London had the means and will of

destroying an empire, and of cruelly oppressing and tyranniz-
ing over millions of men as good as themselves, the charter of
the city of London should prove no sanction to such tyranny
and such oppression. Charters are kept, when their purposes
are maintained: they are violated, when the privilege is
supported against its end and its object.

Now, Sir, I have finished all I proposed to say, as my
reasons for giving my vote to this bill. If I am wrong, it is
not for want of pains to know what is right. This pledge, at
least, of my rectitude I have given to my country.

A Representation to His Majesty

Traditionally the speech from the throne to the two assembled houses at the opening of a new session was a ministerial statement of self-justification and future intent. As such it was usually the subject of debate before the usual address of thanks was voted. At the opening of Parliament in May 1784 the Foxites had little hope of opposing the address successfully, for they had just been heavily defeated in a general election. Burke therefore determined to put his views on permanent record by writing a speech in the form of a motion, which would be recorded in full in the official Journal of the House of Commons. The motion was made on 14 June, and occupies six folio sides in the printed *Journals*. No debate was aroused by Burke's motion, his colleagues not caring to associate themselves with so unusual a proceeding. But he was sufficiently pleased with his work to publish it soon afterwards in pamphlet form, with explanatory notes.

The motion and notes together are of considerable interest as a description, by one of its best-informed Members, of the role of the House of Commons in the late eighteenth century. The Commons were, Burke believed, the 'sole representatives' of the people and as such the 'natural guardians of the Constitution'. Although the people might approach the King or the upper house as individuals, the collective sense of the people could only be transmitted through the Commons; it followed that ministers of the crown could only receive that sense from, not deliver it to the House. Burke further rejected 'hazardous theories' concerning a balance of the constitution, as between monarch, Lords and Commons. Such a balance had been a commonplace of expositions concerning the constitution since the Revolution of 1688, and the concept had also been widely borrowed abroad, not least by Montesquieu and by the Americans. Burke's usual grasp of practicalities was not at fault, however, when he saw that the historical tendency of the British constitution was to elevate the importance of the House of Commons *vis a vis* the crown and the Lords. After this time what Burke called the 'fiction of a balance' gradually ceased to play a preeminent part in British political thinking.

From A Representation to His Majesty, Moved in the House of Commons . . . and Negatived. With a Preface and Notes

PREFACE

The representation now given to the public relates to some of the most essential privileges of the House of Commons.[1] It would appear of little importance, if it were to be judged by its reception in the place where it was proposed. There it was rejected without debate. The subject matter may, perhaps, hereafter appear to merit a more serious consideration. Thinking men will scarcely regard the *penal* dissolution of a Parliament as a very trifling concern. Such a dissolution must operate forcibly as an example; and it much imports the people of this kingdom to consider what lesson that example is to teach.

The late House of Commons was not accused of an interested compliance to the will of a court. The charge against them was of a different nature. They were charged with being actuated by an extravagant spirit of independency. This species of offence is so closely connected with merit, this vice bears so near a resemblance to virtue, that the flight of a House of Commons above the exact temperate medium of independence ought to be correctly ascertained, lest we give encouragement to dispositions of a less generous nature, and less safe for the people; we ought to call for very solid and convincing proofs of the existence, and of the magnitude, too, of the evils which are charged to an independent spirit, before

[1] For the political and constitutional situation which led up to this document see Introduction, pp. 29 and 34.

we give sanction to any measure, that, by checking a spirit so easily damped, and so hard to be excited, may affect the liberty of a part of our Constitution, which, if not free, is worse than useless.

The Editor[1] does not deny that by possibility such an abuse may exist: but, *primâ fronte*, there is no reason to presume it. The House of Commons is not, by its complexion, peculiarly subject to the distempers of an independent habit. Very little compulsion is necessary, on the part of the people, to render it abundantly complaisant to ministers and favorites of all descriptions. It required a great length of time, very considerable industry and perseverance, no vulgar policy, the union of many men and many tempers, and the concurrence of events which do not happen every day, to build up an independent House of Commons. Its demolition was accomplished in a moment; and it was the work of ordinary hands. But to construct is a matter of skill; to demolish, force and fury are sufficient.

The late House of Commons has been punished for its independence. That example is made. Have we an example on record of a House of Commons punished for its servility? The rewards of a senate so disposed are manifest to the world. Several gentlemen are very desirous of altering the constitution of the House of Commons; but they must alter the frame and constitution of human nature itself, before they can so fashion it, by any mode of election, that its conduct will not be influenced by reward and punishment, by fame and by disgrace. If these examples take root in the minds of men, what members hereafter will be bold enough not to be corrupt, especially as the king's highway of obsequiousness is so very broad and easy? To make a passive member of Parliament, no dignity of mind, no principles of honor, no resolution, no ability, no industry, no learning, no experience, are in the least degree necessary. To defend a post of importance against a powerful enemy requires an Eliot; a drunken invalid is qualified to hoist a white flag, or to deliver up the keys of the fortress on his knees.

[1] Burke himself.

The gentlemen chosen into this Parliament, for the purpose of this surrender, were bred to better things, and are no doubt qualified for other service. But for this strenuous exertion of inactivity, for the vigorous task of submission and passive obedience, all their learning and ability are rather a matter of personal ornament to themselves than of the least use in the performance of their duty.

The present surrender, therefore, of rights and privileges without examination, and the resolution to support any minister given by the secret advisers of the crown, determines not only on all the power and authority of the House, but it settles the character and description of the men who are to compose it, and perpetuates that character as long as it may be thought expedient to keep up a phantom of popular representation.

It is for the chance of some amendment before this new settlement takes a permanent form, and while the matter is yet soft and ductile, that the Editor has republished this piece, and added some notes and explanations to it. His intentions, he hopes, will excuse him to the original mover, and to the world. He acts from a strong sense of the incurable ill effects of holding out the conduct of the late House of Commons as an example to be shunned by future representatives of the people.

MOTION

RELATIVE TO

THE SPEECH FROM THE THRONE

LUNÆ, 14° DIE JUNII, 1784.

A motion was made, That a representation be presented to his Majesty, most humbly to offer to his royal consideration, that the address of this House, upon his Majesty's speech from the throne, was dictated solely by our conviction of his Majesty's own most gracious intentions towards his people, which, as we feel with gratitude, so we are ever ready to acknowledge with cheerfulness and satisfaction.

Impressed with these sentiments, we were willing to separate from our general expressions of duty, respect, and veneration to his Majesty's royal person and his princely virtues all discussion whatever with relation to several of the matters suggested and several of the expressions employed in that speech.

That it was not fit or becoming that any decided opinion should be formed by his faithful Commons on that speech, without a degree of deliberation adequate to the importance of the object. Having afforded ourselves due time for that deliberation, we do now most humbly beg leave to represent to his Majesty, that, in the speech from the throne, his ministers have thought proper to use a language of a very alarming import, unauthorized by the practice of good times, and irreconcilable to the principles of this government.

Humbly to express to his Majesty, that it is the privilege and duty of this House to guard the Constitution from all infringement on the part of ministers, and, whenever the occasion requires it, to warn them against any abuse of the authorities committed to them; but it is very lately,* that, in a manner not more unseemly than irregular and preposterous, ministers have thought proper, by admonition from the throne, implying distrust and reproach, to convey the expectations of the people to us, their sole representatives,† and have presumed to caution us, the natural guardians of the Constitution, against any infringement of it on our parts.

This dangerous innovation we, his faithful Commons, think it our duty to mark; and as these admonitions from the throne, by their frequent repetition, seem intended to lead

---

* See King's Speech, Dec. 5, 1782, and May 19, 1784.

† 'I shall never submit to the doctrines I have heard this day from the woolsack, that the other House [House of Commons] are the only representatives and guardians of the people's rights. I boldly maintain the contrary. I say this House [House of Lords] *is equally the representatives of the people.*' – Lord Shelburne's Speech, April 8, 1778. *Vide* Parliamentary Register, Vol. X, p. 392.

gradually to the establishment of an usage, we hold ourselves bound thus solemnly to protest against them.

This House will be, as it ever ought to be, anxiously attentive to the inclinations and interests of its constituents; nor do we desire to straiten any of the avenues to the throne, or to either House of Parliament. But the ancient order in which the rights of the people have been exercised is not a restriction of these rights. It is a method providently framed in favor of those privileges which it preserves and enforces, by keeping in that course which has been found the most effectual for answering their ends. His Majesty may receive the opinions and wishes of individuals under their signatures, and of bodies corporate under their seals, as expressing their own particular sense; and he may grant such redress as the legal powers of the crown enable the crown to afford. This, and the other House of Parliament, may also receive the wishes of such corporations and individuals by petition. The collective sense of his people his Majesty is to receive from his Commons in Parliament assembled. It would destroy the whole spirit of the Constitution, if his Commons were to receive that sense from the ministers of the crown, or to admit them to be a proper or a regular channel for conveying it.

That the ministers in the said speech declare, 'His Majesty has a just and confident reliance that we (his faithful Commons) are animated with the same sentiments of loyalty, and the same attachment to our excellent Constitution which he had the happiness to see so fully manifested in every part of the kingdom.'

To represent, that his faithful Commons have never failed in loyalty to his Majesty. It is new to them to be reminded of it. It is unnecessary and invidious to press it upon them by any example. This recommendation of loyalty, after his Majesty has sat for so many years, with the full support of all descriptions of his subjects, on the throne of this kingdom, at a time of profound peace, and without any pretence of the existence or apprehension of war or conspiracy, becomes in itself a source of no small jealousy to his faithful Commons; as many circumstances lead us to apprehend that therein the ministers have reference to some other measures and principles of loyalty, and to some other ideas of the Constitution, than the laws require, or the practice of Parliament will admit.

No regular communication of the proofs of loyalty and attachment to the Constitution, alluded to in the speech from the throne, have been laid before this House, in order to enable us to judge of the nature, tendency, or occasion of them, or in what particular acts they were displayed; but if we are to suppose the manifestations of loyalty (which are held out to us as an example for imitation) consist in certain addresses delivered to his Majesty, promising support to his Majesty in the exercise of his prerogative, and thanking his Majesty for removing certain of his ministers, on account of the votes they have given upon bills depending in Parliament, – if this be the example of loyalty alluded to in the speech from the throne, then we must beg leave to express our serious concern for the impression which has been made on any of our fellow-subjects by misrepresentations which have seduced them into a seeming approbation of proceedings subversive of their own freedom. We conceive that the opinions delivered in these papers were not well considered; nor were the parties duly informed of the nature of the matters on which they were called to determine, nor of those proceedings of Parliament which they were led to censure.

We shall act more advisedly. – The loyalty we shall manifest will not be the same with theirs; but, we trust, it will be equally sincere, and more enlightened. It is no slight authority which shall persuade us (by receiving as proofs of loyalty the mistaken principles lightly taken up in these addresses) obliquely to criminate, with the heavy and ungrounded charge of disloyalty and disaffection, an uncorrupt, independent, and reforming Parliament.* Above all, we shall take care that none

* In that Parliament the House of Commons by two several resolutions put an end to the American war. Immediately on the change of ministry which ensued, in order to secure their own independence, and to prevent the accumulation of new burdens on the people by the growth of a civil list debt, they passed the Establishment Bill. By that bill thirty-six offices tenable by members of Parliament were suppressed, and an order of payment was framed by which the growth of

of the rights and privileges, always claimed, and since the
accession of his Majesty's illustrious family constantly exercised by this House (and which we hold and exercise in trust
for the Commons of Great Britain, and for their benefit),
shall be constructively surrendered, or even weakened and
impaired, under ambiguous phrases and implications of
censure on the late Parliamentary proceedings. If these claims
are not well founded, they ought to be honestly abandoned; if
they are just, they ought to be steadily and resolutely maintained.

Of his Majesty's own gracious disposition towards the true
principles of our free Constitution his faithful Commons never
did or could entertain a doubt; but we humbly beg leave to

---

any fresh debt was rendered impracticable. The debt on the civil list
from the beginning of the present reign had amounted to one million
three hundred thousand pounds and upwards. Another act was passed
for regulating the office of the Paymaster-General and the offices
subordinate to it. A million of public money had sometimes been in
the hands of the paymasters: this act prevented the possibility of any
money whatsoever being accumulated in that office in future. The
offices of the Exchequer, whose emoluments in time of war were
excessive, and grew in exact proportion to the public burdens, were
regulated, – some of them suppressed, and the rest reduced to fixed
salaries. To secure the freedom of election against the crown, a bill
was passed to disqualify all officers concerned in the collection of the
revenue in any of its branches from voting in elections: a most
important act, not only with regard to its primary object, the freedom
of election, but as materially forwarding the due collection of revenue.
For the same end, (the preserving the freedom of election,) the House
rescinded the famous judgment relative to the Middlesex election, and
expunged it from the journals. On the principle of reformation of their
own House, connected with a principle of public economy, an act
passed for rendering contractors with government incapable of a seat
in Parliament. The India Bill (unfortunately lost in the House of
Lords) pursued the same idea to its completion, and disabled all
servants of the East India Company from a seat in that House for a
certain time, and until their conduct was examined into and cleared.
The remedy of infinite corruptions and of infinite disorders and oppressions, as well as the security of the most important objects of public
economy, perished with that bill and that Parliament. That Parliament also instituted a committee to inquire into the collection of the
revenue in all its branches, which prosecuted its duty with great vigor,
and suggested several material improvements.

express to his Majesty our uneasiness concerning other new and unusual expressions of his ministers, declaratory of a resolution 'to support in their *just balance* the rights and privileges of every branch of the legislature.'

It were desirable that all hazardous theories concerning a balance of rights and privileges (a mode of expression wholly foreign to Parliamentary usage) might have been forborne. His Majesty's faithful Commons are well instructed in their own rights and privileges, which they are determined to maintain on the footing upon which they were handed down from their ancestors; they are not unacquainted with the rights and privileges of the House of Peers; and they know and respect the lawful prerogatives of the crown: but they do not think it safe to admit anything concerning the existence of a balance of those rights, privileges, and prerogatives; nor are they able to discern to what objects ministers would apply their fiction of a balance, nor what they would consider as a just one. These unauthorized doctrines have a tendency to stir improper discussions, and to lead to mischievous innovations in the Constitution.*

---

* If these speculations are let loose, the House of Lords may quarrel with their share of the legislature, as being limited with regard to the origination of grants to the crown and the origination of money bills. The advisers of the crown may think proper to bring its negative into ordinary use, – and even to dispute, whether a mere negative, compared with the deliberative power exercised in the other Houses, be such a share in the legislature as to produce a due balance in favor of that branch, and thus justify the previous interference of the crown in the manner lately used. The following will serve to show how much foundation there is for great caution concerning these novel speculations. Lord Shelburne, in his celebrated speech, April 8th, 1778, expresses himself as follows. (*Vide* Parliamentary Register, Vol. X.)

'The noble and learned lord on the woolsack, in the debate which opened the business of this day, asserted that your Lordships were incompetent to make any alteration in a money bill or a bill of supply. I should be glad to see the matter fairly and fully discussed, and the subject brought forward and argued upon precedent, as well as all its collateral relations. I should be pleased to see the question fairly committed, were it for no other reason but to hear the sleek, smooth contractors from the other House come to this bar and declare, that they, and they only, *could frame a money bill*, and they, and they *only*,

That his faithful Commons most humbly recommend, instead of the inconsiderate speculations of unexperienced men, that, on all occasions, resort should be had to the happy practice of Parliament, and to those solid maxims of government which have prevailed since the accession of his Majesty's illustrious family, as furnishing the only safe principles on which the crown and Parliament can proceed.

We think it the more necessary to be cautious on this head, as, in the last Parliament, the present ministers had thought proper to countenance, if not to suggest, an attack upon the most clear and undoubted rights and privileges of this House.*

---

could dispose of the *property of the peers of Great Britain.* Perhaps some arguments more plausible than those I heard this day from the woolsack, to show that the Commons have an uncontrollable, unqualified right to bind your Lordships' property, may be urged by them. At present, I beg leave to differ from the noble and learned lord; for, until the claim, after a solemn discussion of this House, is openly and directly relinquished, I shall continue to be of opinion that your Lordships have a right to *alter, amend,* or reject a money bill.'

The Duke of Richmond also, in his letter to the volunteers of Ireland, speaks of several of the powers exercised by the House of Commons in the light of usurpations; and his Grace is of opinion, that, when the people are restored to what he conceives to be their rights, in electing the House of Commons, the other branches of the legislature ought to be restored to theirs. – *Vide* Remembrancer, Vol. XVI.

* By an act of Parliament, the Directors of the East India Company are restrained from acceptance of bills drawn from India, beyond a certain amount, without the consent of the Commissioners of the Treasury. The late House of Commons, finding bills to an immense amount drawn upon that body by their servants abroad, and knowing their circumstances to be exceedingly doubtful, came to a resolution providently cautioning the Lords of the Treasury against the acceptance of these bills, until the House should otherwise, direct. The Court Lords then took occasion to declare against the resolution as illegal, by the Commons undertaking to direct in the execution of a trust created by act of Parliament. The House, justly alarmed at this resolution, which went to the destruction of the whole of its superintending capacity, and particularly in matters relative to its own province of money, directed a committee to search the journals, and they found a regular series of precedents, commencing from the remotest of those records, and carried on to that day, by which it appeared that the House interfered, by an authoritative advice and admonition,

Fearing, from these extraordinary admonitions, and from the new doctrines, which seem to have dictated several unusual expressions, that his Majesty has been abused by false representations of the late proceedings in Parliament, we think it our duty respectfully to inform his Majesty, that no attempt whatever has been made against his lawful prerogatives, or against the rights and privileges of the Peers, by the late House of Commons, in any of their addresses, votes, or resolutions; neither do we know of any proceeding by bill, in which it was proposed to abridge the extent of his royal prerogative: but, if such provision had existed in any bill, we protest, and we declare, against all speeches, acts, or addresses, from any persons whatsoever, which have a tendency to consider such bills, or the persons concerned in them, as just objects of any kind of censure and punishment from the throne. Necessary reformations may hereafter require, as they have frequently done in former times, limitations and abridgments, and in some cases an entire extinction, of some branch of prerogative. If bills should be improper in the form in which they appear in the House where they originate, they are liable, by the wisdom of this Constitution, to be corrected, and even to be totally set aside, elsewhere. This is the known, the legal, and the safe remedy; but whatever, by the manifestation of the royal displeasure, tends to intimidate individual members from proposing, or this House from receiving, debating, and passing bills, tends to prevent even the beginning of every reformation in the state, and utterly destroys the deliberative capacity of Parliament. We therefore claim, demand, and insist upon it, as our undoubted right, that no persons shall be deemed proper objects of animadversion by the crown, in any mode whatever, for the votes which they give or the propositions which they make in Parliament.

We humbly conceive, that besides its share of the legislative power, and its right of impeachment, that, by the law and usage of Parliament, this House has other powers and capaci-

---

upon every act of executive government without exception, and in many much stronger cases than that which the Lords thought proper to quarrel with.

ties, which it is bound to maintain. This House is assured that our humble advice on the exercise of prerogative will be heard with the same attention with which it has ever been regarded, and that it will be followed by the same effects which it has ever produced, during the happy and glorious reigns of his Majesty's royal progenitors, – not doubting but that, in all those points, we shall be considered as a council of wisdom and weight to advise, and not merely as an accuser of competence to criminate.* This House claims both capacities; and we trust that we shall be left to our free discretion which of them we shall employ as best calculated for his Majesty's and the national service. Whenever we shall see it expedient to offer our advice concerning his Majesty's servants, who are those of the public, we confidently hope that the personal favor of any minister, or any set of ministers, will not be more dear to his Majesty than the credit and character of a House of Commons. It is an experiment full of peril to put the representative wisdom and justice of his Majesty's people in the wrong; it is a crooked and desperate design, leading to mischief, the extent of which no human wisdom can foresee, to attempt to form a prerogative party in the nation, to be resorted to as occasion shall require, in derogation from the authority of the Commons of Great Britain in Parliament assembled; it is a contrivance full of danger, for ministers to set up the representative and constituent bodies of the Commons of this kindgom as two separate and distinct powers, formed to counterpoise each other, leaving the preference in the hands of secret advisers of the crown.[1] In such a situation of things, these advisers, taking advantage of the

* 'I observe, at the same time, that there is *no charge or complaint* suggested against my present ministers.' – The King's Answer, 25th February, 1784, to the Address of the House of Commons. *Vide* Resolutions of the House of Commons, printed for Debrett, p. 31.

[1] By secret advisers Burke probably chiefly meant those leaders of the court party whom he had castigated in the *Present Discontents*, or their like. Both Charles Jenkinson and John Robinson (1727–1802), Joint Secretary to the Treasury under North, had been involved in the king's decision to remove the Coalition and dissolve Parliament.

differences which may accidentally arise or may purposely be fomented between them, will have it in their choice to resort to the one or the other, as may best suit the purposes of their sinister ambition. By exciting an emulation and contest between the representative and the constituent bodies, as parties contending for credit and influence at the throne, sacrifices will be made by both; and the whole can end in nothing else than the destruction of the dearest rights and liberties of the nation. If there must be another mode of conveying the collective sense of the people to the throne than that by the House of Commons, it ought to be fixed and defined, and its authority ought to be settled: it ought not to exist in so precarious and dependent a state as that ministers should have it in their power, at their own mere pleasure, to acknowledge it with respect or to reject it with scorn.

It is the undoubted prerogative of the crown to dissolve Parliament; but we beg leave to lay before his Majesty, that it is, of all the trusts vested in his Majesty, the most critical and delicate, and that in which this House has the most reason to require, not only the good faith, but the favor of the crown. His Commons are not always upon a par with his ministers in an application to popular judgment; it is not in the power of the members of this House to go to their election at the moment the most favorable for them. It is in the power of the crown to choose a time for their dissolution whilst great and arduous matters of state and legislation are depending, which may be easily misunderstood, and which cannot be fully explained before that misunderstanding may prove fatal to the honor that belongs and to the consideration that is due to members of Parliament.

With his Majesty is the gift of all the rewards, the honors, distinctions, favors, and graces of the state; with his Majesty is the mitigation of all the rigors of the law: and we rejoice to see the crown possessed of trusts calculated to obtain good-will, and charged with duties which are popular and pleasing. Our trusts are of a different kind. Our duties are harsh and invidious in their nature; and justice and safety is all we can expect in the exercise of them. We are to offer salutary, which is not always pleasing counsel: we are to inquire and to accuse; and the objects of our inquiry and charge will be for the most part persons of wealth, power, and extensive connections: we are to make rigid laws for the preservation of revenue, which of necessity more or less confine some action or restrain some function which before was free: what is the most critical and invidious of all, the whole body of the public impositions originate from us, and the hand of the House of Commons is seen and felt in every burden that presses on the people. Whilst ultimately we are serving them, and in the first instance whilst we are serving his Majesty, it will be hard indeed, if we should see a House of Commons the victim of its zeal and fidelity, sacrifices by his ministers to those very popular discontents which shall be excited by our dutiful endeavors for the security and greatness of his throne. No other consequence can result from such an example, but that, in future, the House of Commons, consulting its safety at the expense of its duties, and suffering the whole energy of the state to be relaxed, will shrink from every service which, however necessary, is of a great and arduous nature, – or that, willing to provide for the public necessities, and at the same time to secure the means of performing that task, they will exchange independence for protection, and will court a subservient existence through the favor of those ministers of state or those secret advisers who ought themselves to stand in awe of the Commons of this realm.

A House of Commons respected by his ministers is essential to his Majesty's service: it is fit that they should yield to Parliament, and not that Parliament should be new-modelled until it is fitted to their purposes. If our authority is only to be held up when we coincide in opinion with his Majesty's advisers, but is to be set at nought the moment it differs from them, the House of Commons will sink into a mere appendage of administration, and will lose that independent character which, inseparably connecting the honor and reputation with the acts of this House, enables us to afford a real, effective, and substantial support to his government. It is the deference shown to our opinion, when we dissent from the servants of the crown, which alone can give authority to the proceedings of this House, when it concurs with their measures.

That authority once lost, the credit of his Majesty's crown will be impaired in the eyes of all nations. Foreign powers, who may yet wish to revive a friendly intercourse with this nation, will look in vain for that hold which gave a connection with Great Britain the preference to an alliance with any other state. A House of Commons of which ministers were known to stand in awe, where everything was necessarily discussed on principles fit to be openly and publicly avowed, and which could not be retracted or varied without danger, furnished a ground of confidence in the public faith which the engagement of no state dependent on the fluctuation of personal favor and private advice can ever pretend to. If faith with the House of Commons, the grand security for the national faith itself, can be broken with impunity, a wound is given to the political importance of Great Britain which will not easily be healed.

Speech in opening the Impeachment of Warren Hastings

The cumbersome process of state trial by impeachment at the bar of the House of Lords had not been used for over half a century when Burke revived it. His motive for so doing lay in the difficulty of obtaining in any other way the punishment of those guilty of misgovernment in India. In opening the case on behalf of the Commons his concern was that the long disuse which marked the process of impeachment itself should not lead to a summary acquittal. The danger was a real one, for the King, whose intervention in the Lords in 1783 had brought about the rejection of the Whigs' India Bill, was an ardent supporter of Hastings and might be tempted to repeat his action if a good excuse appeared. Burke in fact succeeded in getting a full hearing, although an initial procedural decision of the Lords to hear all the charges in their sequence before turning to Hastings' defence helped to ensure the eventual acquittal of the defendant. The case continued over seven years, giving the maximum of publicity to Burke's basic contention that a distant empire brought responsibilities as well as advantages to its rulers. Much of what is most characteristic of Burke's political thought came out in the course of his speeches. Conviction that Hastings had infringed a higher morality, even if his deeds could not be punished under the positive laws of nations, lay behind Burke's exclamation 'let him fly where he will from law to law; law (I thank God) meets him everywhere'. But with his concept, a somewhat untypical one in the Age of Enlightenment, of the overall authority of a Law of God, was linked as usual a very practical appreciation, the product of that Age, of the differences between nations and peoples which necessitated different forms of government. Hastings' worst offence, in Burke's view, was not that he was conventionally tyrannical or extortionate, but that he had failed to understand the principles of government. 'If we undertake to govern the inhabitants of such a country', Burke told the House of Lords on the third day of the impeachment proceedings, 'we must govern them upon their own principles and maxims, and not upon ours'.

From a Speech in Opening the Impeachment of Warren Hastings (*15 February 1788*)

My Lords, – The gentlemen who have it in command to support the impeachment against Mr Hastings have directed me to open the cause with a general view of the grounds upon which the Commons have proceeded in their charge against him.[1] They have directed me to accompany this with another general view of the extent, the magnitude, the nature, the tendency, and the effect of the crimes which they allege to have been by him committed. They have also directed me to give an explanation (with their aid I may be enabled to give it) of such circumstances, preceeding the crimes charged on Mr Hastings, or concomitant with them, as may tend to elucidate whatever may be found obscure in the articles as they stand. To these they wished me to add a few illustrative remarks on the laws, customs, opinions, and manners of the people concerned, and who are the objects of the crimes we charge on Mr Hastings. The several articles, as they appear before you, will be opened by other gentlemen with more particularity, with more distinctness, and, without doubt, with infinitely more ability, when they come to apply the evidence which naturally belongs to each article of this accusation. This, my Lords, is the plan which we mean to pursue on the great charge which is now to abide your judgment.

My Lords, I must look upon it as an auspicious circumstance

[1] Apart from Burke himself, the principal managers appointed by the Commons to carry on the impeachment were Fox and Richard Brinsley Sheridan. One of the youngest managers was Charles Grey, later Earl Grey. Francis was recognized to be a personal enemy of Hastings, and was excluded.

to this cause, in which the honor of the kingdom and the fate of many nations are involved, that, from the first commencement of our Parliamentary process to this the hour of solemn trial, not the smallest difference of opinion has arisen between the two Houses.

My Lords, there are persons who, looking rather upon what was to be found in our records and histories than what was to be expected from the public justice, had formed hopes consolatory to themselves and dishonorable to us. They flattered themselves that the corruptions of India would escape amidst the dissensions of Parliament. They are disappointed. They will be disappointed in all the rest of their expectations which they have formed upon everything, except the merits of their cause. The Commons will not have the melancholy unsocial glory of having acted a solitary part in a noble, but imperfect work. What the greatest inquest of the nation has begun its highest tribunal will accomplish. At length justice will be done to India. It is true that your Lordships will have your full share in this great achievement; but the Commons have always considered that whatever honor is divided with you is doubled on themselves.

My Lords, I must confess, that, amidst these encouraging prospects, the Commons do not approach your bar without awe and anxiety. The magnitude of the interests which we have in charge will reconcile some degree of solicitude for the event with the undoubting confidence with which we repose ourselves upon your Lordships' justice. For we are men, my Lords; and men are so made, that it is not only the greatness of danger, but the value of the adventure, which measures the degree of our concern in every undertaking. I solemnly assure your Lordships that no standard is sufficient to estimate the value which the Commons set upon the event of the cause they now bring before you. My Lords, the business of this day is not the business of this man, it is not solely whether the prisoner at the bar be found innocent or guilty, but whether millions of mankind shall be made miserable or happy.

Your Lordships will see, in the progress of this cause, that there is not only a long, connected, systematic series of misdemeanors, but an equally connected system of maxims and principles invented to justify them. Upon both of these you must judge. According to the judgment that you shall give upon the past transactions in India, inseparably connected as they are with the principles which support them, the whole character of your future government in that distant empire is to be unalterably decided. It will take its perpetual tenor, it will receive its final impression, from the stamp of this very hour.

It is not only the interest of India, now the most considerable part of the British empire, which is concerned, but the credit and honor of the British nation itself will be decided by this decision. We are to decide by this judgment, whether the crimes of individuals are to be turned into public guilt and national ignominy, or whether this nation will convert the very offences which have thrown a transient shade upon its government into something that will reflect a permanent lustre upon the honor, justice, and humanity of this kingdom.

My Lords, there is another consideration, which augments the solicitude of the Commons, equal to those other two great interests I have stated, those of our empire and our national character, – something that, if possible, comes more home to the hearts and feelings of every Englishman: I mean, the interests of our Constitution itself, which is deeply involved in the event of this cause. The future use and the whole effect, if not the very existence, of the process of an impeachment of high crimes and misdemeanors before the peers of this kingdom upon the charge of the Commons will very much be decided by your judgment in this cause. This tribunal will be found (I hope it will always be found) too great for petty causes: if it should at the same time be found incompetent to one of the greatest, – that is, if little offences, from their minuteness, escape you, and the greatest, from their magnitude, oppress you, – it is impossible that this form of trial should not in the end vanish out of the Constitution. For we must not deceive ourselves: whatever does not stand with credit cannot stand long. And if the Constitution should be deprived, I do not mean in form, but virtually, of this resource, it is virtually deprived of everything else that is valuable in it. For this process is the cement which binds the whole together; this is the individuating principle that makes England what England is. In this court it is that no subject, in no part of the empire, can fail of competent and proportionable justice; here it is that we provide for that which is the substantial excellence of our Constitution, – I mean, the great circulation of responsibility, by which (excepting the supreme power) no man, in no circumstances, can escape the account which he owes to the laws of his country. It is by this process that magistracy, which tries and controls all other things, is itself tried and controlled. Other constitutions are satisfied with making good subjects; this is a security for good governors. It is by this tribunal that statesmen who abuse their power are accused by statesmen and tried by statesmen, not upon the niceties of a narrow jurisprudence, but upon the enlarged and solid principles of state morality. It is here that those who by the abuse of power have violated the spirit of law can never hope for protection from any of its forms; it is here that those who have refused to conform themselves to its perfections can never hope to escape through any of its defects. It ought, therefore, my Lords, to become our common care to guard this your precious deposit, rare in its use, but powerful in its effect, with a religious vigilance, and never to suffer it to be either discredited or antiquated. For this great end your Lordships are invested with great and plenary powers: but you do not suspend, you do not supersede, you do not annihilate any subordinate jurisdiction; on the contrary, you are auxiliary and supplemental to them all.

Whether it is owing to the felicity of our times, less fertile in great offences than those which have gone before us, or whether it is from a sluggish apathy which has dulled and enervated the public justice, I am not called upon to determine – but, whatever may be the cause, it is now sixty-three years since any impeachment, grounded upon abuse of authority and misdemeanor in office, has come before this tribunal. The last is that of Lord Macclesfield, which happened in the year

1725.[1] So that the oldest process known to the Constitution of this country has, upon its revival, some appearance of novelty. At this time, when all Europe is in a state of, perhaps, contagious fermentation, when antiquity has lost all its reverence and all its effect on the minds of men, at the same time that novelty is still attended with the suspicions that always will be attached to whatever is new, we have been anxiously careful, in a business which seems to combine the objections both to what is antiquated and what is novel, so to conduct ourselves that nothing in the revival of this great Parliamentary process shall afford a pretext for its future disuse.

My Lords, strongly impressed as they are with these sentiments, the Commons have conducted themselves with singular care and caution. Without losing the spirit and zeal of a public prosecution, they have comported themselves with such moderation, temper, and decorum as would not have ill become the final judgment, if with them rested the final judgment, of this great cause.

With very few intermissions, the affairs of India have constantly engaged the attention of the Commons for more than fourteen years. We may safely affirm we have tried every mode of legislative provision before we had recourse to anything of penal process. It was in the year 1774[2] we framed an act of Parliament for remedy to the then existing disorders in India, such as the then information before us enabled us to enact. Finding that the act of Parliament did not answer all the ends that were expected from it, we had, in the year 1782, recourse to a body of monitory resolutions. Neither had we the expected fruit from them. When, therefore, we found that our inquiries and our reports, our laws and our admonitions, were alike despised, that enormities increased in proportion as they were forbidden, detected, and exposed, – when we found that guilt stalked with an erect and upright front, and that legal

[1] Thomas Parker (1666?–1732), first Earl of Macclesfield, was impeached and found guilty of malversation while Lord Chancellor.
[2] 1773.

authority seemed to skulk and hide its head like outlawed guilt, – when we found that some of those very persons who were appointed by Parliament to assert the authority of the laws of this kingdom were the most forward, the most bold, and the most active in the conspiracy for their destruction, – then it was time for the justice of the nation to recollect itself. To have forborne longer would not have been patience, but collusion; it would have been participation with guilt; it would have been to make ourselves accomplices with the criminal.

We found it was impossible to evade painful duty without betraying a sacred trust. Having, therefore, resolved upon the last and only resource, a penal prosecution, it was our next business to act in a manner worthy of our long deliberation. In all points we proceeded with selection. We have chosen (we trust it will so appear to your Lordships) such a crime, and such a criminal, and such a body of evidence, and such a mode of process, as would have recommended this course of justice to posterity, even if it had not been supported by any example in the practice of our forefathers.

First, to speak of the process: we are to inform your Lordships, that, besides that long previous deliberation of fourteen years, we examined, as a preliminary to this proceeding, every circumstance which could prove favorable to parties apparently delinquent, before we finally resolved to prosecute. There was no precedent to be found in the Journals, favorable to persons in Mr Hastings's circumstances, that was not applied to. Many measures utterly unknown to former Parliamentary proceedings, and which, indeed, seemed in some degree to enfeeble them, but which were all to the advantage of those that were to be prosecuted, were adopted, for the first time, upon this occasion. In an early stage of the proceeding, the criminal desired to be heard. He was heard; and he produced before the bar of the House that insolent and unbecoming paper which lies upon our table.[1] It was deliberately given in

[1] Hastings's reply to the charges brought against him in the Commons had been delivered on 1 and 2 May 1786, and had not been well received.

by his own hand, and signed with his own name. The Commons, however, passed by everything offensive in that paper with a magnanimity that became them. They considered nothing in it but the facts that the defendant alleged, and the principles he maintained; and after a deliberation not short of judicial, we proceeded with confidence to your bar.

So far as to the process; which, though I mentioned last in the line and order in which I stated the objects of our selection, I thought it best to dispatch first.

As to the crime which we chose, we first considered well what it was in its nature, under all the circumstances which attended it. We weighed it with all its extenuations and with all its aggravations. On that review, we are warranted to assert that the crimes with which we charge the prisoner at the bar are substantial crimes, – that they are no errors or mistakes, such as wise and good men might possibly fall into, which may even produce very pernicious effects without being in fact great offences. The Commons are too liberal not to allow for the difficulties of a great and arduous public situation. They know too well the domineering necessities which frequently occur in all great affairs. They know the exigency of a pressing occasion, which, in its precipitate career, bears everything down before it, – which does not give time to the mind to recollect its faculties, to reinforce its reason, and to have recourse to fixed principles, but, by compelling an instant and tumultuous decision, too often obliges men to decide in a manner that calm judgment would certainly have rejected. We know, as we are to be served by men, that the persons who serve us must be tried as men, and with a very large allowance indeed to human infirmity and human error. This, my Lords, we knew and we weighed before we came before you. But the crimes which we charge in these articles are not lapses, defects, errors of common human frailty, which, as we know and feel, we can allow for. We charge this offender with no crimes that have not arisen from passions which it is criminal to harbor, – with no offences that have not their root in avarice, rapacity, pride, insolence, ferocity, treachery, cruelty, malignity of temper, – in short, in [with?] nothing that does not argue a total extinction of all moral principle, that does not manifest an inveterate blackness of heart, dyed in grain with malice, vitiated, corrupted, gangrened to the very core. If we do not plant his crimes in those vices which the breast of man is made to abhor, and the spirit of all laws, human and divine, to interdict, we desire no longer to be heard upon this occasion. Let everything that can be pleaded on the ground of surprise or error, upon those grounds be pleaded with success: we give up the whole of those predicaments. We urge no crimes that were not crimes of forethought. We charge him with nothing that he did not commit upon deliberation, – that he did not commit against advice, supplication, and remonstrance, – that he did not commit against the direct command of lawful authority, – that he did not commit after reproof and reprimand, the reproof and reprimand of those who were authorized by the laws to reprove and reprimand him. The crimes of Mr. Hastings are crimes not only in themselves, but aggravated by being crimes of contumacy. They were crimes, not against forms, but against those eternal laws of justice which are our rule and our birthright. His offences are, not in formal, technical language, but in reality, in substance and effect, *high* crimes and high misdemeanors.

So far as to the crimes. As to the criminal, we have chosen him on the same principle on which we selected the crimes. We have not chosen to bring before you a poor, puny, trembling delinquent, misled, perhaps, by those who ought to have taught him better, but who have afterwards oppressed him by their power, as they had first corrupted him by their example. Instances there have been many, wherein the punishment of minor offences, in inferior persons, has been made the means of screening crimes of an high order, and in men of high description. Our course is different. We have not brought before you an obscure offender, who, when his insignificance and weakness are weighed against the power of the prosecution, gives even to public justice something of the appearance of oppression: no, my Lords, we have brought before you the first man of India, in rank, authority, and station. We have brought before you the chief of the tribe, the head of the whole body of Eastern offenders, a captain-general of iniquity, under whom all the fraud, all the peculation, all the tyranny in India are embodied, disciplined, arrayed, and paid. This is the person, my Lords, that we bring before you. We have brought before you such a person, that, if you strike at him with the firm and decided arm of justice, you will not have need of a great many more examples. You strike at the whole corps, if you strike at the head.

So far as to the crime: so far as to the criminal. Now, my Lords, I shall say a few words relative to the evidence which we have brought to support such a charge, and which ought to be equal in weight to the charge itself. It is chiefly evidence of record, officially signed by the criminal himself in many instances. We have brought before you his own letters, authenticated by his own hand. On these we chiefly rely. But we shall likewise bring before you living witnesses, competent to speak to the points to which they are brought.

When you consider the late enormous power of the prisoner, – when you consider his criminal, indefatigable assiduity in the destruction of all recorded evidence, – when you consider the influence he has over almost all living testimony, – when you consider the distance of the scene of action, – I believe your Lordships, and I believe the world, will be astonished that so much, so clear, so solid, and so conclusive evidence of all kinds has been obtained against him. I have no doubt that in nine instances in ten the evidence is such as would satisfy the narrow precision supposed to prevail, and to a degree rightly to prevail, in all subordinate power and delegated jurisdiction. But your Lordships will maintain, what we assert and claim as the right of the subjects of Great Britain, that you are not bound by any rules of evidence, or any other rules whatever, except those of natural, immutable, and substantial justice.

God forbid the Commons should desire that anything should be received as proof from them which is not by nature adapted to prove the thing in question! If they should make such a request, they would aim at overturning the very principles of that justice to which they resort; they would give the nation an evil example that would rebound back on themselves, and bring destruction upon their own heads, and on those of all their posterity.

On the other hand, I have too much confidence in the learning with which you will be advised, and the liberality and nobleness of the sentiments with which you are born, to suspect that you would, by any abuse of the forms, and a technical course of proceeding, deny justice to so great a part of the world that claims it at your hands. Your Lordships always had an ample power, and almost unlimited jurisdiction; you have now a boundless object. It is not from this district or from that parish, not from this city or the other province, that relief is now applied for: exiled and undone princes, extensive tribes, suffering nations, infinite descriptions of men, different in language, in manners, and in rites, men separated by every barrier of Nature from you, by the Providence of God are blended in one common cause, and are now become suppliants at your bar. For the honor of this nation, in vindication of this mysterious Providence, let it be known that no rule formed upon municipal maxims (if any such rule exists) will prevent the course of that imperial justice which you owe to the people that call to you from all parts of a great disjointed world. For, situated as this kingdom is, an object, thank God, of envy to the rest of the nations, its conduct in that high and elevated situation will undoubtedly be scrutinized with a severity as great as its power is invidious.

It is well known that enormous wealth has poured into this country from India through a thousand channels, public and concealed; and it is no particular derogation from our honor to suppose a possibility of being corrupted by that by which other empires have been corrupted, and assemblies almost as respectable and venerable as your Lordships have been directly or indirectly vitiated. Forty millions of money, at least, have within our memory been brought from India into England. In this case the most sacred judicature ought to look to its reputation. Without offence we may venture to suggest that the best way to secure reputation is, not by a proud defiance of public opinion, but by guiding our actions in such a manner as that public opinion may in the end be securely defied, by having been previously respected and dreaded. No direct false judgment is apprehended from the tribunals of this country; but it is feared that partiality may lurk and nestle in the abuse of our forms of proceeding. It is necessary, therefore, that nothing in that proceeding should appear to mark the slightest trace, should betray the faintest odor of chicane. God forbid, that, when you try the most serious of all causes, that, when you try the cause of Asia in the presence of Europe, there should be the least suspicion that a narrow partiality, utterly destructive of justice, should so guide us that a British subject in power should appear in substance to possess rights which are denied to the humble allies, to the attached dependants of this kingdom, who by their distance have a double demand upon your protection, and who, by an implicit (I hope not a weak and useless) trust in you, have stripped themselves of every other resource under heaven!

I do not say this from any fear, doubt, or hesitation concerning what your Lordships will finally do, – none in the world; but I cannot shut my ears to the rumors which you all know to be disseminated abroad. The abusers of power may have a chance to cover themselves by those fences and intrenchments which were made to secure the liberties of the people against men of that very description. But God forbid it should be bruited from Pekin to Paris, that the laws of England are for the rich and the powerful, but to the poor, the miserable, and defenceless they afford no resource at all! God forbid it should be said, no nation is equal to the English in *substantial* violence and in *formal* justice, – that in this kingdom we feel ourselves competent to confer the most extravagant and inordinate powers upon public ministers, but that we are deficient, poor, helpless, lame, and impotent in the means of calling them to account for their use of them! An opinion has been insidiously circulated through this kingdom, and through foreign nations too, that, in order to cover our participation in guilt, and our common interest in the plunder of the East, we have invented a set of scholastic distinctions, abhorrent to the common sense and unpropitious to the common necessities of mankind, by which we are to deny ourselves the knowledge of what the rest of the world knows, and what so great a part of the world both knows and feels. I do not deprecate any appearance which may give countenance to this aspersion from suspicion that any corrupt motive can influence this court; I deprecate it from knowing that hitherto we have moved within the narrow circle of municipal justice. I am afraid, that, from the habits acquired by moving within a circumscribed sphere, we may be induced rather to endeavor at forcing Nature into that municipal circle than to enlarge the circle of national justice to the necessities of the empire we have obtained.

This is the only thing which does create any doubt or difficulty in the minds of sober people. But there are those who will not judge so equitably. Where two motives, neither of them perfectly justifiable, may be assigned, the worst has the chance of being preferred. If, from any appearance of chicane in the court, justice should fail, all men will say, better there were no tribunals at all. In my humble opinion, it would be better a thousand times to give all complainants the short answer the Dey of Algiers gave a British ambassador, representing certain grievances suffered by the British merchants, – 'My friend,' (as the story is related by Dr Shaw,)[1] 'do not you know that my subjects are a band of robbers, and that I am their captain?' – better it would be a thousand times, and a thousand thousand times more manly, than an hypocritical process, which, under a pretended reverence to punctilious ceremonies and observances of law, abandons mankind without help and resource to all the desolating consequences of arbitrary power. The conduct and event of this cause will put an end to such doubts, wherever they may be entertained. Your Lordships will exercise the great plenary powers with which you are invested in a manner that will do honor to the protecting justice of this kingdom, that will completely avenge the great people who are subjected to it. You will not suffer your proceedings to be squared by any rules but by their

[1] Thomas Shaw (1694–1751), Principal of St Edmund Hall, Oxford.

necessities, and by that law of a common nature which cements them to us and us to them. The reports to the contrary have been spread abroad with uncommon industry; but they will be speedily refuted by the humanity, simplicity, dignity, and nobleness of your Lordships' justice.

Reflections on the Revolution in France

The 'gentleman in Paris', mentioned in the full title of this work, was Charles-Jean-François Depont (1767–1796), a young friend of the writer who had sought his views on the Revolution. In a Preface Burke maintained that 'having thrown down his first thoughts in the form of a letter, and, indeed, when he sat down to write, having intended it for a private letter, he found it difficult to change the form of address, when his sentiments had grown into a greater extent and had received another direction.' The original letter which Burke wrote for Depont alone was drafted in November 1789, though not sent till later. The *Reflections*, however, owed little to the private letter except continuity of ideas and the form in which it was cast.

The main stimulus to the writing of the *Reflections* was not Depont's request but the publication of the radical Richard Price's *A Discourse on the Love of our Country*, a sermon preached before the Revolution Society of London at its meeting on 4 November 1789 to commemorate the Revolution of 1688. Price welcomed the recent events in France as similar to Britain's 'Glorious Revolution', a comparison which in Burke's opinion made the former appear less innovatory, and the latter more so, than the cases demanded. In his desire to amend the view that events in France were taking a parallel course to those of Britain in 1688 Burke was led far into discussion of the history and philosophy of government. Despite the title his most important and best-informed reflections concerned not France but Britain. In one major respect, however, Burke proved perceptive on France too. At the time of publication in 1790 the worst excesses of the Revolution were yet to come, but he forecast them with some accuracy. Less perceptive was his treatment of the Old Régime; in his anxiety to see that the existing government of Britain was not overset by a social revolution such as France was experiencing he was led to assert that pre-Revolution French government had been basically satisfactory. Contemporary critics of the *Reflections* denied the truth of his assertion, but after the disasters of 1792–1793 it was Burke's view which triumphed for his own generation. In the longer term his work has not proved to be a satisfactory explanation of the French Revolution, but its comparative analysis of British government remains the best statement of its kind published in the eighteenth century.

Out of Burke's interpretation of British institutions emerged his fullest exposition of the doctrine of prescription, which held that the very fact of a constitution's having survived the tests of time guaranteed to it a large measure of wisdom which should not lightly be put aside by reformers. This doctrine is perhaps the nearest that Burke ever came to an abstract political theory, though it is arguable that he was merely extending the application of legal and constitutional assumptions and the habit which the British had long displayed of deferring to political precedent. His reason for moving as far as he did on to the plane of abstract theory was his belief that the French Revolution had been caused primarily by the speculations of French philosophers based upon the doctrine of the natural rights of man. 'The pretended rights of these theorists', he maintained, 'are all extremes: and in proportion as they are metaphysically true, they are morally and politically false.' Nevertheless theory had to be countered by theory; against the rights of man Burke set the duties of man, owed, he maintained, under a moral code or law of God. And against the concept of *a priori* statemaking held by the French revolutionaries, he set his model of a state built up slowly but soundly, fit to weather the storms of revolution because basically conforming to the needs of its people as demonstrated in the course of centuries.

From Reflections on the Revolution in France, and on the Proceedings in Certain Societies in London relative to that Event: in a Letter intended to have been sent to a Gentleman in Paris (1790)

Whatever may be the success of evasion in explaining away the gross error of *fact*, which supposes that his Majesty (though he holds it in concurrence with the wishes) owes his crown to the choice of his people, yet nothing can evade their full, explicit declaration concerning the principle of a right in the people to choose, – which right is directly maintained, and tenaciously adhered to. All the oblique insinuations concerning election bottom in this proposition, and are referable to it. Lest the foundation of the king's exclusive legal title should pass for a mere rant of adulatory freedom, the political divine proceeds dogmatically to assert,* that, by the principles of the Revolution, the people of England have acquired three fundamental rights, all of which, with him, compose one system, and lie together in one short sentence: namely, that we have acquired a right

1. 'To choose our own governors.'
2. 'To cashier them for misconduct.'
3. 'To frame a government for ourselves.'

This new, and hitherto unheard-of bill of rights, though made in the name of the whole people, belongs to those gentlemen and their faction only.[1] The body of the people of England have no share in it. They utterly disclaim it. They will resist the practical assertion of it with their lives and fortunes. They are bound to do so by the laws of their country, made at the time of that very Revolution which is appealed to in favor of the fictitious rights claimed by the society which abuses its name.

These gentlemen of the Old Jewry, in all their reasonings on the Revolution of 1688, have a revolution which happened in

* P. 34, Discourse on the Love of Our Country, by Dr Price.
[1] Specifically, the members of the Revolution Society meeting at the Old Jewry: in general, the radical reformers.

England about forty years before, and the late French Revolution, so much before their eyes and in their hearts, that they are constantly confounding all the three together. It is necessary that we should separate what they confound. We must recall their erring fancies to the *acts* of the Revolution which we revere, for the discovery of its true *principles*. If the *principles* of the Revolution of 1688 are anywhere to be found, it is in the statute called the *Declaration of Right*. In that most wise, sober, and considerate declaration, drawn up by great lawyers and great statesmen, and not by warm and inexperienced enthusiasts, not one word is said, nor one suggestion made, of a general right 'to choose our own *governors*, to cashier them for misconduct, and to *form* a government for *ourselves*.'

This Declaration of Right (the act of the 1st of William and Mary, sess. 2, ch. 2) is the corner-stone of our Constitution, as reinforced, explained, improved, and in its fundamental principles forever settled. It is called 'An Act for declaring the rights and liberties of the subject, and for *settling* the *succession* of the crown.'[1] You will observe that these rights and this succession are declared in one body, and bound indissolubly together.

A few years after this period, a second opportunity offered for asserting a right of election to the crown. On the prospect of a total failure of issue from King William, and from the princess, afterwards Queen Anne, the consideration of the settlement of the crown, and of a further security for the liberties of the people, again came before the legislature. Did they this second time make any provision for legalizing the crown on the spurious Revolution principles of the Old Jewry? No. They followed the principles which prevailed in the Declaration of Right; indicating with more precision the persons who were to inherit in the Protestant line. This act[2] also incorporated, by the same policy, our liberties and an hereditary succession in the same act. Instead of a right to

[1] The Act referred to by Burke is that which is commonly called the Bill of Rights. It embodies the Declaration of Rights drawn up by Parliament in naming William and Mary joint sovereigns.

[2] The Act of Settlement, 1701.

choose our own governors, they declared that the *succession* in that line (the Protestant line drawn from James the First) was absolutely necessary 'for the peace, quiet, and security of the realm,' and that it was equally urgent on them 'to maintain a *certainty in the succession* thereof, to which the subjects may safely have recourse for their protection.' Both these acts, in which are heard the unerring, unambiguous oracles of Revolution policy, instead of countenancing the delusive gypsy predictions of a 'right to choose our governors,' prove to a demonstration how totally adverse the wisdom of the nation was from turning a case of necessity into a rule of law.

Unquestionably there was at the Revolution, in the person of King William, a small and a temporary deviation from the strict order of a regular hereditary succession; but it is against all genuine principles of jurisprudence to draw a principle from a law made in a special case and regarding an individual person. *Privilegium non transit in exemplum.*[1] If ever there was a time favorable for establishing the principle that a king of popular choice was the only legal king, without all doubt it was at the Revolution. Its not being done at that time is a proof that the nation was of opinion it ought not to be done at any time. There is no person so completely ignorant of our history as not to know that the majority in Parliament, of both parties, were so little disposed to anything resembling that principle, that at first they were determined to place the vacant crown, not on the head of the Prince of Orange, but on that of his wife, Mary, daughter of King James, the eldest born of the issue of that king, which they acknowledged as undoubtedly his.[2] It would be to repeat a very trite story, to recall to your memory all those circumstances which demonstrated that their accepting King William was not properly a *choice*; but to all

[1] A special case does not pass into precedent (a legal maxim). The reader is reminded, as often, that Burke approached political problems from the point of view of a trained lawyer.

[2] Contrary to Burke's assertion the Whigs in 1689 did not contemplate giving the crown to Mary alone; their wish was that William should be sole monarch, but in compromise with the Tories they accepted Mary jointly with her husband.

those who did not wish in effect to recall King James, or to deluge their country in blood, and again to bring their religion, laws, and liberties into the peril they had just escaped, it was an act of *necessity*, in the strictest moral sense in which necessity can be taken.

In the very act in which, for a time, and in a single case, Parliament departed from the strict order of inheritance, in favor of a prince who, though not next, was, however, very near in the line of succession, it is curious to observe how Lord Somers, who drew the bill called the Declaration of Right, has comported himself on that delicate occasion. It is curious to observe with what address this temporary solution of continuity is kept from the eye; whilst all that could be found in this act of necessity to countenance the idea of an hereditary succession is brought forward, and fostered, and made the most of, by this great man, and by the legislature who followed him. Quitting the dry, imperative style of an act of Parliament, he makes the Lords and Commons fall to a pious legislative ejaculation, and declare that they consider it 'as a marvellous providence, and merciful goodness of God to this nation, to preserve their said Majesties' *royal* persons most happily to reign over us *on the throne of their ancestors*, for which, from the bottom of their hearts, they return their humblest thanks and praises.' The legislature plainly had in view the Act of Recognition of the first of Queen Elizabeth, chap. 3rd, and of that of James the First, chap. 1st, both acts strongly declaratory of the inheritable nature of the crown; and in many parts they follow, with a nearly literal precision, the words, and even the form of thanksgiving which is found in these old declaratory statutes.

The two Houses, in the act of King William, did not thank God that they had found a fair opportunity to assert a right to choose their own governors, much less to make an election the *only lawful* title to the crown. Their having been in a condition to avoid the very appearance of it, as much as possible, was by them considered as a providential escape. They threw a politic, well-wrought veil over every circumstance tending to weaken the rights which in the meliorated order of succession they meant to perpetuate, or which might furnish a precedent for any future departure from what they had then settled forever. Accordingly, that they might not relax the nerves of their monarchy, and that they might preserve a close conformity to the practice of their ancestors, as it appeared in the declaratory statutes of Queen Mary* and Queen Elizabeth, in the next clause they vest, by recognition, in their Majesties *all* the legal prerogatives of the crown, declaring 'that in them they are most *fully*, rightfully, and *entirely* invested, incorporated, united, and annexed.' In the clause which follows, for preventing questions, by reason of any pretended titles to the crown, they declare (observing also in this the traditionary language, along with the traditionary policy of the nation, and repeating as from a rubric the language of the preceding acts of Elizabeth and James) that on the preserving 'a *certainty* in the SUCCESSION thereof the unity, peace, and tranquillity of this nation doth, under God, wholly depend.'

They knew that a doubtful title of succession would but too much resemble an election, and that an election would be utterly destructive of the 'unity, peace, and tranquillity of this nation,' which they thought to be considerations of some moment. To provide for these objects, and therefore to exclude forever the Old Jewry doctrine of 'a right to choose our own governors,' they follow with a clause containing a most solemn pledge, taken from the preceding act of Queen Elizabeth, – as solemn a pledge as ever was or can be given in favor of an hereditary succession, and as solemn a renunciation as could be made of the principles by this society imputed to them:–
'The Lords Spiritual and Temporal, and Commons, do, in the name of all the people aforesaid, most humbly and faithfully submit *themselves, their heirs, and posterities forever*; and do faithfully promise that they will stand to, maintain, and defend their said Majesties, and also the *limitation of the crown*, herein specified and contained, to the utmost of their powers,' &c., &c.

So far is it from being true that we acquired a right by the Revolution to elect our kings, that, if we had possessed it

* 1st Mary, sess. 3, ch. 1.

before, the English nation did at that time most solemnly renounce and abdicate it, for themselves, and for all their posterity forever. These gentlemen may value themselves as much as they please on their Whig principles; but I never desire to be thought, a better Whig than Lord Somers, or to understand the principles of the Revolution better than those by whom it was brought about, or to read in the Declaration of Right any mysteries unknown to those whose penetrating style has engraved in our ordinances, and in our hearts, the words and spirit of that immortal law.

It is true, that, aided with the powers derived from force and opportunity, the nation was at that time, in some sense, free to take what course it pleased for filling the throne, – but only free to do so upon the same grounds on which they might have wholly abolished their monarchy, and every other part of their Constitution. However, they did not think such bold changes within their commission. It is, indeed, difficult, perhaps impossible, to give limits to the mere *abstract* competence of the supreme power, such as was exercised by Parliament at that time; but the limits of a *moral* competence, subjecting, even in powers more indisputably sovereign, occasional will to permanent reason, and to the steady maxims of faith, justice, and fixed fundamental policy, are perfectly intelligible, and perfectly binding upon those who exercise any authority, under any name, or under any title, in the state. The House of Lords, for instance, is not morally competent to dissolve the House of Commons, – no, nor even to dissolve itself, nor to abdicate, if it would, its portion in the legislature of the kingdom. Though a king may abdicate for his own person, he cannot abdicate for the monarchy. By as strong, or by a stronger reason, the House of Commons cannot renounce its share of authority. The engagement and pact of society, which generally goes by the name of the Constitution, forbids such invasion and such surrender. The constituent parts of a state are obliged to hold their public faith with each other, and with all those who derive any serious interest under their engagements, as much as the whole state is bound to keep its faith with separate communities: otherwise, competence and power would soon be confounded, and no law be left but the will of a prevailing force. On this principle, the succession of the crown has always been what it now is, an hereditary succession by law: in the old line it was a succession by the Common Law; in the new by the statute law, operating on the principles of the Common Law, not changing the substance, but regulating the mode and describing the persons. Both these descriptions of law are of the same force, and are derived from an equal authority, emanating from the common agreement and original compact of the state, *communi sponsione reipublicæ*,[1] and as such are equally binding on king, and people too, as long as the terms are observed, and they continue the same body politic.

It is far from impossible to reconcile, if we do not suffer ourselves to be entangled in the mazes of metaphysic sophistry, the use both of a fixed rule and an occasional deviation, – the sacredness of an hereditary principle of succession in our government with a power of change in its application in cases of extreme emergency. Even in that extremity (if we take the measure of our rights by our exercise of them at the Revolution), the change is to be confined to the peccant part only, – to the part which produced the necessary deviation; and even then it is to be effected without a decomposition of the whole civil and political mass, for the purpose of originating a new civil order out of the first elements of society.

A state without the means of some change is without the means of its conservation. Without such means it might even risk the loss of that part of the Constitution which it wished the most religiously to preserve. The two principles of conservation and correction operated strongly at the two critical periods of the Restoration and Revolution, when England found itself without a king. At both those periods the nation had lost the bond of union in their ancient edifice: they did not, however, dissolve the whole fabric. On the contrary, in both cases they regenerated the deficient part of the old Constitution through the parts which were not im-

[1] As often, Burke provides his own paraphrase. In this case he may also have invented the tag itself.

paired. They kept these old parts exactly as they were, that the part recovered might be suited to them. They acted by the ancient organized states in the shape of their old organization, and not by the organic *moleculæ* of a disbanded people. At no time, perhaps, did the sovereign legislature manifest a more tender regard to that fundamental principle of British constitutional policy than at the time of the Revolution, when it deviated from the direct line of hereditary succession. The crown was carried somewhat out of the line in which it had before moved; but the new line was derived from the same stock. It was still a line of hereditary descent; still an hereditary descent in the same blood, though an hereditary descent qualified with Protestantism. When the legislature altered the direction, but kept the principle, they showed that they held it inviolable.

On this principle, the law of inheritance had admitted some amendment in the old time, and long before the era of the Revolution. Some time after the Conquest great questions arose upon the legal principles of hereditary descent. It became a matter of doubt whether the heir *per capita* or the heir *per stirpes* was to succeed[1]; but whether the heir *per capita* gave away when the heirdom *per stirpes* took place, or the Catholic heir when the Protestant was preferred, the inheritable principle survived with a sort of immortality through all transmigrations, –

Multosque per annos
Stat fortuna domûs, et avi numerantur avorum.[2]

This is the spirit of our Constitution, not only in its settled course, but in all its revolutions. Whoever came in, or however he came in, whether he obtained the crown by law or by force, the hereditary succession was either continued or adopted.

[1] The heir *per capita* would be a suitable member of the royal family, not necessarily a descendant of the latest monarch. The heir *per stirpes* would be that monarch's personal heir.

[2] 'The family fortunes stand through many years, reckoned by grandsires' grandsires.' Virgil, *Georgics*, iv. 208–9.

The gentlemen of the Society for Revolutions see nothing in that of 1688 but the deviation from the Constitution; and they take the deviation from the principle for the principle. They have little regard to the obvious consequences of their doctrine, though they may see that it leaves positive authority in very few of the positive institutions of this country. When such an unwarrantable maxim is once established, that no throne is lawful but the elective, no one act of the princes who preceded this era of fictitious election can be valid. Do these theorists mean to imitate some of their predecessors, who dragged the bodies of our ancient sovereigns out of the quiet of their tombs? Do they mean to attaint and disable backwards all the kings that have reigned before the Revolution, and consequently to stain the throne of England with the blot of a continual usurpation? Do they mean to invalidate, annul, or to call into question, together with the titles of the whole line of our kings, that great body of our statute law which passed under those whom they treat as usurpers? to annul laws of inestimable value to our liberties, – of as great value at least as any which have passed at or since the period of the Revolution? If kings who did not owe their crown to the choice of their people had no title to make laws, what will become of the statute *De tallagio non concedendo?* of the *Petition of Right?* of the act of *Habeas Corpus?*[1] Do these new doctors of the rights of men presume to assert that King James the Second, who came to the crown as next of blood, according to the rules of a then unqualified succession, was not to all intents and purposes a lawful king of England, before he had done any of those acts which were justly construed into an abdication of his crown? If he was not, much trouble in Parliament might have been saved at the period these gentlemen commemorate. But King James was a bad king with a good title, and not an usurper. The princes who succeeded according to the act of Parliament which settled the crown on the Electress Sophia[2]

---

[1] Statutes or instruments, of 1297, 1628 and 1679 respectively, limiting the powers of the crown.

[2] The Electress Sophia of Hanover, granddaughter of James I and mother of George I.

and on her descendants, being Protestants, came in as much by a title of inheritance as King James did. He came in according to the law, as it stood at his accession to the crown; and the princes of the House of Brunswick came to the inheritance of the crown, not by election, but by the law, as it stood at the several accessions, of Protestant descent and inheritance, as I hope I have shown sufficiently.

The law by which this royal family is specifically destined to the succession is the act of the 12th and 13th of King William.[1] The terms of this act bind 'us, and our *heirs*, and our *posterity*, to them, their *heirs*, and their *posterity*,' being Protestants, to the end of time, in the same words as the Declaration of Right had bound us to the heirs of King William and Queen Mary. It therefore secures both an hereditary crown and an hereditary allegiance. On what ground, except the constitutional policy of forming an establishment to secure that kind of succession which is to preclude a choice of the people forever, could the legislature have fastidiously rejected the fair and abundant choice which our own country presented to them, and searched in strange lands for a foreign princess, from whose womb the line of our future rulers were to derive their title to govern millions of men through a series of ages?

The Princess Sophia was named in the act of settlement of the 12th and 13th of King William, for a *stock* and root of *inheritance* to our kings, and not for her merits as a temporary administratrix of a power which she might not, and in fact did not, herself ever exercise. She was adopted for one reason, and for one only, – because, says the act, 'the most excellent Princess Sophia, Electress and Duchess Dowager of Hanover, is *daughter* of the most excellent Princess Elizabeth, late Queen of Bohemia, *daughter* of our late *sovereign lord* King James the First, of happy memory, and is hereby declared to be the next in *succession* in the Protestant line,' &c., &c.; 'and the crown shall continue to the *heirs* of her body, being Protestants.' This limitation was made by Parliament, that through the Princess Sophia an inheritable line not only was to be con-

[1] The Act of Settlement.

tinued in future, but (what they thought very material) that through her it was to be connected with the old stock of inheritance in King James the First; in order that the monarchy might preserve an unbroken unity through all ages, and might be preserved (with safety to our religion) in the old approved mode by descent, in which, if our liberties had been once endangered, they had often, through all storms and struggles of prerogative and privilege, been preserved. They did well. No experience has taught us that in any other course or method than that of an *hereditary crown* our liberties can be regularly perpetuated and preserved sacred as our *hereditary right*. An irregular, convulsive movement may be necessary to throw off an irregular, convulsive disease. But the course of succession is the healthy habit of the British Constitution. Was it that the legislature wanted, at the act for the limitation of the crown in the Hanoverian line, drawn through the female descendants of James the First, a due sense of the inconveniences of having two or three, or possibly more, foreigners in succession to the British throne? No! – they had a due sense of the evils which might happen from such foreign rule, and more than a due sense of them. But a more decisive proof cannot be given of the full conviction of the British nation that the principles of the Revolution did not authorize them to elect kings at their pleasure, and without any attention to the ancient fundamental principles of our government, than their continuing to adopt a plan of hereditary Protestant succession in the old line, with all the dangers and all the inconveniences of its being a foreign line full before their eyes, and operating with the utmost force upon their minds.

A few years ago I should be ashamed to overload a matter so capable of supporting itself by the then unnecessary support of any argument; but this seditious, unconstitutional doctrine is now publicly taught, avowed, and printed. The dislike I feel to revolutions, the signals for which have so often been given from pulpits, – the spirit of change that is gone abroad, – the total contempt which prevails with you, and may come to prevail with us, of all ancient institutions, when set in opposition to a present sense of convenience, or to the bent of a present inclination, – all these considerations make it not unadvisable, in my opinion, to call back our attention to the true principles of our own domestic laws, that you, my French friend, should begin to know, and that we should continue to cherish them. We ought not, on either side of the water, to suffer ourselves to be imposed upon by the counterfeit wares which some persons, by a double fraud, export to you in illicit bottoms, as raw commodities of British growth, though wholly alien to our soil, in order afterwards to smuggle them back again into this country, manufactured after the newest Paris fashion of an improved liberty.

The people of England will not ape the fashions they have never tried, nor go back to those which they have found mischievous on trial. They look upon the legal hereditary succession of their crown as among their rights, not as among their wrongs, – as a benefit, not as a grievance, – as a security for their liberty, not as a badge of servitude. They look on the frame of their commonwealth, *such as it stands*, to be of inestimable value; and they conceive the undisturbed succession of the crown to be a pledge of the stability and perpetuity of all the other members of our Constitution.

I shall beg leave, before I go any further, to take notice of some paltry artifices which the abettors of election as the only lawful title to the crown are ready to employ, in order to render the support of the just principles of our Constitution a task somewhat invidious. These sophisters substitute a fictitious cause, and feigned personages, in whose favor they suppose you engaged, whenever you defend the inheritable nature of the crown. It is common with them to dispute as if they were in a conflict with some of those exploded fanatics of slavery who formerly maintained, what I believe no creature now maintains, 'that the crown is held by divine, hereditary, and indefeasible right.' These old fanatics of single arbitrary power dogmatized as if hereditary royalty was the only lawful government in the world, – just as our new fanatics of popular arbitrary power maintain that a popular election is the sole lawful source of authority. The old prerogative enthusiasts, it is true, did speculate foolishly, and perhaps impiously too, as if monarchy had more of a divine sanction than any other mode of government, – and as if a right to govern by inheritance were in strictness *indefeasible* in every person who should be found in the succession to a throne, and under every circumstance, which no civil or political right can be. But an absurd opinion concerning the king's hereditary right to the crown does not prejudice one that is rational, and bottomed upon solid principles of law and policy. If all the absurd theories of lawyers and divines were to vitiate the objects in which they are conversant, we should have no law and no religion left in the world. But an absurd theory on one side of a question forms no justification for alleging a false fact or promulgating mischievous maxims on the other.

The second claim of the Revolution Society is 'a right of cashiering their governors for *misconduct.*' Perhaps the apprehensions our ancestors entertained of forming such a precedent as that 'of cashiering for misconduct' was the cause that the declaration of the act which implied the abdication of King James, was if it had any fault, rather too guarded and too circumstantial.* But all this guard, and all this accumulation of circumstances, serves to show the spirit of caution which predominated in the national councils, in a situation in which men irritated by oppression, and elevated by a triumph over it, are apt to abandon themselves to violent and extreme courses; it shows the anxiety of the great men who influenced the conduct of affairs at that great event to make the Revolution a parent of settlement, and not a nursery of future revolutions.

No government could stand a moment, if it could be blown down with anything so loose and indefinite as an opinion of '*misconduct.*' They who led at the Revolution grounded their

---

* 'That King James the Second, having endeavored to *subvert the Constitution* of the kingdom, by breaking the *original contract* between king and people, and, by the advice of Jesuits and other wicked persons, having violated the *fundamental* laws, and *having withdrawn himself out of the kingdom,* hath *abdicated* the government, and the throne is thereby *vacant.*' [Resolution of the Commons, 28 January, 1689. Burke's italics.]

virtual abdication of King James upon no such light and uncertain principle. They charged him with nothing less than a design, confirmed by a multitude of illegal overt acts, to *subvert the Protestant Church and State*, and their *fundamental*, unquestionable laws and liberties: they charged him with having broken the *original contract* between king and people. This was more than *misconduct*. A grave and overruling necessity obliged them to take the step they took, and took with infinite reluctance, as under that most rigorous of all laws. Their trust for the future preservation of the Constitution was not in future revolutions. The grand policy of all their regulations was to render it almost impracticable for any future sovereign to compel the states of the kingdom to have again recourse to those violent remedies. They left the crown, what in the eye and estimation of law it had ever been, perfectly irresponsible. In order to lighten the crown still further, they aggravated responsibility on ministers of state. By the statute of the first of King William, sess. 2d, called '*the act for declaring the rights and liberties of the subject, and for settling the succession of the crown*,' they enacted that the ministers should serve the crown on the terms of that declaration. They secured soon after the *frequent meetings of Parliament*, by which the whole government would be under the constant inspection and active control of the popular representative and of the magnates of the kingdom. In the next great constitutional act, that of the 12th and 13th of King William, for the further limitation of the crown, and *better* securing the rights and liberties of the subject, they provided 'that no pardon under the great seal of England should be pleadable to an impeachment by the Commons in Parliament.' The rule laid down for government in the Declaration of Right, the constant inspection of Parliament, the practical claim of impeachment, they thought infinitely a better security not only for their constitutional liberty, but against the vices of administration, than the reservation of a right so difficult in the practice, so uncertain in the issue, and often so mischievous in the co isequences, as that 'cashiering their governors.'

Dr Price, in this sermon,* condemns, very properly, the practice of gross adulatory addresses to kings. Instead of this fulsome style, he proposes that his Majesty should be told, on occasions of congratulation, that 'he is to consider himself as more properly the servant than the sovereign of his people.' For a compliment, this new form of address does not seem to be very soothing. Those who are servants in name, as well as in effect, do not like to be told of their situation, their duty, and their obligations. The slave in the old play tells his master, '*Hæc commemoratio est quasi exprobratio.*'[1] It is not pleasant as compliment; it is not wholesome as instruction. After all, if the king were to bring himself to echo this new kind of address, to adopt it in terms, and even to take the appellation of Servant of the People as his royal style, how either he or we should be much mended by it I cannot imagine. I have seen very assuming letters signed, 'Your most obedient, humble servant.' The proudest domination that ever was endured on earth took a title of still greater humility than that which is now proposed for sovereigns by the Apostle of Liberty. Kings and nations were trampled upon by the foot of one calling himself 'The Servant of Servants'; and mandates for deposing sovereigns were sealed with the signet of 'The Fisherman.'[2]

I should have considered all this as no more than a sort of flippant, vain discourse, in which, as in an unsavory fume, several persons suffer the spirit of liberty to evaporate, if it were not plainly in support of the idea, and a part of the scheme of 'cashiering kings for misconduct.' In that light it is worth some observation.

Kings, in one sense, are undoubtedly the servants of the people, because their power has no other rational end than that of the general advantage; but it is not true that they are, in the ordinary sense (by our Constitution, at least), anything like servants, – the essence of whose situation is to obey the commands of some other, and to be removable at pleasure. But

---

* P. 22, 23, 24.
[1] 'Such a reminder seems a reproach.' Terence, *Andria*, Act 1, sc. 1.
[2] Papal titles.

the king of Great Britain obeys no other person; all other persons are individually, and collectively too, under him, and owe to him a legal obedience. The law, which knows neither to flatter nor to insult, calls this high magistrate, not our servant, as this humble divine calls him, but '*our sovereign lord the king*'; and we, on our parts, have learned to speak only the primitive language of the law, and not the confused jargon of their Babylonian pulpits.

As he is not to obey us, but we are to obey the law in him, our Constitution has made no sort of provision towards rendering him, as a servant, in any degree responsible. Our Constitution knows nothing of a magistrate like the *Justicia* of Aragon, – nor of any court legally appointed, nor of any process legally settled, for submitting the king to the responsibility belonging to all servants. In this he is not distinguished from the commons and the lords, who, in their several public capacities, can never be called to an account for their conduct: although the Revolution Society chooses to assert, in direct opposition to one of the wisest and most beautiful parts of our Constitution, that 'a king is no more than the first servant of the public, created by it, *and responsible to it.*'

Ill would our ancestors at the Revolution have deserved their fame for wisdom, if they had found no security for their freedom, but in rendering their government feeble in its operations and precarious in its tenure, – if they had been able to contrive no better remedy against arbitrary power than civil confusion. Let these gentlemen state who that *representative* public is to whom they will affirm the king, as a servant, to be responsible. It will be then time enough for me to produce to them the positive statute law which affirms that he is not.

The ceremony of cashiering kings, of which these gentlemen talk so much at their ease, can rarely, if ever, be performed without force. It then becomes a case of war, and not of constitution. Laws are commanded to hold their tongues amongst arms; and tribunals fall to the ground with the peace they are no longer able to uphold. The Revolution of 1688 was obtained by a just war, in the only case in which any war, and much more a civil war, can be just. '*Justa bella quibus* NECESSARIA.'[1] The question of dethroning, or, if these gentlemen like the phrase better, 'cashiering kings,' will always be, as it has always been, an extraordinary question of state, and wholly out of the law: a question (like all other questions of state) of dispositions, and of means, and of probable consequences, rather than of positive rights. As it was not made for common abuses, so it is not to be agitated by common minds. The speculative line of demarcation, where obedience ought to end and resistance must begin, is faint, obscure, and not easily definable. It is not a single act or a single event which determines it. Governments must be abused and deranged indeed, before it can be thought of; and the prospect of the future must be as bad as the experience of the past. When things are in that lamentable condition, the nature of the disease is to indicate the remedy to those whom Nature has qualified to administer in extremities this critical, ambiguous, bitter potion to a distempered state. Times and occasions and provocations will teach their own lessons. The wise will determine from the gravity of the case; the irritable, from sensibility to oppression; the high-minded, from disdain and indignation at abusive power in unworthy hands; the brave and bold, from the love of honorable danger in a generous cause: but, with or without right, a revolution will be the very last resource of the thinking and the good.

The third head of right asserted by the pulpit of the Old Jewry, namely, the 'right to form a government for ourselves,' has, at least, as little countenance from anything done at the Revolution, either in precedent or principle, as the two first of their claims. The Revolution was made to preserve our *ancient* indisputable laws and liberties, and that *ancient* constitution of government which is our only security for law and liberty. If you are desirous of knowing the spirit of our Constitution, and the policy which predominated in that great period which has secured it to this hour, pray look for both

[1] 'To those to whom war is necessary it is just.' Livy, *Hist.* ix. 1.

in our histories, in our records, in our acts of Parliament and journals of Parliament, and not in the sermons of the Old Jewry, and the after-dinner toasts of the Revolution Society. In the former you will find other ideas and another language. Such a claim is as ill-suited to our temper and wishes as it is unsupported by any appearance of authority. The very idea of the fabrication of a new government is enough to fill us with disgust and horror. We wished at the period of the Revolution and do now wish, to derive all we possess as *an inheritance from our forefathers.* Upon that body and stock of inheritance we have taken care not to inoculate any scion alien to the nature of the original plant. All the reformations we have hitherto made have proceeded upon the principle of reference to antiquity; and I hope, nay, I am persuaded, that all those which possibly may be made hereafter will be carefully formed upon analogical precedent, authority, and example.

Our oldest reformation is that of Magna Charta. You will see that Sir Edward Coke, that great oracle of our law, and indeed all the great men who follow him, to Blackstone,* are industrious to prove the pedigree of our liberties.[1] They endeavor to prove that the ancient charter, the Magna Charta of King John, was connected with another positive charter from Henry the First, and that both the one and the other were nothing more than a reaffirmance of the still more ancient standing law of the kingdom. In the matter of fact, for the greater part, these authors appear to be in the right; perhaps not always: but if the lawyers mistake in some particulars, it proves my position still the more strongly; because it demonstrates the powerful prepossession towards antiquity with which the minds of all our lawyers and legislators, and of all the people whom they wish to influence, have been always filled, and the stationary policy of this kingdom in considering their most sacred rights and franchises as an *inheritance.*

In the famous law of the 3rd of Charles the First, called the *Petition of Right,* the Parliament says to the king, 'Your

* See Blackstone's Magna Charta, printed at Oxford, 1759.
[1] Sir Edward Coke (1552–1634) and Sir William Blackstone (1723–1780) were the leading exponents of constitutional law in their times.

subjects have *inherited* this freedom': claiming their franchises, not on abstract principles, 'as the rights of men,' but as the rights of Englishmen, and as a patrimony derived from their forefathers. Selden,[1] and the other profoundly learned men who drew this Petition of Right, were as well acquainted, at least, with all the general theories concerning the 'rights of men' as any of the discoursers in our pulpits or on your tribune: full as well as Dr Price, or as the Abbé Sieyès.[2] But, for reasons worthy of that practical wisdom which superseded their theoretic science, they preferred this positive, recorded, *hereditary* title to all which can be dear to the man and the citizen to that vague, speculative right which exposed their sure inheritance to be scrambled for and torn to pieces by every wild, litigious spirit.

The same policy pervades all the laws which have since been made for the preservation of our liberties. In the 1st of William and Mary, in the famous statute called the Declaration of Right, the two Houses utter not a syllable of 'a right to frame a government for themselves.' You will see that their whole care was to secure the religion, laws, and liberties that had been long possessed, and had been lately endangered. 'Taking* into their most serious consideration the *best* means for making such an establishment that their religion, laws, and liberties might not be in danger of being again subverted,' they auspicate all their proceedings by stating as some of those *best* means, 'in the *first place*,' to do 'as their *ancestors in like cases have usually* done for vindicating their *ancient* rights and liberties, to *declare*';– and then they pray the king and queen 'that it may be *declared* and enacted that *all and singular* the rights and liberties *asserted and declared* are the true *ancient* and indubitable rights and liberties of the people of this kingdom.'

You will observe, that, from Magna Charta to the Declaration of Right, it has been the uniform policy of our Constitu-

[1] John Selden (1584–1654) was, like Coke, a leading lawyer opponent of James I and Charles I.

[2] Emmanuel-Joseph Sieyès (1748–1836), a prominent member of the French Constituent Assembly.

* 1 W. and M.

tion to claim and assert our liberties as an *entailed inheritance*
derived to us from our forefathers, and to be transmitted to
our posterity, – as an estate specially belonging to the people
of this kingdom, without any reference whatever to any other
more general or prior right. By this means our Constitution
preserves an unity in so great a diversity of its parts. We have
an inheritable crown, an inheritable peerage, and a House of
Commons and a people inheriting privileges, franchises, and
liberties from a long line of ancestors.

This policy appears to me to be the result of profound
reflection, – or rather the happy effect of following Nature,
which is wisdom without reflection, and above it. A spirit of
innovation is generally the result of a selfish temper and confined views. People will not look forward to posterity, who
never look backward to their ancestors. Besides, the people of
England well know that the idea of inheritance furnishes a
sure principle of conservation, and a sure principle of transmission, without at all excluding a principle of improvement.
It leaves acquisition free; but it secures what it acquires.
Whatever advantages are obtained by a state proceeding on
these maxims are locked fast as in a sort of family settlement,
grasped as in a kind of mortmain forever. By a constitutional
policy working after the pattern of Nature, we receive, we
hold, we transmit our government and our privileges, in the
same manner in which we enjoy and transmit our property and
our lives. The institutions of policy, the goods of fortune, the
gifts of Providence, are handed down to us, and from us, in
the same course and order. Our political system is placed in a
just correspondence and symmetry with the order of the world,
and with the mode of existence decreed to a permanent body
composed of transitory parts, – wherein, by the disposition
of a stupendous wisdom, moulding together the great mysterious incorporation of the human race, the whole, at one time,
is never old or middle-aged or young, but, in a condition of
unchangeable constancy, moves on through the varied tenor
of perpetual decay, fall, renovation, and progression. Thus, by
preserving the method of Nature in the conduct of the state,
in what we improve we are never wholly new, in what we

retain we are never wholly obsolete. By adhering in this manner and on those principles to our forefathers, we are guided, not by the superstition of antiquarians, but by the spirit of philosophic analogy. In this choice of inheritance we have given to our frame of polity the image of a relation in blood: binding up the Constitution of our country with our dearest domestic ties; adopting our fundamental laws into the bosom of our family affections; keeping inseparable, and cherishing with the warmth of all their combined and mutually reflected charities, our state, our hearths, our sepulchres, and our altars.

Through the same plan of a conformity to Nature in our artificial institutions, and by calling in the aid of her unerring and powerful instincts to fortify the fallible and feeble contrivances of our reason, we have derived several other, and those no small benefits, from considering our liberties in the light of an inheritance. Always acting as if in the presence of canonized forefathers, the spirit of freedom, leading in itself to misrule and excess, is tempered with an awful gravity. This idea of a liberal descent inspires us with a sense of habitual native dignity, which prevents that upstart insolence almost inevitably adhering to and disgracing those who are the first acquirers of any distinction. By this means our liberty becomes a noble freedom. It carries an imposing and majestic aspect. It has a pedigree and illustrating ancestors. It has its bearings and its ensigns armorial. It has its gallery of portraits, its monumental inscriptions, its records, evidences, and titles. We procure reverence to our civil institutions on the principle upon which Nature teaches us to revere individual men: on account of their age, and on account of those from whom they are descended. All your sophisters cannot produce anything better adapted to preserve a rational and manly freedom than the course that we have pursued, who have chosen our nature rather than our speculations, our breasts rather than our inventions, for the great conservatories and magazines of our rights and privileges.

You might, if you pleased, have profited of our example,

and have given to your recovered freedom a correspondent dignity. Your privileges, though discontinued, were not lost to memory. Your Constitution, it is true, whilst you were out of possession, suffered waste and dilapidation; but you possessed in some parts the walls, and in all the foundations, of a noble and venerable castle. You might have repaired those walls; you might have built on those old foundations. Your Constitution was suspended before it was perfected; but you had the elements of a Constitution very nearly as good as could be wished. In your old states[1] you possessed that variety of parts corresponding with the various descriptions of which your community was happily composed; you had all that combination and all that opposition of interests, you had that action and counteraction, which, in the natural and in the political world, from the reciprocal struggle of discordant powers draws out the harmony of the universe. These opposed and conflicting interests, which you considered as so great a blemish in your old and in our present Constitution, interpose a salutary check to all precipitate resolutions. They render deliberation a matter, not of choice, but of necessity; they make all change a subject of *compromise*, which naturally begets moderation; they produce *temperaments*, preventing the sore evil of harsh, crude, unqualified reformations, and rendering all the headlong exertions of arbitrary power, in the few or in the many, forever impracticable. Through that diversity of members and interests, general liberty had as many securities as there were separate views in the several orders; whilst by pressing down the whole by the weight of a real monarchy, the separate parts would have been prevented from warping and starting from their allotted places.

You had all these advantages in your ancient states; but you chose to act as if you had never been moulded into civil society, and had everything to begin anew. You began ill, because you began by despising everything that belonged to you. You set up your trade without a capital. If the last

[1] i.e. the three estates which constituted the States-General, who were summoned in May 1789 for the first time since 1614 but were soon replaced by the Constituent Assembly.

generations of your country appeared without much lustre in your eyes, you might have passed them by, and derived your claims from a more early race of ancestors. Under a pious predilection for those ancestors, your imaginations would have realized in them a standard of virtue and wisdom beyond the vulgar practice of the hour; and you would have risen with the example to whose imitation you aspired. Respecting your forefathers, you would have been taught to respect yourselves. You would not have chosen to consider the French as a people of yesterday, as a nation of low-born, servile wretches until the emancipating year of 1789. In order to furnish, at the expense of your honor, an excuse to your apologists here for several enormities of yours, you would not have been content to be represented as a gang of Maroon slaves,[1] suddenly broke loose from the house of bondage, and therefore to be pardoned for your abuse of the liberty to which you were not accustomed, and were ill fitted. Would it not, my worthy friend, have been wiser to have you thought, what I for one always thought you, a generous and gallant nation, long misled to your disadvantage by your high and romantic sentiments of fidelity, honour, and loyalty; that events had been unfavorable to you, but that you were not enslaved through any illiberal or servile disposition; that, in your most devoted submission, you were actuated by a principle of public spirit; and that it was your country you worshipped, in the person of your king? Had you made it to be understood, that, in the delusion of this amiable error, you had gone further than your wise ancestors, – that you were resolved to resume your ancient privileges, whilst you preserved the spirit of your ancient and your recent loyalty and honor; or if, diffident of yourselves, and not clearly discerning the almost obliterated Constitution of your ancestors, you had looked to your neighbors in this land, who had kept alive the ancient principles and models of the old common law of Europe, meliorated and adapted to its present state, – by following wise examples you would have given new examples of wisdom to the world. You would have rendered the cause of liberty venerable in the eyes of every worthy

[1] Escaped slaves of the West Indies.

mind in every nation. You would have shamed despotism from the earth, by showing that freedom was not only reconcilable, but, as, when well disciplined, it is, auxiliary to law. You would have had an unoppressive, but a productive revenue. You would have had a flourishing commerce to feed it. You would have had a free Constitution, a potent monarchy a disciplined army, a reformed and venerated clergy, – a mitigated, but spirited nobility, to lead your virtue, not to overlay it; you would have had a liberal order of commons, to emulate and to recruit that nobility; you would have had a protected, satisfied, laborious, and obedient people, taught to seek and to recognize the happiness that is to be found by virtue in all conditions, – in which consists the true moral equality of mankind, and not in that monstrous fiction which, by inspiring false ideas and vain expectations into men destined to travel in the obscure walk of laborious life, serves only to aggravate and embitter that real inequality which it never can remove, and which the order of civil life establishes as much for the benefit of those whom it must leave in an humble state as those whom it is able to exalt to a condition more splendid, but not more happy. You had a smooth and easy career of felicity and glory laid open to you, beyond anything recorded in the history of the world; but you have shown that difficulty is good for man.

Compute your gains; see what is got by those extravagant and presumptuous speculations which have taught your leaders to despise all their predecessors, and all their contemporaries, and even to despise themselves, until the moment in which they became truly despicable. By following those false lights, France has bought undisguised calamities at a higher price than any nation has purchased the most unequivocal blessings. France has bought poverty by crime. France has not sacrificed her virtue to her interest; but she has abandoned her interest, that she might prostitute her virtue. All other nations have begun the fabric of a new government, or the reformation of an old, by establishing originally, or by enforcing with greater exactness, some rites or other of religion. All other people have laid the foundations of civil freedom in severer manners, and a system of a more austere and masculine morality. France, when she let loose the reins of regal authority, doubled the license of a ferocious dissoluteness in manners, and of an insolent irreligion in opinions and practices, – and has extended through all ranks of life, as if she were communicating some privilege, or laying open some secluded benefit, all the unhappy corruptions that usually were the disease of wealth and power. This is one of the new principles of equality in France.

France, by the perfidy of her leaders, has utterly disgraced the tone of lenient council in the cabinets of princes, and disarmed it of its most potent topics. She has sanctified the dark, suspicious maxims of tyrannous distrust, and taught kings to tremble at (what will hereafter be called) the delusive plausibilities of moral politicians. Sovereigns will consider those who advise them to place an unlimited confidence in their people as subverters of their thrones, – as traitors who aim at their destruction, by leading their easy good-nature, under specious pretences, to admit combinations of bold and faithless men into a participation of their power. This alone (if there were nothing else) is an irreparable calamity to you and to mankind. Remember that your Parliament of Paris told your king, that, in calling the states together, he had nothing to fear but the prodigal excess of their zeal in providing for the support of the throne. It is right that these men should hide their heads. It is right that they should bear their part in the ruin which their counsel has brought on their sovereign and their country. Such sanguine declarations tend to lull authority asleep, – to encourage it rashly to engage in perilous adventures of untried policy, – to neglect those provisions, preparations, and precautions which distinguish benevolence from imbecility, and without which no man can answer for the salutary effect of any abstract plan of government or of freedom. For want of these, they have seen the medicine of the state corrupted into its poison. They have seen the French rebel against a mild and lawful monarch, with more fury, outrage, and insult than ever any people has been known to rise against the most illegal usurper or the most sanguinary tyrant. Their resistance was made to concession; their revolt was from protection; their blow was aimed at a hand holding out graces, favors, and immunities.

This was unnatural. The rest is in order. They have found their punishment in their success. Laws overturned; tribunals subverted; industry without vigor; commerce expiring; the revenue unpaid, yet the people impoverished; a church pillaged, and a state not relieved; civil and military anarchy made the constitution of the kingdom; everything human and divine sacrificed to the idol of public credit, and national bankruptcy the consequence; and, to crown all, the paper securities of new, precarious, tottering power, the discredited paper securities of impoverished fraud and beggared rapine, held out as a currency for the support of an empire, in lieu of the two great recognized species that represent the lasting, conventional credit of mankind, which disappeared and hid themselves in the earth from whence they came, when the principle of property, whose creatures and representatives they are, was systematically subverted.

Were all these dreadful things necessary? Were they the inevitable results of the desperate struggle of determined patriots, compelled to wade through blood and tumult to the quiet shore of a tranquil and prosperous liberty? No! nothing like it. The fresh ruins of France, which shock our feelings wherever we can turn our eyes, are not the devastation of civil war: they are the sad, but instructive monuments of rash and ignorant counsel in time of profound peace. They are the display of inconsiderate and presumptuous, because unresisted and irresistible authority. The persons who have thus squandered away the precious treasure of their crimes, the persons who have made this prodigal and wild waste of public evils (the last stake reserved for the ultimate ransom of the state), have met in their progress with little, or rather with no opposition at all. Their whole march was more like a triumphal procession than the progress of a war. Their pioneers have gone before them, and demolished and laid everything level at their feet. Not one drop of *their* blood have they shed in the cause of the country they have ruined. They have made no sacrifices to their projects of greater consequence than their shoe-buckles, whilst they were imprisoning their king, murdering their fellow-citizens, and bathing in tears and plunging in poverty and distress thousands of worthy men and worthy families. Their cruelty has not even been the base result of fear. It has been the effect of their sense of perfect safety, in authorizing treasons, robberies, rapes, assassinations, slaughters, and burnings, throughout their harassed land. But the cause of all was plain from the beginning.

This unforced choice, this fond election of evil, would appear perfectly unaccountable, if we did not consider the composition of the National Assembly: I do not mean its formal constitution, which, as it now stands, is exceptionable enough, but the materials of which in a great measure it is composed, which is of ten thousand times greater consequence than all the formalities in the world. If we were to know nothing of this assembly but by its title and function, no colors could paint to the imagination anything more venerable. In that light, the mind of an inquirer, subdued by such an awful image as that of the virtue and wisdom of a whole people collected into one focus, would pause and hesitate in condemning things even of the very worst aspect. Instead of blamable, they would appear only mysterious. But no name, no power, no function, no artificial institution whatsoever, can make the men, of whom any system of authority is composed, any other than God, and Nature, and education, and their habits of life have made them. Capacities beyond these the people have not to give. Virtue and wisdom may be the objects of their choice; but their choice confers neither the one nor the other on those upon whom they lay their ordaining hands. They have not the engagement of Nature, they have not the promise of Revelation for any such powers.

After I had read over the list of the persons and descriptions elected into the *Tiers État*, nothing which they afterwards did could appear astonishing. Among them, indeed, I saw some of known rank, some of shining talents; but of any practical experience in the state not one man was to be found.

The best were only men of theory. But whatever the distinguished few may have been, it is the substance and mass of the body which constitutes its character, and must finally determine its direction. In all bodies, those who will lead must also, in a considerable degree, follow. They must conform their propositions to the taste, talent, and disposition of those whom they wish to conduct: therefore, if an assembly is viciously or feebly composed in a very great part of it, nothing but such a supreme degree of virtue as very rarely appears in the world, and for that reason cannot enter into calculation, will prevent the men of talents disseminated through it from becoming only the expert instruments of absurd projects. If, what is the more likely event, instead of that unusual degree of virtue, they should be actuated by sinister ambition and a lust of meretricious glory, then the feeble part of the assembly, to whom at first they conform, becomes, in its turn, the dupe and instrument of their designs. In this political traffic, the leaders will be obliged to bow to the ignorance of their followers, and the followers to become subservient to the worst designs of their leaders.

To secure any degree of sobriety in the propositions made by the leaders in any public assembly, they ought to respect, in some degree perhaps to fear, those whom they conduct. To be led any otherwise than blindly, the followers must be qualified, if not for actors, at least for judges; they must also be judges of natural weight and authority. Nothing can secure a steady and moderate conduct in such assemblies, but that the body of them should be respectably composed, in point of condition in life, of permanent property, of education, and of such habits as enlarge and liberalize the understanding.

In the calling of the States-General of France, the first thing that struck me was a great departure from the ancient course. I found the representation for the third estate composed of six hundred persons. They were equal in number to the representatives of both the other orders. If the orders were to act separately, the number would not, beyond the consideration of the expense, be of much moment. But when it became apparent that the three orders were to be melted down into one, the policy and necessary effect of this numerous representation became obvious. A very small desertion from either of the other two orders must throw the power of both into the hands of the third. In fact, the whole power of the state was soon resolved into that body. Its due composition became, therefore, of infinitely the greater importance.

Judge, Sir, of my surprise, when I found that a very great proportion of the Assembly (a majority, I believe, of the members who attended) was composed of practitioners in the law. It was composed, not of distinguished magistrates, who had given pledges to their country of their science, prudence, and integrity, – not of leading advocates, the glory of the bar, – not of renowned professors in universities, – but for the far greater part, as it must in such a number, of the inferior, unlearned, mechanical, merely instrumental members of the profession. There were distinguished exceptions; but the general composition was of obscure provincial advocates, of stewards of petty local jurisdictions, country attorneys, notaries, and the whole train of the ministers of municipal litigation, the fomenters and conductors of the petty war of village vexation. From the moment I read the list, I saw distinctly, and very nearly as it has happened, all that was to follow.

The degree of estimation in which any profession is held becomes the standard of the estimation in which the professors hold themselves. Whatever the personal merits of many individual lawyers might have been (and in many it was undoubtedly very considerable), in that military kingdom no part of the profession had been much regarded, except the highest of all, who often united to their professional offices great family splendor, and were invested with great power and authority. These certainly were highly respected, and even with no small degree of awe. The next rank was not much esteemed; the mechanical part was in a very low degree of repute.

Whenever the supreme authority is vested in a body so composed, it must evidently produce the consequences of supreme authority placed in the hands of men not taught habitually to respect themselves, – who had no previous fortune in character at stake, – who could not be expected to bear with moderation or to conduct with discretion a power which they themselves, more than any others, must be surprised to find in their hands. Who could flatter himself that these men, suddenly, and as it were by enchantment, snatched from the humblest rank of subordination, would not be intoxicated with their unprepared greatness? Who could conceive that men who are habitually meddling, daring, subtle, active, of litigious dispositions and unquiet minds, would easily fall back into their old condition of obscure contention, and laborious, low, and unprofitable chicane? Who could doubt but that, at any expense to the state, of which they understood nothing, they must pursue their private interests, which they understood but too well? It was not an event depending on chance or contingency. It was inevitable; it was necessary; it was planted in the nature of things. They must *join* (if their capacity did not permit them to *lead*) in any project which could procure to them a *litigious constitution*, – which could lay open to them those innumerable lucrative jobs which follow in the train of all great convulsions and revolutions in the state, and particularly in all great and violent permutations of property. Was it to be expected that they would attend to the stability of property, whose existence had always depended upon whatever rendered property questionable, ambiguous, and insecure? Their objects would be enlarged with their elevation; but their disposition, and habits, and mode of accomplishing their designs must remain the same.

Well! but these men were to be tempered and restrained by other descriptions, of more sober minds and more enlarged understandings. Were they, then, to be awed by the supereminent authority and awful dignity of a handful of country clowns, who have seats in that assembly, some of whom are said not to be able to read and write, – and by not a greater number of traders, who, though somewhat more instructed, and more conspicuous in the order of society, had never known anything beyond their counting-house? No! both these descriptions were more formed to be overborne and swayed by the intrigues and artifices of lawyers than to become their counterpoise. With such a dangerous disproportion, the whole must needs be governed by them.

To the faculty of law was joined a pretty considerable proportion of the faculty of medicine. This faculty had not, any more than that of the law, possessed in France its just estimation. Its professors, therefore, must have the qualities of men not habituated to sentiments of dignity. But supposing they had ranked as they ought to do, and as with us they do actually, the sides of sick-beds are not the academies for forming statesmen and legislators. Then came the dealers in stocks and funds, who must be eager, at any expense, to change their ideal paper wealth for the more solid substance of land. To these were joined men of other descriptions, from whom as little knowledge of or attention to the interests of a great state was to be expected, and as little regard to the stability of any institution, – men formed to be instruments, not controls. – Such, in general, was the composition of the *Tiers État* in the National Assembly; in which was scarcely to be perceived the slightest traces of what we call the natural landed interest of the country.

We know that the British House of Commons, without shutting its doors to any merit in any class, is, by the sure operation of adequate causes, filled with everything illustrious in rank, in descent, in hereditary and in acquired opulence, in cultivated talents, in military, civil, naval, and politic distinction, that the country can afford. But supposing, what hardly can be supposed as a case, that the House of Commons should be composed in the same manner with the *Tiers État* in France, – would this dominion of chicane be borne with patience, or even conceived without horror? God forbid I should insinuate anything derogatory to that profession which is another priesthood, administering the rights of sacred justice! But whilst I revere men in the functions which belong to them, and would do as much as one man can do to prevent their exclusion from any, I cannot, to flatter them, give the lie to Nature. They are good and useful in the composition; they must be mischievous, if they preponderate so as virtually to become the whole. Their very excellence in their peculiar functions may be far from a qualification for others. It cannot escape observation, that, when men are too much confined to professional and faculty habits, and, as it were, inveterate in the recurrent employment of that narrow circle, they are rather disabled than qualified for whatever depends on the knowledge of mankind, on experience in mixed affairs, on a comprehensive, connected view of the various, complicated, external, and internal interests which go to the formation of that multifarious thing called a State.

After all, if the House of Commons were to have an wholly professional and faculty composition, what is the power of the House of Commons, circumscribed and shut in by the immovable barriers of laws, usages, positive rules of doctrine and practice, counterpoised by the House of Lords, and every moment of its existence at the discretion of the crown to continue, prorogue, or dissolve us? The power of the House of Commons, direct or indirect, is, indeed, great: and long may it be able to preserve its greatness, and the spirit belonging to true greatness, at the full! – and it will do so, as long as it can keep the breakers of law in India from becoming the makers of law for England. The power, however, of the House of Commons, when least diminished, is as a drop of water in the ocean, compared to that residing in a settled majority of your National Assembly. That assembly, since the destruction of the orders, has no fundamental law, no strict convention, no respected usage to restrain it. Instead of finding themselves obliged to conform to a fixed constitution, they have a power to make a constitution which shall conform to their designs. Nothing in heaven or upon earth can serve as a control on them. What ought to be the heads, the hearts, the dispositions, that are qualified, or that dare, not only to make laws under a fixed constitution, but at one heat to strike out a totally new constitution for a great kingdom, and in every part of it, from the monarch on the throne to the vestry of a parish? But

'Fools rush in where angels fear to tread.'

In such a state of unbounded power, for undefined and undefinable purposes, the evil of a moral and almost physical inaptitude of the man to the function must be the greatest we can conceive to happen in the management of human affairs.

Having considered the composition of the third estate, as it stood in its original frame, I took a view of the representatives of the clergy. There, too, it appeared that full as little regard was had to the general security of property, or to the aptitude of the deputies for their public purposes, in the principles of their election. That election was so contrived as to send a very large proportion of mere country curates to the great and arduous work of new-modelling a state: men who never had seen the state so much as in a picture; men who knew nothing of the world beyond the bounds of an obscure village; who, immersed in hopeless poverty, could regard all property, whether secular or ecclesiastical, with no other eye than that of envy; among whom must be many who, for the smallest hope of the meanest dividend in plunder, would readily join in any attempts upon a body of wealth in which they could hardly look to have any share, except in a general scramble. Instead of balancing the power of the active chicaners in the other assembly, these curates must necessarily become the active coadjutors, or at best the passive instruments, of those by whom they had been habitually guided in their petty village concerns. They, too, could hardly be the most conscientious of their kind, who, presuming upon their incompetent understanding, could intrigue for a trust which led them from their natural relation to their flocks, and their natural spheres of action, to undertake the regeneration of kingdoms. This preponderating weight, being added to the force of the body of chicane in the *Tiers État*, completed that momentum of ignorance, rashness, presumption, and lust of plunder, which nothing has been able to resist.

To observing men it must have appeared from the beginning, that the majority of the third estate, in conjunction with such a deputation from the clergy as I have described, whilst it pursued the destruction of the nobility, would inevitably become subservient to the worst designs of individuals in that class. In the spoil and humiliation of their own order these individuals would possess a sure fund for the pay of their new followers. To squander away the objects which made the happiness of their fellows would be to them no sacrifice at all. Turbulent, discontented men of quality, in proportion as they are puffed up with personal pride and arrogance, generally despise their own order. One of the first symptoms they discover of a selfish and mischievous ambition is a profligate disregard of a dignity which they partake with others. To be attached to the subdivision, to love the little platoon we belong to in society, is the first principle (the germ, as it were) of public affections. It is the first link in the series by which we proceed towards a love to our country and to mankind. The interest of that portion of social arrangement is a trust in the hands of all those who compose it; and as none but bad men would justify it in abuse, none but traitors would barter it away for their own personal advantage.

There were, in the time of our civil troubles in England (I do not know whether you have any such in your Assembly in France), several persons, like the then Earl of Holland,[1] who by themselves or their families had brought an odium on the throne by the prodigal dispensation of its bounties towards them, who afterwards joined in the rebellions arising from the discontents of which they were themselves the cause: men who helped to subvert that throne to which they owed, some of them, their existence, others all that power which they employed to ruin their benefactor. If any bounds are set to the rapacious demands of that sort of people, or that others are permitted to partake in the objects they would engross, revenge and envy soon fill up the craving void that is left in their avarice. Confounded by the complication of distempered passions, their reason is disturbed; their views become vast and perplexed, – to others inexplicable, to themselves uncertain. They find, on all sides, bounds to their unprincipled ambition in any fixed order of things; but in the fog and haze

---

[1] Henry Rich (1560–1649), first Earl of Holland, changed sides several times during the Civil War and was finally beheaded by the parliamentary army.

of confusion all is enlarged, and appears without any limit.

When men of rank sacrifice all ideas of dignity to an ambition without a distinct object, and work with low instruments and for low ends, the whole composition becomes low and base. Does not something like this now appear in France? Does it not produce something ignoble and inglorious: a kind of meanness in all the prevalent policy; a tendency in all that is done to lower along with individuals all the dignity and importance of the state? Other revolutions have been conducted by persons who, whilst they attempted or affected changes in the commonwealth, sanctified their ambition by advancing the dignity of the people whose peace they troubled. They had long views. They aimed at the rule, not at the destruction of their country. They were men of great civil and great military talents, and if the terror, the ornament of their age. They were not like Jew brokers contending with each other who could best remedy with fraudulent circulation and depreciated paper the wretchedness and ruin brought on their country by their degenerate councils. The compliment made to one of the great bad men of the old stamp (Cromwell) by his kinsman, a favorite poet of that time, shows what it was he proposed, and what indeed to a great degree he accomplished in the success of his ambition:–

'Still as *you* rise, the *state*, exalted too,
Finds no distemper whilst't is changed by *you:*
Changed like the world's great scene, when without noise
The rising sun night's *vulgar* lights destroys.'[1]

These disturbers were not so much like men usurping power as asserting their natural place in society. Their rising was to illuminate and beautify the world. Their conquest over their competitors was by outshining them. The hand, that, like a destroying angel, smote the country, communicated to it the force and energy under which it suffered. I do not say (God forbid!) I do not say that the virtues of such men were to be taken as a balance to their crimes; but they were some cor-

[1] Edmund Waller (1606–1687), *Panegyric to My Lord Protector*, 1655.

rective to their effects. Such was, as I said, our Cromwell.
Such were your whole race of Guises, Condés, and Colignys.[1]
Such the Richelieus, who in more quiet times acted in the
spirit of a civil war. Such, as better men, and in a less dubious
cause, were your Henry the Fourth, and your Sully, though
nursed in civil confusions, and not wholly without some of
their taint. It is a thing to be wondered at, to see how very
soon France, when she had a moment to respire, recovered
and emerged from the longest and most dreadful civil war that
ever was known in any nation. Why? Because, among all their
massacres, they had not slain the *mind* in their country. A
conscious dignity, a noble pride, a generous sense of glory and
emulation, was not extinguished. On the contrary, it was
kindled and inflamed. The organs also of the state, however
shattered, existed. All the prizes of honor and virtue, all the
rewards, all the distinctions, remained. But your present
confusion, like a palsy, has attacked the fountain of life itself.
Every person in your country, in a situation to be actuated by
a principle of honor, is disgraced and degraded, and can
entertain no sensation of life, except in a mortified and
humiliated indignation. But this generation will quickly pass
away. The next generation of the nobility will resemble the
artificers and clowns, and money-jobbers, usurpers, and Jews,
who will be always their fellows, sometimes their masters.
Believe me, Sir, those who attempt to level never equalize.
In all societies consisting of various descriptions of citizens,
some description must be uppermost. The levellers, therefore,
only change and pervert the natural order of things: they load
the edifice of society by setting up in the air what the solidity
of the structure requires to be on the ground. The associations
of tailors and carpenters, of which the republic (of Paris, for
instance) is composed, cannot be equal to the situation into
which, by the worst of usurpations, an usurpation on the
prerogatives of Nature, you attempt to force them.

The Chancellor of France,[2] at the opening of the States,
said, in a tone of oratorial flourish, that all occupations were

[1] Turbulent French nobles of the sixteenth century.
[2] Jean-Sylvan Bailly (1736–1793), the astronomer.

honorable. If he meant only that no honest employment was disgraceful, he would not have gone beyond the truth. But in asserting that anything is honorable, we imply some distinction in its favor. The occupation of a hair-dresser, or of a working tallow-chandler, cannot be a matter of honor to any person – to say nothing of a number of other more servile employments. Such descriptions of men ought not to suffer oppression from the state; but the state suffers oppression, if such as they, either individually or collectively, are permitted to rule. In this you think you are combating prejudice, but you are at war with Nature.*

I do not, my dear Sir, conceive you to be of that sophistical, captious spirit, or of that uncandid dullness, as to require, for every general observation or sentiment, an explicit detail of the correctives and exceptions which reason will presume to be included in all the general propositions which come from reasonable men. You do not imagine that I wish to confine power, authority, and distinction to blood and names and titles. No, Sir. There is no qualification for government but virtue and wisdom, actual or presumptive. Wherever they are actually found, they have, in whatever state, condition, profession, or trade, the passport of Heaven to human place and honor. Woe to the country which would madly and impiously reject the service of the talents and virtues, civil, military, or religious, that are given to grace and to serve it; and would

---

* Ecclesiasticus, chap. xxxviii. ver. 24, 25. 'The wisdom of a learned man cometh by opportunity of leisure: and he that hath little business shall become wise. How can he get wisdom that holdeth the plough, and that glorieth in the goad; that driveth oxen, and is occupied in their labors, and whose talk is of bullocks?'

Ver. 27. 'So every carpenter and workmaster, that laboreth night and day,' &c.

Ver. 33. 'They shall not be sought for in public counsel, nor sit high in the congregation: they shall not sit on the judge's seat, nor understand the sentence of judgment: they cannot declare justice and judgment, and they shall not be found where parables are spoken.'

Ver. 34. 'But they will maintain the state of the world.'

I do not determine whether this book be canonical, as the Gallican Church (till lately) has considered it, or apocryphal, as here it is taken. I am sure it contains a great deal of sense and truth.

condemn to obscurity everything formed to diffuse lustre and glory around a state! Woe to that country, too, that, passing into the opposite extreme, considers a low education, a mean, contracted view of things, a sordid, mercenary occupation, as a preferable title to command! Everything ought to be open – but not indifferently to every man. No rotation, no appointment by lot, no mode of election operating in the spirit of sortition or rotation, can be generally good in a government conversant in extensive objects; because they have no tendency, direct or indirect, to select the man with a view to the duty, or to accommodate the one to the other. I do not hesitate to say that the road to eminence and power, from obscure condition, ought not to be made too easy, nor a thing too much of course. If rare merit be the rarest of all rare things, it ought to pass through some sort of probation. The temple of honor ought to be seated on an eminence. If it be opened through virtue, let it be remembered, too, that virtue is never tried but by some difficulty and some struggle.

Nothing is a due and adequate representation of a state, that does not represent its ability, as well as its property. But as ability is a vigorous and active principle, and as property is sluggish, inert, and timid, it never can be safe from the invasions of ability, unless it be, out of all proportion, predominant in the representation. It must be represented, too, in great masses of accumulation, or it is not rightly protected. The characteristic essence of property, formed out of the combined principles of its acquisition and conservation, is to be *unequal.* The great masses, therefore, which excite envy, and tempt rapacity, must be put out of the possibility of danger. Then they form a natural rampart about the lesser properties in all their gradations. The same quantity of property which is by the natural course of things divided among many has not the same operation. Its defensive power is weakened as it is diffused. In this diffusion each man's portion is less than what, in the eagerness of his desires, he may flatter himself to obtain by dissipating the accumulations of others. The plunder of the few would, indeed, give but a share inconceivably small in the distribution to the many. But the many are not capable of making this calculation; and those who lead them to rapine never intend this distribution.

The power of perpetuating our property in our families is one of the most valuable and interesting circumstances belonging to it, and that which tends the most to the perpetuation of society itself. It makes our weakness subservient to our virtue; it grafts benevolence even upon avarice. The possessors of family wealth, and of the distinction which attends hereditary possession (as most concerned in it), are the natural securities for this transmission. With us the House of Peers is formed upon this principle. It is wholly composed of hereditary property and hereditary distinction, and made, therefore, the third of the legislature, and, in the last event, the sole judge of all property in all its subdivisions. The House of Commons, too, though not necessarily, yet in fact, is always so composed, in the far greater part. Let those large proprietors be what they will (and they have their chance of being amongst the best), they are, at the very worst, the ballast in the vessel of the commonwealth. For though hereditary wealth, and the rank which goes with it, are too much idolized by creeping sycophants, and the blind, abject admirers of power, they are too rashly slighted in shallow speculations of the petulant, assuming, short-sighted coxcombs of philosophy. Some decent, regulated preëminence, some preference (not exclusive appropriation) given to birth, is neither unnatural, nor unjust, nor impolitic.

It is said that twenty-four millions ought to prevail over two hundred thousand. True; if the constitution of a kingdom be a problem of arithmetic. This sort of discourse does well enough with the lamp-post for its second: to men who *may* reason calmly it is ridiculous. The will of the many, and their interest, must very often differ; and great will be the difference when they make an evil choice. A government of five hundred country attorneys and obscure curates is not good for twenty-four millions of men, though it were chosen by eight-and-forty millions; nor is it the better for being guided by a dozen of persons of quality who have betrayed their trust in order to obtain that power. At present, you seem in everything to have strayed out of the high road of Nature. The property of France does not govern it. Of course property is destroyed, and rational liberty has no existence. All you have got for the present is a paper circulation, and a stock-jobbing constitution: and as to the future, do you seriously think that the territory of France, upon the republican system of eighty-three independent municipalities (to say nothing of the parts that compose them), can ever be governed as one body, or can ever be set in motion by the impulse of one mind? When the National Assembly has completed its work, it will have accomplished its ruin. These commonwealths will not long bear a state of subjection to the republic of Paris. They will not bear that this one body should monopolize the captivity of the king, and the dominion over the assembly calling itself national. Each will keep its own portion of the spoil of the Church to itself; and it will not suffer either that spoil, or the more just fruits of their industry, or the natural produce of their soil, to be sent to swell the insolence or pamper the luxury of the mechanics of Paris. In this they will see none of the equality, under the pretence of which they have been tempted to throw off their allegiance to their sovereign, as well as the ancient constitution of their country. There can be no capital city in such a constitution as they have lately made. They have forgot, that, when they framed democratic governments, they had virtually dismembered their country. The person whom they persevere in calling king has not power left to him by the hundredth part sufficient to hold together this collection of republics. The republic of Paris will endeavor, indeed, to complete the debauchery of the army, and illegally to perpetuate the Assembly, without resort to its constituents, as the means of continuing its despotism. It will make efforts, by becoming the heart of a boundless paper circulation, to draw everything to itself: but in vain. All this policy in the end will appear as feeble as it is now violent.

If this be your actual situation, compared to the situation to which you were called, as it were by the voice of God and man, I cannot find it in my heart to congratulate you on the choice you have made, or the success which has attended your endeavors. I can as little recommend to any other nation a conduct grounded on such principles and productive of such effects. That I must leave to those who can see further into your affairs than I am able to do, and who best know how far your actions are favorable to their designs. The gentlemen of the Revolution Society, who were so early in their congratulations, appear to be strongly of opinion that there is some scheme of politics relative to this country, in which your proceedings may in some way be useful. For your Dr Price, who seems to have speculated himself into no small degree of fervor upon this subject, addresses his auditors in the following very remarkable words:– 'I cannot conclude without recalling *particularly* to your recollection a consideration which I have *more than once alluded to*, and which probably your thoughts have *been all along anticipating;* a consideration with which *my mind is impressed more than I can express:* I mean the consideration of the *favorableness of the present times to all exertions in the cause of liberty.*'

It is plain that the mind of this *political* preacher was at the time big with some extraordinary design; and it is very probable that the thoughts of his audience, who understood him better than I do, did all along run before him in his reflection, and in the whole train of consequences to which it led.

Before I read that sermon, I really thought I had lived in a free country; and it was an error I cherished, because it gave me a greater liking to the country I lived in. I was, indeed, aware that a jealous, ever-waking vigilance, to guard the treasure of our liberty, not only from invasion, but from decay and corruption, was our best wisdom and our first duty. However, I considered that treasure rather as a possession to be secured than as a prize to be contended for. I did not discern how the present time came to be so very favorable to all *exertions* in the cause of freedom. The present time differs from any other only by the circumstances of what is doing in France. If the example of that nation is to have an influence on this, I can easily conceive why some of their proceedings which have an unpleasant aspect, and are not quite reconcilable to humanity, generosity, good faith, and justice, are palliated with so much milky good-nature towards the actors, and borne with so much heroic fortitude towards the sufferers. It is certainly not prudent to discredit the authority of an example we mean to follow. But allowing this, we are led to a very natural question:– What is that cause of liberty, and what are those exertions in its favor, to which the example of France is so singularly auspicious? Is our monarchy to be annihilated, with all the laws, all the tribunals, and all the ancient corporations of the kingdom? Is every landmark of the country to be done away in favor of a geometrical and arithmetical constitution? Is the House of Lords to be voted useless? Is Episcopacy to be abolished? Are the Church lands to be sold to Jews and jobbers, or given to bribe new-invented municipal republics into a participation in sacrilege? Are all the taxes to be voted grievances, and the revenue reduced to a patriotic contribution or patriotic presents? Are silver shoe-buckles to be substituted in the place of the land-tax and the malt-tax, for the support of the naval strength of this kingdom? Are all orders, ranks, and distinctions to be confounded, that out of universal anarchy, joined to national bankruptcy, three or four thousand democracies should be formed into eighty-three, and that they may all, by some sort of unknown attractive power, be organized into one? For this great end is the army to be seduced from its discipline and its fidelity, first by every kind of debauchery, and then by the terrible precedent of a donative in the increase of pay? Are the curates to be seduced from their bishops by holding out to them the delusive hope of dole out of the spoils of their own order? Are the citizens of London to be drawn from their allegiance by feeding them at the expense of their fellow-subjects? Is a compulsory paper currency to be substituted in the place of the legal coin of this kingdom? Is what remains of the plundered stock of public revenue to be employed in the wild project of maintaining two armies to watch over and to fight with each other? If these are the ends and means of the Revolution Society, I admit they are well

assorted; and France may furnish them for both with precedents in point.

I see that your example is held out to shame us. I know that
we are supposed a dull, sluggish race, rendered passive by
finding our situation tolerable, and prevented by a mediocrity
of freedom from ever attaining to its full perfection. Your
leaders in France began by affecting to admire, almost to
adore, the British Constitution; but as they advanced, they
came to look upon it with a sovereign contempt. The friends
of your National Assembly amongst us have full as mean an
opinion of what was formerly thought the glory of their
country. The Revolution Society has discovered that the
English nation is not free. They are convinced that the inequality in our representation is a 'defect in our Constitution
so gross and palpable as to make it excellent chiefly in *form and
theory*';*– that a representation in the legislature of a kingdom
is not only the basis of all constitutional liberty in it, but of
'*all legitimate government;* that without it a *government* is
nothing but an *usurpation*';– that, 'when the representation is
partial, the kingdom possesses liberty only *partially;* and if
extremely partial, it gives only a *semblance;* and if not only
extremely partial, but corruptly chosen, it becomes a *nuisance.*'
Dr Price considers this inadequacy of representation as our
fundamental grievance; and though, as to the corruption of this
semblance of representation, he hopes it is not yet arrived to
its full perfection of depravity, he fears that 'nothing will be
done towards gaining for us this *essential blessing,* until some
great abuse of power again provokes our resentment, or some
great calamity again alarms our fears, or perhaps till the
acquisition of a *pure and equal representation by other countries,*
whilst we are *mocked* with the *shadow,* kindles our shame.' To
this he subjoins a note in these words:– 'A representation
chosen chiefly by the Treasury, and a *few* thousands of the
dregs of the people, who are generally paid for their votes.'

You will smile here at the consistency of those democratists
who, when they are not on their guard, treat the humbler part
of the community with the greatest contempt, whilst, at the

* Discourse on the Love of our Country, 3rd edit. p. 39.

same time, they pretend to make them the depositories of all power. It would require a long discourse to point out to you the many fallacies that lurk in the generality and equivocal nature of the terms 'inadequate representation.' I shall only say here, in justice to that old-fashioned Constitution under which we have long prospered, that our representation has been found perfectly adequate to all the purposes for which a representation of the people can be desired or devised. I defy the enemies of our Constitution to show the contrary. To detail the particulars in which it is found so well to promote its ends would demand a treatise on our practical Constitution. I state here the doctrine of the revolutionists, only that you and others may see what an opinion these gentlemen entertain of the Constitution of their country, and why they seem to think that some great abuse of power, or some great calamity, as giving a chance for the blessing of a Constitution according to their ideas, would be much palliated to their feelings; you see *why they* are so much enamored of your fair and equal representation, which being once obtained, the same effects might follow. You see they consider our House of Commons as only 'a semblance,' 'a form,' 'a theory,' 'a shadow,' 'a mockery,' perhaps 'a nuisance.'

These gentlemen value themselves on being systematic, and not without reason. They must therefore look on this gross and palpable defect of representation, this fundamental grievance, (so they call it), as a thing not only vicious in itself, but as rendering our whole government absolutely *illegitimate*, and not at all better than a downright *usurpation*. Another revolution, to get rid of this illegitimate and usurped government, would of course by perfectly justifiable, if not absolutely necessary. Indeed, their principle, if you observe it with any attention, goes much further than to an alteration in the election of the House of Commons; for, if popular representation, or choice, is necessary to the *legitimacy* of all government, the House of Lords is, at one stroke, bastardized and corrupted in blood. That House is no representative of the people at all, even in 'semblance' or 'in form.' The case of the crown is altogether as bad. In vain the crown may endeavor to screen itself against these gentlemen by the authority of the establishment made on the Revolution. The Revolution, which is resorted to for a title, on their system, wants a title itself. The Revolution is built, according to their theory, upon a basis not more solid than our present formalities, as it was made by a House of Lords not representing any one but themselves, and by a House of Commons exactly such as the present, that is, as they term it, by a mere 'shadow and mockery' of representation.

Something they must destroy, or they seem to themselves to exist for no purpose. One set is for destroying the civil power through the ecclesiastical; another for demolishing the ecclesiastic through the civil. They are aware that the worst consequences might happen to the public in accomplishing this double ruin of Church and State; but they are so heated with their theories, that they give more than hints that this ruin, with all the mischiefs that must lead to it and attend it, and which to themselves appear quite certain, would not be unacceptable to them, or very remote from their wishes. A man amongst them of great authority, and certainly of great talents, speaking of a supposed alliance between Church and State, says, 'Perhaps *we must wait for the fall of the civil powers*, before this most unnatural alliance be broken. Calamitous, no doubt, will that time be. But what convulsion in the political world ought to be a subject of lamentation, if it be attended with so desirable an effect?'[1] You see with what a steady eye these gentlemen are prepared to view the greatest calamities which can befall their country!

It is no wonder, therefore, that, with these ideas of everything in their Constitution and government at home, either in Church or State, as illegitimate and usurped, or at best as a vain mockery, they look abroad with an eager and passionate enthusiasm. Whilst they are possessed by these notions, it is vain to talk to them of the practice of their ancestors, the fundamental laws of their country, the fixed form of a Constitution whose merits are confirmed by the solid test of long

[1] Joseph Priestley (1733–1804), pioneer chemist, Unitarian and radical pamphleteer, *A History of the Corruptions of Christianity* (1782). The italics are Burke's.

experience and an increasing public strength and national prosperity. They despise experience as the wisdom of unlettered men; and as for the rest, they have wrought under ground a mine that will blow up, at one grand explosion, all examples of antiquity, all precedents, charters, and acts of Parliament. They have 'the rights of men.' Against these there can be no prescription; against these no argument is binding: these admit no temperament and no compromise: anything withheld from their full demand is so much of fraud and injustice. Against these their rights of men let no government look for security in the length of its continuance, or in the justice and lenity of its administration. The objections of these speculatists, if its forms do not quadrate with their theories, are as valid against such an old and beneficent government as against the most violent tyranny or the greenest usurpation. They are always at issue with governments, not on a question of abuse, but a question of competency and a question of title. I have nothing to say to the clumsy subtilty of their political metaphysics. Let them be their amusement in the schools.

> *Illa* se jactet in aula
> Æolus, et clauso ventorum carcere regnet.[1]

But let them not break prison to burst like a Levanter,[2] to sweep the earth with their hurricane, and to break up the fountains of the great deep to overwhelm us!

Far am I from denying in theory, full as far is my heart from withholding in practice (if I were of power to give or to withhold), the *real* rights of men. In denying their false claims of right, I do not mean to injure those which are real, and are such as their pretended rights would totally destroy. If civil society be made for the advantage of man, all the advantages for which it is made become his right. It is an institution of beneficence; and law itself is only beneficence acting by a rule. Men have a right to live by that rule; they have a right to justice, as between their fellows, whether their fellows are in politic

[1] 'Let Æolus reign and rule the winds in captivity.' Virgil, *Aeneid*, i. 140.
[2] The strong east wind of the Mediterranean.

function or in ordinary occupation. They have a right to the fruits of their industry, and to the means of making their industry fruitful. They have a right to the acquisitions of their parents, to the nourishment and improvement of their off-spring, to instruction in life and to consolation in death. Whatever each man can separately do, without trespassing upon others, he has a right to do for himself; and he has a right to a fair portion of all which society, with all its combinations of skill and force, can do in his favor. In this partnership all men have equal rights; but not to equal things. He that has but five shillings in the partnership has as good a right to it as he that has five hundred pounds has to his larger proportion; but he has not a right to an equal dividend in the product of the joint stock. And as to the share of power, authority, and direction which each individual ought to have in the management of the state, that I must deny to be amongst the direct original rights of man in civil society; for I have in my contemplation the civil social man, and no other. It is a thing to be settled by convention.

If civil society be the offspring of convention, that convention must be its law. That convention must limit and modify all the descriptions of constitution which are formed under it. Every sort of legislative, judicial, or executory power are its creatures. They can have no being in any other state of things; and how can any man claim, under the conventions of civil society, rights which do not so much as suppose its existence – rights which are absolutely repugnant to it? One of the first motives to civil society, and which becomes one of its fundamental rules, is, *that no man should be judge in his own cause.* By this each person has at once divested himself of the first fundamental right of uncovenanted man that is, to judge for himself, and to assert his own cause. He abdicates all right to be his own governor. He inclusively, in a great measure, abandons the right of self-defence, the first law of Nature. Men cannot enjoy the rights of an uncivil and of a civil state together. That he may obtain justice, he gives up his right of determining what it is in points the most essential to him. That he may secure some liberty, he makes a surrender in trust of the whole of it.

Government is not made in virtue of natural rights, which may and do exist in total independence of it – and exist in much greater clearness, and in a much greater degree of abstract perfection: but their abstract perfection is their practical defect. By having a right to everything they want everything. Government is a contrivance of human wisdom to provide for human *wants*. Men have a right that these wants should be provided for by this wisdom. Among these wants is to be reckoned the want, out of civil society, of a sufficient restraint upon their passions. Society requires not only that the passions of individuals should be subjected, but that even in the mass and body, as well as in the individuals, the inclinations of men should frequently be thwarted, their will controlled, and their passions brought into subjection. This can only be done *by a power out of themselves*, and not, in the exercise of its function, subject to that will and to those passions which it is its office to bridle and subdue. In this sense the restraints on men, as well as their liberties, are to be reckoned among their rights. But as the liberties and the restrictions vary with times and circumstances, and admit of infinite modifications, they cannot be settled upon any abstract rule; and nothing is so foolish as to discuss them upon that principle.

The moment you abate anything from the full rights of men each to govern himself, and suffer any artificial, positive limitation upon those rights, from that moment the whole organization of government becomes a consideration of convenience. This it is which makes the constitution of a state, and the due distribution of its powers, a matter of the most delicate and complicated skill. It requires a deep knowledge of human nature and human necessities, and of the things which facilitate or obstruct the various ends which are to be pursued by the mechanism of civil institutions. The state is to have recruits to its strength and remedies to its distempers. What is the use of discussing a man's abstract right to food or medicine? The question is upon the method of procuring and administering

them. In that deliberation I shall always advise to call in the aid
of the farmer and the physician, rather than the professor of
metaphysics.

The science of constructing a commonwealth, or renovating
it, or reforming it, is like every other experimental science, not
to be taught *a priori*. Nor is it a short experience that can
instruct us in that practical science; because the real effects of
moral causes are not always immediate, but that which in the
first instance is prejudicial may be excellent in its remoter
operation, and its excellence may arise even from the ill
effects it produces in the beginning. The reverse also happens;
and very plausible schemes, with very pleasing commence-
ments, have often shameful and lamentable conclusions. In
states there are often some obscure and almost latent causes,
things which appear at first view of little moment, on which a
very great part of its prosperity or adversity may most essentially depend. The science of government being, therefore, so
practical in itself, and intended for such practical purposes, a
matter which requires experience, and even more experience
than any person can gain in his whole life, however sagacious
and observing he may be, it is with infinite caution that any
man ought to venture upon pulling down an edifice which has
answered in any tolerable degree for ages the common purposes
of society, or on building it up again without having models and
patterns of approved utility before his eyes.

These metaphysic rights entering into common life, like
rays of light which pierce into a dense medium, are, by the
laws of Nature, refracted from their straight line. Indeed, in
the gross and complicated mass of human passions and concerns, the primitive rights of men undergo such a variety of
refractions and reflections that it becomes absurd to talk of
them as if they continued in the simplicity of their original
direction. The nature of man is intricate; the objects of society
are of the greatest possible complexity: and therefore no
simple disposition or direction of power can be suitable either
to man's nature or to the quality of his affairs. When I hear the
simplicity of contrivance aimed at and boasted of in any new
political constitutions, I am at no loss to decide that the arti-

ficers are grossly ignorant of their trade or totally negligent of their duty. The simple governments are fundamentally defective, to say no worse of them. If you were to contemplate society in but one point of view all these simple modes of polity are infinitely captivating. In effect each would answer its single end much more perfectly than the more complex is able to attain all its complex purposes. But it is better that the whole should be imperfectly and anomalously answered than that while some parts are provided for with great exactness, others might be totally neglected, or perhaps materially injured, by the over-care of a favorite member.

The pretended rights of these theorists are all extremes; and in proportion as they are metaphysically true, they are morally and politically false. The rights of men are in a sort of *middle*, incapable of definition, but not impossible to be discerned. The rights of men in governments are their advantages; and these are often in balances between differences of good – in compromises sometimes between good and evil, and sometimes between evil and evil. Political reason is a computing principle: adding, subtracting, multiplying, and dividing, morally, and not metaphysically or mathematically, true moral denominations.

By these theorists the right of the people is almost always sophistically confounded with their power. The body of the community, whenever it can come to act, can meet with no effectual resistance; but till power and right are the same, the whole body of them has no right inconsistent with virtue, and the first of all virtues, prudence. Men have no right to what is not reasonable, and to what is not for their benefit; for though a pleasant writer said, '*Liceat perire poetis*,' when one of them, in cold blood, is said to have leaped into the flames of a volcanic revolution, '*ardentum frigidus Ætnam insiluit*,'[1] I consider such a frolic rather as an unjustifiable poetic licence than as one of the franchises of Parnassus; and whether he

[1] Horace writes in *De Arte Poetica* 464–66, 'Empedocles, desiring to be thought immortal, coolly threw himself into burning Etna (ardentum frigidus Aetnam insiluit); poets may kill themselves if they wish (liceat perire poetis).'

were poet, or divine, or politician, that chose to exercise this kind of right, I think that more wise, because more charitable, thoughts would urge me rather to save the man than to preserve his brazen slippers as the monuments of his folly.

The kind of anniversary sermons to which a great part of what I write refers, if men are not shamed out of their present course, in commemorating the fact, will cheat many out of the principles and deprive them of the benefits of the Revolution they commemorate. I confess to you, Sir, I never liked this continual talk of resistance and revolution, or the practice of making the extreme medicine of the Constitution its daily bread. It renders the habit of society dangerously valetudinary; it is taking periodical doses of mercury sublimate, and swallowing down repeated provocatives of cantharides to our love of liberty.[1]

This distemper of remedy, grown habitual, relaxes and wears out, by a vulgar and prostituted use, the spring of that spirit which is to be exerted on great occasions. It was in the most patient period of Roman servitude that themes of tyrannicide made the ordinary exercise of boys at school – *cum perimit sœvos classis numerosa tyrannos.*[2] In the ordinary state of things, it produces in a country like ours the worst effects, even on the cause of that liberty which it abuses with the dissoluteness of an extravagant speculation. Almost all the high-bred republicans of my time have, after a short space, become the most decided, thorough-paced courtiers; they soon left the business of a tedious, moderate, but practical resistance, to those of us whom, in the pride and intoxication of their theories, they have slighted as not much better than Tories. Hypocrisy, of course, delights in the most sublime speculations; for, never intending to go beyond speculation, it costs nothing to have it magnificent. But even in cases where rather levity than fraud was to be suspected in these ranting speculations, the issue has been much the same. These pro-

[1] Patent remedies.
[2] 'While a large class is attacking cruel tyrants.' Juvenal, *Satires*, vii. 151.

fessors, finding their extreme principles not applicable to cases which call only for a qualified, or, as I may say, civil and legal resistance, in such cases employ no resistance at all. It is with them a war or a revolution, or it is nothing. Finding their schemes of politics not adapted to the state of the world in which they live, they often come to think lightly of all public principle, and are ready, on their part, to abandon for a very trivial interest what they find of very trivial value. Some, indeed, are of more steady and persevering natures; but these are eager politicians out of Parliament, who have little to tempt them to abandon their favorite projects. They have some change in the Church or State, or both, constantly in their view. When that is the case, they are always bad citizens, and perfectly unsure connections. For, considering their speculative designs as of infinite value, and the actual arrangement of the state as of no estimation, they are, at best, indifferent about it. They see no merit in the good, and no fault in the vicious management of public affairs; they rather rejoice in the latter, as more propitious to revolution. They see no merit or demerit in any man, or any action, or any political principle, any further than as they may forward or retard their design of change; they therefore take up, one day, the most violent and stretched prerogative, and another time the wildest democratic ideas of freedom, and pass from the one to the other without any sort of regard to cause, to person, or to party.

In France you are now in the crisis of a revolution, and in the transit from one form of government to another: you cannot see that character of men exactly in the same situation in which we see it in this country. With us it is militant, with you it is triumphant; and you know how it can act, when its power is commensurate to its will. I would not be supposed to confine those observations to any description of men, or to comprehend all men of any description within them – no, far from it! I am as incapable of that injustice as I am of keeping terms with those who profess principles of extremes, and who, under the name of religion, teach little else than wild and dangerous politics. The worst of these politics of revolution is this: they temper and harden the breast, in order to prepare it for the desperate strokes which are sometimes used in extreme occasions. But as these occasions may never arrive, the mind receives a gratuitous taint; and the moral sentiments suffer not a little, when no political purpose is served by the depravation. This sort of people are so taken up with their theories about the rights of man, that they have totally forgot his nature. Without opening one new avenue to the understanding, they have succeeded in stopping up those that lead to the heart. They have perverted in themselves, and in those that attend to them, all the well-placed sympathies of the human breast.

This famous sermon of the Old Jewry breathes nothing but this spirit through all the political part. Plots, massacres, assassinations, seem to some people a trivial price for obtaining a revolution. A cheap, bloodless reformation, a guiltless liberty, appear flat and vapid to their taste. There must be a great change of scene; there must be a magnificent stage effect; there must be a grand spectacle to rouse the imagination, grown torpid with the lazy enjoyment of sixty years' security, and the still unanimating repose of public prosperity. The preacher found them all in the French Revolution. This inspires a juvenile warmth through his whole frame. His enthusiasm kindles as he advances; and when he arrives at his peroration, it is in a full blaze. Then viewing, from the Pisgah of his pulpit, the free, moral, happy, flourishing, and glorious state of France, as in a bird-eye landscape of a promised land, he breaks out into the following rapture:—

'What an eventful period is this! I am *thankful* that I have lived to it; I could almost say, *Lord, now lettest thou thy servant depart in peace, for mine eyes have seen thy salvation.* – I have lived to see a *diffusion* of knowledge which has undermined superstition and error. – I have lived to see *the rights of men* better understood than ever, and nations panting for liberty which seemed to have lost the idea of it. – I have lived to see *thirty millions of people*, indignant and resolute, spurning at slavery, and demanding liberty with an irresistible voice; *their king led in triumph, and an arbitrary monarch surrendering himself to his subjects.*'*

* Another of these reverend gentlemen, who was witness to some of

Before I proceed further, I have to remark that Dr Price seems rather to overvalue the great acquisitions of light which he has obtained and diffused in this age. The last century appears to me to have been quite as much enlightened. It had, though in a different place, a triumph as memorable as that of Dr. Price; and some of the great preachers of that period partook of it as eagerly as he has done in the triumph of France. On the trial of the Reverend Hugh Peters for high treason, it was deposed, that, when King Charles was brought to London for his trial, the Apostle of Liberty in that day conducted the *triumph*.[1] 'I saw,' says the witness, 'his Majesty in the coach with six horses, and Peters riding before the king *triumphing*.' Dr Price, when he talks as if he had made a discovery, only follows a precedent; for, after the commencement of the king's trial, this precursor, the same Dr Peters, concluding a long prayer at the royal chapel at Whitehall (he had very triumphantly chosen his place), said, 'I have prayed and preached these twenty years; and now I may say with old Simeon, *Lord, now lettest thou thy servant depart in peace, for mine eyes have seen thy salvation*.'* Peters had not the fruits of his prayer; for he neither departed so soon as he wished, nor in peace. He became (what I heartily hope none of his followers may be in this country) himself a sacrifice to the triumph which he led as pontiff. They dealt at the Restoration, perhaps, too hardly with this poor good man. But we owe it to his memory and his sufferings, that he had as much illumination and as much zeal, and had as effectually undermined all *the superstition and error* which might impede the great business he was engaged in, as any who follow and repeat after him in this age, which would assume to itself an exclusive title to the knowl-

the spectacles which Paris has lately exhibited, expresses himself thus: – '*A king dragged in submissive triumph by his conquering subjects* is one of those appearances of grandeur which seldom rise in the prospect of human affairs, and which, during the remainder of my life, I shall think of with wonder and gratification.' These gentlemen agree marvellously in their feelings.

[1] Hugh Peters (1598–1660), the independent divine, was executed for his part in obtaining the death of Charles I.

* State Trials, Vol. II, p. 360, 363.

edge of the rights of men, and all the glorious consequences of that knowledge.

After this sally of the preacher of the Old Jewry, which differs only in place and time, but agrees perfectly with the spirit and letter of the rapture of 1648,[1] the Revolution Society, the fabricators of governments, the heroic band of *cashierers* of monarchs, electors of sovereigns, and leaders of kings in triumph, strutting with a proud consciousness of the diffusion of knowledge, of which every member had obtained so large a share in the donative, were in haste to make a generous diffusion of the knowledge they had thus gratuitously received. To make this bountiful communication, they adjourned from the church in the Old Jewry to the London Tavern, where the same Dr Price, in whom the fumes of his oracular tripod were not entirely evaporated, moved and carried the resolution, or address of congratulation, transmitted by Lord Stanhope to the National Assembly of France.[2]

I find a preacher of the Gospel profaning the beautiful and prophetic ejaculation, commonly called '*Nunc dimittis*,' made on the first presentation of our Saviour in the temple, and applying it, with an inhuman and unnatural rapture, to the most horrid, atrocious, and afflicting spectacle that perhaps ever was exhibited to the pity and indignation of mankind. This '*leading in triumph*,' a thing in its best form unmanly and irreligious, which fills our preacher with such unhallowed transports, must shock, I believe, the moral taste of every well-born mind. Several English were the stupefied and indignant spectators of that triumph. It was (unless we have been strangely deceived) a spectacle more resembling a procession of American savages entering into Onondaga after some of their murders called victories,[3] and leading into hovels hung round with scalps their captives overpowered with the scoffs and buffets of women as ferocious as themselves, much more

[1] i.e. the execution of Charles I, which fell in 1648 by the Old Style dating.

[2] Charles Stanhope (1753–1816), third Earl Stanhope, chairman of the Revolution Society.

[3] Onondaga was an Indian village and missionary station of the French Jesuits.

than it resembled the triumphal pomp of a civilized martial
nation; – if a civilized nation, or any men who had a sense of
generosity, were capable of a personal triumph over the fallen
and afflicted.

This, my dear Sir, was not the triumph of France. I must
believe, that, as a nation, it overwhelmed you with shame and
horror. I must believe that the National Assembly find themselves in a state of the greatest humiliation in not being able to
punish the authors of this triumph or the actors in it, and that
they are in a situation in which any inquiry they may make
upon the subject must be destitute even of the appearance of
liberty or impartiality. The apology of that assembly is found
in their situation; but when we approve what they *must* bear, it
is in us the degenerate choice of a vitiated mind.

With a compelled appearance of deliberation, they vote
under the dominion of a stern necessity. They sit in the heart,
as it were, of a foreign republic: they have their residence in a
city whose constitution has emanated neither from the charter
of their king nor from their legislative power. There they are
surrounded by an army not raised either by the authority of
their crown or by their command, and which, if they should
order to dissolve itself, would instantly dissolve them. There
they sit, after a gang of assassins had driven away some hundreds of the members; whilst those who held the same moderate
principles, with more patience or better hope, continued every
day exposed to outrageous insults and murderous threats.
There a majority, sometimes real, sometimes pretended,
captive itself, compels a captive king to issue as royal edicts, at
third hand, the polluted nonsense of their most licentious and
giddy coffee-houses. It is notorious that all their measures are
decided before they are debated. It is beyond doubt, that,
under the terror of the bayonet, and the lamp-post, and the
torch to their houses, they are obliged to adopt all the crude
and desperate measures suggested by clubs composed of a
monstrous medley of all conditions, tongues, and nations.
Among these are found persons in comparison of whom Cati-
line would be thought scrupulous, and Cethegus a man of

sobriety and moderation.[1] Nor is it in these clubs alone that the public measures are deformed into monsters. They undergo a previous distortion in academies, intended as so many seminaries for these clubs, which are set up in all the places of public resort. In these meetings of all sorts, every counsel, in proportion as it is daring and violent and perfidious, is taken for the mark of superior genius. Humanity and compassion are ridiculed as the fruits of superstition and ignorance. Tenderness to individuals is considered as treason to the public. Liberty is always to be estimated perfect as property is rendered insecure. Amidst assassination, massacre, and confiscation, perpetrated or meditated, they are forming plans for the good order of future society. Embracing in their arms the carcasses of base criminals, and promoting their relations on the title of their offences, they drive hundreds of virtuous persons to the same end, by forcing them to subsist by beggary or by crime.

The Assembly, their organ, acts before them the farce of deliberation with as little decency as liberty. They act like the comedians of a fair, before a riotous audience; they act amidst the tumultuous cries of a mixed mob of ferocious men, and of women lost to shame, who, according to their insolent fancies, direct, control, applaud, explode them, and sometimes mix and take their seats amongst them – domineering over them with a strange mixture of servile petulance and proud, presumptuous authority. As they have inverted order in all things, the gallery is in the place of the house. This assembly, which overthrows kings and kingdoms, has not even the physiognomy and aspect of a grave legislative body – *nec color imperii, nec frons erat ulla senatûs*[2] They have a power given to them, like that of the Evil Principle, to subvert and destroy – but none to construct, except such machines as may be fitted for further subversion and further destruction.

Who is it that admires, and from the heart is attached to national representative assemblies, but must turn with horror

[1] Conspirators against the Roman Republic.
[2] Lucan, Pharsalia, IX. 207. Burke gives *erat* for *erit* and provides his own paraphrase.

and disgust from such a profane burlesque and abominable perversion of that sacred institute? Lovers of monarchy, lovers of republics, must alike abhor it. The members of your Assembly must themselves groan under the tyranny of which they have all the shame, none of the direction, and little of the profit. I am sure many of the members who compose even the majority of that body must feel as I do, notwithstanding the applauses of the Revolution Society. Miserable king! miserable assembly! How must that assembly be silently scandalized with those of their members who could call a day which seemed to blot the sun out of heaven '*un beau jour*'!* How must they be inwardly indignant at hearing others who thought fit to declare to them, 'that the vessel of the state would fly forward in her course towards regeneration with more speed than ever,' from the stiff gale of treason and murder which preceded our preacher's triumph! What must they have felt, whilst, with outward patience and inward indignation, they heard of the slaughter of innocent gentlemen in their houses, that 'the blood spilled was not the most pure'! What must they have felt, when they were besieged by complaints of disorders which shook their country to its foundations, at being compelled coolly to tell the complainants that they were under the protection of the law, and that they would address the king (the captive king) to cause the laws to be enforced for their protection, when the enslaved ministers of that captive king had formally notified to them that there were neither law nor authority nor power left to protect! What must they have felt at being obliged, as a felicitation on the present new year, to request their captive king to forget the stormy period of the last, on account of the great good which *he* was likely to produce to his people – to the complete attainment of which good they adjourned the practical demonstrations of their loyalty, assuring him of their obedience when he should no longer possess any authority to command!

This address was made with much good-nature and affection, to be sure. But among the revolutions in France must be

* 6th of October, 1789. [Viz. the day on which the French royal family were carried from Versailles to Paris.]

reckoned a considerable revolution in their ideas of politeness. In England we are said to learn manners at second-hand from your side of the water, and that we dress our behavior in the frippery of France. If so, we are still in the old cut, and have not so far conformed to the new Parisian mode of good breeding as to think it quite in the most refined strain of delicate compliment (whether in condolence or congratulation) to say, to the most humiliated creature that crawls upon the earth, that great public benefits are derived from the murder of his servants, the attempted assassination of himself and of his wife, and the mortification, disgrace, and degradation that he has personally suffered. It is a topic of consolation which our ordinary of Newgate would be too humane to use to a criminal at the foot of the gallows. I should have thought that the hangman of Paris, now that he is liberalized by the vote of the National Assembly, and is allowed his rank and arms in the Herald's College of the rights of men, would be too generous, too gallant a man, too full of the sense of his new dignity, to employ that cutting consolation to any of the persons whom the *lèze-nation* might bring under the administration of his *executive powers*.

A man is fallen indeed, when he is thus flattered. The anodyne draught of oblivion, thus drugged, is well calculated to preserve a galling wakefulness, and to feed the living ulcer of a corroding memory. Thus to administer the opiate portion of amnesty, powdered with all the ingredients of scorn and contempt, is to hold to his lips, instead of 'the balm of hurt minds,' the cup of human misery full to the brim, and to force him to drink it to the dregs.

Yielding to reasons at least as forcible as those which were so delicately urged in the compliment on the new year, the king of France will probably endeavor to forget these events and that compliment. But History, who keeps a durable record of all our acts, and exercises her awful censure over the proceedings of all sorts of sovereigns, will not forget either those events, or the era of this liberal refinement in the intercourse of mankind. History will record, that, on the morning of the sixth of October, 1789, the king and queen of France, after a day of confusion, alarm, dismay, and slaughter, lay down, under the pledged security of public faith, to indulge nature in a few hours of respite, and troubled, melancholy repose. From this sleep the queen was first startled by the voice of the sentinel at her door, who cried out to her to save herself by flight – that this was the last proof of fidelity he could give – that they were upon him, and he was dead. Instantly he was cut down. A band of cruel ruffians and assassins, reeking with his blood, rushed into the chamber of the queen, and pierced with a hundred strokes of bayonets and poniards the bed, from whence this persecuted woman had but just time to fly almost naked, and, through ways unknown to the murderers, had escaped to seek refuge at the feet of a king and husband not secure of his own life for a moment.

This king, to say no more of him, and this queen, and their infant children, (who once would have been the pride and hope of a great and generous people), were then forced to abandon the sanctuary of the most splendid palace in the world, which they left swimming in blood, polluted by massacre, and strewed with scattered limbs and mutilated carcasses. Thence they were conducted into the capital of their kingdom. Two had been selected from the unprovoked, unresisted, promiscuous slaughter which was made of the gentlemen of birth and family who composed the king's body-guard. These two gentlemen, with all the parade of an execution of justice, were cruelly and publicly dragged to the block, and beheaded in the great court of the palace. Their heads were stuck upon spears, and led the procession; whilst the royal captives who followed in the train were slowly moved along, amidst the horrid yells, and shrilling screams, and frantic dances, and infamous contumelies, and all the unutterable abominations of the furies of hell, in the abused shape of the vilest of women. After they had been made to taste, drop by drop, more than the bitterness of death, in the slow torture of a journey of twelve miles, protracted to six hours, they were, under a guard composed of those very soldiers who had thus conducted them through this famous triumph, lodged in one of the old palaces of Paris, now converted into a Bastile for kings.

Is this a triumph to be consecrated at altars, to be commemorated with grateful thanksgiving, to be offered to the Divine Humanity with fervent prayer and enthusiastic ejaculation? – These Theban and Thracian orgies, acted in France, and applauded only in the Old Jewry, I assure you, kindle prophetic enthusiasm in the minds but of very few people in this kingdom: although a saint and apostle, who may have revelations of his own, and who has so completely vanquished all the mean superstitions of the heart, may incline to think it pious and decorous to compare it with the entrance into the world of the Prince of Peace, proclaimed in an holy temple by a venerable sage, and not long before not worse announced by the voice of angels to the quiet innocence of shepherds.

At first I was at a loss to account for this fit of unguarded transport. I knew, indeed, that the sufferings of monarchs make a delicious repast to some sort of palates. There were reflections which might serve to keep this appetite within some bounds of temperance. But when I took one circumstance into my consideration, I was obliged to confess that much allowance ought to be made for the society, and that the temptation was too strong for common discretion: I mean, the circumstance of the Io Pæan of the triumph, the animating cry which called for '*all* the BISHOPS to be hanged on the lamp-posts,'* might well have brought forth a burst of enthusiasm on the foreseen consequences of this happy day. I allow to so much enthusiasm some little deviation from prudence. I allow this prophet to break forth into hymns of joy and thanksgiving on an event which appears like the precursor of the Millennium, and the projected Fifth Monarchy, in the destruction of all Church establishments.[1] There was, however (as in all human affairs there is), in the midst of this joy, something to exercise the patience of these worthy gentlemen, and to try the long-suffering of their faith. The actual murder of the king and queen, and their child, was wanting to the other auspicious

* 'Tous les Évêques à la lanterne!'
[1] The reference is intended to associate Price, in the minds of Burke's readers, with the seventeenth-century extremist sect of 'Fifth Monarchy Men'.

circumstances of this *'beautiful day.'* The actual murder of the bishops, though called for by so many holy ejaculations, was also wanting. A group of regicide and sacrilegious slaughter was, indeed, boldly sketched, but it was only sketched. It unhappily was left unfinished, in this great history-piece of the massacre of innocents. What hardy pencil of a great master, from the school of the rights of men, will finish it, is to be seen hereafter. The age has not yet the complete benefit of that diffusion of knowledge that has undermined superstition and error; and the king of France wants another object or two to consign to oblivion, in consideration of all the good which is to arise from his own sufferings, and the patriotic crimes of an enlightened age.*

* It is proper here to refer to a letter written upon this subject by an eyewitness. That eyewitness was one of the most honest, intelligent, and eloquent members of the National Assembly, one of the most active and zealous reformers of the state. He was obliged to secede from the Assembly; and he afterwards became a voluntary exile, on account of the horrors of this pious triumph, and the dispositions of men, who, profiting of crimes, if not causing them, have taken the lead in public affairs. [This was Trophime Gérard, Marquis de Lally-Tollendal (1758–1830).]

Extract of M. de Lally Tollendal's Second Letter to a Friend.
'Parlons du parti que j'ai pris; il est bien justifié dans ma conscience. – Ni cette ville coupable, ni cette assemblée plus coupable encore, ne méritoient que je me justifie; mais j'ai à cœur que vous, et les personnes qui pensent comme vous, ne me condamnent pas. – Ma santé, je vous jure, me rendoit mes fonctions impossibles; mais même en les mettant de côté il a été au-dessus de mes forces de supporter plus longtems l'horreur que me causoit ce sang, – ces têtes, – cette reine *presque égorgée*, – ce roi, amené *esclave*, entrant à Paris anu milieu de ses assassins, et précédé des têtes de ses malheureux gardes, – ces perfides janissaires, ces assassins, ces femmes cannibales, – ce cri de TOUS LES ÉVÊQUES À LA LANTERNE, dans le moment où le roi entre sa capitale avec deux évêques de son conseil dans sa voiture, – un *coup de fusil*, que j'ai vu tirer dans un *des carrosses de la reine*, – M. Bailly appellant cela *un beau jour*, – l'assemblée ayant déclaré froidement le matin, qu'il n'étoit pas de sa dignité d'aller toute entière environner le roi, – M. Mirabeau disant impunément dans cette assemblée, que le vaisseau de l'état, loin d'être arrêté dans sa course, s'élanceroit avec plus de rapidité que jamais vers sa régénération, – M. Barnave, riant avec lui, quand des flots de sang couloient autour de nous, – le vertueux Mounier* échappant par miracle à vingt assassins, qui

Although this work of our new light and knowledge did not go the length that in all probability it was intended it should be carried, yet I must think that such treatment of any human creatures must be shocking to any but those who are made for accomplishing revolutions. But I cannot stop here. Influenced by the inborn feelings of my nature, and not being illuminated by a single ray of this new-sprung modern light, I confess to you, Sir, that the exalted rank of the persons suffering, and particularly the sex, the beauty, and the amiable qualities of the descendant of so many kings and emperors, with the tender age of royal infants, insensible only through infancy and innocence of the cruel outrages to which their parents were exposed, instead of being a subject of exultation, adds not a little to my sensibility on that most melancholy occasion.

---

avoient voulu faire de sa tête un trophée de plus: Voilà ce qui me fit jurer de ne plus mettre le pied *dans cette caverne d'Antropophages* [the National Assembly], où je n'avois plus de force d'élever la voix, où depuis six semaines je l'avois élevée en vain.

'Moi, Mounier, et tous les honnêtes gens, ont pensé que le dernier effort à faire pour le bien étoit d'en sortir. Aucune idée de crainte ne s'est approchée de moi. Je rougirois de m'en défendre. J'avois encore reçù sur la route de la part de ce peuple, moins coupable que ceux qui l'ont enivré de fureur, des acclamations, et des applaudissements, dont d'autres auroient été flattés, et qui m'ont fait frémir C'est à l'indignation, c'est à l'horreur, c'est aux convulsions physiques, que le seul aspect du sang me fait éprouver que j'ai cédé. On brave une seule mort; on la brave plusieurs fois, quand elle peut être utile. Mais aucune puissance sous le ciel, mais aucune opinion publique ou privée n'ont le droit de me condamner à souffrir inutilement mille supplices par minute, et à périr de désespoir, de rage, au milieu des *triomphes*, du crime que je n'ai pu arrêter. Ils me proscriront, ils confisqueront mes biens. Je labourerai la terre, et je ne les verrai plus. Voilà ma justification. Vous pourrez la lire, la montrer, la laisser copier; tant pis pour ceux qui ne la comprendront pas; ce ne sera alors moi qui auroit eu tort de la leur donner.'

This military man had not so good nerves as the peaceable gentlemen of the Old Jewry. – See Mons. Mounier's narrative of these transactions: a man also of honor and virtue and talents, and therefore a fugitive.

*N. B. M. Mounier was then speaker of the National Assembly. He has since been obliged to live in exile, though one of the firmest assertors of liberty. [Jean-Joseph Mounier (1758–1806).]

I hear that the august person who was the principal object of our preacher's triumph, though he supported himself, felt much on that shameful occasion. As a man, it became him to feel for his wife and his children, and the faithful guards of his person that were massacred in cold blood about him; as a prince, it became him to feel for the strange and frightful transformation of his civilized subjects, and to be more grieved for them than solicitous for himself. It derogates little from his fortitude, while it adds infinitely to the honor of his humanity. I am very sorry to say it, very sorry indeed, that such personages are in a situation in which it is not unbecoming in us to praise the virtues of the great.

I hear, and I rejoice to hear, that the great lady, the other object of the triumph, has borne that day, (one is interested that beings made for suffering should suffer well), and that she bears all the succeeding days, that she bears the imprisonment of her husband, and her own captivity, and the exile of her friends, and the insulting adulation of addresses, and the whole weight of her accumulated wrongs, with a serene patience, in a manner suited to her rank and race, and becoming the off-spring of a sovereign distinguished for her piety and her courage; that, like her, she has lofty sentiments; that she feels with the dignity of a Roman matron; that in the last extremity she will save herself from the last disgrace; and that, if she must fall, she will fall by no ignoble hand.

It is now sixteen or seventeen years since I saw the queen of France, then the Dauphiness, at Versailles; and surely never lighted on this orb, which she hardly seemed to touch, a more delightful vision. I saw her just above the horizon, decorating and cheering the elevated sphere she just began to move in – glittering like the morning-star, full of life and splendor and joy. Oh! what a revolution! and what an heart must I have, to contemplate without emotion that elevation and that fall! Little did I dream, when she added titles of veneration to those of enthusiastic, distant, respectful love, that she should ever be obliged to carry the sharp antidote against disgrace concealed in that bosom! little did I dream that I should have lived to see such disasters fallen upon her in a nation of gallant men, in a nation of men of honor, and of cavaliers! I thought ten thousand swords must have leaped from their scabbards to avenge even a look that threatened her with insult. But the age of chivalry is gone. That of sophisters, economists, and calculators has succeeded; and the glory of Europe is extinguished forever. Never, never more, shall we behold that generous loyalty to rank and sex, that proud submission, that dignified obedience, that subordination of the heart, which kept alive, even in servitude itself, the spirit of an exalted freedom! The unbought grace of life, the cheap defence of nations, the nurse of manly sentiment and heroic enterprise, is gone! It is gone, that sensibility of principle, that chastity of honour, which felt a stain like a wound, which inspired courage whilst it mitigated ferocity, which ennobled whatever it touched, and under which vice itself lost half its evil by losing all its grossness!

This mixed system of opinion and sentiment had its origin in the ancient chivalry; and the principle, though varied in its appearance by the varying state of human affairs, subsisted and influenced through a long succession of generations, even to the time we live in. If it should ever be totally extinguished, the loss, I fear, will be great. It is this which has given its character to modern Europe. It is this which has distinguished it under all its forms of government, and distinguished it to its advantage, from the states of Asia, and possibly from these states which flourished in the most brilliant periods of the antique world. It was this, which, without confounding ranks, had produced a noble equality, and handed it down through all the gradations of social life. It was this opinion which mitigated kings into companions, and raised private men to be fellows with kings. Without force or opposition, it subdued the fierceness of pride and power; it obliged sovereigns to submit to the soft collar of social esteem, compelled stern authority to submit to elegance, and gave a domination, vanquisher of laws, to be subdued by manners.

But now all is to be changed. All the pleasing illusions which made power gentle and obedience liberal, which harmonized the different shades of life, and which by a bland assimilation incorporated into politics the sentiments which beautify and soften private society, are to be dissolved by this new conquering empire of light and reason. All the decent drapery of life is to be rudely torn off. All the superadded ideas, furnished from the wardrobe of a moral imagination, which the heart owns and the understanding ratifies, as necessary to cover the defects of our naked, shivering nature, and to raise it to dignity in our own estimation, are to be exploded, as a ridiculous, absurd, and antiquated fashion.

On this scheme of things, a king is but a man, a queen is but a woman, a woman is but an animal – and an animal not of the highest order. All homage paid to the sex in general as such, and without distinct views, is to be regarded as romance and folly. Regicide, and parricide, and sacrilege, are but fictions of superstition, corrupting jurisprudence by destroying its simplicity. The murder of a king, or a queen, or a bishop, or a father, are only common homicide – and if the people are by any chance or in any way gainers by it, a sort of homicide much the most pardonable, and into which we ought not to make too severe a scrutiny.

On the scheme of this barbarous philosophy, which is the offspring of cold hearts and muddy understandings, and which is as void of solid wisdom as it is destitute of all taste and elegance, laws are to be supported only by their own terrors, and by the concern which each individual may find in them from his own private speculations, or can spare to them from his own private interests. In the groves of *their* academy, at the end of every visto, you see nothing but the gallows. Nothing is left which engages the affections on the part of the commonwealth. On the principles of this mechanic philosophy, our institutions can never be embodied, if I may use the expression, in persons – so as to create in us love, veneration, admiration, or attachment. But that sort of reason which banishes the affections is incapable of filling their place. These public affections, combined with manners, are required sometimes as supplements, sometimes as correctives, always as aids to law. The precept given by a wise man, as well as a great critic, for the construction of poems, is equally true as to states:– '*Non*

satis est pulchra esse poemata, dulcia sunto.'[1] There ought to be
a system of manners in every nation which a well-formed mind
would be disposed to relish. To make us love our country, our
country ought to be lovely.

But power, of some kind or other, will survive the shock in
which manners and opinions perish; and it will find other and
worse means for its support. The usurpation, which, in order
to subvert ancient institutions, has destroyed ancient principles,
will hold power by arts similar to those by which it has
acquired it. When the old feudal and chivalrous spirit of
fealty, which, by freeing kings from fear, freed both kings and
subjects from the precautions of tyranny, shall be extinct in the
minds of men, plots and assassinations will be anticipated by
preventive murder and preventive confiscation, and that long
roll of grim and bloody maxims which form the political code
of all power not standing on its own honor and the honor of
those who are to obey it. Kings will be tyrants from policy,
when subjects are rebels from principle.

When ancient opinions and rules of life are taken away, the
loss cannot possibly be estimated. From that moment we have
no compass to govern us, nor can we know distinctly to what
port we steer. Europe, undoubtedly, taken in a mass, was in a
flourishing condition the day on which your Revolution was
completed. How much of that prosperous state was owing to
the spirit of our old manners and opinions is not easy to say;
but as such causes cannot be indifferent in their operation, we
must presume, that, on the whole, their operation was beneficial.

We are but too apt to consider things in the state in which
we find them, without sufficiently adverting to the causes by
which they have been produced, and possibly may be upheld.
Nothing is more certain than that our manners, our civilization, and all the good things which are connected with manners and with civilization, have, in this European world of ours,
depended for ages upon two principles, and were, indeed, the
result of both combined: I mean the spirit of a gentleman, and

[1] 'It is not enough that poems be pretty: they must be sweet.'
Horace, *De Arte Poetica*, 99.

the spirit of religion. The nobility and the clergy, the one by profession, and the other by patronage, kept learning in existence, even in the midst of arms and confusions, and whilst governments were rather in their causes than formed. Learning paid back what it received to nobility and to priesthood, and paid it with usury, by enlarging their ideas, and by furnishing their minds. Happy, if they had all continued to know their indissoluble union, and their proper place! Happy, if learning, not debauched by ambition, had been satisfied to continue the instructor, and not aspired to be the master! Along with its natural protectors and guardians, learning will be cast into the mire and trodden down under the hoofs of a swinish multitude.*

If, as I suspect, modern letters owe more than they are always willing to own to ancient manners, so do other interests which we value as much as they are worth. Even commerce, and trade, and manufacture, the gods of our economical politicians, are themselves perhaps but creatures, are themselves but effects, which, as first causes, we choose to worship. They certainly grew under the same shade in which learning flourished. They, too, may decay with their natural protecting principles. With you, for the present at least, they all threaten to disappear together. Where trade and manufactures are wanting to a people, and the spirit of nobility and religion remains, sentiment supplies, and not always ill supplies, their place; but if commerce and the arts should be lost in an experiment to try how well a state may stand without these old fundamental principles, what sort of a thing must be a nation of gross, stupid, ferocious, and at the same time poor and sordid barbarians, destitute of religion, honor, or manly pride, possessing nothing at present, and hoping for nothing hereafter?

* See the fate of Bailly and Condorcet, supposed to be here particularly alluded to. Compare the circumstances of the trial and execution of the former with this prediction. [This note by an early editor is in partial explanation of Burke's use of the term 'swinish multitude', for which he was much criticised. The execution of Bailly in 1793 and suicide of Jean-Antoine, Marquis de Condorcet (1743–1794) the following year, after his arrest, fulfilled the prediction.]

I wish you may not be going fast, and by the shortest cut, to that horrible and disgustful situation. Already there appears a poverty of conception, a coarseness and vulgarity, in all the proceedings of the Assembly and of all their instructors. Their liberty is not liberal. Their science is presumptuous ignorance. Their humanity is savage and brutal.

It is not clear whether in England we learned those grand and decorous principles and manners, of which considerable traces yet remain, from you, or whether you took them from us. But to you, I think, we trace them best. You seem to me to be *gentis incunabula nostræ*.[1] France has always more or less influenced manners in England; and when your fountain is choked up and polluted, the stream will not run long or not run clear with us, or perhaps with any nation. This gives all Europe, in my opinion, but too close and connected a concern in what is done in France. Excuse me, therefore, if I have dwelt too long on the atrocious spectacle of the sixth of October, 1789, or have given too much scope to the reflections which have arisen in my mind on occasion of the most important of all revolutions, which may be dated from that day: I mean a revolution in sentiments, manners, and moral opinions. As things now stand, with everything respectable destroyed without us, and an attempt to destroy within us every principle of respect, one is almost forced to apologize for harboring the common feelings of men.

Why do I feel so differently from the Reverend Dr Price, and those of his lay flock who will choose to adopt the sentiments of his discourse? – For this plain reason: Because it is *natural* I should; because we are so made as to be affected at such spectacles with melancholy sentiments upon the unstable condition of mortal prosperity, and the tremendous uncertainty of human greatness; because in those natural feelings we learn great lessons; because in events like these our passions instruct our reason; because, when kings are hurled from their thrones by the Supreme Director of this great drama, and become the objects of insult to the base and of pity to the good, we behold

[1] 'The cradle of our race.' Virgil, *Aeneid*, iii. 105.

such disasters in the moral as we should behold a miracle in the physical order of things. We are alarmed into reflection; our minds (as it has long since been observed) are purified by terror and pity; our weak, unthinking pride is humbled under the dispensations of a mysterious wisdom. Some tears might be drawn from me, if such a spectacle were exhibited on the stage. I should be truly ashamed of finding in myself that superficial, theatric sense of painted distress, whilst I could exult over it in real life. With such a perverted mind, I could never venture to show my face at a tragedy. People would think the tears that Garrick formerly, or that Siddons not long since,[1] have extorted from me, were the tears of hypocrisy; I should know them to be the tears of folly.

Indeed, the theatre is a better school of moral sentiments than churches where the feelings of humanity are thus outraged. Poets who have to deal with an audience not yet graduated in the school of the rights of men, and who must apply themselves to the moral constitution of the heart, would not dare to produce such a triumph as a matter of exultation. There, where men follow their natural impulses, they would not bear the odious maxims of a Machievelian policy, whether applied to the attainment of monarchical or democratic tyranny. They would reject them on the modern, as they once did on the ancient stage, where they could not bear even the hypothetical proposition of such wickedness in the mouth of a personated tyrant, though suitable to the character he sustained. No theatric audience in Athens would bear what has been borne in the midst of the real tragedy of this triumphal day: a principal actor weighing, as it were in scales hung in a shop of horrors, so much actual crime against so much contingent advantage – and after putting in and out weights, declaring that the balance was on the side of the advantages. They would not bear to see the crimes of new democracy posted as in a ledger against the crimes of old despotism, and the bookkeepers of politics finding democracy still in debt, but by no means unable or unwilling to pay the balance. In the theatre,

[1] David Garrick (1717–1779), the actor-manager, and Mrs Sarah Siddons (1755–1831), the actress.

the first intuitive glance, without any elaborate process of reasoning, would show that this method of political computation would justify every extent of crime. They would see, that, on these principles, even where the very worst acts were not perpetrated, it was owing rather to the fortune of the conspirators than to their parsimony in the expenditure of treachery and blood. They would soon see that criminal means, once tolerated, are soon preferred. They present a shorter cut to the object than through the highway of the moral virtues. Justifying perfidy and murder for public benefit, public benefit would soon become the pretext, and perfidy and murder the end – until rapacity, malice, revenge, and fear more dreadful than revenge, could satiate their insatiable appetites. Such must be the consequences of losing, in the splendor of these triumphs of the rights of men, all natural sense of wrong and right.

But the reverend pastor exults in this 'leading in triumph,' because, truly, Louis the Sixteenth was 'an arbitrary monarch': that is, in other words, neither more nor less than because he was Louis the Sixteenth, and because he had the misfortune to be born king of France, with the prerogatives of which a long line of ancestors, and a long acquiescence of the people, without any act of his, had put him in possession. A misfortune it has indeed turned out to him, that he was born king of France. But misfortune is not crime, nor is indiscretion always the greatest guilt. I shall never think that a prince, the acts of whose whole reign were a series of concessions to his subjects, who was willing to relax his authority, to remit his prerogatives, to call his people to a share of freedom not known, perhaps not desired, by their ancestors – such a prince, though he should be subject to the common frailties attached to men and to princes, though he should have once thought it necessary to provide force against the desperate designs manifestly carrying on against his person and the remnants of his authority – though all this should be taken into consideration, I shall be led with great difficulty to think he deserves the cruel and insulting triumph of Paris, and of Dr Price. I tremble for the cause of liberty, from such an example to kings. I tremble for the cause of humanity, in the unpunished outrages of the most wicked of mankind. But there are some people of that low and degenerate fashion of mind that they look up with a sort of complacent awe and admiration to kings who know to keep firm in their seat, to hold a strict hand over their subjects, to assert their prerogative, and, by the awakened vigilance of a severe despotism, to guard against the very first approaches of freedom. Against such as these they never elevate their voice. Deserters from principle, listed with fortune, they never see any good in suffering virtue, nor any crime in prosperous usurpation.

If it could have been made clear to me that the king and queen of France (those, I mean, who were such before the triumph) were inexorable and cruel tyrants, that they had formed a deliberate scheme for massacring the National Assembly (I think I have seen something like the latter insinuated in certain publications), I should think their captivity just. If this be true, much more ought to have been done, but done, in my opinion, in another manner. The punishment of real tyrants is a noble and awful act of justice; and it has with truth been said to be consolatory to the human mind. But if I were to punish a wicked king, I should regard the dignity in avenging the crime. Justice is grave and decorous, and in its punishments rather seems to submit to a necessity than to make a choice. Had Nero, or Agrippina, or Louis the Eleventh, or Charles the Ninth been the subject – if Charles the Twelfth of Sweden, after the murder of Patkul, or his predecessor, Christina, after the murder of Monaldeschi,[1] had fallen into your hands, Sir, or into mine, I am sure our conduct would have been different.

If the French king, or king of the French (or by whatever name he is known in the new vocabulary of your Constitution), has in his own person and that of his queen really deserved these unavowed, but unavenged, murderous attempts, and those frequent indignities more cruel than murder, such a

[1] Johann Reinhold Patkul (1660–1707), a Livonian, and Gian Renaldo Monaldeschi (d. 1657), an Italian, were put to death at the behest of the Swedish monarchs mentioned.

person would ill deserve even that subordinate executory trust which I understand is to be placed in him; nor is he fit to be called chief in a nation which he has outraged and oppressed. A worse choice for such an office in a new commonwealth than that of a deposed tyrant could not possibly be made. But to degrade and insult a man as the worst of criminals, and afterwards to trust him in your highest concerns, as a faithful, honest, and zealous servant, is not consistent in reasoning, nor prudent in policy, nor safe in practice. Those who could make such an appointment must be guilty of a more flagrant breach of trust than any they have yet committed against the people. As this is the only crime in which your leading politicians could have acted inconsistently, I conclude that there is no sort of ground for these horrid insinuations. I think no better of all the other calumnies.

In England, we give no credit to them. We are generous enemies; we are faithful allies. We spurn from us with disgust and indignation the slanders of those who bring us their anecdotes with the attestation of the flower-de-luce on their shoulder. We have Lord George Gordon fast in Newgate; and neither his being a public proselyte to Judaism, nor his having, in his zeal against Catholic priests and all sorts of ecclesiastics, raised a mob (excuse the term, it is still in use here) which pulled down all our prisons, have preserved to him a liberty of which he did not render himself worthy by a virtuous use of it.[1] We have rebuilt Newgate, and tenanted the mansion. We have prisons almost as strong as the Bastile, for those who dare to libel the queens of France. In this spiritual retreat let the noble libeller remain. Let him there meditate on his Talmud, until he learns a conduct more becoming his birth and parts, and not so disgraceful to the ancient religion to which he has become a proselyte – or until some persons from your side of the water, to please your new Hebrew brethren, shall ransom him. He may then be enabled to purchase, with the old hoards of the synagogue, and a very small poundage on the long compound interest of the thirty pieces of silver (Dr Price has

[1] Lord George Gordon (1751–1793), instigator of the Gordon Riots of 1780, was imprisoned in Newgate for libel from 1788 until his death.

shown us what miracles compound interest will perform in
1790 years), the lands which are lately discovered to have been
usurped by the Gallican Church. Send us your Popish Arch-
bishop of Paris, and we will send you our Protestant Rabbin.
We shall treat the person you send us in exchange like a gentleman and an honest man, as he is: but pray let him bring with
him the fund of his hospitality, bounty, and charity; and,
depend upon it, we shall never confiscate a shilling of that
honorable and pious fund, nor think of enriching the Treasury
with the spoils of the poorbox.

To tell you the truth, my dear Sir, I think the honor of our
nation to be somewhat concerned in the disclaimer of the proceedings of this society of the Old Jewry and the London
Tavern. I have no man's proxy. I speak only from myself,
when I disclaim, as I do with all possible earnestness, all communion with the actors in that triumph, or with the admirers
of it. When I assert anything else, as concerning the people of
England, I speak from observation, not from authority; but I
speak from the experience I have had in a pretty extensive and
mixed communication with the inhabitants of this kingdom, of
all descriptions and ranks, and after a course of attentive
observation, begun in early life, and continued for near forty
years. I have often been astonished, considering that we are
divided from you but by a slender dike of about twenty-four
miles, and that the mutual intercourse between the two
countries has lately been very great, to find how little you seem
to know of us. I suspect that this is owing to your forming a
judgment of this nation from certain publications, which do,
very erroneously, if they do at all, represent the opinions and
dispositions generally prevalent in England. The vanity,
restlessness, petulance, and spirit of intrigue of several petty
cabals, who attempt to hide their total want of consequence in
bustle and noise, and puffing and mutual quotation of each
other, makes you imagine that our contemptuous neglect of
their abilities is a general mark of acquiescence in their opinions. No such thing, I assure you. Because half a dozen grass-
hoppers under a fern make the field ring with their importunate chink, whilst thousands of great cattle reposed beneath

the shadow of the British oak chew the cud and are silent, pray do not imagine that those who make the noise are the only inhabitants of the field – that, of course, they are many in number – or that, after all, they are other than the little, shrivelled, meagre, hopping, though loud and troublesome insects of the hour.

I almost venture to affirm that not one in a hundred amongst us participates in the 'triumph' of the Revolution Society. If the king and queen of France and their children were to fall into our hands by the chance of war, in the most acrimonious of all hostilities (I deprecate such an event, I deprecate such hostility), they would be treated with another sort of triumphal entry into London. We formerly have had a king of France in that situation: you have read how he was treated by the victor in the field, and in what manner he was afterwards received in England. Four hundred years have gone over us; but I believe we are not materially changed since that period. Thanks to our sullen resistance to innovation, thanks to the cold sluggishness of our national character, we still bear the stamp of our forefathers. We have not (as I conceive) lost the generosity and dignity of thinking of the fourteenth century; nor as yet have we subtilized ourselves into savages. We are not the converts of Rousseau; we are not the disciples of Voltaire; Helvetius has made no progress amongst us. Atheists are not our preachers; madmen are not our lawgivers. We know that *we* have made no discoveries, and we think that no discoveries are to be made, in morality – nor many in the great principles of government, nor in the ideas of liberty, which were understood long before we were born altogether as well as they will be after the grave has heaped its mould upon our presumption, and the silent tomb shall have imposed its law on our pert loquacity. In England we have not yet been completely embowelled of our natural entrails: we still feel within us, and we cherish and cultivate, those inbred sentiments which are the faithful gaurdians, the active monitors of our duty, the true supporters of all liberal and manly morals. We have not been drawn and trussed, in order that we may be filled, like stuffed birds in a museum, with chaff and rags, and paltry, blurred shreds of paper about the rights of man. We preserve the whole of our feelings still native and entire, unsophisticated by pedantry and infidelity. We have real hearts of flesh and blood beating in our bosoms. We fear God; we look up with awe to kings, with affection to Parliaments, with duty to magistrates, with reverence to priests, and with respect to nobility.* Why? Because, when such ideas are brought before our minds, it is *natural* to be so affected; because all other feelings are false and spurious, and tend to corrupt our minds, to vitiate our primary morals, to render us unfit for rational liberty, and, by teaching us a servile, licentious, and abandoned insolence, to be our low sport for a few holidays, to make us perfectly fit for and justly deserving of slavery through the whole course of our lives.

You see, Sir, that in this enlightened age I am bold enough to confess that we are generally men of untaught feelings: that, instead of casting away all our old prejudices, we cherish them to a very considerable degree; and, to take more shame to ourselves, we cherish them because they are prejudices; and the longer they have lasted, and the more generally they have prevailed, the more we cherish them. We are afraid to put men to live and trade each on his own private stock of reason; because we suspect that the stock in each man is small, and that the individuals would do better to avail themselves of the general bank and capital of nations and of ages. Many of our men of speculation, instead of exploding general prejudices, employ their sagacity to discover the latent wisdom which prevails in them. If they find what they seek (and they seldom fail), they think it more wise to continue the prejudice, with the reason involved, than to cast away the coat of prejudice, and to leave nothing but the naked reason; because prejudice, with its

* The English are, I conceive, misrepresented in a letter published in one of the papers, by a gentleman thought to be a Dissenting minister. When writing to Dr Price of the spirit which prevails at Paris, he says, – 'The spirit of the people in this place has abolished all the proud *distinctions* which the *king* and *nobles* had usurped in their minds: whether they talk of *the king, the noble, or the priest*, their whole language is that of the most *enlightened and liberal amongst the English.*' If this gentleman means to confine the terms *enlightened and liberal* to one set of men in England, it may be true. It is not generally so.

reason, has a motive to give action to that reason, and an affection which will give it permanence. Prejudice is of ready application in the emergency; it previously engages the mind in a steady course of wisdom and virtue, and does not leave the man hesitating in the moment of decision, skeptical, puzzled, and unresolved. Prejudice renders a man's virtue his habit, and not a series of unconnected acts. Through just prejudice, his duty becomes a part of his nature.

Your literary men, and your politicians, and so do the whole clan of the enlightened among us, essentially differ in these points. They have no respect for the wisdom of others; but they pay it off by a very full measure of confidence in their own. With them it is a sufficient motive to destroy an old scheme of things, because it is an old one. As to the new, they are in no sort of fear with regard to the duration of a building run up in haste; because duration is no object to those who think little or nothing has been done before their time, and who place all their hopes in discovery. They conceive, very systematically, that all things which give perpetuity are mischievous, and therefore they are at inexpiable war with all establishments. They think that government may vary like modes of dress, and with as little ill effect; that there needs no principle of attachment, except a sense of present conveniency, to any constitution of the state. They always speak as if they were of opinion that there is a singular species of compact between them and their magistrates, which binds the magistrate, but which has nothing reciprocal in it, but that the majesty of the people has a right to dissolve it without any reason but its will. Their attachment to their country itself is only so far as it agrees with some of their fleeting projects: it begins and ends with that scheme of polity which falls in with their momentary opinion.

These doctrines, or rather sentiments, seem prevalent with your new statesmen. But they are wholly different from those on which we have always acted in this country.

I hear it is sometimes given out in France, that what is doing among you is after the example of England. I beg leave to affirm that scarcely anything done with you has originated from the practice or the prevalent opinions of this people, either in the act or in the spirit of the proceeding. Let me add, that we are as unwilling to learn these lessons from France as we are sure that we never taught them to that nation. The cabals here who take a sort oι share in your transactions as yet consist of but a handful of people. If, unfortunately, by their intrigues, their sermons, their publications, and by a confidence derived from an expected union with the counsels and forces of the French nation, they should draw considerable numbers into their faction, and in consequence should seriously attempt anything here in imitation of what has been done with you, the event, I dare venture to prophesy, will be, that, with some trouble to their country, they will soon accomplish their own destruction. This people refused to change their law in remote ages from respect to the infallibility of Popes, and they will not now alter it from a pious implicit faith in the dogmatism of philosophers – though the former was armed with the anathema and crusade, and though the latter should act with the libel and the lamp-iron.

Formerly your affairs were your own concern only. We felt for them as men; but we kept aloof from them, because we were not citizens of France. But when we see the model held up to ourselves, we must feel as Englishmen, and, feeling, we must provide as Englishmen. Your affairs, in spite of us, are made a part of our interest – so far at least as to keep at a distance your panacea or your plague. If it be a panacea, we do not want it: we know the consequences of unnecessary physic. If it be a plague, it is such a plague that the precautions of the most severe quarantine ought to be established against it.

I hear on all hands, that a cabal, calling itself philosophic, receives the glory of many of the late proceedings, and that their opinions and systems are the true actuating spirit of the whole of them. I have heard of no party in England, literary or political, at any time, known by such a description. It is not with you composed of those men, is it? whom the vulgar, in their blunt, homely style, commonly call Atheists and Infidels? If it be, I admit that we, too, have had writers of that description, who made some noise in their day. At present they repose in lasting oblivion. Who, born within the lasty forty years, has read one word of Collins, and Toland, and Tindal, and Chubb, and Morgan, and that whole race who called themselves Freethinkers?[1] Who now reads Bolingbroke? Who ever read him through? Ask the booksellers of London what is become of all these lights of the world. In as few years their few successors will go to the family vault of 'all the Capulets.' But whatever they were, or are, with us they were and are wholly unconnected individuals. With us they kept the common nature of their kind, and were not gregarious. They never acted in corps, nor were known as a faction in the state, nor presumed to influence in that name or character, or for the purposes of such a faction, on any of our public concerns. Whether they ought so to exist, and so be permitted to act, is another question. As such cabals have not existed in England, so neither has the spirit of them had any influence in establishing the original frame of our Constitution, or in any one of the several reparations and improvements it has undergone. The whole has been done under the auspices, and is confirmed by the sanctions, of religion and piety. The whole has emanated from the simplicity of our national character, and from a sort of native plainness and directness of understanding, which for a long time characterized those men who have successively obtained authority among us. This disposition still remains – at least in the great body of the people.

We know, and, what is better, we feel inwardly, that religion is the basis of civil society, and the source of all good, and of all comfort.* In England we are so convinced of this, that

---

[1] Anthony Collins (1676–1729), John Toland (1670–1722), Matthew Tindal (1657–1733), Thomas Chubb (1679–1747), and Thomas Morgan (d. 1743).

* Sit igitur hoc ab initio persuasum civibus, dominos esse omnium rerum ac moderatores deos; eaque, quæ gerantur, corum geri vi, ditione, ac numine; eosdemque optime de genere hominum mereri; et qualis quisque sit, quid agat, quid in se admittat, qua mente, qua pietate colat religiones intueri: piorum et impiorum habere rationem. His enim rebus imbutæ mentes haud sane abhorrebunt ab utili et a vera sententia. – Cic. de Legibus, l. 2. ['So in the very beginning we must persuade our citizens that the gods are the lords and rulers of all things, and that what is done, is done by their will and authority; that they are likewise great benefactors of man, observing the character of

there is no rust of superstition, with which the accumulated absurdity of the human mind might have crusted it over in the course of ages, that ninety-nine in a hundred of the people of England would not prefer to impiety. We shall never be such fools as to call in an enemy to the substance of any system to remove its corruptions, to supply its defects, or to perfect its construction. If our religious tenets should ever want a further elucidation, we shall not call on Atheism to explain them. We shall not light up our temple from that unhallowed fire. It will be illuminated with other lights. It will be perfumed with other incense than the infectious stuff which is imported by the smugglers of adulterated metaphysics. If our ecclesiastical establishment should want a revision, it is not avarice or rapacity, public or private, that we shall employ for the audit or receipt or application of its consecrated revenue. Violently condemning neither the Greek nor the Armenian, nor, since heats are subsided, the Roman system of religion, we prefer the Protestant: not because we think it has less of the Christian religion in it, but because, in our judgment, it has more. We are Protestants, not from indifference, but from zeal.

We know, and it is our pride to know, that man is by his constitution a religious animal; that atheism is against, not only our reason, but our instincts; and that it cannot prevail long. But if, in the moment of riot, and in a drunken delirium from the hot spirit drawn out of the alembic of hell, which in France is now so furiously boiling, we should uncover our nakedness, by throwing off that Christian religion which has hitherto been our boast and comfort, and one great source of civilization amongst us, and among many other nations, we are apprehensive (being well aware that the mind will not endure a void) that some uncouth, pernicious, and degrading superstition might take place of it.

For that reason, before we take from our establishment the

---

every individual, what he does, of what wrong he is guilty, and with what intentions and with what piety he fulfills his religious duties; and they take note of the pious and the impious. For surely minds which are imbued with such ideas will not fail to form true and useful opinions.' *De Legibus* II. vii.]

natural, human means of estimation, and give it up to contempt, as you have done, and in doing it have incurred the penalties you well deserve to suffer, we desire that some other may be presented to us in the place of it. We shall then form our judgment.

On these ideas, instead of quarrelling with establishments, as some do, who have made a philosophy and a religion of their hostility to such institutions, we cleave closely to them. We are resolved to keep an established church, an established monarchy, an established aristocracy, and an established democracy, each in the degree it exists, and in no greater.

An Appeal from the New to the Old Whigs

When Burke published the *Reflections* he had not been without hope that his argument would wean his party colleagues from their belief that the recent events in France were similar to the universally-respected Revolution of 1688. In the following months it became clear that no such conversion had taken place, and on 6 May 1791 the quarrel between Burke and Fox reached its climax. In the course of a debate on the Quebec Bill Burke insisted upon speaking in condemnation of the new French constitution, and Fox found it necessary to make his own position equally clear. Amid a deeply-moved House Burke thereupon stood up to renounce his last ties with the party leader. On 12 May the *Morning Chronicle*, which supported Fox, announced that the rupture was complete, that the majority of the party adhered to Fox as the exponent of the Whigs' 'pure doctrines', and that Burke was consequently to retire from Parliament. Stung by this hint that he should go, and ny the implication that it was he who had deserted the party's principles, Burke sat down to vindicate himself on paper. The result, *An Appeal from the New to the Old Whigs*, was published anonymously in August and only referred to Burke in the third person; but its authorship was well known in the political circles for which it was principally written.

The main contention of the *Appeal* was that it was Burke's attitude to the French Revolution, and not Fox's, which expressed the true 'Whig principles' of the Revolution of 1688; in short that the Foxites were 'New Whigs' failing to carry out the party traditions. 'These new Whigs hold that the sovereignty ... did not only originate *from* the people ... but that in the people the same sovereignty constantly and unalienably resides; that the people may lawfully depose kings, not only for misconduct, but without any misconduct at all; that they may set up any new fashion of government for them-

selves, or continue without any government, at their pleasure
. . .' This, he maintained, had not been the position occupied
by the first Whigs. To support his contention he quoted at
large (in passages too long for inclusion in the present selection) from the speeches made by leading Whig lawyers at the
trial of Dr Henry Sacheverell in 1710 for preaching the pre-
Revolution Tory doctrine of non-resistance to kings; Burke
was able to show that those Whigs were only against unlimited
non-resistance, in short that they approved of non-resistance
to lawful established government except in extreme instances.
In thus choosing his authorities from 1710, nearly a generation
after the English Revolution, Burke was able to gloss over the
much more extreme views which had been put forward by the
first Whigs from 1679–88, which bore a closer resemblance to
those of Fox.

*From An Appeal from the New to the Old Whigs, in consequence
of some late Discussions in Parliament relative to the Reflections
on the French Revolution (1791)*

Mr Burke has been also reproached with an inconsistency
between his late writings and his former conduct, because he
had proposed in Parliament several economical, leading to
several constitutional reforms. Mr Burke thought, with a
majority of the House of Commons, that the influence of the
crown at one time was too great; but after his Majesty had, by
a gracious message, and several subsequent acts of Parliament,
reduced it to a standard which satisfied Mr Fox himself, and,
apparently at least, contented whoever wished to go farthest in
that reduction, is Mr Burke to allow that it would be right for
us to proceed to indefinite lengths upon that subject? that it
would therefore be justifiable in a people owing allegiance to a
monarchy, and professing to maintain it, not to *reduce*, but
wholly to *take away all* prerogative and *all* influence whatsoever? Must his having made, in virtue of a plan of economical
regulation, a reduction of the influence of the crown compel
him to allow that it would be right in the French or in us to

bring a king to so abject a state as in function not to be so respectable as an under-sheriff, but in person not to differ from the condition of a mere prisoner? One would think that such a thing as a medium had never been heard of in the moral world.

This mode of arguing from your having done *any* thing in a certain line to the necessity of doing *every* thing has political consequences of other moment than those of a logical fallacy. If no man can propose any diminution or modification of an invidious or dangerous power or influence in government, without entitling friends turned into adversaries to argue him into the destruction of all prerogative, and to a spoliation of the whole patronage of royalty, I do not know what can more effectually deter persons of sober minds from engaging in any reform, nor how the worst enemies to the liberty of the subject could contrive any method more fit to bring all correctives on the power of the crown into suspicion and disrepute.

If, say his accusers, the dread of too great influence in the crown of Great Britain could justify the degree of reform which he adopted, the dread of a return under the despotism of a monarchy might justify the people of France in going much further, and reducing monarchy to its present nothing. – Mr Burke does not allow that a sufficient argument *ad hominem* is inferable from these premises. If the horror of the excesses of an absolute monarchy furnishes a reason for abolishing it, no monarchy once absolute (all have been so at one period or other) could ever be limited. It must be destroyed; otherwise no way could be found to quiet the fears of those who were formerly subjected to that sway. But the principle of Mr Burke's proceeding ought to lead him to a very different conclusion – to this conclusion – that a monarchy is a thing perfectly susceptible of reform, perfectly susceptible of a balance of power, and that, when reformed and balanced, for a great country it is the best of all governments. The example of our country might have led France, as it has led him, to perceive that monarchy is not only reconcilable to liberty, but that it may be rendered a great and stable security to its perpetual enjoyment. No correctives which he proposed to the power of the crown could lead him to approve of a plan of a republic (if so it may be reputed) which has no correctives, and which he believes to be incapable of admitting any. No principle of Mr Burke's conduct or writings obliged him from consistency to become an advocate for an exchange of mischiefs; no principle of his could compel him to justify the setting up in the place of a mitigated monarchy a new and far more despotic power, under which there is no trace of liberty, except what appears in confusion and in crime.

Mr Burke does not admit that the faction predominant in France have abolished their monarchy, and the orders of their state, from any dread of arbitrary power that lay heavy on the minds of the people. It is not very long since he has been in that country. Whilst there he conversed with many descriptions of its inhabitants. A few persons of rank did, he allows, discover strong and manifest tokens of such a spirit of liberty as might be expected one day to break all bounds. Such gentlemen have since had more reason to repent of their want of foresight than I hope any of the same class will ever have in this country. But this spirit was far from general, even amongst the gentlemen. As to the lower orders, and those little above them, in whose names the present powers domineer, they were far from discovering any sort of dissatisfaction with the power and prerogatives of the crown. That vain people were rather proud of them: they rather despised the English for not having a monarch possessed of such high and perfect authority. *They* had felt nothing from *lettres de cachet*. The Bastile could inspire no horrors into *them*. This was a treat for their betters. It was by art and impulse, it was by the sinister use made of a season of scarcity, it was under an infinitely diversified succession of wicked pretences wholly foreign to the question of monarchy or aristocracy, that this light people were inspired with their present spirit of levelling. Their old vanity was led by art to take another turn: it was dazzled and seduced by military liveries, cockades, and epaulets, until the French populace was led to become the willing, but still the proud and thoughtless, instrument and victim of another domination. Neither did that people despise or hate or fear their nobility :

on the contrary, they valued themselves on the generous qualities which distinguished the chiefs of their nation.

So far as to the attack on Mr Burke in consequence of his reforms.

To show that he has in his last publication abandoned those principles of liberty which have given energy to his youth, and in spite of his censors will afford repose and consolation to his declining age, those who have thought proper in Parliament to declare against his book ought to have produced something in it which directly or indirectly militates with any rational plan of free government. It is something extraordinary, that they whose memories have so well served them with regard to light and ludicrous expressions, which years had consigned to oblivion, should not have been able to quote a single passage in a piece so lately published, which contradicts anything he has formerly ever said in a style either ludicrous or serious. They quote his former speeches and his former votes, but not one syllable from the book. It is only by a collation of the one with the other that the alleged inconsistency can be established. But as they are unable to cite any such contradictory passage, so neither can they show anything in the general tendency and spirit of the whole work unfavorable to a rational and generous spirit of liberty; unless a warm opposition to the spirit of levelling, to the spirit of impiety, to the spirit of proscription, plunder, murder, and cannibalism, be adverse to the true principles of freedom.

The author of that book is supposed to have passed from extreme to extreme; but he has always kept himself in a medium. This charge is not so wonderful. It is in the nature of things, that they who are in the centre of a circle should appear directly opposed to those who view them from any part of the circumference. In that middle point, however, he will still remain, though he may hear people who themselves run beyond Aurora[1] and the Ganges cry out that he is at the extremity of the West.

In the same debate[2] Mr Burke was represented by Mr Fox

---

[1] Roman goddess of dawn; viz. the East.
[2] i.e. on the Quebec Bill.

as arguing in a manner which implied that the British Constitution could not be defended, but by abusing all republics ancient and modern. He said nothing to give the least ground for such a censure. He never abused all republics. He has never professed himself a friend or an enemy to republics or to monarchies in the abstract. He thought that the circumstances and habits of every country, which it is always perilous and productive of the greatest calamities to force, are to decide upon the form of its government. There is nothing in his nature, his temper, or his faculties which should make him an enemy to any republic, modern or ancient. Far from it. He has studied the form and spirit of republics very early in life; he has studied them with great attention, and with a mind undisturbed by affection or prejudice. He is, indeed, convinced that the science of government would be poorly cultivated without that study. But the result in his mind from that investigation has been and is, that neither England nor France, without infinite detriment to them, as well in the event as in the experiment, could be brought into a republican form; but that everything republican which can be introduced with safety into either of them must be built upon a monarchy – built upon a real, not a nominal monarchy, *as its essential basis;* that all such institutions, whether aristocratic or democratic, must originate from their crown, and in all their proceedings must refer to it; that by the energy of that mainspring along those republican parts must be set in action, and from thence must derive their whole legal effect (as amongst us they actually do), or the whole will fall into confusion. These republican members have no other point but the crown in which they can possibly unite.

This is the opinion expressed in Mr Burke's book. He has never varied in that opinion since he came to years of discretion. But surely, if at any time of his life he had entertained other notions (which, however, he has never held or professed to hold), the horrible calamities brought upon a great people by the wild attempt to force their country into a republic might be more than sufficient to undeceive his understanding, and to free it forever from such destructive fancies. He is certain that many, even in France, have been made sick of their theories by their very success in realizing them.

To fortify the imputation of a desertion from his principles, his constant attempts to reform abuses have been brought forward. It is true, it has been the business of his strength to reform abuses in government, and his last feeble efforts are employed in a struggle against them. Politically he has lived in that element; politically he will die in it. Before he departs, I will admit for him that he deserves to have all his titles of merit brought forth, as they have been, for grounds of condemnation, if one word justifying or supporting abuses of any sort is to be found in that book which has kindled so much indignation in the mind of a great man. On the contrary, it spares no existing abuse. Its very purpose is to make war with abuses – not, indeed, to make war with the dead, but with those which live, and flourish, and reign.

The *purpose* for which the abuses of government are brought into view forms a very material consideration in the mode of treating them. The complaints of a friend are things very different from the invectives of an enemy. The charge of abuses on the late monarchy of France was not intended to lead to its reformation, but to justify its destruction. They who have raked into all history for the faults of kings, and who have aggravated every fault they have found, have acted consistently, because they acted as enemies. No man can be a friend to a tempered monarchy who bears a decided hatred to monarchy itself. He, who, at the present time, is favorable or even fair to that system, must act towards it as towards a friend with frailties who is under the prosecution of implacable foes. I think it a duty, in that case, not to inflame the public mind against the obnoxious person by any exaggeration of his faults. It is our duty rather to palliate his errors and defects, or to cast them into the shade, and industriously to bring forward any good qualities that he may happen to possess. But when the man is to be amended, and by amendment to be preserved, then the line of duty takes another direction. When his safety is effectually provided for, it then becomes the office of a friend to urge his faults and vices with all the energy of enlightened affection, to paint them in their most vivid colors, and to bring the moral patient to a better habit. Thus I think with regard to individuals; thus I think with regard to ancient and respected governments and orders of men. A spirit of reformation is never more consistent with itself than when it refuses to be rendered the means of destruction.

I suppose that enough is said upon these heads of accusation. One more I had nearly forgotten, but I shall soon dispatch it. The author of the Reflections, in the opening of the last Parliament, entered on the journals of the House of Commons a motion for a remonstrance to the crown,[1] which is substantially a defence of the preceding Parliament, that had been dissolved under displeasure. It is a defence of Mr Fox. It is a defence of the Whigs. By what connection of argument, by what association of ideas, this apology for Mr Fox and his party is by him and them brought to criminate his and their apologist, I cannot easily divine. It is true that Mr Burke received no previous encouragement from Mr Fox, nor any the least countenance or support, at the time when the motion was made, from him or from any gentleman of the party – one only excepted, from whose friendship, on that and on other occasions, he derives an honor to which he must be dull indeed to be insensible.* If that remonstrance, therefore, was a false or feeble defence of the measures of the party, they were in no wise affected by it. It stands on the journals. This secures to it a permanence which the author cannot expect to any other work of his. Let it speak for itself to the present age and to all posterity. The party had no concern in it; and it can never be quoted against them. But in the late debate it was produced, not to clear the party from an improper defence in which they had no share, but for the kind purpose of insinuating an inconsistency between the principles of Mr Burke's defence of the dissolved Parliament and those on which he proceeded in his late Reflections on France.

It requires great ingenuity to make out such a parallel

---

[1] The motion of 14 June, 1784, for which see above, pp. 251-62.
* Mr Windham [William Windham (1750–1810), M.P. for Norwich, who had seconded the motion].

between the two cases as to found a charge of inconsistency in
the principles assumed in arguing the one and the other. What
relation had Mr Fox's India Bill to the Constitution of France?
What relation had that Constitution to the question of right in
an House of Commons to give or to withhold its confidence
from ministers, and to state that opinion to the crown? What
had this discussion to do with Mr Burke's idea in 1784 of the
ill consequences which must in the end arise to the crown from
setting up the commons at large as an opposite interest to the
commons in Parliament? What has this discussion to do
with a recorded warning to the people of their rashly forming
a precipitate judgment against their representatives? What
had Mr Burke's opinion of the danger of introducing new
theoretic language, unknown to the records of the kingdom,
and calculated to excite vexatious questions, into a Parliamentary proceeding, to do with the French Assembly,
which defies all precedent, and places its whole glory in
realizing what had been thought the most visionary theories?
What had this in common with the abolition of the French
monarchy, or with the principles upon which the English
Revolution was justified – a Revolution in which Parliament,
in all its acts and all its declarations, religiously adheres to 'the
form of sound words,' without excluding from private discussions such terms of art as may serve to conduct an inquiry
for which none but private persons are responsible? These
were the topics of Mr Burke's proposed remonstrance; all of
which topics suppose the existence and mutual relation of our
three estates – as well as the relation of the East India Company
to the crown, to Parliament, and to the peculiar laws, rights,
and usages of the people of Hindostan. What reference, I say,
had these topics to the Constitution of France, in which there
is no king, no lords, no commons, no India Company to
injure or support, no Indian empire to govern or oppress?
What relation had all or any of these, or any question which
could arise between the prerogatives of the crown and the
privileges of Parliament, with the censure of those factious
persons in Great Britain whom Mr Burke states to be engaged,

not in favor of privilege against prerogative, or of prerogative against privilege, but in an open attempt against our crown and our Parliament, against our Constitution in Church and State, against all the parts and orders which compose the one and the other?

No persons were more fiercely active against Mr Fox, and against the measures of the House of Commons dissolved in 1784, which Mr Burke defends in that remonstrance, than several of those revolution-makers whom Mr Burke condemns alike in his remonstrance and in his book. These revolutionists, indeed, may be well thought to vary in their conduct. He is, however, far from accusing them, in this variation, of the smallest degree of inconsistency. He is persuaded that they are totally indifferent at which end they begin the demolition of the Constitution. Some are for commencing their operations with the destruction of the civil powers, in order the better to pull down the ecclesiastical – some wish to begin with the ecclesiastical, in order to facilitate the ruin of the civil; some would destroy the House of Commons through the crown, some the crown through the House of Commons, and some would overturn both the one and the other through what they call the people. But I believe that this injured writer will think it not at all inconsistent with his present duty or with his former life strenuously to oppose all the various partisans of destruction, let them begin where or when or how they will. No man would set his face more determinedly against those who should attempt to deprive them, or any description of men, of the rights they possess. No man would be more steady in preventing them from abusing those rights to the destruction of that happy order under which they enjoy them. As to their title to anything further, it ought to be grounded on the proof they give of the safety with which power may be trusted in their hands. When they attempt without disguise, not to win it from our affections, but to force it from our fears, they show, in the character of their means of obtaining it, the use they would make of their dominion. That writer is too well read in men not to know how often the desire and design of a tyrannic domination lurks in the claim of an extravagant liberty. Perhaps in the beginning it *always* displays itself in that manner. No man has ever affected power which he did not hope from the favor of the existing government in any other mode.

The attacks on the author's consistency relative to France are (however grievous they may be to his feelings) in a great degree external to him and to us, and comparatively of little moment to the people of England. The substantial charge upon him is concerning his doctrines relative to the Revolution of 1688. Here it is that they who speak in the name of the party have thought proper to censure him the most loudly and with the greatest asperity. Here they fasten, and, if they are right in their fact, with sufficient judgment in their selection. If he be guilty in this point, he is equally blamable, whether he is consistent or not. If he endeavors to delude his countrymen by a false representation of the spirit of that leading event, and of the true nature and tenure of the government formed in consequence of it, he is deeply responsible, he is an enemy to the free Constitution of the kingdom. But he is not guilty in any sense. I maintain that in his Reflections he has stated the Revolution and the Settlement upon their true principles of legal reason and constitutional policy.

His authorities are the acts and declarations of Parliament, given in their proper words. So far as these go, nothing can be added to what he has quoted. The question is, whether he has understood them rightly. I think they speak plain enough. But we must now see whether he proceeds with other authority than his own constructions, and, if he does, on what sort of authority he proceeds. In this part, his defence will not be made by argument, but by wager of law. He takes his compurgators, his vouchers, his guaranties, along with him. I know that he will not be satisfied with a justification proceeding on general reasons of policy. He must be defended on party grounds, too, or his cause is not so tenable as I wish it to appear. It must be made out for him not only that in his construction of these public acts and monuments he conforms himself to the rules of fair, legal, and logical interpretation, but it must be proved that his construction is in perfect harmony with that of the ancient Whigs, to whom, against the sentence of the modern, on his part, I here appeal.

This July it will be twenty-six years* since he became connected with a man[1] whose memory will ever be precious to Englishmen of all parties, as long as the ideas of honor and virtue, public and private, are understood and cherished in this nation. That memory will be kept alive with particular veneration by all rational and honorable Whigs. Mr Burke entered into a connection with that party through that man, at an age far from raw and immature – at those years when men are all they are ever likely to become – when he was in the prime and vigor of his life – when the powers of his understanding, according to their standard, were at the best, his memory exercised, his judgment formed, and his reading much fresher in the recollection and much readier in the application than now it is. He was at that time as likely as most men to know what were Whig and what were Tory principles. He was in a situation to discern what sort of Whig principles they entertained with whom it was his wish to form an eternal connection. Foolish he would have been at that time of life (more foolish than any man who undertakes a public trust would be thought) to adhere to a cause which he, amongst all those who were engaged in it, had the least sanguine hopes of as a road to power.

There are who remember, that, on the removal of the Whigs in the year 1766, he was as free to choose another connection as any man in the kingdom. To put himself out of the way of the negotiations which were then carrying on very eagerly and through many channels with the Earl of Chatham, he went to Ireland very soon after the change of ministry, and did not return until the meeting of Parliament. He was at that time free from anything which looked like an engagement. He was further free at the desire of his friends; for, the very day of his return, the Marquis of Rockingham wished him to accept an employment under the new system. He believes he might have had such a situation; but again he cheerfully took his fate with the party.

* July 17th, 1765.   [1] Rockingham.

It would be a serious imputation upon the prudence of my friend, to have made even such trivial sacrifices as it was in his power to make for principles which he did not truly embrace or did not perfectly understand. In either case the folly would have been great. The question now is, whether, when he first practically professed Whig principles, he understood what principles he professed, and whether in his book he has faithfully expressed them.

When he entered into the Whig party, he did not conceive that they pretended to any discoveries. They did not affect to be better Whigs than those were who lived in the days in which principle was put to the test. Some of the Whigs of those days were then living. They were what the Whigs had been at the Revolution – what they had been during the reign of Queen Anne – what they had been at the accession of the present royal family.

What they were at those periods is to be seen. It rarely happens to a party to have the opportunity of a clear, authentic, recorded declaration of their political tenets upon the subject of a great constitutional event like that of the Revolution. The Whigs had that opportunity – or to speak more properly, they made it. The impeachment of Dr Sacheverell[1] was undertaken by a Whig ministry and a Whig House of Commons, and carried on before a prevalent and steady majority of Whig peers. It was carried on for the express purpose of stating the true grounds and principles of the Revolution – what the Commons emphatically called their *foundation*. It was carried on for the purpose of condemning the principles on which the Revolution was first opposed and afterwards calumniated, in order, by a juridical sentence of the highest authority, to confirm and fix Whig principles, as they had operated both in the resistance to King James and in the subsequent settlement, and to fix them in the extent and with the limitations with which it was meant they should be understood by posterity. The ministers and managers for the Com-

---

[1] Henry Sacheverell (1674?–1724), a High Church clergyman impeached in 1710 for reviving pre-Revolution Tory doctrines. He received a nominal sentence.

mons were persons who had, many of them, an active share in the Revolution. Most of them had seen it at an age capable of reflection. The grand event, and all the discussions which led to it and followed it, were then alive in the memory and conversation of all men. The managers for the Commons must be supposed to have spoken on that subject to prevalent ideas of the leading party in the Commons, and of the Whig ministry. Undoubtedly they spoke also their own private opinions; and the private opinions of such men are not without weight. They were not *umbratiles doctores*, men who had studied a free Constitution only in its anatomy and upon dead systems. They knew it alive and in action.

In this proceeding the Whig principles, as applied to the Revolution and Settlement, are to be found, or they are to be found nowhere. I wish the Whig readers of this Appeal first to turn to Mr Burke's Reflections, from page 20 to page 50,[1] and then to attend to the following extracts from the trial of Dr Sacheverell. After this, they will consider two things: first, whether the doctrine in Mr Burke's Reflections be consonant to that of the Whigs of that period; and, secondly, whether they choose to abandon the principles which belonged to the progenitors of some of them, and to the predecessors of them all, and to learn new principles of Whiggism, imported from France, and disseminated in this country from Dissenting pulpits, from Federation societies, and from the pamphlets, which (as containing the political creed of those synods) are industriously circulated in all parts of the two kingdoms. This is their affair, and they will make their option.

These new Whigs hold that the sovereignty, whether exercised by one or many, did not only originate *from* the people (a position not denied nor worth denying or assenting to), but that in the people the same sovereignty constantly and unalienably resides; that the people may lawfully depose kings, not only for misconduct, but without any misconduct at all; that they may set up any new fashion of government for themselves, or continue without any government, at their pleasure; that the people are essentially their own rule, and their will the

---

[1] In the present edition, pp. 279–99.

measure of their conduct; that the tenure of magistracy is not a proper subject of contract, because magistrates have duties, but no rights; and that, if a contract *de facto* is made with them in one age, allowing that it binds at all, it only binds those who are immediately concerned in it, but does not pass to posterity. These doctrines concerning *the people* (a term which they are far from accurately defining, but by which, from many circumstances, it is plain enough they mean their own faction, if they should grow, by early arming, by treachery, or violence, into the prevailing force) tend, in my opinion, to the utter subversion, not only of all government, in all modes, and to all stable securities to rational freedom, but to all the rules and principles of morality itself.

I assert that the ancient Whigs held doctrines to tally different from those I have last mentioned. I assert, that the foundations laid down by the Commons, on the trial of Dr Sacheverell, for justifying the Revolution of 1688, are the very same laid down in Mr Burke's Reflections – that is to say, a breach of the *original contract*, implied and expressed in the Constitution of this country, as a scheme of government fundamentally and inviolably fixed in King, Lords, and Commons – that the fundamental subversion of this ancient Constitution, by one of its parts, having been attempted, and in effect accomplished, justified the Revolution; – that it was justified *only* upon the *necessity* of the case, as the *only* means left for the recovery of that *ancient* Constitution formed by the *original contract* of the British state, as well as for the future preservation of the *same* government. These are the points to be proved.[1]

---

[1] In the original edition there follow extracts, together with Burke's glosses on them, from the speeches of the following Whig managers at Sacheverell's trial: Nicholas Lechmere (1675–1727); Sir John Hawles (1645–1716); James Stanhope (1673–1721), later first Earl Stanhope; Robert Walpole (1676–1745), later first Earl of Orford; Sir Joseph Jekyll (*c.* 1662–1738); and Sir Robert Eyre (1666–1735). The full speeches are to be found in T. B. Howell (ed.), *A Complete Collection of State Trials*, vol. xv (1812).

Short Bibliography

Burke's *Correspondence* is available in a modern edition published under the general editorship of Thomas W. Copeland. A new edition of the collected *Works* is also to be published under the direction of Professor Copeland.

Aspects of Burke's Life and Thought

BREWER, JOHN. 'Party and the Double Cabinet: two facets of Burke's *Thoughts*', *The Historical Journal*, xiv (1971).

CANAVAN, F. *The Political Reason of Edmund Burke* (North Carolina, 1960).

COBBAN, ALFRED. *Edmund Burke and the Revolt against the Eighteenth Century* (2nd ed., London, 1960).

CONE, CARL B. *Burke and the Nature of Politics*, 2 vols (Kentucky, 1957–1964).

COPELAND, THOMAS W. *Our Eminent Friend Edmund Burke* (New Haven, 1949).

COURTNEY, C. P. *Montesquieu and Burke* (Oxford, 1963).

HILL, B. W. 'Fox and Burke: the Whig Party and the question of Principles, 1784–1789', *English Historical Review*, lxxxix (1974).

LUCAS, PAUL. 'On Edmund Burke's doctrine of prescription; or, an appeal from the new to the old lawyers', *The Historical Journal* xl (1968).

MAHONEY, T. H. D. *Edmund Burke and Ireland* (Harvard, 1960).

O'GORMAN, FRANK. *Edmund Burke, His Political Philosophy* (London, 1973).

PARKIN, CHARLES, *The Moral Basis of Burke's Political Thought* (Cambridge, 1956).

POCOCK, J. G. A. 'Burke and the Ancient Constitution – a

problem in the history of ideas', *The Historical Journal*, iii (1960).

SUTHERLAND, L. S. 'Edmund Burke and the First Rockingham Ministry', *English Historical Review*, xlvii (1932).

TODD, WILLIAM B. *A Bibliography of Edmund Burke* (London, 1964).

WILKINS, B. T. *The Problems of Burke's Political Philosophy* (Oxford, 1967).

General Reading on the Period

BROOKE, JOHN. *King George III* (London, 1972).

BUTTERFIELD, H. *George III and the Historians* (London, 1957).

CANNON, JOHN. *The Fox-North Coalition* (Cambridge, 1969).

CHRISTIE, IAN R. *Myth and Reality in Late-Eighteenth-Century British Politics* (London, 1970).

DERRY, JOHN. *Charles James Fox* (London, 1972).

FOORD, ARCHIBALD S. 'The Waning of the "Influence of the Crown" ', *English Historical Review* lxii (1947).

GEORGE, MRS ERIC. 'Fox's Martyrs; the General Election of 1784', *Transactions of the Royal Historical Society*, 4th series, xxi (1939).

GUTTRIDGE, G. H. *English Whiggism and the American Revolution* (California, 1942).

HILL, B. W. 'Executive Monarchy and the Challenge of Parties, 1689–1832', *The Historical Journal*, xiii (1970).

LANGFORD, P. *The First Rockingham Administration, 1765–1766* (Oxford, 1973).

MARSHALL, P. J. *The Impeachment of Warren Hastings* (Oxford, 1965).

MITCHELL, L. G. *Charles James Fox and the Disintegration of the Whig Party 1782–1794* (Oxford, 1971).

NAMIER, SIR LEWIS. *England in the Age of the American Revolution* (2nd ed., London, 1961).

O'GORMAN, F. *The Whig Party and the French Revolution* (London, 1967).

O'GORMAN, F. *The Rise of Party in England: the Rockingham Whigs, 1760-1782* (London, 1975).

PARES, RICHARD. *King George III and the Politicians* (Oxford, 1954).

SUTHERLAND, LUCY S. *The East India Company in Eighteenth-Century Politics* (Oxford, 1952).

WATSON, J. STEVEN. *The Reign of George III, 1760–1815* (Oxford, 1960).

Index